Jewish Dogs

STANFORD STUDIES IN JEWISH HISTORY AND CULTURE

EDITED BY *Aron Rodrigue and Steven J. Zipperstein*

Jewish Dogs

An Image and Its Interpreters

Continuity in the Catholic-Jewish Encounter

Kenneth Stow

STANFORD UNIVERSITY PRESS
STANFORD, CALIFORNIA
2006

Stanford University Press
Stanford, California

©2006 by the Board of Trustees of the Leland Stanford Junior University. All rights reserved.

No part of this book may be reproduced or transmitted in any form or by any means, electronic or mechanical, including photocopying and recording, or in any information storage or retrieval system without the prior written permission of Stanford University Press.

Printed in the United States of America
on acid-free, archival-quality paper

Library of Congress Cataloging-in-Publication Data
Stow, Kenneth R.
  Jewish dogs : an image and its interpreters : continuity in the Catholic-Jewish encounter / Kenneth Stow.
     p. cm.—(Stanford studies in Jewish history and culture)
  Includes documents in Latin as well as documents translated into English from Hebrew and Latin.
  Includes bibliographical references and index.
  ISBN 0-8047-5281-8 (cloth : alk. paper)
  1. Blood accusation—History. 2. Catholic Church—Relations—Judaism. 3. Judaism—Relations—Catholic Church. 4. Bollandists. I. Title. II. Series.

BM585.2.S755 2006
261.2'609—dc22   2005033001

Original Printing 2006

Last figure below indicates year of this printing:
15 14 13 12 11 10 09 08 07 06

Typeset by Classic Typography in 10.5/14 Galliard

for e.

Contents

	Preface	ix
	Introduction: Equality, Supersession, and Anxiety	1
1.	Ambivalence and Continuity	37
2.	The Bollandists and Their Work	55
3.	Richard of Pontoise and Philip Augustus	75
4.	The Jewish Version: The Bollandist Reconstruction Vindicated	99
5.	A Usable Past	119
6.	Purity and Its Discontents	133
7.	Denouement	158
	Appendix One: Bollandist and Parallel Texts	177
	Appendix Two: Translation of the Blois Letters	198
	Notes	203
	Select Bibliography	293
	Index	309

Preface

> Shylock: Thou call'dst me dog before thou hadst a cause;
> But, since I am a dog, beware my fangs.
>
> Shakespeare, *The Merchant of Venice* 3.3.6-7

Works of history are supposed to be dispassionate, their authors detached, and the books they write judgmentally neutral. By these standards, this book is a failure. Engagement and emotion are visible on every page.

To produce such a book was far from my mind when I began to write. My intention was to perform a simple scholarly exercise contrasting the discussions of purported ritualistic murders by Jews of Christian children as these discussions appear in late twelfth- and early thirteenth-century Jewish and Christian narrative sources. But a wrinkle soon appeared. I discovered that the key to understanding the medieval Christian narrative lies in the writings of the still little known Jesuit Bollandists of Antwerp and Louvain, or Leuven, the seventeenth-century authors of the multivolume *Acta Sanctorum*.[1] Theirs was the first attempt accurately to establish and report saints' lives; their purpose was to winnow the false from the true. Yet, in the process, and faithful to their own interpretative standards, they came to validate reports of ritual murder, giving these reports full, and sometimes, forceful credence. But why? My reading quickly became two-layered, and the result was historiography within historiography: to ask why, at least in this instance, medieval historical writing is so well interpreted through the lens of similar writing, and its underlying motivation, in early modernity, each of the two in its own time-specific context.

It then remained to ask whether the Bollandists had opened a window only on twelfth- and thirteenth-century writing and thought. Or does their perspicacity shed light on the actual experiences of twelfth- and early thirteenth-century Jews independently of contemporary chroniclers and their biases? It does. In particular, their writings provide a direct path into the thinking—and policies—of King Philip II Augustus of France (1179–1223). To complicate matters, John McCulloh, who graciously read an early draft of this study, asked me whether the modern successors of the original Bollandists, still known by this name and still resident in Belgium, perpetuated their predecessors' outlook. With respect to the ritual murder charge, they most certainly did not. Rather, early twentieth-century Bollandist scholars forcefully repudiated the ritual murder accusations their predecessors thought they had validated. Even more forcefully, modern Bollandists locked horns with early twentieth-century proponents of the ritual murder charge, many of whom were members of the Bollandists' own Jesuit Order. Belief in ritual murder had been continuous over eight centuries.

This unbroken line says much about how Christianity, especially Catholic Christianity, confronted Jews over the *longue durée*, hence the subtitle *Continuity in the Catholic-Jewish Encounter*. Tracing the roots of this eight-hundred-year belief and following their continuity into the twentieth century became central to the study. These roots lie in the writings of Paul, although, more precisely, as we shall see, they lie in subsequent elaborations.

This is not to presage a blanket condemnation of Catholicism or of individual Catholics (nor does it serve as a pretext to censure the recently much discussed Pius XII, whose name will reappear but once in the entire book). On the contrary, this study has Catholic "heroes," and, as is easy to guess, these heroes are the twentieth-century Bollandists (and Catholics of like mind), who not only denounced the ritual murder myth but continued to do so in the face of sometimes virulent censure. No papal denunciation of this accusation, beginning with that of Innocent IV in 1247, had ever been so blunt. Ironically, the source of the modern Bollandist denunciation was strict adherence to the traditions of rigorous hagiographic scholarship established by the first Bollandists. Bollandist sophistication had grown enormously over the centuries. To this irony and its effects, I shall devote considerable space.

The study originated with the question of how Jews perceived one instance of the ritual murder myth, that at Blois on the Loire in 1171.

And as research on occasion felicitously does, this study began in the classroom. My students and I had set out to read a group of Hebrew letters apparently related to the burning at Blois of about thirty Jews, who perished in a great bonfire ordered by Theobald, count of Blois, brother-in-law of King Louis VII, the father of Philip Augustus. It is commonly assumed that these letters were composed very shortly after the events, and, at the start, not expecting surprises, my students and I thought unraveling the letters would take no more than one or two classroom sessions. We spent nearly the whole year on the project. Each class meeting produced new questions and generated the need for ever-closer textual reading.[2]

Ostensibly, the principal actor in these Hebrew letters is King Louis VII. The subject is his reactions to the burnings. In fact, our classroom discussions brought us to agree that the king really meant is either Louis's son, Philip Augustus, or (less probably) the later Louis IX. This discovery prompted me, now independently, to investigate anew the texts relating to Philip Augustus's interaction with the Jews. The investigation confirmed the known picture, but it added an important detail, that Philip's demonstrable belief that Jews killed Christian children was not only important, but pivotal in his Jewry policies. Philip may also have thought Jews capable of "sacrificing and devouring little Christian children's hearts," the full-blown "blood libel," where the blood of the ritual murder victim is alleged to be used for ritual or magical purposes. Yet Philip would have imagined this alleged crime a full decade or more before the first actual accusation of murdering a Christian child to extract and use its blood was made at Fulda, in Germany, in 1235.

To verify these findings, I set out, with some admitted serendipity, to investigate the fortunes of medieval ritual murder accusations as they are reported in the *Acta Sanctorum*. These reports are as sophisticated as they are disturbing—and they also influenced future thought. This last I realized thanks to the promptings of John McCulloh, but also to the good fortune of reading, at about this point in my research, the writings of Giovanni Miccoli and David Kertzer, now reinforced by the work of Tomasso Caliò. Everything came together. The Bollandists' representation of the fate of the alleged victims—victims they called martyrs, for reasons we shall see below—adumbrates late nineteenth- and early twentieth-century imaginings, which are framed as a perennial Jewish assault on Catholic integrity and purity. The early Bollandists themselves portray this assault as a never-ending attack on the Eucharist. The victims (as was also the case with Catholics martyring themselves rather than submit to Protestant demands in the Bollandists' own day) were deemed eucharistic surrogates.

Almost consequentially, the ritual murder narratives of the *Acta Sanctorum* were the font from which Italian Jesuits of the late nineteenth and early twentieth centuries drew to publish essays (in *La civiltà cattolica* and similar journals) touting ritual murder as a fact. As Félix Vernet observed a century ago,[3] the Bollandists' early modern seventeenth-century narrations of supposedly true medieval events influenced the twentieth-century audience: the fideistic line adopted and the unswerving belief professed by twentieth-century Italian Jesuit writers (and by others, too) who launched the libels anew were identical to the positions espoused by medieval and early modern narrators. The message ritual murder tales conveyed to their audience had clearly remained constant over time. The only change was the message's reslanting to promote contemporary goals.

The key allowing succeeding layers of narrators to exploit tales of ritual murder for immediate needs may be a unanimity of credence. Unwavering faith in the veracity of the tales has, for over eight hundred years, facilitated interpreting—and reinterpreting—them in the light of what I would like to call the "authorial present." In one way or another, those writing of ritual murder did so within their own temporal context. Discussing highly different events, Gabrielle Spiegel has called writing of the past in the present tense "Romancing the Past."[4] The idea of the past interpreted in presentist terms also underlies Karl Morrison's portrayal of medieval historical writing, which he describes as the creation of "instruments of [aesthetic] cognition." By visually and verbally stimulating readers to confront gaps that authors purposefully left in order to stoke the imagination, seal in memories, instill values, and "discipline the soul," images were created in readers' minds that "opened . . . a multitude of speculative doors."[5] Jean-Claude Schmitt goes a step further. Discussing the nature of medieval "chronicles" and "histories," he asks how "despite professing [their devotion] to truth [*vérité*], the [authors of these histories] willingly incorporate the most marvelous fictions." His answer is simple: "For them [these authors], history is a discourse of *vérité*, par excellence, but their perception of history and *vérité* is quite different from ours."[6]

With respect to tales of ritual murder, this definition and terms like "romancing the past" or "authorial present" are most apt. One would be hard pressed to find a better example than ritual murder of remolding historical materials to suit contemporary, even sectorial, needs.[7] We have just noted that the twentieth-century Jesuit heirs of the original Bollandists were repudiating the ritual murder libel at the same time that other Jesuits were fostering it, principally Jesuits living in Rome and writing in *La civiltà cattolica*. For the modern Bollandists, the charge of ritual murder was "inane." This was their "authorial present," and we shall see that what guided them was their ability to detach themselves, as scholars, from the theo-political issues of ecclesiastical self-confidence, and its absence, that plagued the ritual murder charge's twentieth-century defenders. These latter feared for ecclesiastical purity, and they feared even more for the survival of the Church as they knew it, just as those who came before them had done in centuries past. Understanding the reasons for the firm stance of the twentieth-century Bollandists decrying the ritual murder charge—even when to do so meant openly clashing with their Italian Jesuit counterparts—has been one of the more intriguing, if not uplifting, aspects of the present study.[8]

A second result, important to me historiographically, is that my reading of the Bollandist work, as I had hoped from the start, allowed me to corroborate the interpretations my students and I had reached for the so-called Blois letters. For reasons of a more orderly presentation, these Hebrew texts are discussed second and the Bollandist material first. This editorial decision has not affected the conclusions.

Yet once the task of corroboration and mutual corroboration was achieved, I began to ask whether John McCulloh's question about the continuity of Bollandist thought from the seventeenth century to modern times might not be posed in reverse. Might reading Bollandist material also point backward, to help understand earlier periods, and especially the thinking of those who lived well before the times of the imputed ritual murders in the twelfth and thirteenth centuries? The results of the inquiry were electrifying. I was carried back to Christian origins, and what finally emerged was a demonstrable continuity in attitudes toward Jews that has survived through not eight hundred years but nearly two thousand. In the words of my friend Robert Stacey, I had chanced upon an enduring "exegetical matrix." There was no choice for me but to follow this matrix as it took its full course. Put otherwise, Bollandist thinking both forced and allowed me to put order into issues I had been struggling with for years. What I had at first imagined would be the end of the study turned out to be its beginning.

This book addresses a wide audience, or at least so it is hoped. I recognize that many readers will find parts of the book daunting, especially the technical discussions of the policies of King Philip Augustus of France and, perhaps more, the analysis of the Blois Letters. Nor will the discussion of martyrdom, particularly that of Werner of Oberwesel, found in Chapter 2, lack complexity. I ask forbearance. Readers may decide first to read rapidly, to follow the overall sense, and then to revisit sections most attuned to their personal and scholarly interests. They are asked also keep in mind that this book is *primarily a history of continuous and continuing mentality*, which seeks to explain, or at least to offer one plausible explanation for, why the subject of Jews has been so consistently problematic in the history of the Christian, especially the Catholic, West, and why a constant set of unchanging principles has underlain periodic variations. The roots of attitudes toward Jews are as deep as they have resisted decay. With this thought fixed in his or her mind, the reader's compass will hopefully point always north.

The story will not be told conventionally, proceeding century by century. Instead, it will be set out principally by theme, beginning with an overall discussion, in the Introduction, of imagery based on interpretations of the scenario presented in Matthew 15:26: Matthew's statement, put in the mouth of Christ, that "the bread" that he, Christ, has brought for "the children" should not be "thrown to the dogs"; in the text of the Latin Vulgate, "non est bonum sumere panem filiorum et mittere canibus." Exegetically, this verse was transmogrified into an image of Christian children hungering for the Eucharist, which "Jewish dogs" incessantly plot to steal, consume, savage, or pollute. This identification dates from no later than the fourth century.

Yet we have already indicated that often imagined Jewish plots against the Eucharist were expressed in later times in terms of ritual murder or the blood libel, the victims called martyrs, and every martyr considered a eucharistic surrogate. As though by definition, all imagined Jewish assaults against "innocent children" came to be identified as assaults against the Eucharist. It is the perennially perceived interchangeability of martyr-victim with eucharistic purity and its defense, or simply the idea of defending eucharistic purity from its pretended enemies, that unites centuries of thinking. It also is the line that runs through and unites the various sections of this book. Its chronological progression from ancient origins to modern ambivalence, back to medieval anxieties, and finally to modern and general thematic concerns should not confuse. The central question is always the Eucharist and those who are said to threaten it, the so-called "Jewish dogs"—and sometimes Jewish responses to this anxiety.

Two motifs are woven through the book, sometimes more, sometimes less visibly. The reader is urged to keep both constantly in mind. In one way or another, they are linked to the image of the "Jewish dog," which itself often lies, or should I say lies in waiting, in the shadows of the discussion. One of these, as might be imagined, is purity and its maintenance in the face of suspected Jewish aggression. Achieving victory required adopting dual and often overlapping strategies. First, physical contact was proscribed. Contact with the perennially "unclean" Jews was called contaminating, especially sexual contact, but also the contact of common commensality. Second, special Jewish nefariousness was memorialized through purposefully concocted tales. These demonstrated the unexceptional triumph of martyrdom against all attempts at depredation, in this case, the triumph of the surrogate Eucharist, the victim of ritual murder; by survival, I mean of the victim's eucharistic body, not the physical one.

Moreover, unsullied Christian purity was a prerequisite to participate in Christian ritual acts, most particularly, to receive—or give—the Eucharist. It goes without saying that formal teaching holds unexceptionally that nothing can affect the Eucharist itself, which is considered God incarnate, as was Christ himself. Informal belief was less sure, heightening fears. Purity also referred to the physical purity of holy spaces and objects. These, too, had to be defended. No less important was the desire to demonstrate purity's merits. Here, martyrdom and its commemoration played a particular role. So essential was the testimony of martyrdom to demonstrate eucharistic resilience and purity that martyrs were fictionally created. To this, the repetition of ritual murder tales over the centuries both contributed and unerringly attests.

The second motif is that of "supersession."[9] Christian teaching claims that Christianity is the bearer, actually, the sole legitimate possessor, of the divine promise and choice, and that it has inherited the mantle of *Verus Israel*, the True Israel, which the Jews once asserted was exclusively theirs (or so Christian theology has framed it). In Paul's candid words: "We [believers], my brothers, are we not like Isaac, the sons of the promise . . . [and thus] free? . . . The covenant . . . of Sinai [Judaism] gives birth to slavery" (Gal. 4:28/24, in that order). However, the Church sought authentication for "supersession" by demonstrating that the faith (faith, not deeds) of the newly chosen Christians was integral, pure, and unblemished, but, most of all, capable of withstanding challenge. This last was revealed best through the ability to repulse alleged Jewish aggression.

It is at this point that the motifs of purity and supersession meet; "fuse" might be a more precise word. For what Jewish aggression and wrongful contact most endangered was that highest form of Christian purity, unity in Christ, a unity that also bestows upon every Christian a eucharistic aspect. By partaking of the Eucharist, every Christian, individually, became a metaphoric limb of the Christian body, an integral member of the social unity constituted by Paul's Christian fellowship (as Paul defines it most precisely in 1 Cor. 10:16–18). Unity in Christ, as Paul explained it in Romans, also made the Christian into the spiritual child of Abraham, replacing the children of Abraham's flesh. But this coveted status and its purity might easily be corrupted. To paraphrase Paul in 1 Corinthians 5:6 and 6:15–16: A little leaven sours the whole loaf; do not eat with the sinful. Nor may one unite with a whore (literally or metaphorically understood), lest he or she destroy the bond to, and unity in, Christ. In Galatians, Paul exhorts: "expel the son of the servant woman" (4:30), by which he meant avoid Jewish practice, even if the practitioners are Christians. Later, this would become avoid Jewish plots, which subvert. The concepts of supersession and the preservation of Christian purity had become conjoint twins.

Yet purity and its conservation is not a Christian invention. It has been a central theme throughout the human past. It featured already in Hittite conceptions of the Temple Gate as early as the second millennium B.C.E. But so, tellingly, did the dog. Who might pass through the gate? Neither pigs nor dogs, for they were considered foci of impurity. No attempt will be made here *directly* to trace the transmission of this Hittite concept to the future. Yet one cannot but note the parallel to the prophet Isaiah, who contrasts the antinomies of proper sacrifice, an ox or a lamb and incense, with the unclean sacrifice of a dog, a pig, or idolatry.[10] Adepts of the ancient Dead Sea Sect, too, may have used the canine image as a marker of impurity.[11] That members of this sect linked the sense of their own purity with the idea of being chosen goes without saying.

It is in these terms that the notion of dogs and pigs, but especially dogs, will be at the heart of this book; the arch-locus of impurity, dogs—read here, "Jewish dogs"—were to be kept from entering "the temple," now, the Christian temple. They must especially be kept away from (Matthew's [15:26]) "bread." Were not Hittites admonished: "let not a pig or a dog stay at the door of the place [the temple] where the *loaves* are broken?" And were they not further told: "Since a dog approached the [altar] table and consumed the daily [sacrificial offering of] bread, they 'consume' [destroy] the table." The near identity of Matthew and the Hittite texts is breathtaking. This sense Matthew 7:6 reinforces, warning believers not to give the holy to dogs, their "pearls" to swine. About the tenth century, this last verse was applied directly to Jews. The images of dogs (and pigs) and (Eucharistic) loaves (and regardless of Matthew's original intention) seem almost destined to become focal in Christian confrontational teachings regarding Jews.

The drama of the hermeneutic was also going to be applied to supposedly real confrontations. In the ritual murder story of Simonino of Trent in 1475, the Jews are said literally "to bark." In 1870, Pius IX would use this same word to speak of Jews liberated from the Ghetto, now free, he was implying, to wander about like dogs and befoul the city of Rome. However verbalized and whatever the context, the image of the contaminating "Jewish dog" seems to have been one that facilely reached the tip of the tongue. This was so even as the modes of confrontational expression evolved over time, even when they became politicized within the framework of the modern state, and even when they were framed in terms of race. What often seems to have been qualitative change is really "the old in a new container," or so I believe.[12]

Apprehension about Jews began with the founding of the Church itself, and it has endured, and still endures, to the detriment of all. Some express their apprehension with reserve, and still others through words of excruciating hate. However, for all, the source of apprehension, the fear of being compromised and of losing pride of place, is in refusing to accept the idea perhaps first put forth by the Italian Jew David de Pomis, who wrote, as early as the late sixteenth century, that "nothing is more a matter of individual will than belief."[13] By definition, there are no hierarchies, no preferences, no belief that is better than another, certainly none that guarantees. God, de Pomis, may have been thinking, has no preference, but desires only mutual human respect.

De Pomis may also have been reflecting on the words of Isaiah about the nature of fasting. The fast, Isaiah said, must be accompanied by care for one's neighbor—by itself fasting yields nothing—for only then "will your dawn break forth" (Isa. 58:8). Dismiss haughtiness, Isaiah was saying. Do not vaunt yourself to claim that your way is better than mine. That is sin, and as the Gospel would later say, "the wages of sin are death." Yet even in the early twenty-first century, there are some who refuse to accept this message. They claim theological preeminence and broadcast hate. And they do this both on the Internet, as will be amply illustrated below, and on the cinema screen. They have produced cinematic blood libels in reverse, in which the ritual murder victim is Christ himself. For such people, as I see it, the "light of the dawn" will never break forth.

As I said at the start of this Preface, I did not embark on writing this book to make a statement like this. My intentions were purely scholarly, in the strictest sense of the term; and my hope is that what I have said will be judged by the strict scholarly standards that determined my every written word. I most definitely did not intend, therefore, to end by calling for the cessation of all supersessionist teaching, nor was my purpose to urge quashing its motivating fears; it matters little how this teaching is framed or the manner in which the fears are expressed. This call came on its own, the day after I wrote the closing words in the last chapter. By the time the reader presses through what is not always a neat thicket, I hope he or she, too, will agree that this call needs to be made, even in this work of rigorous historical study. Or perhaps just because of it.

*

The research on this book has sometimes been unconventional. The libraries of the University of Haifa and Columbia University have served me well, as have those of Smith College, the University of Massachusetts at Amherst, and Amherst College. And, of course, the Biblioteca Apostolica Vaticana. But the Internet, too, has been a fruitful source, and not only for ready information such as dates or for online texts. The "Net" is one of the best (read, worst) places to find scurrilous libels and reprints of earlier attacks. These sites will be referred to more than once. Happily, the noxious Melvig.org now vends consumer products, not lies; one suspects a change of domain. Holywar.org, the most salacious of these sites, is still going strong. Its condemnations of the late Pope John Paul II for heresy, alongside so much more that it contains, should make Catholics shudder.

I thank those who have made this book possible. Friends have read the manuscript in whole or in part, including John McCulloh, David Malkiel, John O'Malley, Haym Soloveitchik, Ronald Florence, and Kevin Madigan, who reviewed the central medieval chapters and gave important advice. William Chester Jordan helped in matters pertaining to French history, as only he knows how to do, and Esther Cohen shared with me her limitless knowledge of medieval ways. The full manuscript was read and vetted in detail and to my profit by Johannes

Heil, Lisa Lampert, and Magda Teter. Magda offered precious help in pointing to additional important materials, including the portrait that graces the dust jacket and is reproduced in the book. My colleague at Haifa, J. H. Chajes made pertinent suggestions. Robert Stacey read every last comma, and his comments have been indispensable in creating the final product. A full reading was also given by Jeannine Horowitz, my colleague at Haifa, who has an especially rich knowledge of medieval Christianity and medieval France, its history and literature. Judith Tydor Baumel, Maurice Kriegel, Yael Zerubavel, and my student Federica Francesconi read the text and encouraged me greatly, as did Wanda Needleman, whose psychoanalytic expertise was the font of insightful remarks. Elin and Herb Brockman gave encouragement. Especially valuable was the reading of Marjorie Agosín, a consummate writer, whose tale of the *perro judío* set me off in search of the "Jewish dog."

Special thanks go to Stephen Zipperstein and Aaron Rodrigue, and to Norris Pope of Stanford University Press, for believing in this book. Angie Michaelis, and Mariana Raykov, also of the Press, attentively shepherded the book through the stages of production, often with sage counsel. Rob Ehle's cover design is a true example of making a picture say more than a thousand words. The meticulous editing of Peter Dreyer has earned my deepest gratitude.

The best reading of all, and so much encouragement and patience, came from my wife, Estela Harretche, Carmit, to whom this book is dedicated.

HAIFA, ISRAEL

Jewish Dogs

Introduction
Equality, Supersession, and Anxiety

On March 26, 2000, Pope John Paul II placed a prayer in a chink between the stones of the Western Wall. This is the Wailing Wall, the last remnant of the Temple destroyed by the Romans in Jerusalem in 70 C.E. Referring to "Abraham and his descendants," yet carefully refraining from specifying the precise identity of Abraham's children, whether Jews, Christians, or Muslims, the prayer and its message bespeak traditional Christian theology.[1] Christians may easily see this prayer as applying to them. Yet thanks to its intentionally opaque wording, Jews and Muslims may see the prayer as applying to them as well. However, much more was at stake here than the identity of Abraham's offspring. The real importance of the event was the site where it took place: a Jewish holy site, to the extent that Judaism recognizes sites as being holy.[2] What is holy for Jews, the pope was saying, is independently, and unconditionally, holy unto itself. After 2,000 years of dissension, Pope John Paul had accepted Judaism as incontrovertibly valid. Theologically, for Catholicism, as espoused by the pope, Judaism's continuity was no longer justified by the expected ultimate fusion of the Jews into the Catholic fold, as St. Paul had said in Romans 11. The pope was working a revolution, and many within the Church share the sentiment.

However, this papal turn has not been universal. The *Christus dominus* or *Dominus Iesus* text, issued on August 6, 2000, by the then Cardinal Joseph Ratzinger (and afterward Pope Benedict XVI) implies the opposite, reiterating the supremacy of Catholicism as the "only true Church" and decrying "a religious relativism that leads to the belief that one religion is as good as another."[3] Non-Catholic faith is wanting.[4]

This does not rule out temporary, or what might better be named temporizing, tolerance, the kind most commonly read into the preaching of St. Paul (in Romans) and espoused by the Vatican II Council of 1965 in the encyclical *Nostra aetate*, "In Our Times;" it is temporizing, for even *Nostra aetate* looks forward to the time when there will be one flock and one pastor (John 10:16), the conversion of all to Catholicism. Yet the willingness of those for whom the Catholic structure is preeminent to abide with teachings that are consonant with Church doctrine and history does not imply a willingness to abide with much else. And this creates a contradiction. One cannot espouse interreligious dialogue, or respect for other religions, as Pope Benedict (when he was still Cardinal Ratzinger) said he does, yet continue to defend supersessionism by saying: "The Pope has offered respect, but also a theology: Christ is the fulfillment of Abraham."[5] Moreover, almost by definition, initiatives for change must originate in the Catholic camp. Recent attempts to point to negative Jewish attitudes or to minimize suspicions about Catholic motives, however worthy, obscure the fundamental problem.

Besides, there are, and always have been, those who wish for no peace at all. Concern for Catholic preeminence has often led in far less accommodating directions than even the one taken by Cardinal Ratzinger. Catholic integralists have been preoccupied with forces they presume capable of weakening Catholic purity and unity, and their preoccupation has bred repugnance for even the slightest deviation.[6] It has also made Catholic integralism perennially uneasy about Judaism, which is assumed to stimulate an ever-present Judaizing potential that eventually corrupts both the individual Christian believer and the Church as a body. Both ancient and, as we shall see, modern Catholic theologians have sometimes argued precisely this. They have also lumped Jewish acts, real and imagined, together, as one with the supposed designs of the Church's (other) alleged enemies, whether external or internal. Jews and these other "enemies" have been censured and sometimes cursed in the same breath. The reasons have been as politic—centered on the struggle for ecclesiastical power—as they have been religious or theological.[7]

This pattern is still alive, especially on the Internet. The anxiety-driven web site Holywar.org (there are many others like it) openly links and applauds virulently expressed hatred of Jews, hatred of Zionism, denial of the Shoah, and charges of ritual murder. Yet it does so hand in hand with condemnations of internal theological "error" *within* the ecclesiastical hierarchy.[8] The late Pope John Paul is accused of over one hundred heresies, one of the most notable being his espousal of "freedom of conscience," attributed to a (regretfully unconfirmable) statement the pope is said to have made in the official Vatican newspaper, the *Osservatore romano*, on September 1, 1980. John Paul's defense of this freedom is then juxtaposed with its rejection by Gregory XVI—and its repetition by Pius IX, in 1864—who said that to espouse freedom of conscience and religious belief as fundamental human rights was a "delirium."[9]

Sentiments like these are often masked and sometimes expressed unawares. Nevertheless, these sentiments exist, as the following quizzical riddle, part of a children's game, reveals. This riddle provides the leitmotif underlying the entire study, pithily epitomizing the darker side of the relationship between the Jews and the Church during the past two millennia.

A Parable: The Dogs and the Bread

> ¿Quién robó los panes del horno?
> Los perros judíos, los perros judíos.
>
> Who has stolen the loaves from the oven?
> The Jewish dogs, the Jewish dogs.

This unsettling riddle, or refrain, sung by Chilean schoolchildren (my example is from the 1960s, but I am told it is still sung today),[10] is none other than a disguised Host libel, the charge of intentionally desecrating the eucharistic Host. The bread in the refrain is the Eucharist, the sacrament whose ritual and communal ingestion, as put by Paul in 1 Corinthians 10:16–17, creates a union of all Christians in the true body and blood of Christ.[11] This same union features throughout the New Testament. In Matthew 15:36, it appears in reverse order, in the miracle of the loaves, in which Christ's body, for which the loaves stand, is infinitely divisible. The loaves move outward from Christ the person to feed the throng. However, Christ's body provides a banquet only for those whose identity we learn ten verses earlier (15:26), when Matthew reports Jesus to say: "It is not meet to take the children's bread and cast it to the dogs."[12]

For Matthew himself, these children were the "lost sheep of the house of Israel" to whom Christ had referred in verse 15:24. Yet thanks to Paul and subsequent Christian exegesis (especially of Gal. 4:21–31), the Jews shed their original identity. No longer "the children," they have become "carnal," "carnal Jews," as Paul calls them in 1 Corinthians 10:18. Their place as "children" has been taken by the new true and spiritual Israel, "the children of the promise" (Rom. 4, 8, and 9, and Gal. 4:28).[13] It is the "carnal Jews" who are now "the dogs." The late fourth-century John Chrysostom says this outright in the commentary on Matthew 15:24–26 in his *Homilies Against the Jews*:

> Although those Jews had been called to the adoption of sons, *they fell to kinship with dogs; we who were dogs received the strength, through God's grace*, to put aside the irrational nature, which was ours, and to rise to the honor of sons. How do I prove this? Christ said: "It is not fair to take the children's bread and to cast it to the dogs." Christ was speaking to the Canaanite woman when He called the Jews children and the Gentiles dogs. But see how *thereafter the order was changed about: they became dogs, and we became the children.*[14]

Chrysostom's insistence was born of anxiety. The bulk of his homilies against the Jews reveal how much he dreaded the Jews, who were persistently refuting his teachings. They were bent, as he saw it, on reclaiming both the "bread" and the title of being the "children" for themselves. Daily, he said, Jews seduced Christians (in his city of Antioch) into Jewish practice. The Chilean refrain is this anxiety's final evolution. Its origin may also be traced to Paul, at least as Paul had come to be interpreted.

In Galatians 5:1–9, Paul called for the ostracism of Judaizers—he meant Gentile Christians, not Jews—whose weak faith led them to circumcise themselves. But what Paul said of Judaizers would soon be applied to Jews. So would a similar denunciation in Philippians 3:2. The commentary on Matthew 15:26 by the English Protestant divine Matthew Henry (1662–1714) is unambiguous:

The Gentiles were looked upon by the Jews with great contempt, were called and counted dogs; and, in comparison with the house of Israel, who were so dignified and privileged, Christ here seems to allow it, and therefore thinks it not meet that the Gentiles should share in the favors bestowed on the Jews. But see how the tables are turned; after the bringing of the Gentiles into the church, the Jewish zealots for the law are called dogs, Phil. 3:2 [and 3, where Paul says: "Beware of those dogs and their malpractices. Beware of those who insist on mutilation—'circumcision' I will not call it; we are the circumcised [he means, of the heart], we whose worship is spiritual"].[15]

The metaphor of the Jewish dog and its accompanying anxiety, which pictured this dog as a threat, had taken hold. What ensured its continuity, not to mention its facile incorporation into the Chilean refrain, was catholicity of belief—alongside the catholicity of the metaphor's invocation, regardless of whether the context was social, intellectual, ecclesiastical, popular, or a combination of all four.[16] Examples abound. The tenth-century Pope Leo VII is (apocryphally) credited with having spoken of Jews citing Matthew 7:6, saying: "Give not that which is holy unto the dogs, neither cast your pearls before the swine, lest haply they trample them under their feet, and turn and rend you." And Gregory the Great (followed by various Church councils) spoke of forced converts "returning to their vomit [like a dog]."[17] So common did the image of the "Jewish dog" become that the *Life* of Herman the Jew, a convert to Christianity about the mid twelfth century, has Herman, while still a Jew, berate a "fictitious" Rupert of Deutz (whom we shall meet speaking his own words below) denouncing the Christian custom of calling Jews "dog carcasses." Herman's objection went unheeded. The transcript of a mid sixteenth-century Roman trial cites a young woman scolding a Jewish customer in her father's store, calling him a *cagnaccio sciattato*. "You ritually slaughtered little dog," she says, the insult compounded by her resort to Judaeo-Romanesco, colloquial Roman Jewish speech; *sciattato* is a transformation of the Hebrew *shehitah*, the kosher slaughtering of meat.[18] Whether spoken or unspoken, the metaphoric image of the Jew as the ravaging dog—by itself, or as some transposed equivalent—seems to have been on the tip of many tongues. Eventually, one could speak with secular ease, as does Shakespeare, of the "dog Jew" and the "currish Jew."[19]

The image of the Jewish dog surfaced especially in the context of "the children's bread" and those who endangered it or its recipients: those who might abscond with this food, leaving the children to hunger, or those who might rip it apart, as dogs are wont to do with food. Exegetically, the Jew had become, and would continue to be seen as, the hungry thief, the "trampler" of the true Christian food. We are reminded of the dog in the Hittite text, cited in the Preface, consuming the altar-bread. But the allusion is also more ominous, to the various libels directed at Jews, the charge of desecrating the Host, the rightful diet of the "children," and the accusation of killing Christian children and draining the "eucharistic blood" that flowed when the "dogs" mutilated the victim's body. This last would literally be said as part of the accusation that Jews had murdered Simonino of Trent in 1475. Jews were also accused of befouling and contaminating their surroundings, like dogs, which, as we shall see below, they were said to do even through sight and raucous noise. Their presence itself was contaminating, and that contamination they transferred to others.

Moreover, the Body of Christ that the Jewish dogs were said to pursue was more than the Host itself or the individual ritual murder victim. It was also, if not principally, the Christian collective, the *Corpus Christi*, in what we shall come to see were that body's political and social guises, both of which were often pictured eucharistically, just as Paul himself had pictured them in 1 Corinthians 10:16–17; the centrality of this passage cannot be overemphasized. Thus the earlier ninth-century cleric Amalric of Metz elaborated on Paul in his *Liber Officialis*, a book of instruction on how to perform the mass and other ritual: "We are one bread in Christ that must have one heart" (Sicut unus panis [the term is Paul's] sumus in Christo, sic et unum cor debemus habere). This seamless unity Amalric contrasted with the body of the Jews. We are, he said, expanding on his words elsewhere in the tract—and citing verbatim the Venerable Bede (d. 735)—a *convocatio*, a "unity" and a "harmonious accord." This is wholly unlike, and in distinction to, the synagogue, a *congregation*, which is (literally, from the Latin *con* and *grex*) a gathering place of "sheep and inanimate objects."[20] By (interpreted) Pauline definition, an attack by the

Jewish dogs—the sheep of the synagogue—on a Christian individual was an attack on the Christian *convocatio*, the whole, the sum of the articulated Christian parts.[21] Individuals were not to be neatly distinguished from the broader Christian *corpus*, the earthly embodiment of the *Corpus Christi*. This point is cardinal, and the reader is urged to keep it constantly at the back of his or her mind.

Pauline Unity and Purity in Christ

Powerfully enhancing anxiety about the potential Jewish threat was the Pauline image of leaven and fermentation. This second image complemented and, eventually, melded with that of the dog, especially with the notion of the dog's noted filth. Paul speaks most memorably of this leaven in Galatians 4 and 5, referring to the Judaizing of Gentile Christians. But leaven as an image is not exclusively Pauline. Matthew 15 and 16, too, speak of the leaven of the Pharisees and Sadducees, a perception that certainly facilitated redirecting Paul's remonstrations about leaven to the Jews (which chronologically preceded those of Matthew). Specifically, Paul speaks of the "little leaven," the fermentation, that can spoil the whole lump (of dough) (Gal. 5:9), the leaven of corruption and wickedness that ruins the true unleavened Passover matzoh. The one corrupted is at once the individual Christian, whom Paul calls "unleavened Passover bread," and, by implication, Christ himself and Christ's entire social body. Amalric echoes and elaborates on Paul by calling Christian society, not only Paul's fellowship of believers, *unus panis*, one loaf with a single heart, in Christ—"for indeed our Passover has begun; the sacrifice is offered, Christ himself" (1 Cor. 5:6–8). It was only to be expected that the canons, from earliest times, would—as they did—prohibit Christians from consuming Jewish unleavened bread.[22]

Paul's extrapolation in 1 Corinthians 6:15–19 (on the basis of the leaven image of chapter 5) makes the point more forcefully yet; and through proximity, the two chapters—both of which deal with sexual immorality and its effects, and, hence, with carnality and its rejection—become thematically one. "Do you not," asks Paul, "know that your bodies are limbs and organs of Christ? Shall I then take from

Christ his bodily parts and make them over to a harlot? Never! You surely know that anyone who links himself with a harlot becomes physically one with her, but he who links himself with Christ is one with him spiritually. Shun fornication."

Eventually, throughout canon law and ecclesiastical thinking, this shunning came to mean flight from all things Jewish; Paul's original intention of Judaizers was wholly transposed. Like union with the harlot or any forbidden sexual union, contact with Jews and Judaism was deemed corrupting. Both were a fermenting leaven. Paul himself, therefore, may have demanded that Christians avoid "loose livers," with whom Christians "should not even dine" (1 Cor. 5:11), but people like John Chrysostom began to apply Paul's language and terms like "loose living" and "harlotry" to Jews. Calling upon the reserves of his hyperbolically pernicious rhetoric, Chrysostom repeatedly named the synagogue a bordello and its doings prostitution, just as he invoked these same affronts to preach the horrors awaiting Judaizers who frequented synagogues and participated in Jewish rites.[23]

However, the origins of the figure of leaven and carnality are not Pauline. This figure was invented by the rabbis; and this is significant in the context of Christianity's, and particularly Paul's, claim that Christianity had superseded Judaism. Paul's figure may derive from a saying that would eventually be inserted into the Talmudic tractate *Berakhot* 17a: "Our will is to perform Thy will, and what prevents us [from doing so] is the yeast in the dough of our nature," the *yezer ha-rʿa*, by which rabbinic teaching means the "bodily drive."[24] Paul would remake this saying, or one very much like it, into the idea of the leaven that is the carnality against which man's spiritual drive wages a constant war. This is just as the (spiritually driven) Christian fellowship of 1 Corinthians 10:16–17 sits unspokenly, yet patently, contrasted in verse 10:18 with the "carnal [fellowship of the] Jews." This contrast recurs in the Epistle to the Romans (especially chapters 9 to 11): carnality versus faith, purity versus contamination. It is also reinforced by a second rabbinic teaching, which explains that almost alone of the creatures on Noah's Ark, the dog dared copulate, promiscuously at that, while waiting out the Flood.[25] It was just such a portrait of promiscuity that John Chrysostom was recalling, when, commenting on Matthew, he said that the Christians, who have become the true children, have shed their "irrational [pagan, carnal, and, in context, doglike] nature."²⁶ And for Chrysostom, as we have seen, the dogs were now the Jews and their synagogues, kennels.

The pairing of a doglike, animalistic nature, and irrationality would continue to be articulated. It was said in the high Middle Ages that by rejecting Christ, the Jews revealed their irrationality. Yet was not *rationality* humanity's sine qua non? If so, rational beings were Christian and human. Non-Christians must be irrational and inhuman. Thomas Aquinas summed up this thinking well. The Jews, he said, embody the inverse of Christian virtue: if it is natural (read rational and human) to believe, then unbelief (the state of the Jews) is contrary to nature.²⁷ The Jews' humanity was in doubt.

Martin Luther displaced this figure onto the Church. It was Catholicism, he implied, that fostered irrationality: "If I had been a Jew [he wrote] and had seen such idiots and blockheads [the Catholics] ruling and teaching the Christian religion, I would rather have been a sow than a Christian. For they have dealt with the Jews as if they were dogs and not human beings. . . . If . . . we use brute force and slander them, saying that they need the blood of Christians to get rid of their stench and I know not what other nonsense of that kind and treat them like dogs, what food can we expect of them?"²⁸ Consummate exegete that he was, Luther had upended the dog-children dichotomy of Matthew; to be a Catholic was clearly worse than being a pig, and by allusion, Catholics, not Jews, were the dogs. The pope, he said elsewhere, was the child of Hagar, the bondwoman. Catholics, therefore, not Jews, were those God had rejected. They were not at all the *Verus Israel* they claimed to be.²⁹ Nonetheless, Luther could have expressed himself this way only because Matthew's canine image as a marker of Jewish identity had become a commonplace—just as had the idea of impurity.³⁰

Luther himself was likely unaware that his comments point to a third rabbinic-pharisaic idea, the brotherhood of the "clean of hands." This idea, too, influenced Christian thinking about Jews, and that of Paul in particular. "What food can we expect, . . . if [the Jews] are treated as dogs," Luther asks, figuratively equating Jews (who convert) with "food." How, in other words, can we expect Jews to join in the covenant of the clean of hand—to join with those who devour and become (the *unus panis*), one with "the food"—if we treat them as inhuman and unworthy? This thought perfectly reflects Paul's sense of who might be rightfully "within," who "without." In his anxiety to preserve the purity not only of the individual believer but also of the Christian fellowship's united membership, had not Paul admonished against dining with carnal "loose livers"? It was cleanliness, the purity of hands—and, of course, the purity of the food itself—that was prerequisite to dine at the common (pharisaic or eucharistic) table, to participate in the closed Christian fellowship of 1 Corinthians 10:16–17.[31] Yet for Luther, too, communion and community were synonymous.[32] Ardent student of Paul that he was, Luther equated Jewish conversion with food.

As one might imagine, the epitome of all these ideas was also Jewish, namely, the biblical verse Ezekiel 44:7. The prophet admonishes the priests who were to rebuild the Jerusalem temple: "You have . . . brought the uncircumcised of heart and of body, outsiders, into my sanctuary; they pollute my house by offering the sacrifice, my bread, which is the fat and the blood; their abominations violate my covenant." This verse (which again recalls Hittite temple prohibitions) demonstrably influenced Paul. Though Paul did not quote it, its words sustain his claim in 1 Corinthians 10:18 (intended to reinforce what he had just said in verses 16 and 17): Jews who sacrifice a sacrifice of fat and blood—which Ezekiel, so providentially for Paul (and then Matthew), calls "bread"—become "members" of the altar. However, this is to the exclusion of all others.[33] Paul considered it essential that Christians emulate this behavior. Only exclusivity would safeguard the purity of the eucharistic "dough" and ward off the "leaven."

That Paul had borrowed so much from Judaism boded only ill. Resting, as it did, on Jewish intellectual origins, the Pauline vision of purity and exclusivity was destined to compete with that of the Jews, the same Jews whom the Christians, according to Paul, had "superseded," the Jews, as he had put it in Ephesians 2:14–16, who were destined ultimately to self-destruct by uniting in Christ. United, the two would form "a single new humanity in [Christ] himself." Moreover, the borrowings that encouraged such competition did not stop with Paul. The third-century Bishop Cyprian of Carthage, too, leaned heavily on Jewish ideas in fashioning his own special concepts of purity.

Purity According to Cyprian

With respect to Corinthians itself, Paul's immediate context was not Jews, but the threat to Christian purity posed by pagan ritual, which Paul viewed as universally contaminating. In 1 Corinthians 10:21, he elaborated: "You cannot partake of the Lord's table and the table of demons," nor of pagan wine as compared to the cup of the Lord, the blood. This challenge would not disappear. Laws from 742 and 769, (wrongly) attributed to Charlemagne, still warned—bishops and priests, in particular—to steer clear of "filthy" gentile practice, "lest God's people finds itself indulging in paganism" (ut populus Dei paganias non faciat, sed omnes spurcitias gentilitatis abiciat et respuat). The specific practices the laws prohibited were magic, dismay about which would eventually enter stories of profaning the Host, as well as stories of ritual murder.[34]

Catholic thinkers would eventually transfer Paul's concerns about idolatry to Jews. However, during the five hundred years prior to these eighth-century laws, it was not pagan magic but pagan sacrifice that became a Christian rallying cry—and in a time of real Christian crisis. The capacity of this sacrifice to pollute was deemed enormous. The one aroused was Cyprian.

Speaking of those had taken part in this sacrifice, especially priests, who had done so in order to escape the Decian Persecution of the year 250—the issue was not Jews or Judaism—Cyprian admonished: "Nor let the people [who participated in pagan sacrifice] flatter themselves that they can be free from the contagion of sin, while communicating with a priest who is a sinner.... [As] Hosea the prophet [9:4] forewarns: 'Their sacrifices shall be as the *bread* [emphasis added] of mourning; all that eat thereof shall be polluted.'"[35] Cyprian must also have had in mind the proviso of Ezekiel 44:13 that only *pure* Levites may offer the fat and the blood, which is what Ezekiel, only six verses earlier (44:7), had called "the bread" (of the sacrifice), the "bread" that Paul had equated with the Eucharist. The exclusion of nonadepts from the sacrifice in Ezekiel thus presages what Cyprian would mean, just as Ezekiel's words came to inform the thinking of Paul. Cyprian's conceptuality, if not his precise biblical citations, follow Paul to the letter. Yet Cyprian carried the teachings of sacrificial, eucharistic purity to new heights. In the tract "On the Lapsed," Cyprian enunciated a fully articulated doctrine of purity, which is also heavily Levitical:

> Returning from the altars of the devil, they draw near to the holy place of the Lord, with hands filthy and reeking with smell, still almost breathing of the plague-bearing idol-meats; and even with jaws still exhaling their crime, and reeking with the fatal contact, they intrude on the body of the Lord, although the sacred Scripture stands in their way, and cries, saying, "Every one that is clean shall eat of the flesh; and whatever soul eats of the flesh of the saving sacrifice, which is the Lord's, having his uncleanness upon him, that soul shall be cut off from his people" [Lev. 7:19–21]. Also, the apostle testifies, and says, "You cannot drink the cup of the Lord and the cup of devils; you cannot be partakers of the Lord's table and of the table of devils" [1 Cor. 10:21]. He threatens, moreover, the stubborn and denounces them, saying, "Whosoever eats the bread or drinks the cup of the Lord unworthily, is guilty of desecrating the body and blood of the Lord" [1 Cor. 11:27].[36]

Cyprian had bundled together the purity concepts of Ezekiel, Leviticus, and Hosea with those of Paul, who in 1 Corinthians 6 says, "touch nothing unclean," and in 1 Corinthians 11:23–32, specifies: "One should not dine with the unworthy, . . . which is to sin against the body and blood of the Lord."

For Cyprian, as for Hosea, consuming the sacrifice offered (hence, touched) by a lapsed Christian, or *lapsus,* transmits pollution;[37] and for both, this pollution is physical, not spiritual.[38] A fourth Jewish concept, therefore, one that concretizes the previous three, has been brought to bear on eucharistic purity. Real physical contact pollutes, not only that of the metaphorical kind, as might be understood of ideas like leaven, fermentation, and animalistic behavior. Touching profane demonic sacrifice renders one unfit to offer sacrifice, or to receive it, and this contagion passes from one communicant to another.

It endangers the contaminated when they approach the eucharistic altar. There is even a hint that the contagion—the "desecration" Cyprian speaks of, by way of "violence . . . [done] to His body and blood,"[39]— passes to the sacrifice itself (however theologically improbable the idea of contaminating what is held to be God Himself may be).[40] Cyprian is horrified by forbidden contact, including marriages between Christians and gentiles, which he views as the wedding of Christianity to harlotry (1 Cor. 6:19). The very thought of them prompts him to quote Paul's warning (2 Cor. 6:14–17) in full: "What has righteousness to do with wickedness? Can light consort with darkness? Can Christ agree with Belial . . . a compact between the temple of God and the idols of the heathen? . . . Separate yourselves, says the Lord: *touch nothing unclean.*"[41]

However, despite the location of this passage in Cyprian's *Three Books of Testimonies Against the Jews*, the one who applied it to Jews was not Cyprian but Pope Stephen III, about the year 770, who adopted these verses to warn of the excessive contact with Jews that resulted from domestic service (and, by implication, the concubinage that regularly accompanied it).[42] Yet, by this time, Pope Stephen was expressing the norm. More than once in this study, we shall see churchmen equating Judaism with "idolatry" and paralleling contact with Judaism and Jews with "idolatry's pollution." This was certainly true of John Chrysostom. Commenting on 1 Corinthians 10:16–20, Chrysostom melded idolatrous contamination with that which he pictured stemming from Jews. Christians, he writes, partake of the body of God, Christ; Jews "partake of the altar" of mundane sacrifice. Their altar is pagan. Chrysostom's rhetorical skills enable him to say this so deftly that one is persuaded without reflecting that the interchangeability of Jewish with pagan altars is self-understood.[43] For many, it indeed was. The emperor Gratian's law *Christianorum ad aras* of 383 c.e., which was contemporary with Chrysostom and reproduced in the Theodosian Code of 438 c.e. (Book 16, title 7. law 3), recalls Paul's warnings about "leavening" and directs Christians to shun not only pagan ritual but also that of the Jews. The syncopation of this law in the so-called *Monk's Epitome* of the eighth century is clearer yet: "The crime of Christians passing over to altars and temples"—the law seems to paraphrase Cyprian, directly—"or those who pollute themselves with the

Jewish contagions should be punished."⁴⁴ The two crimes, as far as the *Epitome*'s author is concerned, are one. So are "Jewish contagions" (rites) and "pagan altars." Eventually, it became common (ecclesiastical) wisdom to equate Jewish with pagan practice, whether overtly or only implicitly. Both, equally, might pollute and endanger the individual Christian. They threatened the well-being of the entire eucharistic Christian fellowship.

Nor was the issue one of assertive or Jewish behavior or initiatives. Acts as otherwise innocent as (secular) dining in common might be called infectious. This notion was inevitable, thanks to Paul's picture in Corinthians of the exclusivity of the Christian fellowship and his fear of dining with "loose livers." Victorinus Africanus's commentary on Galatians extends Paul's prohibition against Judaizing through circumcision to embrace mixed dining as early as the second century.⁴⁵ For Victorinus, it was patently obvious: like circumcision, mixed dining cut one off from the faith. To be circumcised or share a Jew's table was now, as Paul said in 1 Corinthians 6:12, "fornicating against one's own body." It was to unite with harlotry rather than with God through the Eucharist received in purity. It was tantamount to reverting to the Christian's previous, unbaptized state, and it would be considered ever more so as time went on. It was also to behave like a promiscuous dog and to give the dogs the "bread" intended for the "children," whether that bread be eucharistic or the simple loaf shared during table fellowship. To dine with a Jew was the same as sharing the table and cup of the demon. In 388, shortly after *Christianorum ad aras* was issued, John Chrysostom—who besides the dog, likened Jews to any animal fit for slaughter—said this outright:

> Tell me, then: How do you Judaizers have the boldness, after dancing with demons [i.e., Jews], to come back to the assembly of the apostles? After you have gone off and shared [bread or ritual] with those who shed the blood of Christ, how is it that you do not shudder to come back and share in his sacred banquet, to partake of his precious blood? Do you not shiver, are you not afraid when you commit such outrages? Have you so little respect for that very banquet?⁴⁶

The tenth-century Bishop Ratherius of Verona was even more decisive. He accuses Christians dining with Jews of violating the admonition of 1 Corinthians 5:11 not to eat with "loose livers" and idolaters, even though Paul neither mentions Jews in this verse nor intended it to apply to them.[47] For Ratherius, dining with a Jew was contaminating.[48] The same had been said at various Church councils. The ninth-century Agobard of Lyon cites the edicts of these councils repeatedly.

Purity, Jews, and Agobard of Lyon

Agobard considered dining with Jews anathema, and in expressing his fear of impurity transferred by touch, he went beyond even Cyprian. He refers to the stark Haggai 2:12–15, which speaks of a chain reaction in which personal impurity passes from "toucher" to touched; Agobard's emphasis is on the Christian social body, far more than on the individual. Special care must be taken not to dine with a Jew and then a priest. Agobard also suggested following the lead of Cyprian—Donatistic overtones aside, for the issue is not orthodoxy, but how Agobard viewed the act—that a contaminated priest passed on his impurity to all who received the Eucharist at his hands. Perhaps the altar itself became contaminated.

Agobard is insistent. He returns to the theme on every second page of his lengthy letters excoriating Jewish behavior: Dining with a Jew makes one impure; Jews pollute through food at the table; Jewish company of any kind contaminates; and to eat with Jews is to dine with the anti-Christ.[49] One must be on constant guard not to accept gifts from Jews at holiday time, especially the Passover matzoh, that surrogate for Christ's sacrifice, the true matzoh, as Paul calls it in 1 Corinthians 5. There can be no question that Agobard was thinking of 1 Corinthians 10:21 and 11:27 in precisely the same context as Cyprian had centuries earlier. However, Agobard was speaking of Jews, not lapsed priests. It is with reference to Jews that he says: "You cannot drink the cup of the Lord and the cup of devils; you cannot be partakers of the Lord's table and of the table of devils" (1 Cor. 10:21), for "whosoever eats the bread or drinks the cup of the Lord unworthily is guilty of desecrating the body and blood of the Lord" (1 Cor. 11:27).

Following Chrysostom, Agobard judged it an offense to know of violations and not speak up. To dine or have any prohibited social intercourse with Jews, Agobard calls "an act that leads to the yoking of the free to the harness of idolatry" (idolatriae autem iugo libertatem animi inclinarent). By linking idolatry with the yoke of servitude, Judaism's present state as Paul had spelled it out in Romans, Agobard seamlessly fused Judaism with idolatry and its pernicious effects. Socializing with Jews leads to idolatry, which is the loss of Christian liberty. So much the more reason for Christians to beware, lest Jews seduce them "into their errors." To buttress his arguments, Agobard cites the same texts in Corinthians and Matthew to which Cyprian, Chrysostom, and Pope Stephen resorted, which were also invoked at the councils held at Agde, Clermont, and Laodicea in the fifth century (whose edicts were then reiterated at the important council at Meaux in 845–46, roughly contemporary with Agobard himself). Agobard was bent on making an airtight case.[50]

It remained only for Agobard to cite Matthew 15:26, which he did, and then to contextualize this verse with the verses from Haggai mentioned above, as well as with the warning of 2 Corinthians 6:14–15 against joining light with darkness. This allows Agobard to weave together all his charges in one brief paragraph. Since this people, the Jews, he writes, is "so polluted with impurities," they see fulfilled in them the prophecy of Haggai, who says that the touch of one who has had contact with the dead defiles all the food or drink it touches, and so "this people. . . . whatever they offer [on the altar] is defiled." "What, indeed," Agobard goes on, "has light to do with darkness, Christ with Belial?" The Jews must be separated "from all the mysteries of the faithful, . . . and from their society and table." Did not Christ tell the Canaanite woman that he had come to feed the children, not the dogs, and that what the children ate would be "the bread that descended from heaven"? For good measure, Agobard adds to the citation of Matthew the openly eucharistic John 6:53–58, which speaks of union with Christ through the wine and the blood.[51] In the nexus of contact and impurity, especially at the table, and of the dangers with which impurity threatened his cherished *societas fidei*, as he called it (a term that dates back to at least the second-century Ignatius), Agobard had ascribed to the Jews a potentially destructive role.[52]

We cannot know whether, in citing Haggai, Agobard was thinking of Leviticus 22:4-8 as well, which also speaks of the need for priests to be pure (Agobard rarely cites the Hebrew Bible in his writings against the Jews). Priests, this verse says, must be unsullied by contact with the dead prior to partaking of the sacrificial meal. Indicatively, this meal is called in Hebrew *lahmo*, his (the priest's) bread. But if Agobard had indeed been thinking of this passage, his dread would be unmistakable. He would have been anticipating Johannes Buxtorf, who, in 1603, purposefully conflated Leviticus 22:8 with the admonition in Exodus 22:31: "Sanctified, or specially set aside people you shall be unto me and carrion meat you shall not eat, but you shall throw it to the dogs."[53] Christians receiving their "bread" must, like priests, distance themselves from the swill that is fit only for dogs, the Jews, and especially from that which the Jews themselves reject. Otherwise, and this was Agobard's ultimate fear, Christians, polluted by sharing a common Jewish table, would revert to what John Chrysostom had call their "original canine state."

This same spirit animates *The Corrector*, part of the *Decretum* of the early eleventh-century Burchard of Worms. Effectively summing up Agobard's thinking, Burchard writes: "Did you eat of the food of Jews or others, pagans, which they had prepared for themselves? If you did, do penance ten days on bread and water" (to cleanse yourself of the sin and restore purity).[54] No less direct is Agobard's contemporary Rabanus Maurus, who speaks of the need *emundari*, to cleanse, persons who (elsewhere) are said to have become *inquinati*, profaned.[55] Until they are purified, they must be *conpiscendum*, kept away, from Christian *consortio*, or kept back from *communione*. Persons who have been defiled through *convivia*, sharing Jewish food, should not eat bread with a cleric.[56] Turning matters upside down, but arriving at the same conclusion, Raymundus of Peñaforte wrote in his thirteenth-century *Summa de poenitentia et matrimoniae* (Summa on Penitence and Marriage) that Jewish contempt for Christian food *impugned* the faith.[57] Raymundus was the principal editor of the *Decretals* of Gregory IX, which from 1234 to the early twentieth century served as the official body of Canon Law.

The problem was not only one of the table. Shades of Paul on harlotry, mixed Jewish-Christian sexuality was also said to threaten. Agobard railed against Jews and Christians sexually uniting. So, too, even more pointedly, did Sicard of Cremona (d. 1215). Both, and, indeed, so many others after them, may have been focused, not only on Paul, but once again on Leviticus 22:4: "Whoever touches any one that is unclean by the dead; or from whomsoever the flow of seed goes out" is unclean to eat *lahmo*, the sacrificial bread. Tainted food, impure sexuality, and pollution went hand in hand. A married couple, Sicard wrote, in which one spouse had converted, while the other tarried, must refrain from sexual contact until both partners were baptized, lest the taking of the sacrament be compromised. Once again, Jewish contact had to be shunned. It threatened the Christian purity of the individual, and, through him or her, it imperiled the purity of the earthly *Corpus Christi* as a whole.[58]

The sixteenth-century Marquardus de Susannis agreed. These concepts and anxieties were resilient—not to mention that what began as theology had acquired legal standing. "The commingling is obnoxious" (Et est odiosa talis commixtio), whether the Christian be man or woman; "it defames both baptism and Christianity" (quia sit per eam iniuria baptismo et universae religioni Christianae), de Susannis wrote of sexual contact between a Christian and a Jew. It thus endangers the entirety of Christian society, not only the individual offender. Besides, de Susannis added, Jews sometimes commit this offense intentionally, particularly in relations with a prostitute, where they believe the nature of the woman will mask the *contemptum*.[59] Marriage between a Jew and a Christian is out of the question. Not only does such a marriage possess none of the signification of the marital sacrament—the union of Christ and the Church; by its nature, such a marriage "prostitutes a limb of Christ among the Gentiles." In support, de Susannis cites Augustine, who, in turn, cites Cyprian. Both say precisely this, basing their thinking, no doubt, on the admonition of 1 Corinthians 6:15: do not join the limbs of Christ with harlotry.[60]

The legal collection known as the *Schwabenspiegel*, compiled by a German cleric in about 1275, went to the point directly. "If a Christian lies with a Jewess, or a Jew with a Christian woman, they are both guilty of superharlotry [*überhure*]," and they must be burned, "for the Christian has denied the Christian faith [by joining his limbs to harlotry and so alienating himself from Christ's body]." One French judge in the fourteenth century added that sex with a Jew merited burning as "bestiality," since "to have sexual relations with a Jewish woman is to have sexual relations with a dog."⁶¹ In sexuality of this kind, as it was put in Catalayud, in Spain, there was concern lest "these faithless dirty people infect the purity of Christians."⁶² Purity, canine bestiality, and harlotry—one and interchangeable—endanger the *societas fidei*. "Bestiality" is also the word Christian witnesses used to describe Jewish life in testimony before the Modenese Inquisition in 1602.⁶³ These witnesses were all servants, lower-class laity. The view of Judaism, if not of Jews themselves, as bestial was no clerical monopoly.

Fears for Christian purity, we have noted, extended to domestic service. De Susannis, citing 2 Corinthians 6, writes that servitude to Jews is to join light with darkness. The *Summa Coloniensis* of 1169 explains more precisely: through servitude, Christians are stained (*maculati*), and so, too, is Christianity.⁶⁴ Fear of "pollution" is the reason why the age-old but never applied restriction on domestic service began to be reemphasized about the time of this *Summa*. The restriction applied to employing both Christian men and women. Charters issued to Jews by bishops and secular rulers through the thirteenth century reveal that previously Jews had regularly been exempted from this rule. The Third Lateran Council of 1179 renewed it, and Pope Alexander III made strenuous—and successful—efforts to have this edict applied. The culmination would be the decree of the Fourth Lateran Council of 1215 ordering distinct Jewish dress—it, too, intended to avoid pollution. About these councils and especially about Alexander III's initiative, I shall have more to say below.⁶⁵

Concern about the contamination effected by servitude to Jews was ancient. Gregory the Great had already spoken out on the subject, and so had Stephen III. Pope Stephen, as noted, pressed the case perhaps even more strongly than had Gregory by citing the inflammatory language of 2 Corinthians 6:14–15, why "should a believer unite with an unbeliever," which he linked to Matthew 7:6: why should "the holy be given to dogs." Gregory the Great, however, had been especially clear, twice in fact. His special fear was the damage that servitude to Jews did to Christ himself: "Were not all Christians the members of Christ? Do we not know that Christ is the head of the members, whom we honor? . . . So how can we honor the head and permit his enemies [literally] to boot the members around?" To diminish Christ's members was to diminish Christ himself.[66] Because of the unity of all members in Christ, to diminish one of them was to diminish the entire *Corpus Christi*. There were those who saw the danger of contamination as so great that it justified expulsion.

Surprisingly, Agobard had not considered this possibility. At one point, he backtracks, recalling Paul, to say that Jews should be treated piously.[67] Yet, as though responding to Agobard's stricture, a text (falsely) ascribed to Pope Leo VII in 938 defended its call to expel recalcitrant Jews who resisted preaching and refused to convert, citing Matthew 7:6 and 2 Corinthians 6:14–15.[68] The threatened expulsion, like the text itself, was imaginary, not fact. Nonetheless, it—and especially the citation of Matthew 7:6—exemplify how persistent were the metaphors of Jewish identity and, in particular, the metaphor of the dog and its noxious acts.[69]

Impurity Through Servitude and Touch

Jews rendered things unclean, especially through touch. This was much as did the *lapsus*, and we recall Agobard's citation of Haggai with respect to dining with Jews. Amplified through the prism of 2 Corinthians 6:17—"one should touch nothing unclean"—the fear that the Jewish touch polluted led to some startling legislation. Laws passed by lay councils in southern France and Perugia in Italy in the fourteenth and fifteenth centuries prohibited Jews from touching all food in the marketplace and required them to purchase food they did touch.[70] These prohibitions likely originated much earlier, and they were apparently more widespread than we know. So common were they, it seems, that voiding them required special privilege. The 1264 charter of Boleslaw the Pious to Jews in Poland decreed: "We also order that Jews may sell and buy all things freely and *may touch bread* as do Christians." The 1388 charter to the Jews of Brest issued by Grand Duke Witold Alexander of Lithuania said the same.[71] Notably, it was specifically bread, with its ever-present eucharistic overtones, that these charters authorized Jews to touch.

Yet legislation like this argues that all food was viewed as susceptible to corruption. It helps explain why shunning the Jewish table defended purity and signified Christian fidelity. In defense of the Dominican bishop of Ventimiglia, Battista de' Giudici, the apostolic commissioner sent to investigate the conduct of the trial at Trent concerning Simonino in 1475, who raised doubts about its propriety, it was said that the bishop had never dined with Jews. De' Giudici was *not* a *lapsus*. He had neither compromised Christian purity nor rendered himself or those he dined with unclean by partaking of the Jewish—read, pagan—table/sacrifice.[72] The thirteenth-century Johannes Teutonicus employed the same reasoning. Jews, said Johannes, "deceive people between courses."[73] De Susannis agreed and quoted Johannes verbatim. One suspects that those who attacked and defended de' Giudici also knew Johannes's dictum. Its ready acceptance reflects not so much Johannes's pithiness but that he had clarified—and raised—the stakes.

Johannes's idea of deception as a reason to avoid the Jewish table also added something new. This was something Agobard, and possibly others, too, had forcefully implied. But it remained to be said explicitly. Pollution occurred not only passively, when the Christian came into contact with Jews, or unilaterally sought Jews out. The nefarious might be initiated by the Jews themselves, as when they "deceived people between courses." Contrary to the passivity Alexander II attributed Jews in 1062, saying "they always accept Christian rule" (semper parati servire sunt), a statement made into an often cited and influential canon, others saw Jews as intentionally dangerous. For Agobard and Chrysostom, Jews were provocateurs, whether as seducers of Christian women, owners of Christian slaves, or diffusers of Jewish and Judaizing propaganda. Seemingly, the Jew is attributed the place of the Roman emperor Decius, who, by demanding obligatory pagan worship, forced Christians "to lapse."

To minimize danger and pollution, Jews had to be controlled. What Chrysostom and Agobard were preaching was not simply exegetical rhetoric or an equally rhetorical fidelity to what they believed Paul had said of Jews—notwithstanding that theirs was an exegetical world where the meaning of scriptural verses carried enormous weight. For Chrysostom and Agobard, the desire, the need, to control Jewishly caused pollution was a reaction to what for them, as believers in eucharistic purity, was real trauma. It was just as, in the case of Cyprian, the trauma of the Decian persecutions of the mid third century, when *lapsi* truly existed, was real, and the fear of contamination in specifically Pauline terms was fully justified.

If we accept Chrysostom's accusations, Jews were encouraging precisely what he feared: accommodating Christians in their synagogues and providing them with medical and perhaps magical remedies. One imagines that covertly or overtly, Antioch's Jews, in this early Christian day, were also proselytizing. Agobard's fears are less easily substantiated by pointing to Jewish acts. Much of what he ascribes to Jews reflects his vision of reality, or how he wanted to see it, or have it seen, not necessarily what really was. Agobard was perfectly capable of saying—as he did—that Jews speaking well of Judaism in public were proselytizing. And he viewed the support given Jews by imperial officials, the *missi*, as traitorous, accusing them, alongside the emperor, of betraying the purity of the *societas fidei*. To attain such a "society of the faith" was Agobard's primary hope.

Agobard was literally overcome with anxiety as he saw Emperor Louis the Pious favoring Jews with broad commercial privileges, interpreting laws concerning Jewish ownership of Christian slaves to Jewish advantage, and allowing Jews to express themselves freely—no doubt negatively—about Christianity's merits.[74] There should be little surprise that Agobard called Jews the minions of the Antichrist, and it is no less surprising that Agobard never drew the logical conclusion from his warnings about Jews threatening "the society of faith." He never said—as the eventual laws about touching food exhibited in the marketplace imply—that whether actively or passively, intentionally or accidentally, Jews threatened the Eucharist itself. Perhaps it was only the inchoate state of eucharistic theology in the early ninth century that held him back.

The Jewish Response

Jews certainly did speak ill of the Eucharist, which Christians knew, including the content of Jewish verbal sallies. We have no direct evidence for earlier periods, but for *Sefer Yosef HaMekane* and the *Nizzahon Yashan*, from the middle and later thirteenth (or early fourteenth) century respectively, the Eucharist was polluted and polluting. To make their point, these two polemicists cleverly cited the same verses in Hosea as had Cyprian (whose works were well known in the Middle Ages) to glorify the Eucharist and insist on eucharistic purity. That medieval Jews consistently called Christianity idolatry needs no repeating. The response of these two Hebrew works to Christian accusations was most sophisticated. It is the Christians, not Jews, who "bark," says the *Nizzahon Yashan*, cleverly inverting the by now common image. We shall revisit these polemics in greater detail below. Suffice it for the moment to say that Christians reading these books—and Christians did have access to Hebrew by this time—must have been infuriated.[75] They might also have thought that, unwilling to limit themselves to parody and aspersion, Jews, in their discontent, might seek ways to act their parodies out. Jews, after all, were increasingly being viewed as aggressive, as witnessed by the remark by Johannes Teutonicus cited above.

Innocent III spoke of Jewish antagonism without hesitation. In a letter filled with complaints sent to the count of Nevers in 1208, Pope Innocent complained that at the time of the grape harvest, Jews pressed the grapes wearing linen boots, took the best quality wine for their own ritual and pleasure, and sloughed off the rest, which they found virtually disgusting, to Christians. There was danger that this bilge might later become the blood of Christ in the sacrament.[76] A few years earlier, at an episcopal synod held in Paris about the year 1200, Odo of Sully ordered priests "to forbid Christians every Sunday during the grape harvest from acquiring the residue of the grapes, which the Jews press in the way they do to produce horrid filth in contempt of the sacrament, a residue that should rather be thrown to the pigs or spread as fertilizer."[77] By implication, the eucharistic sacrament that might be effected from this foul wine was somehow dirtied.

Yet implied here was the also possibility of a final escalation. It was a timely one as well, coming soon after Innocent III declared the Eucharist to be an annual obligation for all in 1215. By the end of the thirteenth century, it was said Jews plotted to savage the Eucharist itself. Their plots, of course, would fail, for theologically, was not destroying the Eucharist impossible? Frustrated, the Jews were said to seek an alternative mark, and this they found in that prime eucharistic surrogate, individual Christians, some of whom they martyred.

The Creation of Martyrs

Time and again, Christian martyrs are described and understood in eucharistic terms. The second-century Ignatius is said to have imagined himself metamorphosed into the bread of Christ in his martyrdom, and in the sixteenth century, Edmund Campion called martyrs "holy Hosts and oblations."[78] Spokesmen of the Church fought bitterly to maintain this ideal. Cyprian especially spoke out in praise of the martyr's bodily purity and transfiguration, which also reified the eucharistic nature of the true and united Christian conventicle. In this context, Cyprian's excoriation of *lapsi* makes all the more sense. His writings on martyrdom were cited repeatedly throughout the centuries; he himself was put to death in 258.[79]

There was actually a "need" for eucharistic martyrdom, which was assigned the same purpose as that assigned to the Eucharist itself. In the words of Augustine, "Christians partake of the Eucharist to gain not immortality for the body, but eternal life for the spirit."[80] Through their deaths, martyrs were believed to embody this miracle in its glory, and this made of martyrs a necessary piece of ritual paraphernalia on the road to salvation. As Karl Morrison puts it, "More than any act other than the Eucharist, martyrdom rendered God's Kingdom incarnate."[81] Good Werner of Oberwesel was said literally to have suffered, indeed, to have undergone a passion, *in loco Christi*, *pro Christo*, and *propter Christo*, in place of Christ, for Christ, and for the sake of Christ, in the late thirteenth century. So glorious was the martyriological ideal that there was reason to maintain it even in the *absence* of persecution. This might be accomplished by creating martyrs (and martyrdom) out of whole cloth—and, *superfluo dictu*, in the Middle Ages and into the modern period, those most regularly accused of creating (eucharistic) martyrs were Jews. The story of Werner of Oberwesel, who may be the martyr par excellence at Jewish hands, illustrates how fully tales of martyrdom could meld the wishful and fantastic under the rubric of Jewish maliciousness. A thorough discussion of the Werner episode, which follows in Chapter 2, is essential.[82]

Once More the Dog, or Canine Cannibalism

Just beneath the surface in fantasies like this one is the metaphor of the Jewish dog, which by Werner's day had also been elaborated. A fourteenth-century Flemish poet called the Jews who attacked Werner "dirty Jews, the stinking dogs" (sales Juifs, les chiens puants). The allusion, no doubt, was to the odor Jews were said to exude, a function of the male menstruation attributed them from the fourteenth century (at the latest).[83] Yet, as we may recall, the aggressive Jewish dogs do more than pollute the "bread of the children" through their stench. They also lust to steal the bread, which they do by murdering the *unus panis*, the one loaf, represented by Christian children. As a fifteenth-century German poem put it: "A stone was found/secretly in a place/on which Jewish dogs murdered/many children."[84] The early twelfth-century Rupert of Deutz made the same point exegetically in his *De Sancte Trinitate*. Commenting on Lamentations 4:2–5, Rupert wrote:

> Though even the lamia [a kind of female demon] bares her breast to feed her pups, the daughter of my people is cruel like the ostrich.... The lamia is a monstrous animal. Its name means tearing.... Yet it has a natural affection toward its young [and feeds them].... But the daughter of my people is very cruel and has not even bared her breast [like the ostrich that scatters its eggs in the desert].... On top of that, she killed it, saying, "his blood is on us" [Matt. 27:25]. [Hence] from then until today, the tongue of the nursing infant clings to its palate; and there is no one to break bread for the children who are asking it. They have too much hunger and thirst to hear the word of God, not because they want the word of God, but because *they [the mothers] prefer [the children] to perish* rather than to break for themselves the bread of the scriptures that they might live from the marrow of spiritual understanding.

Willis Johnson, focusing on the emphasized phrase, has correctly identified this passage (the translation and collation of Rupert's own texts is his) as a condemnation of Jewish cruelty. It refers specifically to the slaughter by mothers (and fathers) of their children during the First Crusade Rhineland massacres of 1096; following the subject-object logic of the passage, Johnson correctly, I believe, interpolates and reads "prefer *them* [the children] to perish."[85] Yet Rupert's reference to the blood of Christ in Matthew implies that the infants who perished were already Christians, baptized Jewish children, who were not being sustained (or instructed in how to sustain themselves) with the bread of the scriptures. Rupert, therefore, was accusing Jewish mothers—the Crusade mothers—of killing their children who had been baptized in the Crusade mayhem, as many indeed were, rather than see these children eucharistically nourished. Rupert himself lived near enough to the Rhineland in the decade or so following 1096 to have received direct reports of events.

But why does Rupert consider these mothers worse than the lamia? The animal corresponding to the lamia in twelfth-century bestiaries, Johnson explains, is the hyena, "who lives in graveyards and feeds on dead bodies" (in sepulcros mortuorum habitans, eorumque corpora vescens). The lamia is thus a wild dog "to which [says the bestiary] may be likened the Children of Israel" (huic assimilantur filii Israel), the Jews, the carnal sons of Israel (Jacob). Yet, worse than the hyena and its depredations, Jewish mothers commit a second, truly enormous crime. Beyond stealing the "bread," they also destroy the children who yearn for it; indeed, they kill their very own.[86]

This accusation was fatal. How distant is it from accusing Jewish mothers of slaughtering their baptized children to saying that Jews might potentially kill any Christian child? Jews might also be charged with attacking the "bread," the Host itself. To say that the Jewish mother withheld the "bread" and killed the child is also to say that the mother "stole the bread from the oven." Nor is this extension of Rupert's meaning a recherché attempt at a reprise of the refrain with which we began. By the time of Rupert, tales intertwining the elements of eucharistic bread, "the oven," and children had been told for centuries. Afterward, and certainly later, the bread in the oven, the explicit Eucharist, and the (Christian, Christlike) child were viewed interchangeably as one and the same. In the case of Werner of Oberwesel, we shall see all three eucharistic figures invoked in the same breath.

Already in the sixth century, Gregory of Tours, followed by (pseudo-)Bede in the mid eighth century, injected the imagery of bread, oven, and Eucharist directly into episodes of fictional Jewishly perpetrated martyrdom. Gregory narrates the story of the Jewish boy of Bourges. The boy's father, enraged that his young son has tasted the Eucharist, throws the boy into an oven, from which the Virgin saves him, transfigured. In the fifteenth-century Croxton *Play of the Sacrament*, the Host in the oven is baked into a bloodied child, completing the eucharistic martyriological fusion.[87] This fusion is visible even earlier. In 1322, in the Spanish town of Sogorb, Jews were accused of molding the figure of Christ *out of bread* and burning it in an oven.[88] The German chronicler Friedrich Cosener reports that Jews tried to burn a host in an oven, but it remained unconsumed, whence the Virgin appeared to charge the Jews with murdering her son.[89]

Earlier, there were tales of figures molded out of wax that were tortured to death like Christ. These tales were especially potent. Through identifying with such persecuted waxen figures, every Christian might vicariously acquire for him or herself a martyr's identity. One and all could benefit from the Virgin's loving succor. It is the Virgin herself who reveals a Jewish plot to torture a waxen image, Christlike in appearance, in thirteenth-century Toledo; so goes a tale told by Gonzalo de Berceo. The goal, as the text says, was to sing the Virgin's praise as she foils the Jews' plan to reenact the passion of Christ anew.[90] Yet de Berceo could not have been ignorant that wax assumes infinite forms. Anyone might imagine the waxen figure in the tale being refashioned into his or her own personal image. The passion would be played out on their own persons. And here there was something thrilling. The eucharistic potential inherent in each and every Christian might be realized. As Odo of Cambrai said in the twelfth century: "He feeds us with his blood and body, so that we unite in one body in him, and so that we are him, and he is one with us," whether in life or the throes of death.[91] And as phrased even more pertinently, and most recently by Abbot Clement of St. Andrew's Benedictine Abbey in Cleveland: "The Eucharist doesn't turn into us, but we turn into Jesus."[92] Why not through suffering his passion as well? As both individual and eucharistic surrogate, whether for Christ himself or for the entire Christian collective, there was all the more reason why each Christian might avidly foster visions of Jewish perversity and perversion. Did not this also elicit a renewed sensation of Christ himself suffering in the blood?[93] Except that through the medium of wax, the sufferer was now "everyman." Martyrdom perpetrated by Jews no longer had to be limited to events witnessed at a remove, through hearing, reading, or imagining. The projection of the supposed victim's agonies onto the individual imagination might also be perfected.

Imagination might also run rife. Drawings of Simonino of Trent picture the Jews draining this supposed child-martyr's blood in the same way one drains the blood of slaughtered pigs. But this was not the first recourse to this image. In 1255, it was said that Jews "had stuck Hugh of Lincoln [another alleged child martyr] like a pig."[94] Whether the pig is intended to be associated with Christ, or, as is also said, with the Jews themselves—making this a very strange charge—the motif of seeking to drain every last drop of Christian blood, the negation of the Eucharist, seems very clear.[95]

This end might also be accomplished through the "ubiquitous social plague" of lending at interest, which was depicted as the letting of vital blood. As with the waxen image, blood-martyrdom in its various guises could be inserted into a social setting to stress the dangers threatening the collective Christian body, beside that of the individual. The Jews guilty of this practice were also called dogs, or so they were named by the fifteenth-century bishop Ruggero Mandosi of Amelia.[96] In 1468, the Observantine Franciscan friar Fortunato Coppoli da Perugia went further to say that Jews: "'were truly wild and thirsty dogs, who have sucked and go on sucking our blood,' and who devour poor Christians [through lending] 'as rust devours iron.'"[97] The contemporary German writer Hans Folz dubbed Jewish lenders "bloodhounds [who] suck and milk/The poor Christians' blood."[98]

That blood, as the friars (and Folz) saw it, was the blood of Christ, and they equated the payment of interest with eucharistic martyrdom. Money, said contemporary homilists, referring specifically to the money Jews took in interest, was the blood of the town, the town itself being the *Corpus Christi*.[99] By "sucking" this blood, the dogs were stealing anew the "lost children's (eucharistic) food." This time, it was the sacred blood of the collective *Corpus Christi*, the so-called "warmth of the town." No wonder that Franciscan Observantine Friars railed against lending in extravagant terms! Their preoccupation was not (or not alone) to uphold the canon law principle that to take interest was to wage war. For them, taking interest directly assaulted the Host, if not the entire *societas Christiana*. The anxieties differed little from those of Agobard centuries before. The private wealth that lending generated seems also to have symbolized for the Observantines the corruption of an idealized state of Christian communal property: read, the Franciscan concept of Apostolic Poverty, that Jesus and his disciples owned nothing—now transposed, it appears, to society as a whole. One wonders how the Observantines would have reacted had they known the opinion of the late eleventh-century Jewish exegete Rabbi Solomon Yitzhaki, known as Rashi. Commenting on the dictum of the Talmud, tractate Shabbat 63a, that "he who lends [money] is greater than he who performs charity," Rashi said: "[the money] may suffice to make the poor man independent," in other words, to solidify his private estate.[100]

Yet the Observantines had not pushed the metaphor of the dog to its limits. These were reached in the narrative of the humanist physician Dr. Tiberino retelling the passion of Simonino of Trent. When the boy was brought in, Tiberino recounts, the Jews began to *ululare*, to howl or bark.[101] By likening the Jews torturing Simonino to dogs, Tiberino seems to have been uniting Chrysostom's interpretation of Matthew with an image of the crucified Christ surrounded by dogs. Such an image had appeared regularly in Christian plastic art from the ninth century on, and it would continue to appear in it through the time (and works) of Hieronymus Bosch (ca. 1450-1516), and even later. The origin of this image is apparently Psalm 21:17. "Many dogs have surrounded me" (Circumdederunt me canes multi), the psalmist says of his enemies, a passage that was commonly applied to Christ.[102] Yet since ritual murder victims were likened to Christ—was not Werner of Oberwesel said to have suffered *in loco Christo?*—Tiberino had really offered readers a chilling recreation of the Crucifixion. He was confident that readers would tie his description and the fate of Simonino to depictions of Christ himself on the Cross. An eighteenth-century painting that still hangs in the cathedral church of Sandomierz, a small town in southeastern Poland, explicitly renders the two scenes as one (see fig. 1). Going beyond even Dr. Tiberino, Carol de Prevot's panoramic blood libel depicts the martyred child first as Christ in swaddling clothes, then

Figure 1. Carol de Prevot, *Martyriologium Romanum*, Sandomierz, Poland, ca. 1725.

rolled and tortured in a barrel lined with sharp nails, then dismembered. Jews collect the blood, and the Christ child—who, indeed, is pictured as crucified in the center of the painting—is finally devoured by a horrendously vicious dog, metonymously standing in for the Jews in general.[103]

So canine was the Jews' image that even synagogal chanting was likened to "barking." More than one papal text invokes the term for barking, *ululare*, to refer to the *clamore* attached to the synagogue service. A letter by King Henry III of England in 1253 employs *ululare*, as well as the companion term *strepitum*, a racket. The term appears again in a text of Philip V of France in 1320, which speaks in nearly the same breath of "their braying" (suos latratos), and also "their barking" (suos ululates). Philip directed that the offending synagogue from whose walls these sounds were emanating be removed; its "noise competed" (concurrenter emittere) with the prayer of a nearby church.[104] Jewish prayer, if not all Jewish practice, seems universally to have been sensed as the yelping of dogs "pra/eying" to devour the host. In the case of Simonino of Trent, the Jewish dog was also braying in anticipation of the (eucharistic) blood feast that the martyred Simonino was about to furnish, placed on the Cross (in another painting of his passion) and polluted through circumcision.

Eventually, all Jewish sounds, noise, and perhaps even speech might be likened to barking. Having experienced the dismemberment of the papal state and the simultaneous fall of the Roman Ghetto just months before, Pius IX was moved in 1871 to complain that Jews were aurally polluting the city's sacred space. They were "barking" (*latrare*) up and down Roman streets.[105] By extension, the smelly Jewish dogs were spreading the infamous "Jewish stench" throughout out the city. This thought may have also recalled for Pius the "stinking" and "revolting" rabbinic lore (foetida et foeda . . . scribarum sapientia) that Ramon Martí had deplored in his *Pugio fidei* of about 1278.[106] It was, in this context, so very easy for Pius (and, as we shall see, for others, too) to deem the now ubiquitous "Jewish dogs" symbolic of modernity itself. Did the Jews not symbolize that other cur, the new Italian monarchy, which had replaced the papal state? As for the defunct Roman Ghetto, to carry the imagery to its extreme, it had been a kennel for the three hundred years of its existence.[107] *Latrare*, I stress, was Pius IX's own word. Yet had he not been preceded in using it, or words like it, by

Chrysostom, Agobard, Rupert of Deutz, Henry III, Philip V, Fortunato Coppoli, and Dr. Tiberino, to name but a few? The figure of the Jewish dog was not invented to facilitate historical hermeneutic.

Combining all purported Jewish treachery under the rubric of canine eucharistic cannibalism immeasurably increased the desire to be avenged on the Jews. This was so regardless of whether vengeance took the form of excising Paul's anxiety-raising "leaven" through expulsion or whether it ended in violence, as happened at Trent in 1475, Lincoln in 1255, or, as we shall see, at Blois in 1171. Bitterly ironic, as desirable as it was for Jews to create eucharistic martyrs to strengthen the faith, the fruit of Jewish "cooperation" in this endeavor was mayhem. Each of the three above libels resulted in tens of Jews, men and women, losing their lives. The Host libel of 1298 that provoked the Rindfleisch massacres led to the deaths of hundreds, if not thousands.

Violence also produced forced conversion. In the earlier Middle Ages, any number of bishops resorted to force, for instance, one at Arles, whom Gregory the Great reprimanded.[108] Conversion, these bishops must have thought, would end Jewish pollution. It would certainly end the Jewish presence; the means were secondary. Other clergy knew that the theologically wrong had to be masked, and they invented marvelous narratives vividly disguising force as free will. Gregory of Tours, a rough contemporary of Gregory the Great, writes of three hundred Jews who had previously refused baptism now dressed in white and hastening to be baptized after hearing the Gospel of John preached.[109]

Admittedly, the resort to force was the exception, and so was the spilling of blood. Doctrinally, force, for any reason, was unthinkable. Besides, Paul's references to Jews and Judaism encompassed more than rage against Judaizing. Paul was a Jew himself. He felt his Judaism and proclaimed it—at least three times in chapters 9–11 in his Epistle to the Romans. And these three chapters provide a corrective to Paul's chronologically earlier words in Corinthians and Galatians, where, in the event, he was decrying the leaven of Judaizing, not the faults of actual Jews. Did not his admonition to drive out the son of Hagar (Gal. 4:30) refer exclusively to expunging Jewish practices, especially circumcision, which some *Gentile* believers had adopted?

But there is some doubt whether Paul's contemporaries understood this. Perhaps already Gentile Christians in Rome, who shared a common conventicle with Jewish Christians, were asking, as they mulled over Paul's words about Christian unity in the cup and bread, whether their still Judaizing counterparts should not be severed from the fellowship. One wonders whether Paul's somewhat conciliatory attitude toward Jewish-Christian believers in the later chapters of Romans was enough to satisfy them. As though in response to such uneasiness, Paul in Romans emphasizes that God's covenant is everlasting. Or perhaps Paul independently understood the pejorative implications of Galatians for actual Jews? This, of course, we cannot know. Yet Paul did insist that the Jews, including those still unbelieving, as well as Jewish Christians, would one day enter the united Christian fold. They would *have to enter*, as Paul saw it, before the parousia could arrive. This was the destiny of mankind. Jews, accordingly, were (temporarily) enemies of God, for the sake of the Gospel, but they were also (constantly) dear to God, thanks to the merits of the patriarchs (Rom. 11:22 and 11:28 especially).

Yet these words promoted only an armistice. They did not announce a treaty of peace. They left room for suspicion and an ambiguity of obligation. To explain why removing the "clamor" (*clamore*) of a synagogue required affording the Jews an alternate place of prayer, Gregory the Great based himself not on theology but on Roman law.[110] This law alone, in Gregory's day (although ever less afterward) was the principal guarantor of Jewish rights and privileges. Neither Paul nor (what, most arguably, is said about) Augustine's discussion of Jewish witness afforded security.[111] It is notable that fifteen hundred years later, Marquardus de Susannis understood the ambivalence perfectly. Jews living as *pacificos*, he wrote, must be sustained. The rule of *caritas* vouchsafes this, and by *caritas*, de Susannis (following medieval legal tradition) meant the justice on which the world stands. Nothing could be firmer, or so one might think. For the rule has its exceptions, de Susannis continues: Jews who plot against Christianity may be expelled *iure optimo*. This was a piece of legal shorthand, which meant that all agree, but no firm law or precedent can be adduced in support. Thus, for allegedly creating havoc in the town of Udine in 1556, the Jews *were* expelled. The town's leaders called the event an "opportunity to get rid of the Jews" (occasione discaciar gli ebrei). De Susannis himself lived in Udine, and the author of the text describing the expulsion was his cousin Pagano. This section of de Susannis's long legal disquisition was anything but theory.[112]

To this must be added that Paul himself, however knowingly, nourished ambivalence. By making the Jews, not unlike the pig, "half-kosher," at once God's "friends" and "enemies," he could only have aroused doubt.[113] Thus it came to be that the Jew was to be pushed away, yet Jews were also to be brought close and loved. This is precisely the theme Augustine took up in the last chapter of his *Adversus Iudaeos*. Following nine chapters that speak of Jewish carnality and servitude, in chapter 10, Augustine tells his listener and reader to follow the example of Paul and to "love" Jews. Even Agobard acquiesced. Did he not admit, at the end of his tirades, and to his certain distaste, that Jews must be treated piously, reiterating Paul's hope in Romans 11 of ultimate Jewish conversion?[114] Ambiguity about Jews had, therefore, become a permanent factor of life, which, in the light of what has just been said, might aptly be named "the Agobardian predicament." However, the one who best summed up this ambiguity was Chrétien de Troyes (d. 1189/90). He also attenuated it by interjecting a note of indebtedness into his *Contes du Graal*. His comments, fortuitously, are framed within the present study's special terms of reference:

> The wicked Jews, whom we should kill like dogs,
> Brought harm to themselves and did us great good,
> When in their malice they raised him on the cross:
> They damned themselves and saved us.[115]

The Supersessionist Dilemma

Yet how different was "Agobard's predicament" from the ambiguity bespoken by Pope Benedict XVI as Cardinal Ratzinger: "respect" for Judaism along with unbending supersessionism (Pope Benedict's certain disquiet at hearing himself cited *on Jews* in the same breath with Agobard notwithstanding)?[116] The ambiguity of both is so clearly rooted not only in Paul, but in the original metaphor in Matthew of the children, the "bread," and the dogs. Supersessionism is what the dog analogy was intended to shore up from the start. It is the crux of the Catholic-Jewish conundrum. Chrysostom said it outright: "we who were dogs *received the strength*, through God's grace." The claim to inherit was, therefore, to be tirelessly protected, and alongside it, eucharistic purity and the oneness of the variegated *Corpus Christi*.

The ambiguity inherent in the supersessionist reliance on the metaphor of "the children and the dogs" also foreshadowed instability. To say that the Church holds Judaism dear as "an older brother" offers little solace. Indeed, it only entrenches the children-"dog" antinomy. When Paul spoke of the "elder brother," citing Genesis 25:23 (in Romans 9), he himself meant the carnal children of Israel, who had been superseded by the spiritual ones, children he interpretatively called Ishmael and Isaac, Esau and Jacob.[117] And through the ages, for Christian exegetes, the rejected Ishmael and Esau have been the Jews.

By Augustine's day, in the early fifth century, this exegesis represented what to many seemed solid fact. The testimony Augustine says Jews bring to validate Christianity is not the witness of a free man. Nor, as is so often said, is it that of demonstrating the venerability and, hence, the truth of the biblical text, which Jews are said to preserve. Rather, the so-called Jewish testimony is that of the slave, living in slavery. In every context in which Augustine raises the idea of Jewish witness, he portrays the Jews as *capsarii*, the older slaves who carry the young master's books to school.[118] The young master, the Christian, as Augustine also points out, rules over the defeated Jews. The "prophecy" of Genesis 49:10 has been fulfilled: "the staff shall not be removed from Judah, until Shiloh [the messiah] arrives." These "enslaved" Jews, Augustine adds, are identical with the carnal Jews of his own day (how many Jews Augustine encountered in real life is a mystery). By repeating the acts of their fathers, contemporary Jews are guilty, as were their fathers, of Christ's death. The mark of Cain, which Augustine also said Jews bear, does not signify, as is sometimes said, "spare them." That mark is Judaism itself, which, in its essence, is murderous.[119] Accordingly, even those who advocate preaching love and the sweetness of lips to bring the Jews to the light, as did Augustine (following his long chastisement for carnality) stand balanced on a thin wire.[120]

From this wire, it has been, and still is, easy to slip off. Anxieties over a besieged *unus panis*, to recall the warning of Paul as restated by the ninth-century Amalric of Metz, ended by privileging accusations and, sometimes, violent acting out. Fearing for the integrity of his cherished *societas fidei*, Amalric's rough contemporary Agobard, despite his Pauline strictures, toed the line only with difficulty. His complaints of beatings by royal *missi* and an episode in which he may have forcibly baptized Jewish children suggest that at least once he overstepped the bounds.[121]

Yet to live within the black and white supersessionist matrix is to fall back on comfortably seductive reassurances: not only of eucharistic verity, the guarantees of faith in Christ, and membership in the united Christian fellowship but, above all, of the rewards of maintaining exclusive Christian purity. Because it confers all these benefits, this vision of reality is too enticing easily to let go, regardless of the cost to others. It certainly has sustained ambivalence. And it is with the very clear manifestations of ambivalence sometimes present in modern Catholic discussions of ritual murder that our study now proceeds. Even in recent decades ambivalence, rather than radical innovation, has (too) often been espoused. The image of the "Jewish dog," suspected of threatening to reclaim for itself the mantle of chosenness, whether violently or through surreptitious infiltration, has proved tenacious, even when it is not framed in words. I ask readers to bear this in mind constantly as they go through the long sections of the book in which the "dog" is hidden from sight. In one way or another, verbalized or deeply *internalized*, the "Jewish dog" has secreted itself just beneath the surface. Its image never really goes away.

One Ambivalence and Continuity

At the far edge of the balcony in the reading room of the Vatican Library, so far left that going any further would mean literally falling off and onto the floor below, there is a section labeled "Judaica." This small Judaica collection (the stacks have a large and admirable one) contains a Babylonian Talmud. This is the same Talmud that was first burned in Paris in 1240 by papal order and again, in Rome itself, in 1553. Afterward, the Talmud was placed on the Index of Prohibited Books. The ban itself no longer exists. Hesitancy about the Talmud apparently does. One reaches the Judaica section only intentionally. Nobody passes by on the way to somewhere else. The possibility of chance encounter piquing a reader's bibliographic curiosity is minimal to nil.

Ambivalence about things Jewish is present elsewhere in the reading room, too. In the entries on ritual murder in the *Enciclopedia cattolica*, issued at Rome in 1953 and prominently displayed on the left side of the reading room's main floor, the watchword is indecision. Indecision features in similar entries in the adjacently shelved *New Catholic Encyclopedia* (issued in 1967 by the Catholic University of America Press) as well. The ritual murder accusation, both encyclopedias imply, was fabricated, and the *New Catholic Encyclopedia* uses words like "infamous," and "delusion." Yet an alleged victim such as Hugh of Lincoln (1255) is listed as St. Hugh, and on the subject of Simonino of Trent (1475), one reads: "The incident still awaits critical historical investigation." The *Enciclopedia cattolica* is unabashedly tentative. On Simonino, called "santo, martire"—even though Simonino was never actually canonized—the entry says that "public opinion, like the [records of the] trial itself, . . . attributes the Jews with guilt. . . . a fully critical study is still awaited" (L'opinione pubblica e il processo . . . attribuirono agli Ebrei la colpa. . . . uno studio critico ancora manca). For the editors of the two encyclopedias, the jury was still out.[1]

The same reserve is found as late as 1968 in the *Bibliotheca Sanctorum*, a modern review of sainthood produced at the Pontifical Lateran University's John XXIII Institute. Father Gérard Mathon of the Catholic University of Lille, the author of the entry on Richard of Pontoise, another "supposed victim" (pretese vittime) of ritual murder (about whom we shall have much to say below), first casts doubt on it, writing, "these supposed crimes are today much contested" (questi pretesi crimini sono oggi assai contestati). But he goes on to say that "it would be best to hold off judgment" (sarà bene attenersi a una valutazione prudente), much as does F. D. Lazenby, the author of the *Catholic Encyclopedia*'s 1967 essay on Simonino of Trent.[2]

This recent scholarship marks a step backward. Much earlier, the *Catholic Encyclopedia* of 1910–12, published by Appleton, and bearing an imprimatur, said about William of Norwich (the first alleged ritual murder victim): "This [charge] has been well named 'one of the most notable and disastrous lies of history.'"[3] And, in 1938, Donald Attwater, commenting on Richard of Pontoise in the revised, Thurston edition of Alban Butler's eighteenth-century *Lives of the Saints*, said that perhaps an "unbalanced" Jew might have murdered a Christian, but that the Jewish people as a whole were to be "acquitted." He repeated himself in the new printing of Butler in 1956.[4] In 1965, at the time of the Vatican II Council, which at last formally absolved the Jews of guilt for Jesus' death, Attwater clarified matters still further, echoing the 1910 *Catholic Encyclopedia*. In the entry on William of Norwich in *The Penguin Dictionary of Saints*, he now declared unambiguously: "No instance of the charge has been substantiated."[5]

Attwater knew, of course, that opinions were not unanimous. W. H. Hart, the editor of the chronicles and charters of Gloucester, writing in the 1860s, had wondered whether many of the stories "would pass scrutiny." However, this did not prevent him from adding that "it is not my intention here to discuss the truth of these charges, . . . but the frequency . . . is sufficient to demand our attention."[6] Yet if Hart seems disingenuous, what should we say of Paul Guerin? In his *Petits Bol-*

landistes, of about 1888, summarizing and often imaginatively retelling the episodes found in the original Bollandist *Acta Sanctorum*, Guerin describes the deaths of five martyrs to "Jewish savagery." Richard of Pontoise, Guerin tells, was struck with a fury found only among the "children of the race of Canaan." This, apparently, is an allusion to the Canaanite woman, the children, and the dogs of Matthew 15:26, which is reinforced when Guerin cites Dr. Tiberino's canine perception of the Jews of Trent (1475) in retelling the story of Simonino. But Guerin then steps back to say that it is contrary to "natural equity" to accuse the whole people of these atrocities. Have not the popes, many times, but specifically Alexander II, saved Jews from the wrath of mobs and princes?[7] What Guerin really believed we are left to guess.

Other scholars were transparent. In the 1880s, the Anglican Reverend Sabine Baring-Gould called the ritual murder charge a canard. The lie so incensed him that throwing caution to the winds, he queried, in his *Lives of the Saints*, whether the Jews, as persecuted and despised as they were in the Middle Ages, did not have the unassailable right to hate Christians.[8] They most certainly did not, would have been the answer of many in the late nineteenth- and early twentieth-century Catholic establishment, whose campaign to resurrect the ritual murder charge makes even ambivalence seem radically rejectionist. Within the Church, the 1880s through the first decades of the twentieth century witnessed a wholesale revival of ritual murder accusations—and their widespread acceptance.[9]

Fin de siècle and Catholic Modernism

The story of the revival is laid out splendidly by Elphège Vacandard in a virtually, and regrettably, forgotten essay of 1913.[10] Vacandard criticizes works like August Rohling's 1872 *Der Talmudjude* (The Talmud Jew), which accuse Jews of murdering Christian children and ritually using their blood. Rebuttals, like that by the Protestant Hebraist Franz Delitzsch in 1882, Vacandard notes, left Rohling and others unmoved.[11] Nor did they deter Father Henri Desportes. In the later 1880s, Desportes compiled a list of 150 alleged ritual murders in his *Le*

Mystère du sang chez les juifs. This list was faithfully reprinted, Vacandard is chagrined to say, in the Milanese *Osservatore cattolico*.[12] Ritual murder and blood-libel accusations were also rampant in the late nineteenth- and early twentieth-century Roman Jesuit organ *La civiltà cattolica*.[13] That various medieval popes roundly condemned these accusations seems not to have mattered.[14]

Yet late nineteenth-century Catholic clerical support for ritual murder accusations was not wall-to-wall. The charge, wrote Georg Kopp, bishop of Fulda and later cardinal of Breslau, was "grounded neither in Judaism nor history . . . a thoroughly outrageous lie" (weder durch die jüdische Religion, noch durch die Geschichte begründen . . . eine entschiedene frevelentliche Unwahrheit).[15] Kopp, unlike others in Germany who opposed the charge, stood high in Vatican esteem. But he had also played the role of intermediary during the *Kulturkampf* between the imperial Chancellor Bismarck and Rome—a man of compromise, it would appear, who knew where to draw the line. Joseph Hubert Reinkins, rector of the University of Breslau and, after 1873, Old-Catholic bishop of Germany, was more outspoken. He called ritual murder "a groundless malicious slander" (eine grundlose und durchaus boshafte Verleumdung) and said that it was "a disgrace" (eine Schmach) for anyone who called himself a Christian to make such allegations. Such people had forgotten the origins of Jesus the person, and they were ignoring the words of Paul in Romans 11:18, where he referred to God's everlasting promise (to the Jews). Protestants, too, expressed opposition. Beside Delitzsch, in Protestant academic circles even Paul de Lagarde, otherwise noted for his racist pan-Germanism, called the charge of ritual murder a fraud. Joining them were Protestant divines and scholars who held posts in important universities, including in faculties of theology.[16]

Our interest here, however, is principally in the Catholic reaction, which was sometimes highly critical—and acerbic, splitting religious orders down the middle, which happened with the Jesuits. Roman Jesuits were among the most vocal supporters of the charge of ritual murder. Jesuits outside Rome, including the Bollandist scholars Hippolyte Delehaye and François Halkin, unabashedly voiced condemnation (as noted in the Preface). Writing in 1925 and 1926, respectively,

Delehaye and Halkin called the charge "inane" and "a murderous and absurd calumny." Adding to their cry was a third Jesuit, the medievalist Peter Browe. At one point, Browe criticized medieval canon law for merely tolerating Jews rather than calling the right of Jews to live in Christian society unimpeachable.

Browe was a major student of the Eucharist, which gives his work great force. He condemned the Host libel in 1926 and decried the practice of forcing Jews to attend missionizing sermons. Browe's essays on the Eucharist appeared in 1929 and 1933, to culminate in 1938, in the two-volume *Die eucharistichen Wunder des Mittelalters*.[17] In 1941, at the height of the Nazi era, Browe stressed the repugnance of canon law for discriminating against converts because of their Jewish blood. This he did, even though his objections ran counter to Jesuit traditions, which had discriminated against descendants of Jews since shortly after the Order's founding in the mid sixteenth century.[18] Browe did write that in his opinion, medieval French and German Jews, as opposed to Italian ones, expressed odium of Christianity, and he admitted to his hopes for Jewish conversion. Yet saying these things may have made his otherwise unpopular stance more palatable. Besides, what disturbed Browe were the remarks in the Hebrew Crusade chronicles calling Christ "the hanged one" or churches places of impurity. In the context of the widespread massacres of Rhenish Jewry in 1096, these remarks are perhaps understandable. No doubt, they rubbed Browe's sensibilities the wrong way.[19]

Nonetheless, opposing stances on ritual murder rested on more than personal feeling. Delehaye, Halkin, and Browe, as well as others, knew that they were speaking out about Jews and ritual murder in the shadow of what is known as the "modernist" crisis. This is the name given to the struggle during the late nineteenth and early twentieth centuries over the compatibility of orthodox Catholic doctrine with modern social, scholarly, and scientific teachings. In the words of George Tyrell, an English Jesuit, although not referring to Jews, modernism sought "a synthesis of Catholicism and Science. It was not asserting the latter's supremacy."[20] Modernism's exponents were Catholic believers, not liberal secularists, and this made them all the more a threat.

This threat was enhanced by the modernist condemnations of ritual murder as myth. Anti-modernists, known also as integralists or ultramontanists, were among the myth's most fervent supporters. Centered principally at Rome, anti-modernists opposed all change that might emend the Catholic status quo, whether theological or political, and their position gained special force with the demise of the papal state in 1870 and its replacement by the secular Italian monarchy.

Yet discussions of the opposition between modernism and anti-modernism have consistently ignored how often Jews were the subject of anti-modernist discourse,[21] while the same clerics who condemned ritual murder were often modernists who spoke out with great animus against integralism, especially its demands for disciplinary conformity and insistence on humiliating scholarly concession. Hippolyte Delehaye's recent biographer Bernard Joassart writes that Delehaye resented being stymied by "the abominable fundamentalist campaign [l'abominable campagne intégriste] . . . which appeared in *L'unità cattolica* and the *La Critique du libéralisme*" at the moment when Delehaye was completing the third edition of his classic *Légendes hagiographiques* in 1927.[22] The attack on Delehaye had begun years earlier, orchestrated by Delehaye's longtime opponent, the papal Secretary of state Cardinal Merry del Val, who used every tool at his disposal to thwart Delehaye's scholarly studies, which more than once had debunked venerable hagiographic myths. Not coincidentally, Merry del Val was one of the ritual murder charge's chief protagonists.

The parallelism thus was four-pronged: modernism versus anti-modernism, belief in ritual murder libels versus their denunciation. And one may perhaps add two prongs more. For as André Vauchez comments, it was only with the ultramontanist anti-modernist victory in the twentieth century, alongside that of popular Catholicism, that child saints began to be canonized. This was the same kind of child-martyr sainthood that was opposed in the fifteenth century by Bishop Battista de' Giudici of Ventimiglia, the prelate who suffered humiliation when he questioned the martyrdom of Simonino of Trent.[23]

It must have specially irritated the Roman establishment that Delehaye took his positions, whether promoting scholarly investigation or urging ritual murder's condemnation, as a continuator, not as a radical. Correctly, Delehaye perceived himself to be following investigative principles that the early seventeenth-century Bollandists had first established. Scholarship, he argued—accurately read texts, not theological wish—revealed true saints and martyrs. Delehaye wrote in his short history of Bollandism that his was the same scholarly path that the original Bollandists had laid out (minus, of course, their support for ritual murder charges, which they had based on *their* understanding of the texts).[24] Delehaye was willing to go to the limit to defend his historical method, refusing to balk even when his ground-breaking *Les Légendes hagiographiques* was threatened with inclusion on the Index of Prohibited Books—together with five books of Alfred Loisy, one of modernism's chief ideological exponents.[25]

The pairing of modernism and opposition to ritual murder repeated in France, notably, in the writings of Vacandard and Félix Vernet. It repeated in Germany, too. The Old-Catholic Joseph Reinkens denounced the teachings of ritual murder as fervently as he decried Roman integralism. He also rejected the corollary doctrine of papal infallibility, which was proclaimed at the First Vatican Council of 1870. Nobody, however, surpassed the theologian Ignaz von Döllinger. So intensely was Döllinger censured for his modernism, that prior to 1881, he voluntarily stopped serving as a priest.

What distinguished Döllinger was his view that condemning ritual murder and attacking integralism were inseparably one. This was unlike Delehaye and Halkin, for whom denouncing ritual murder was an expression of principle that visibly paralleled, but was not of itself vital to renouncing integralist positions. In his famous address of 1881, *The Jews in Europe*, Döllinger declared that the Jews, whatever their faults, were not to blame for their sorry state. The culprit was Christianity. The ritual murder libel was "an utterly false and impossible" (unwahrscheinlichsten oder unmöglichen) charge.[26] As Jacques Kornberg has correctly observed, Döllinger realized that integralism had made stigmatizing Judaism essential to its antimodernist assault.[27] The threat to the *Corpus Christi* that integralism attributed to Judaism and modernism was one and the same.

Yet Döllinger's motivation in speaking out may also have been personal. His 1881 address may have responded to something more specific than integralist ultramontanism per se. That something was not August Rohling's strident *Der Talmudjude* (1872), which may first come to mind. Rather, in the years preceding Döllinger's lecture, Ludwig Erler, then a member of the cathedral chapter in Mainz, a position of no mean importance, had written a series of long, extraordinarily erudite essays on medieval Judaism. For the information they contain, and especially their dense bibliography, these essays are still valid tools of research; they appeared in the influential *Archiv für katholisches Kirchenrecht*, the same periodical in which Browe would publish his essay on Jewish toleration in 1938. Erler's position was the opposite of Döllinger's. The popes, Erler wrote, were forced to restrain Jewish insolence and pride, as well as hatred. He expressed himself cautiously about ritual murder, yet not so cautiously as to hide his belief that some of these murders took place. To support his argument, Erler cited a much earlier book, *Heidenthum und Judenthum*, published in Regensburg in 1857. Its author was Döllinger, who at one point refers to "the Jews' enormous contempt and hatred of other peoples" (hochmüthige Verachtung und feindselige Gehässigkeit der Juden gegen alle anderen Völker).[28] In 1881, Döllinger seems to have been doing a rigorous penance for what he had come to consider his own sins of a quarter-century before.[29]

The meeting of clerical discipline and free scholarly expression did not always result in sparks. This was particularly so when the scholarship appeared in an "approved" Catholic publication. The lengthy entry on "Modernism" in the 1910–12 *Catholic Encyclopedia* produced by Appleton in New York is a study in compromise, appropriate to what seems to be the encyclopedia's liberal bent. Its essay on Jewish history, written by François Gigot, could easily have been the work of a Jewish author. It weighs issues openly and betrays no theological bias. Its stance on ritual murder is one of disdain. Yet conforming to the bull *Pascendi* issued by Pope Pius X in 1907, the encyclopedia calls modernism an error. After which, it hedges. Though stigmatized, modernism is still credited with positive qualities. The writings of Alfred Loisy are cited admiringly, even though Loisy was excommunicate (as well as a professor at the secular Collège de France) at the time of the entry's composition.[30] Such an attitude would have been impossible in Rome.

Shelter from integralism's thrusts was also sought in sophisticated avoidance, and sometimes esotericism. Open speech might be seen as an excessive liberty in clerical circles even in the mid twentieth century. The entry on Simonino of Trent in the *Bibliotheca Sanctorum*, composed in 1968 by Father Iginio Rogger, a teacher of theology at a seminary in Trent, was written in the knowledge that Simonino's cult had been suppressed three years earlier. The overwhelming evidence, Rogger felt free to say, required rejecting the libel. Why, then, does the entry begin "Simone di Trento, beato, martire"? Was this the editor, reluctant to abandon the *santo, martire* of the earlier *Enciclopedia cattolica*? Or was this the wording of a cautious author? Rogger was possibly aware that a year earlier, in 1967—also after the cult's suppression— F. D. Lazenby, writing of Simonino in the American *New Catholic Encyclopedia*, had eschewed a firm stance.[31]

One wonders what Gérard Mathon would have written were the veneration of Richard of Pontoise also to have been suppressed. The apparent vacillation in his entry on Richard (found in the same volume of the *Bibliotheca Sanctorum* as that of Rogger on Simonino) is really great subtlety. Mathon must have judged that prudence dictated an indirect, if not an esoteric, approach, and he concluded his sentence (cited above) beginning "we had best delay judgment until all the facts are in" (sarà bene attenersi a una valutazione prudente) by saying "following the example of Vacandard" (sull'essempio di [Elphège] Vacandard). Vacandard, as we have seen, was enraged by accusations of ritual murder, especially those made in the early twentieth century.

Rogger's discussion of Simonino, too, resorted to the esoteric, or at the least to sleight of hand. Inserted in the bibliography to Rogger's entry on Simonino of Trent is a paired reference: first, to G. Divina's 1902 life of Simonino, the *Storia del beato Simone*, which favors sainthood for the supposed martyr, and, second, to a highly negative review of Divina, a priest in the diocese of Trent, by the Jesuit Bollandist François van Ortroy. The review appeared in the *Analecta Bollandiana* in 1904, and it had created a scandal, as Rogger had to have known even sixty years later. It certainly could not have escaped him that the first to cite these two items together was Hippolyte Delehaye, who had watched the scandal unfold at first hand and whose back-to-back reference to Divina and van Ortroy was unquestionably intentional. Delehaye was writing in an entry on Simonino in a jointly authored volume produced in 1940, known as the *Propylaeum* for December, which is a (teaching) summary of sections of the original *Acta Sanctorum*, with the addition of later bibliography. Joining Delehaye as authors were his fellow Bollandists P. Peeters, M. Coens, B. de Gaiffier, P. Grosjean, and F. Halkin. The achievement was signal. The *Proplyaeum*, with its rich notation of sources and additional bibliography, is also one of the first places an author like Rogger would look as he began his own research on Simonino.[32]

The entry in the *Propylaeum* begins traditionally: "the passion of the boy Simonino of Trent, cruelly murdered by the Jews, who afterward was resplendent in the light of his many miracles" (Tridenti passio sancti Simeonis pueri, a Iudaeis saevissime trucidati, qui multis postea miraculis coruscavit). The text then proceeds to say not simply that Simonino was killed, but *fertur*—it is said, or it is told, as in a story—that he was killed. The reader has been prepared for the following bibliographical reference: "*Acta SS.*, Mart. t. III, p. 494–502 [the location of the original Bollandist discussion]; G. Divina, *Storia del beato Simone* . . . , Trento, 1902; *Anal. Boll.*, t. XXIII, p.122–24." This last is a shorthand reference to van Ortroy's review, which dismantles Divina's reaffirmation of Simonino's martyrdom, charging Divina with presenting only parts of the trial testimony and accusing him of naïve textual reading. The chronological authenticity of a document, says van Ortroy, does not guarantee the veracity of its contents. This lesson the 1953 *Enciclopedia cattolica* seems blissfully to have ignored in citing "the trial record," alongside public opinion, in suspending judgment on Simonino's case.

That van Ortroy had so deftly dismantled Divina, Delehaye and company were certainly aware, just as they clearly knew about the acid exchanges van Ortroy's review had provoked when it first appeared; more will be said below about the review itself and contemporary reaction. It may also be taken for granted that Delehaye sided with van Ortroy; one cannot call the libels "inane" one day and praise an alleged victim of ritual murder the next. Yet neither could Delehaye and his fellows openly contradict those whom they reverenced as intellectual forebears, a reverence that Delehaye's book on "three hundred years" of Bollandism so well illustrates. The demands of filial piety necessitated a cryptic response. That response came in the form of a recondite bibliographical note, yet one whose message was clear: the original Bollandist claim notwithstanding, the accusation of murdering Simonino was nonsense.

Yet in taking this forceful stance and arousing certain displeasure in the Roman Curia, the twentieth-century Bollandists were paradoxically following in their forebears' footsteps, gainsaying conclusions, but espousing methods, as well as reliving early Bollandist trials. Delehaye recounts with great detail the struggle of the seventeenth-century Bollandists with the Roman Curia, when they, too, called received myth into question.[33] Curial displeasure with the Bollandists in Delehaye's day was nothing new. Only now, beyond scholarly method and questions of sainthood, the Curialists were lambasting Bollandist attitudes toward Jews.

The person especially incensed by van Ortroy's review was Cardinal Merry del Val, Delehaye's arch-opponent and, as said, one of the ritual murder libel's chief proponents, who ordered a pre-publication censorship of van Ortroy's text. Del Val's behavior is a sterling example of how opposition to modernism and fear of Jews stemmed from the same font. But were not the late nineteenth-century popes who raged at modernist doctrines (apart from their rage at modernity's purely political manifestations) also appalled at the Ghetto's dismantling? Their record on ritual murder accusations was no better. Indeed, in the strife over the veracity of these accusations, the ferocity of integralist opposition to modernism—and modernity—came directly to the fore. As the late nineteenth-century popes Pius IX, Pius X, and Leo XIII correctly understood, modernist doctrines undermined their authority. They reacted tyrannically, establishing the doctrine of papal (doctrinal) infallibility in 1870 and attacking modernism head-on in the bull *Pascendi* in 1907. Yet, likewise, these popes broke with precedent and approved charges of ritual murder, albeit indirectly, by permitting articles supporting the charge to appear in the Jesuit *La civiltà cattolica*, which was published under papal supervision. Moreover, guided by Merry del Val, first Leo XIII, in 1899, and then Pius X, in

1913, refused to allow medieval letters written by papal predecessors denouncing the blood libel to be republished, particularly the unambiguous denunciation issued by Innocent IV in 1247. The conjoint fears of Judaism and modernism had provoked consternation. Just as the integralist fortress allowed no chinks in the Catholic theological wall, so it discarded the balanced perspective vis-à-vis the Jews, and especially ritual murder, that Innocent IV, and even Innocent III, had once maintained.

Jews and the Modern Polity

The purported Jewish threat had also taken on a political dimension. There is no escaping the thought that the renewal of ritual murder charges by official Catholic publications was related to the demise of the papal state in 1870, which was also the moment when Jews throughout Europe had at last achieved civil equality, evoking political—and racial—anti-Semitism. The fear of Jews and the fear of modernism, if not of modernity itself, especially political modernity, neatly coalesced. For supporters of the concept that the *Corpus Christi* was at once political and spiritual, and that both were one, Judaism and modernism—whether doctrinal, secular, or political—were but two strands in a single thread.

It is in this political light that the refusal to republish medieval papal letters decrying the blood libel has attracted scholarly attention, especially that of students of (secular) political modernism and its ecclesiastical response. Giovanni Miccoli explains that politics were as central to antimodernism as was "right" belief. More was at stake than doctrine and ecclesiastical discipline. Yet recalling doctrines like that of Agobard of Lyon about the *societas fidei*, or even Paul's corporatist view of the Christian fellowship, the *unus panis*, the anti-modernist struggle against the modern state should strike us as continuity, not something new. For members of the Curia, this point was self-evident. The *Corpus Christi* as the earthly embodiment of the saving Christ had always had its lines of political demarcation, and these lines had to be defined and protected. Now that the political *Corpus Christi* as the Church defined it was in the process of being usurped by the political body of the secular modern state, these lines required special protection. What also required defending was the Church as a spiritual unity. Almost by definition this meant defending against the destructive potential that had traditionally been ascribed to the Jews.

The underlying focus of concern would, as always, be the Jewish threat to the mystical body of believers, which, we shall see, was then being denounced in just so many words. But in 1899 and 1913, opposing modernism and reasserting papal political clout, two ends that integralists considered identical to shielding the *Corpus Christi*, might also be accomplished by failing to condemn charges of ritual murder. For did not the ritual murder victim symbolize the *Corpus Christi* itself? Thus it was virtually preordained that the commission established in response to a murder libel made at Polna in Bohemia would rebuff a request for the papacy to reconfirm medieval bulls of condemnation. Setting the tone with respect to the outcome, the commission was said "justly" to be headed by Cardinal Merry del Val, one of whose ancestors the Jews were said to have "crucified." [34] So avid was the commission for a negative result that even the intervention of distinguished English Catholics, including peers and the Lord Justice Russell, could not move it.[35] The furor was international, stretching from England through eastern Europe and southward to Italy. This was not a local incident. Religion and politics had perfectly mixed. Merry del Val would be elusive a second time, in 1913, when once again papal letters were solicited—to no avail—in connection with the Beilis ritual murder trial in Kiev.[36]

"The Jews, symbol of modernity," as Giovanni Miccoli has put it so well—in particular, of political modernity, which threatened the lifeblood of the institutional Church.[37] Was not the detested secular (post-1870) Italian state,[38] headed by the secular monarchy, exercising dominion in territories the pope had ruled politically for centuries? To protest the erection in 1889, in the Campo dei Fiori in Rome, of the statue of the renegade Dominican Giordano Bruno, burned at the stake in 1600 and venerated as a precursor by the secular Roman civic leadership, the pope declared a public fast.[39]

Purported Jewish assertiveness created the same anxiety. During the Dreyfus affair at the end of the nineteenth century, when the French

Jewish Captain Alfred Dreyfus was falsely accused of espionage, exacerbating already existing rifts in French society, the alleged bond between Jews, Judaizing, and the corrosive threat to the Church of secular modernism was stated explicitly. The papal nuncio in France, Monsignor Lorenzelli, condemned the Limousin Abbé Pichot, a teacher of mathematics and modern science, as "the ultimate Dreyfusard and Judaizer among the priests" (il sacerdote più dreyfusardo e più giudiazzante che si conosca). Pichot was guilty of manifesting a spirit that was both "umanitario [i.e., lay and secular—in short, secular humanism] e dreyfusardo [once again, Judaizing]." The (traitorous) Jew and secular modernity were one, together with the secular state—or so Lorenzelli believed, who was echoed in Germany by the Catholic biweekly the *Historisch-politischen Blätter*, which called liberalism "nothing other than denationalized Jewry [seeking to] erect the empire of so-called humanity on the ruins of the Christian world-order. . . . [And] were not the so-called 'modern ideas' rejected by the Syllabus [of Errors] actually of Jewish origin?"[40]

Pius IX, who was horrified, as we have seen, by Jewish emancipation, civil enfranchisement, and the simultaneous ending of the Roman Ghetto and the establishment of Rome as the capital of the secular Italian state (on September 20, 1870), anticipated both these comments. It was in a state of disbelief that he referred in 1871 to the now liberated Jews, saying, "we hear them barking up and down the streets" (li sentiamo per tutte le vie latrare).[41] Both Jewishly and politically, the Jews were polluting the sacred space of the Eternal City.[42] How Pius IX must have envied Gregory the Great (his letters, which survive, had long been known). To prevent the sound of Jewish prayer from penetrating the walls of a nearby church, Gregory had simply ordered that the "offending" synagogue be relocated.[43]

Jewish actions were said to pollute in other ways, too. Jews sitting alongside Christian children in the schools, warned the Jesuit Giovanni Oreglia in 1882, were generating a "dangerous familiarity" (pericolosa famigliarità). Worse, wrote the pseudonymous Ascar in the *Gazzettino illustrato* of January 26, 1935, the Jews had thrown off the outer shell of their Judaism and assimilated ("vanno sgiudaizzandosi per diventare la maggior parte liberi pensatori"), yet, all the while, they remained Jews at heart. Theological and political issues had become indistinguishable. Oreglia and Ascar had identified the Jews as the "deceptive lovers of self" of 2 Timothy 3, who furtively destroy from within by corrupting all they come near; Agobard of Lyon had cited this passage in addressing Emperor Louis the Pious in the ninth century. Hovering below the surface, too, are the remonstrations of earlier times about Jews polluting through physical contact, to wit, Johannes Teutonicus's warning against the perils of "deception between courses." The line was exceedingly thin that distinguished Sicard of Cremona's fear of sexual defilement from the physical proximity on the school bench that irked Giovanni Oreglia—certainly as Oreglia's imagination must have perceived it.

One is hard pressed to differ between the preoccupations and recriminations of Lorenzelli, Desportes, Ascar, and Oreglia and those of so many medievals. *La civiltà cattolica* of 1881 carries an essay Oreglia composed extolling the martyrdom of Simonino of Trent.[44] Oreglia was followed in 1889, by Bishop Antonio de Pol of Vicenza. The Jews, said de Pol, "who deceive" Christians about Lorenzino of Marostica, a purported (fifteenth-century) victim of ritual murder, "desire more to murder Christianity itself than to kill one single Christian" (aspirano non tanto ad uccidere un cristiano, quanto ad uccidere lo stesso Cristianesimo).[45] A French near contemporary, Roger Gougenot des Mousseaux, carried the image even further, writing of "the man of Talmudic faith, whose fanaticism and implacable malice stirred him up against Christian civilization" (le homme de la foi talmudique, celui que son zèle et d'implacables rancunes animent contre la civilisation chrétienne). More extreme, as well as pertinent, was an anonymous manuscript from about 1840, which said that Jewish obstinacy in refusing to accept Jesus was such that "that they had persuaded themselves that to dine on Christian blood as a horrendous surrogate for the Eucharist would grant them salvation in heaven" (sono persuasi che un orrendo equivalente dell'eucarestia, il cibarsi di sangue cristiano, possa permettere loro di accedere alla salvezza nell'aldilà). This echoes precisely an accusation first made no later than the early fourteenth century.[46] Times since Chrysostom and Agobard had changed. Underlying ideas had not.

The early nineteenth-century parallel is also instructive in which great clerical efforts were made to "resacralize" the French state. For had not that essential element of the French Revolution, the creation of a direct bond between citizen and state, substituted, laicized, and secularized, however consciously (or, more likely, unconsciously, for the revolutionaries themselves), the concept of Corinthians that "the cup of blessing which we bless, is it not communion in the blood of Christ? The bread which we break, is it not the communion of the body of Christ? For we being many are one bread, and one body: for we are all partakers of that one bread."[47] Citizens, as the Revolution perceived them, were one in the body of the state, the *corpus reipublicae mysticum*, whose own sempiternal body had now wholly replaced that of the *patria communis*, the *corpus ecclesiae mysticum* of the (medieval) Church.[48]

With this revolutionary perception, the Church sought to compete. It hoped to resurrect the past and reestablish its claim to what it considered properly its own by staging elaborate processions that were akin to the rogations intended to define sacred boundaries, including especially those of the political *Corpus Christi*, which, for the Church was synonymous with the state. Only now the images suspended on the crosses carried in such processions were not those of Jesus, but of the "martyred" Louis XVI and Marie Antoinette. Iconographically substituting Christ, the royal "martyrs" eucharistically metaphorized and metonymized the *corpus mysticum* of the restored Bourbon monarchy. By patent transference, however—and continuing the metaphor—were not the revolutionary regicides of the eighteenth century (Christ-killing) Jews?[49]

The memory, at the least, of these efforts, was surely alive at the nineteenth century's end. But then there were neither intermediaries nor metaphor. Jews, Judaizing, and the secular state—modernity—were openly and mutually identified, and stigmatized. Perhaps borrowing from the "sacralizers," Gougenot des Mousseaux couched his vituperations against Jews in openly eucharistic terms. This was the context of his unrelenting support for the accusation of ritual murder.

What alone was missing, or seems to have been missing, from this scenario was direct reference to the eucharistic Host. Yet such reference had been made, if implicitly, in the eighteenth-century preaching manual of the Lazarist Joseph Lambert.[50] As part of his invective against "false communion," the reception of the Eucharist without previously confessing and receiving absolution, Lambert denounced the "magicians" who tortured the sacrament, "stabbing it, trampling it, throwing it into the flames, . . . and making of it an instrument of death." Host desecration, exactly as it had been ascribed to Jews, was now ascribed to Christians. The passage from this metaphor to that of the crucified (eucharistic) Louis XVI and his consort was simple. The implied identity between Judaizing and the subversion of the French state's rightful sacral nature was so firm that it was unnecessary to evoke it by name—although, as we have seen, that evocation would not tarry as the nineteenth century wore on. Lorenzelli's condemnation of Pichot as *giudaizzante* at that century's end culminated a process well under way.

Lorenzelli's contribution was his explicitness, openly applying the stigma of modernity, which he clearly perceived in the term's political, as well as its theological, sense. Subversion through Judaizing had become absolute. Yet were not those accusing the Jews of subversion also those who accused them of ritual murder, to wit, Desportes, Gougenot, and especially Italian Jesuits?[51] The two accusations were linked as inextricably as they were intimately bound up. Yet as we saw in the Introduction, this is what they had always been.

Ironically, it was the Protestant Ludwig Feuerbach who, in 1841, made it possible to understand this linkage in modern terms. The Jews, Feuerbach said, have an "alimentary view of theology." By this, says Kalman Bland, Feuerbach was depicting Jews as egoistic, carnal, and parochial. Feuerbach's figure, couched in a mordant excoriation of supposed Jewish bodily appetites in distinction to a Christian abstract appreciation of art and beauty, had modernized the metaphor of Paul. It was an anthropological and racial version of Paul's vision of the carnal Jewish altar that stood opposed to the spiritual Christian one, on which the mystical (spiritual) body of Christ was consumed in place of the carnal meat of the Jewish Temple sacrifice. Moreover, by implication, the appetites of Feuerbach's Jews were insatiable. Jews were gluttons, and they were as guilty for Feuerbach as they had been for John Chrysostom of wanting, like dogs, to steal the "children's bread." The Jews' so-called alimentary theology was one that not only desired to subvert Christianity's spiritual purity. It also ravenously sought to swallow it up. Feuerbach had recast in a more contemporary idiom the traditionally expressed anxieties of Catholic clerics like Oreglia, "Ascar," and, most of all, Antonio Pol, who accused Jews of plotting to murder Christianity itself. Feuerbach's imagery also reflects contemporary German thought as a whole: German apprehensions of *Verjudung*, Judaization, the Germans' own word, "in which," as Steven Aschheim explains, "the 'Jewish spirit' had somehow permeated German life and its key institutions . . . to undermine the German psyche. . . . [acting] as a potentially corrupting agent, dissolutive of society . . . [engendering] pollution and powerlessness."[52] This was precisely what Pol, Oreglia, Pius IX, and those of their ilk so greatly feared for the Church.

Hence, despite their verbal reconfiguration, attitudes had not changed. This applies especially to ritual murder. The conclusion of Robert Stacey with respect to ritual murder in the thirteenth century, that its evolution reflects unfolding chapters in the history of Christian piety, seems to apply equally to the nineteenth century.[53] Yet what the libel reflects most at this later moment is continuity. Piety's forms, its modes of expression, even its politics had varied little over time.[54] One reason for this continuity, certainly for its perpetuation, is the irreplaceable library of saints' lives known as the *Acta Sanctorum* bequeathed to posterity by the Bollandists. Their legacy includes what is perhaps the most complete repository of ritual murder tales that we possess.

Two The Bollandists and Their Work

We know little about the early Bollandists, whose history remains mostly unwritten. Perched on the doorstep of the early modern world, and perhaps just because of this, the Bollandists provide a window onto the medieval past from which they themselves had not fully emerged and with whose outlook they still had much in common. At the same time, like many Flemish humanists of the day, the Bollandists were highly devoted to collating and preserving true original texts. What they lacked were sophisticated tools to help them discern textual accuracy.[1]

On the subject of ritual murder, blood libels, and medieval Host accusations, the early Bollandists had much to say. These were the same Bollandists about whom Félix Vernet commented, in condemning the ritual murder libel in his extensive essay of 1910-12 on "Juifs et Chrétiens" in the *Dictionnaire apologétique de la foi catholique*: "Once this charge [of ritual murder] was considered true, and not only in the Middle Ages, but in the seventeenth and eighteenth centuries. The very learned and admirable Bollandists [were] the great authority among those who sustained the existence of ritual murder, 'the princes of historical certainty,' as Gougenot des Mousseaux called them in his *Le Juif, le judaïsme et la judaïsation des peuples chrétiens* (p. 197)."[2]

Vernet's indignation was bidirectional. Going one way, toward the past, Vernet criticized the Bollandists, whose analytical rigor stopped when it came to accepting a medieval lie; and, as Vernet correctly understood, the early Bollandists deeply believed the accusations in their every detail. With respect to modernity, Vernet was attacking contemporary purveyors of the ritual murder charge. He was enraged by people like Gougenot des Mousseaux, who had incorporated Bollandist writings on ritual murder into his clearly troublesome book, whose title implies the same linkage Lorenzelli had made between Judaizing and the corruption of the state.

In suggesting a direct line from seventeenth-century Bollandist thinking to that of their late nineteenth- and early twentieth-century successors, Vernet was right. The solid edifice the seventeenth-century Bollandists erected had nurtured the belief of nineteenth- and twentieth-century authors, whether lay or clerical, in the iniquity of Jews and Judaism. This belief these moderns then fused with their conviction that modernity and modern civilizations were the fonts of iniquity. It is superfluous to recall that for the fundamentally orthodox, the "romancing"—the exegetical interpretations—of one period easily impinge, in the manner of filial piety, on the interpretations of a second. Such piety certainly contributed to the (above-noted) radical, as well as radically pursued, early nineteenth-century French Jesuit political program of Bourbon restoration.

Yet had Vernet asked whether Bollandist thinking might be used to delve into attitudes of earlier epochs, he would have seen something else. Bollandist thinking and writings illuminate accusations that developed in northern France toward the end of the twelfth century and the beginning of the thirteenth, and, in particular, they help unravel Capetian royal policies vis-à-vis French Jews. Bollandist writings provide us with a true bridge. Through them, we may tie together not two but three temporally distant periods: the twelfth, the seventeenth, and the twentieth centuries. In addition, studying the Bollandist ritual murder narratives allows those whose first interest is the Jews themselves to penetrate twelfth- and early thirteenth-century Jewish mentalities. As observed in the Preface, with respect to ritual murder, medieval Christian and Jewish outlooks are mutually corroborative.

The Eucharist, Hosts, Magic, and Protestant Heresy

The Bollandists, first John Bolland, then Godfrey Hinschius (Hinschenius) and Daniel Papebroch, set out from their center in Antwerp to verify true sainthood and martyrdom. Verification would come from adopting the ways of other Flemish humanists, whose goal was to preserve ancient texts and to base their arguments on (what they considered) incontrovertible textual proof. Three hundred years later, Hippolyte Delehaye, a successor of the original Bollandists, was still championing this same method, if, to be sure, with greater sophistication.[3] The Bollandist goal was to discount false saints and enhance the credibility of those they deemed true.[4] What found its way into the *Acta Sanctorum* carried the seal of Bollandist conviction. Moreover, what appears in the *Acta* is a joint Bollandist product, at least with regard to the narratives of ritual murder. With two exceptions, the story of Werner of Oberwesel, whose author was probably Daniel Papebroch (whose initials are to the right of the entry at its start), and that of Hugh of Lincoln, authored by J. B. Sollerius,[5] all the entries on ritual murder are unsigned or unascribed, suggesting that they were the fruit of a combined effort. Accordingly, the Bollandists and their works will be referred to collectively.[6]

The original Bollandists, one modern successor has said, intended to instruct the faithful.[7] No other student of the Bollandists argues this point directly, but the Bollandists were creatures of their times, and it was inevitable that their writings would didactically reinforce contemporary convictions. They might also parry offensive thrusts. To demonstrate true Catholic sainthood was to respond to Protestant charges of Catholic fraud. Narratives, recounting the saving intervention of the Virgin, the enduring truth of the Eucharist, the unity of the Christian fellowship and, perhaps, most of all, martyrdom worked similarly, especially when these motifs were intertwined. This judgment embraces narratives of ritual murder, too. It was no accident that the Saints Days of the most prominent of the child martyrs allegedly murdered by Jews fall on the 24 and 25 March. This was both close to, and on, the Day of the Annunciation,[8] most likely because the Virgin was often assigned a leading role in the miracle of the child's death and its aftermath—or she was said to have intervened herself. Catholic Reformation piety and ritual murder charges seem to have fit together like the proverbial hand in a glove. However consciously, the story that the Bollandists told of ritual murder and its martyrs adds another chapter to the master narrative of successful proofs and adventures of the Eucharist in this world. This was the very sacrament, need it be recalled, that Protestantism so resoundingly rejected, just as Luther rejected the Host libel, one of whose purposes was to validate the Eucharist's salvific efficacy.

For the Bollandists, it appears, strengthening belief in ritual murder and the Host libel was tantamount to strengthening belief in two of Catholicism's central devotional foci, the Virgin and the Eucharist. The Bollandists were no less interested in demonstrating the resilience of the *Corpus Christi*, whether in its political, spiritual, or even its human embodiment. This was the same resilience, as we shall see, that was the grist of later sixteenth- and early seventeenth-century accounts of contemporary Catholic martyrdom. Yet was not demonstrating this resilience also the aim of nineteenth- and early twentieth-century Italian Jesuits? Was not their will to prove the invincibility of the *Corpus Christi* (in their case, against the supposed thrusts of modernity) the propellant that drove them to add modern examples of their own to the list of older ritual murder stories in the original Bollandist portfolio?[9]

However, seventeenth-century Bollandist accounts of ritual murder ranged wider than demonstrating the *Corpus Christi*'s unshakable wholeness. For one, the Bollandists linked ritual murder to imputed Jewish magic—for which they had "good historical reason." It seems more than happenstance that the Bollandists record ritual murders for the years 1540, 1579, 1592, nearly contemporary with the expulsion of the Jews from the papal state by Pius V and Clement VIII, in 1569 and 1593. The bulls of expulsion in both cases charge the Jews with practicing black magic.[10] Magic and ritual murder had been paired for centuries. A prototype of the ritual murder charge ascribed to 1066 accuses Jews of using a waxen figure to torture a bishop to death. Two centuries later, Berthold of Regensburg said that Jews crucify waxen images and sometimes kill Christian children—the essence being the pairing, which puts the two on the same level.[11] This also explains why a waxen image like that met above in the story told by Gonzalo de Berceo might be likened to the *Corpus Christi*.[12] The Jews piercing the image were charged with committing true ritual murder; the image itself was a clear surrogate for a desecrated Host.[13]

These pairings of magic and ritual murder recall the medieval tendency to identify magic with paganism, whose practice by Christians,

Paul had said, threatened the seamless oneness of the eucharistic Christian fellowship. How effortless it was to attach this last accusation to Jewish acts, for were not Judaism and paganism often viewed interchangeably? Charges of profaning the Host sometimes implicated Jewish magic directly.[14] The theme of Jewish magic and ritual murder reached its apparent apogee in the late fourteenth-century *Nova legenda angliae* of John Capgrave, who interjects into the story of Hugh of Lincoln, allegedly murdered in 1255, the observation, "that Hugh was eviscerated—it is said for purposes of necromancy or augury."[15] The Bollandists cited this passage verbatim.

The Bollandists also associated ritual murder with the great bugbear of Protestantism. In discussing Richard of Pontoise, they refer to the *English Martyrology* of John Wilson (1640), which, they say, speaks of Richard's corpse being translated to England, yet whose remains were saved from the (Anglican) heretics;[16] martyrdom conquers all, a theme to which we shall soon return, and in this specifically Anglican context. A parallel provocation may have been the increasing emergence from the shadows of crypto-Jews in (nearby) Amsterdam, which the Bollandists themselves were witnessing; false conversion features in their discussion of events in France in 1182.[17]

Nonetheless, the Bollandists' primary concern was eucharistic piety and its martyriological connections. This was the same brand of piety that was becoming ever more central in the post-Tridentine world, as doctrines and catechisms solidified and inquisitors became moral disciplinarians, confessors, and directors of souls (apart from being prosecutors of heresy).[18] Special emphasis was also being placed on the Eucharist's sacrificial nature. Accordingly, we might expect the Bollandists to highlight ritual murder narratives that laud the body of Christ, the Eucharist, confession, and virginity and praise the self-sacrifice of martyrs, all of which bespeak the ecclesiastical unity embodied in the *Corpus Christi*. The Bollandists thus speak of William of Norwich (1144) and use the occasion to offer a list of similar "martyrs." However, their discussion of William, the earliest supposed ritual murder victim, is not their most intensive. This honor they reserved for the "martyrdom" of the Good Werner of Oberwesel, in 1287, in whose story, Marian and eucharistic piety, in the context of ecclesiastical seamlessness, come directly to the fore.[19]

The Good Werner

The two main narrative sources the Bollandists mine for their argument about Werner require special attention, as does the manner of their use. One source is said to be nearly contemporary, although it is preserved in a later manuscript found in the Bollandist house at Antwerp; a second is a transcript from a trial that took place in 1427 promoting Werner's sainthood.[20] These texts reflect an authorial present that stretches from the thirteenth through the fifteenth centuries and into the Bollandists' own day. As they appear in the *Acta Sanctorum*, the texts have been edited. The Bollandists were master editors in the name of what they considered properly derived truth. They were editors, however, not distorters, their editorial method being the collation of what they believed were reliable testimonies, hence, a naïve, but fair adumbration of modern scholarly method. Yet as the Bollandists expressed it in the pithy statement that opens their long account of Werner's travails, their notions of truth and reliability are disturbing:

> Immane seculis omnibus in Christum & Christianos Iudæorum odium fuit, qui illos quotidie devovent, & atrociter persequuntur, eorum pueros furtim abducunt & crudeliter mactant.

> Through the centuries Jewish hate of Christ and the Christians was enormous. They cursed Christians daily and atrociously persecuted them, stealing Christian children in secret and cruelly killing them.

True as it was to their beliefs, Bollandist editing casts their achievement into the mold of what Hayden White has called "(historiographical) politicization."[21] White means a historiographic process at least as unconscious as it is intentional, whose purpose is to direct the historical narrative toward publicist, as well as historiographic, goals.[22] With respect to ritual murder, the Bollandists were perpetuating so-called martyrdoms in the collective memory and converting the tales that recount them into what they themselves might have called "usable narrative."[23]

With Werner, the narrative agenda emerges from the way the trial of 1427 is discussed. Werner is lauded not only for his wonders—forty pages of lauds and ninety miracles—but also for his tenderness, his veneration of the Virgin (whose aid he invokes alongside that of God himself), his confession to priests, and his subsequent taking of the Eucharist. His faith is steadfast. All together, this is a great Counter-Reformation encomium. In addition, as Miri Rubin has recently noted, two witnesses at this trial equate the boy with the Eucharist. This realizes the identity so common in Eucharistic iconography between child images and the Host: the sacrament is transformed into an actual child and then consumed. Rubin explains that the source of this iconography is the tale met above of the Jewish Boy, The Jew of Bourges. Angered that his son has been taken with Christianity and the Eucharist, the father propels him into a fiery furnace. The Virgin intervenes. She saves the boy; the father is condemned; his mother and sisters convert.[24]

The so-called "near contemporary" account of Werner clarifies the matter a bit further; the material in italics is the Bollandists' own editorial syncopation of the lengthy original:

> Primo namque iste Martyr inclytus, *loco Christi passus est: quia dum Judæi ipsum corpus Christi verum habere non poterant, exarserunt* in ipsum corpus mysticum. Secundo *in* ipso Christus passus est: videntes namque Judæi quod corpus Christi verum ex ipso extorquere non possent, *illud tamen venerabile Sacramentum*, cui contumeliam inferre intendebant, *affecerunt tormentorum contumeliis in ipso puero*.[25]

To paraphrase and explain: the Jews were looking for the "True Body" of Christ, a Host, but unable to obtain one, even by literally shaking it out of Werner suspended upside down (as the text later explains), they vented their rage on the boy himself. The Jews were also furious that Werner had refused to procure a Host for them. However, they raged at Werner not as a child but as the surrogate, substitute, and true equal of the Host, the "Mystical Body" (of Christ, the Church). This latter they saw in the form of (the third, the real, physical body of Christ) Werner's person, so that in place of the Eucharist, they tortured Werner in the flesh and (as the text goes on to say) drained his blood.[26]

In the story of Werner, the eucharistic image implicit in the story of the Jewish boy of Bourges has become explicit, and its parallel, the increasing insertion of eucharistic elements into ritual crucifixion stories has reached its apogee. As described by Robert Stacey, the thirteenth-century Adam of Bristol was taunted by his Jewish tormentors as the *deus christianorum* or even as the *corpus dei Christianorum* while he was being roasted on a spit (read: cooked, oven). Adam is both the physical body of Christ and the True Eucharistic one. Werner is the *corpus mysticum*, too, the *three* bodies of Christ unified. Yet had not Paul's teaching in 1 Corinthians 10 on the unity of individual Christians in Christ and in the Christian fellowship—and the subsequent interpretation of this teaching vis-à-vis the Jews and their alleged threat to that unity—made arriving at this point almost inevitable?

Moreover, from the time of Werner, or, more precisely, from the time that people began recounting his story in ways the Bollandists so pointedly highlight, the imagery was not only repeated, it was inverted, too.[27] We may recall that in the fifteenth-century English Croxton play, based on a story told about events in Aragon in the 1460s, the Jews torture the Host by putting it into an oven, and what emerges is a bloodied child.[28] Host and blood libels have fused—in which latter, Jews ritually reenact the murder of Christ and then (most often) magically use his blood. The fusion is bidirectional: Host desecration into blood libel, or vice versa. This is fearsome. On the one hand, reflecting on the stories of Werner, Adam of Bristol, and the Croxton play, Jewish attacks on the Eucharist had become tantamount to assaulting the *Corpus mysticum*, the body of the Church, in its entirety and its unity. Yet these assaults could just as easily be seen, as in fact they sometimes were, as plots against the body of every individual Christian.

This conclusion is especially striking in the context of sixteenth-century Catholic martyrdom *not involving Jews*. Werner, we just saw, is said to suffer vicariously—actually, to have undergone, like Christ, a "passion"—*loco Christi*, "in place of Christ." Going further, Christ himself is said to suffer "through Werner," *in ipso*. In other words, Werner's passion prolongs the passion of Christ himself. The text immediately elaborates.

> Tertio *in Christo* passus est, quia per illud venerabile Sacramentum fuit ille benedictus puer *Christo incorporatus*, in Christo manens, & Christus cum eo. Quarto Martyr Christi passus est *cum Christo*, quia eodem tempore, & eodem die, quibus illud mysterium ab Ecclesia frequentatur; vel quia realiter per passionem secutus est servus

Dominum suum. Quinto *pro Christo*, quia dum perfidi Christum regnantem in cælis persequi non possunt, persequuntur pro eo Christianum ejus cultorem. Sexto *pro Christo*, quia sicut Christus passus est, ut fieret & salvaretur Christianus, sic Christianus patitur *propter* Christum, ut exaltetur fides [Col. 0699E] Christiana, & glorificetur Deus. Beatus ergo qui persecutionem patitur *propter* Christum.

Werner suffers, undergoes a passion, this text says, "in [*in*] Christ," for, through the sacrament, he has been "incorporated into Christ"; the identity between the two is total. He also suffers "with [*cum*] Christ . . . on the same day," heightening the mutual identity. Further, Werner suffers "instead of [*pro*] Christ": the unbelievers, who could not pursue Christ reigning in heaven, persecuted his devotee in his place. Finally, Werner suffers, "for the good of Christ" (the second *pro Christo*): "Since just as Christ suffered, so that the Christian may exist and be saved, so the Christian [read, Werner] suffers for the sake of Christ [*propter*], to exalt the Christian faith and glorify God. Blessed, therefore, is he who undergoes martyrdom for [again *propter*] Christ's sake."

What exactly does this all mean? The text is apparently suggesting that Werner not only suffers vicariously for Christ, he suffers for Christ's benefit as well, as though his martyrdom redeems Christ himself. Yet is this not tantamount to saying that Werner's martyrdom redeems the entire *corpus mysticum?* By implication—and returning to the theme first seen in the Introduction—the Christian martyr renews and perpetuates Christ's own salvific sacrificial act, which is also the longed for culmination of the reciprocity bespoken by the twelfth-century Odo of Cambrai: "He feeds us with his blood and body so that . . . we are him and he is one with us." As John Colet put it even more forcefully in the early sixteenth century, "One is the food by which we are fed . . . so that all men, nourished by the One, may be one in that by which they are nourished."[29] The passion (through the martyrdom) of one is thus also the passion of all, including of Christ himself. What is more, and by implication, to keep the salvific process alive Christ's passion must be necessarily repeated—"passus est" is said at least six times. Werner's sacrifice perfectly embodies this repetition and its effects.

Whether the Bollandists themselves intended this message is moot. Their express purpose in gathering and publishing external, and earlier, sources was to verify martyrdoms, not to express opinion. Yet, in the spirit of Hayden White's historiographic "politicization," one hesitates to disallow that they may have understood the above text as just suggested, as well as that they may have wished to disseminate just this understanding. Their account of Richard of Pontoise, which we are about to see, seems purposefully publicist. Even Hippolyte Delehaye, though he begins his *Les Origines du culte des martyrs* averring that his is to be a scholarly study, separating the chaff of false sainthood from the wheat of true martyrs, could not restrain the pious enthusiasm he no doubt longed to transmit. Martyrs, he wrote, are a source of glory, and of the "grandeur d'âme," the majesty of the soul.[30] His seventeenth-century predecessors, devout Jesuits like Delehaye himself, could have been no less enthused. They may have been even more disposed than Delehaye to praising martyrdom's glory. For they were writing against the backdrop of Catholic martyrdom as they had witnessed it renewed in the later sixteenth and early seventeenth centuries.

For Catholics, this period was one during which the example of martyrdom was vivid and its praise lavish. The example was being set by those known as the Henrican martyrs, the English Thomas More and Bishop John Fisher of Rochester, who preferred death to swearing allegiance to King Henry VIII as head of an English Church. Works praising these English martyrs were not lacking, especially between 1580 and about 1640, when a veritable flood of them coursed its way through the Continent, including to Antwerp, the Bollandist seat. I have mentioned in the Introduction that these English martyrdoms were often perceived in eucharistic terms. Edmund Campion, to be martyred himself in 1582, referred to martyrs as "holy hosts and oblations" pleasing to God. The martyr, like the Eucharist, also stood for the whole. In the words of John Geninges, the martyr brought back solidarity, not only with Christ, "but also between one member and another [in the Church, for] the passions of the saints are always suffered for the common good of the whole body."[31]

This idea may also be rephrased contrapositively, to say that had those challenged to sacrifice themselves shirked martyrdom, the solidarity of the *corpus mysticum* would have suffered. Brad Gregory has said of these English martyrs that "the Henrican martyrs understood the denial of papal authority to violate the Church's essence—that it is one, holy, catholic, and apostolic. The royal supremacy undermined ecclesiastical unity and catholicity, rending Christ's mythical body by repudiating his earthly vicar, the guarantor of its corporate coherence and continuity. It trampled the Church's holiness . . . [martyrdom was] the highest form of the imitation of Christ." The imitation was in fact so great that its limits required definition. It had to be decided whether the martyr completed, or in some way sustained, the momentum of Christian salvation.[32]

This conundrum, as Gregory explains, is seen in the gloss of the (Catholic) Douai-Rheims New Testament of 1582 to Colossians 1:24. There Paul says: "I am now rejoicing in my sufferings for your sake, and in my flesh I am completing what is lacking in Christ's afflictions for the sake of his body, that is, the Church." Paul, as Gregory suggests, seems to be intimating that "Christ's sufferings were incomplete . . . and [this] invited Catholic exegetes to discuss the relationship between Christ's passion and the meritorious sufferings of Christians."[33] The Douai glossators were clear: "As Christ the head and his body make one person mystical and one full Christ . . . so the passions of the head and the afflictions of the body and members make one complete mass of passion. . . . And not only those passions which he suffered in himself, which were fully ended in his death, and were in themselves fully sufficient for the redemption of the world and remission of all sins." Paul's apparent intimation is being countered.

Nevertheless, the Douai gloss continues directly: "but all those which his body and members suffer [the martyrs], are his also, and of him they receive the condition, quality, and force to be meritorious and satisfactory." With what looks like intentional obfuscation, the commentary is apparently questioning what it has just denied. Does not the martyr, who receives the "condition" of Christ, function *pro Christo* to perpetuate Christ's saving act? And does not he or she also become a "holy host and oblation," to repeat Campion's words?

This returns us to the image of the "bread"—for it, too, is the body of Christ—and to the words spoken by the early martyr Ignatius, who said before his death: "May I become the food of the beasts, through which I will be able to have the pleasure of God. I am the wheat of

God, to be ground by the teeth of the beasts, so that I may be found to be *the pure bread of God*."[34] It was also said that the martyr underwent a "baptism of blood," through which all possible "stain was wiped from his soul." The martyr's body and blood revivify the sacrifice of Christ, and in his person, the martyr realizes the image of Odo of Cambrai that "we are one with him and he is one with us."[35]

In terms of the Henrican martyrs, this image is glorious. In terms of the supposed victims of ritual murder, it is ominous. For what the attack on Werner conjures up, who was said to suffer *pro* and *propter*, as well as *in loco Christo*, is the articulated eucharistic image: at once the Host, the bread, and the blood. Ritual murder not only repeats the crucifixion, it is a premeditated assault by Matthew's Jewish "dogs" intended to deprive the rightful children of their (eucharistic) food. The Jews are bent on "stealing the bread from the oven," the very bread that, in the words on the Eucharist of the Council of Trent, "is most efficacious toward the attainment of eternal glory. For it is written: He that eateth my flesh, and drinketh my blood, hath everlasting life."[36] To destroy or "devour" the Host, the "bread," the true sacrifice as described by Paul and Ezekiel, but now incarnated in the guise of the ritual murder victim, is to destroy salvation.

Yet here is a major paradox. As the faithful might comprehend it, what really occurs in ritual murder is not destruction. Rather, the victim is transfigured, unified with Christ, and accorded Christ's merits. Instead of thwarting salvation, ritual murder verifies and sustains it. Moreover, just as the Host in the Host libel is never desecrated, so the ritual murder victim perseveres through, and over, death. Through their individual passions *pro Christo*, Werner and all other martyrs who are "baptized in blood" promote salvation. Through their indestructibility, the assaulted Host and the (Host-)martyr created by ritual murder reveal the invincibility of the Catholic *Corpus Christi*, whatever its aspect. Exactly as the Trent Catechism propounds, martyred victims "attain eternal glory." Both the assaulted host and the martyr perpetuate Christ's *eucharistic* sacrifice—or, as the Henrican martyrs saw it of themselves, they perpetuate the Roman Church. No wonder that Luther, for all his other accusations against Jews, gave the Host libel the lie!

In less expansive terms, the martyr infuses new spirit into the Church in desperate moments. It seems clear that had there been no martyrs to perpetuate the passion's merits, there would have been a rush to create them—and there was—by inventing ritual murder accusations, blood, and Host libels of every sort. These stories were all the more effective since the perpetrators were that perpetual eucharistic menace, the thieving Jewish "dogs." This goes beyond what Gavin Langmuir perspicaciously intuited with respect to Thomas of Monmouth. Thomas, Langmuir wrote, concocted the story of William of Norwich's murder, the first ritual murder victim, "to assure himself of a local supernatural protector . . . a patron saint assigned by God to Norwich."[37] By demonstrating the invincibility of the collective *Corpus Christi*, martyrs created by Jews were far more necessary in the economy of salvation than Thomas's intercessory figure. Again paradoxically, therefore, the fear inherent in ritual murder tales presaged hope. And this would be even more so should the child victim be likened to, or even called, a sacrifice outright. This indeed occurred, as we shall see in the chapter to follow.

It was not only, therefore, that the victim of a blood libel or ritual murder dispelled doubt about the verity of the miracle of the wine and the bread.[38] For that, the numerous miracle stories involving Hosts, but not involving Jews, were more than sufficient.[39] Rather, the victim (of the Jewish assault) also—and in my opinion this is more important—dispels doubt about the Eucharist's salvific efficacy: about its power to unite all in Christ, and about its capacity to forward salvation's progress. It also dispels doubt about salvation's renewability through the Eucharist. And in so doing, it confirms the Eucharist's power to ward off evil, including that directed against the Eucharist itself. Moreover, personifying simultaneously the real body of Christ, the eucharistic *corpus verum*, and the *corpus mysticum* bound into one, the ritual murder victim in tales like that of Werner advertises the resilience of the *corpus ecclesiae*, the body of the Church, in its broadest sense. It publicizes the perpetual ability of the Church to overcome existential threat, and it testifies to the power of the Church to heal its wounds and defeat alienation. Finally, it proclaims the ability of a world that sees itself as besieged from all sides to recreate harmony where only dissonance is visible.[40] Was it not in this spirit that Thomas Aquinas, with no reference to ritual murder, ascribed the ordinance of the Fourth Lateran Council to partake of the Eucharist annually to the "reign of impiety and the growing cold of charity?"[41] The eucharistic miracle would counter both.

It was also in this spirit that the people of Modena, about 1604, embellished on the episode of seven Jews hanged in Mantua in 1602. The Jews' offense, it was said, was not—as the Mantuan records report it—mocking an itinerant Franciscan preacher. It was swinging an image of Christ on a rope. One witness at Modena, Barbara, the wife of the artisan Giovanni Rubbiano, claimed that loud noises emanating on the night of Holy Thursday from a Jewish house, apparently from a game on a *pingolo*, a kind of swing, were the cries of Jewish youth, who were singing "kill the man." As she saw it, they were reenacting the alleged Mantuan offense. No opportunity, it seems, was being missed to seek out new martyrs, to validate the Eucharist anew, especially on the vigil of Easter, and even if the invented martyrdom was "bloodless," as it was here.[42] Moreover, this kind of thinking was not limited to clerical circles or to the clerical imagination.

Martyrdom, like the act of communion itself, as Thomas so eloquently had written, renewed hope and rekindled the flame of salvation for all. And with respect to that assaulted and victorious Eucharistic incarnation, the victim of ritual murder, this was precisely the narrative point. Centuries later, in 1899, Bishop Antonio de Pol of Vicenza wrote, as we have seen, of Lorenzino of Marostica, saying that the Jews sought "more to murder Christianity itself than to kill one single Christian" (non tanto ad uccidere un cristiano, quanto ad uccidere lo stesso Cristianesimo). By implication, de Pol was also saying that despite their efforts, the Jews had not succeeded. They had murdered the body of the boy Lorenzino, but, in the process, they had created Lorenzino the martyr, vouchsafed with miraculous powers.

By then, the challenge itself had changed. De Pol was writing to oppose Jewish and Christian proximity in a modern world in which the Roman Ghetto no longer existed, the Jews standing metaleptically for the new that was challenging tradition. Hence, although de Pol's immediate concerns may have been far distant from the heretical schism and the royal acts that had moved the Henricans, the anxiety remained the same. Would the benefits conferred by Christ's passion and realized through the Roman Church survive "Jewishly driven" modernity? Lorenzino's martyrdom, his private passion, even after hundreds of years had passed, reassured that they would. Superfluous to say, once a tale of martyrdom was created, it acquired resiliency and took on a life of its own, to be invoked each time a need was felt for a martyr's salvific powers.[43]

We may, of course, ask: which was the horse, which the cart? Did the Bollandists, unquestionably aware of the Henrican martyrs and their attributed virtues, shape and edit their picture of the ritual murder victim, and of Werner in particular, to fit a preexisting sixteenth-century Catholic martyriological image? And was their intention to enhance the glory of these later martyrdoms and to perpetuate ideas like those just suggested? Or was their image of Werner and those like him a traditional one inherited from the past and derived from those many patristic citations in praise of martyrdom that had found their way into sixteenth-century martyriological texts? Much had been absorbed from the writings of Church Fathers like Cyprian, regardless of these citations' independence of the Jews or Jewish involvement. This inherited image the Bollandists then applied, almost unawares, as they wrote of Werner and his ilk. More than likely, the two images were essentially one.

Cyprian's vision is clearest in book 3, paragraph 16, of his *Treatise XII, Three Books of Testimonies Against the Jews*—the location should not escape us, as one may imagine it also did not escape accusers of ritual murder.[44] Speaking of the benefits of martyrdom and citing Paul, Cyprian said: "Of this same thing to the Romans, 'We are the sons of God: but if sons and heirs of God, we are also joint heirs with Christ; *we suffer together* [emphasis added] that we may also be magnified together'" (493 = Rom. 8:16-17). Christ himself, Cyprian is saying, is magnified through martyrdom. Yet as Cyprian understood from Paul, and possibly from the writings of Ignatius, too, the martyr was eucharistically Christ. Martyrdom, union in Christ, and the martyr's salvific function went hand in hand. The idea of Eucharistic union has also endured. In July 2000, John Gallen, an American Jesuit priest, unambiguously paraphrased

Corinthians, saying: "And that eucharistic bread and wine in the sharing then makes us, members of the assembly, more and more completely into the Christ that we are."[45] Whatever border there may be between the true Christ and his members, through the Eucharist this border melts away. How much the more when the eucharistic incarnation is crowned by martyrdom! In the Introduction, we saw that there are those who still think this way, including with respect to machinations they ascribe to Jews.

Social Threat

The road to this end was not direct. Despite the Pauline theology that made it inevitable that ritual murder would be identified with assaults on the *unus panis*—whether as an eucharistic, ecclesiastical, political, or social unity—the Host and ritual murder libels have clearly independent roots. Specifically, the ritual murder accusation and then the blood libel—the first known cases were in 1144 and 1235, respectively—seem to have grown in the milieu following the First Crusade in 1096.[46] The roots of the Host libel may be older. Even in the early Middle Ages, canons prohibited Jews from standing in open windows as the Host was carried publicly in procession, which suggests that any Jewish contact, even visual, with the Eucharist was considered contaminating. Eventually, the canons forbade Jews from leaving their homes at all during Holy Week; and these canons were apparently enforced. A nonessential—and thus highly believable—item in Thomas of Monmouth's twelfth century account of William of Norwich says that what raised suspicions was Jews (violating the canons and) wandering about on Maundy Thursday.[47]

Anxieties about eucharistic contamination were soon joined to condemnations of Jewish magic. In his autobiographical *Life*, Guibert de Nogent tells of the monk who desires to gain a Jewish magician's help in mastering the "black arts." To this end, the monk makes a pact with the Devil to "deny his Christianity" [by making] "a libation of his seed . . . [and then to] taste it . . . as a celebrant [of the sacrament] ought to do . . . [thus] to cast the dishonor of sacrilege on the priesthood and the Blessed Host." The parallel is direct to Agobard of Lyon, who warns lest "anyone who has become impure through fraternizing and dining with the Jews break bread with [a] priest [who would then offer the sacrament]."[48] Guibert feared Jewish sexuality no less than did Agobard.

Jewish subversive intentions and the Jews' desire to defile the sacrament, or at least its recipients and celebrants, were said to be universal. Fears like those in Guibert's tale, of Jewish plots to have believers trade their faith for magical secrets, were constant. As if confirming this fear's durability and its diffusion, Ramon Martí said that "Jews challenged God continually with magic, and blasphemy" (semper Judaei magis provocarunt Deum verbis, et blasphemiis).[49] The idea of Jewish magic corrupting faith appears also in the early medieval story of Theophilos, who is miraculously saved from Jewish wiles by the Virgin. The Virgin snatches Theophilos from his deathbed to bear him to heavenly safety, much as she snatches the Jewish boy from the (oven) door of death in the tale of the Jew of Bourges.[50]

The idea of exchanging faith for magic resurfaces again in the eighteenth-century preaching manual of the Lazarist Joseph Lambert, who condemns Christians approaching the communion table without receiving absolution as Host-desecrating "magicians." These Christians he equates indirectly with Jews, and he calls for their ostracism—exactly as Paul had said with regard to Judaizers in Galatians 4 (and implicitly in 1 Cor. 10).[51] However knowingly, Lambert was building on a decree of the Council of Carthage of 419, which also reminds us of the antiquity of anxieties about Jews contaminating Christian ritual. "A person observing auguries and incantations," says the decree "must be separated from the Church's communion [*conventu ecclesiae*]; similarly [thus equating the two], one who adheres to Jewish superstitions and holidays." We must be struck by the direct parallel between this prohibition and that seen above in the (so-called) Laws of Charlemagne linking paganism and magic. The roots of the decree in Corinthians should also not be overlooked. The decree was cited again by the tenth-century Regino of Prum, whose text is but another example of how paganism, magic, and Judaism came to be treated as one: all three deemed equally pernicious, all three to be distanced from the Christian altar, all three a eucharistic threat.[52]

Lambert's condemnation also presupposes the medieval escalation from charges that Jews magically defiled the Eucharist, or tried to defile it, to the full-blown Host libel that centuries later he was projecting onto supposed Christian perpetrators. This escalation had occurred by 1290,[53] when the first known libel was made—precisely when the Eucharist itself had attained a greater sacramental and canonical force, as well as, and perhaps crucially, when it had achieved an emotional hold on the popular mind.[54] Jews were said not only to threaten the Eucharist's integrity, they were accused of procuring sanctified Hosts in order to torture them. In their simplest form, such accusations underlie what Miri Rubin has called useful tales of exemplification. But she also points to the bond between tales and action: the tale itself confers legitimacy; it confirms the truth of Jewish behavior—and legitimizes Christian response.[55]

Why, however, did the Host accusation meld quickly enough with that of ritual murder? Simply put, and as noted above, the vectors of Pauline theology had come to be applied to the medieval civic body, that is, to society as a whole, not only to the body of the Church. Agobard of Lyon, and others, too, had envisioned Christian society organized according to the Pauline eucharistic image already in the ninth century, if not before. And by the time of the first Host libel in 1290, vision had become fact. From then on, the civic body was viewed regularly as a personification of the *Corpus Christi,* represented and celebrated, for that matter, in annual *Corpus Christi* festivals and processions. The *Corpus Christi* thus had become omnipresent, whether as the *corpus verum* of the Eucharist, the *corpus mysticum* of the Church, or the civic *Corpus Christi* of the town or other political units.[56]

Yet was not the *Corpus Christi* also embodied in the person of each and every Christian, making it inevitable that ritual murder victims, themselves individual "bodies of Christ," would be identified with that *Corpus's* civic, social, and ecclesiastical realizations? The way to this eventuality is already apparent in the stories of Guibert de Nogent and the tale of Theophilos, whose accusations of Jewish magic threatening the faith and integrity of the collective body of Christ focus on that body (again following 1 Cor. 10) as realized in the Christian individual. In the story of Werner of Oberwesel, the elements coalesce; the varying realizations of Christ's body unite in him as though through inertia. Threats to the individual ritual murder victim had become the same as threats to the whole. Apart, therefore, from Werner's function as martyriological paradigm of eucharistic and ecclesiastical invincibility (the invincibility of the *corpus mysticum*), Werner is paradigmatic of the steadfastness of the *Corpus Christi* cum Christian polity as it parried the dangers Jews were said to pose.

The Bollandist story of Werner carries these themes to perfection. The boundary between Werner the individual and Werner the personification of the three manifestations of Christ's body—the *Corpus verum*, the *Corpus mysticum*, and Christ's physical presence—is fluid; and by stressing this fluidity, the Bollandists had fused attacks on any aspect of the *Corpus Christi* into attacks on the indivisible whole, as well as on the individuals who comprised the Christian fellowship, not to mention the Eucharist. Yet had not the second-century Ignatius aptly named this fellowship the *societas fidei*, to be followed by the likes of Agobard?[57] The Werner story thus is one of all-embracing eucharistic "sacrifice," but also of the danger the Jewish menace constantly poses to the entire Christian fellowship. No wonder the Jew came to be viewed as the perpetual Christian enemy, which was so whether in Werner's time or in the Bollandists' much later day—or even afterward.

It was this chilling narrative of unabating Jewish aggression and challenge to the eucharistic essence—in all its manifestations—that eighteenth-century protagonists such as Père Lambert absorbed, to be followed in the nineteenth and twentieth centuries by the ilk of Henry Desportes, the editors of *La civiltà cattolica*, and especially Gougenot des Mousseaux, who referred explicitly to Bollandist texts. Nor should we omit Antonio de Pol, whose words, revisited shortly above, remind us of the ultimate justification for viewing Jews as ever-ready aggressors. Their always failed aggression reassured a troubled mankind of salvation's indestructible promise.[58]

May I dare, then, to take one ultimate step further, to suggest that in this vision, we may explain the tenacity of Pius IX after 1859, when Pius unflinchingly refused to return the secretly baptized and kidnapped Jewish child Edgardo Mortara to his parents?[59] Edgardo, especially in his eventual vest as believer and priest, became more than a martyr. He was a counter-martyr, rescued alive from nefarious Jewish hand, indeed, one who had been brought to life from his previous (Jewish) state of limbo, even from spiritual death. For Pius IX, Edgardo symbolized survival. Edgardo was, in a manner of speaking, the ritual murder "victim" who, unlike others, survived *both* in body and soul.

Moreover, Pius may have been an integralist, but he was certainly no fool. He had to have foreseen that one way or another, sooner or later, the Church would falter. Its temporal power would be lost and its spiritual power threatened. There was only one place for a man like him to turn: to Christ—or, more particularly, to Christ's earthly embodiment and its signs of salvific durability. For Pius IX, that embodiment was Edgardo. Pius himself, in this scenario, if we may permit ourselves to imagine the fantasies evolving in his brain, was also the Virgin, rescuing the boy Edgardo from the oven into which Edgardo's real father, Salomone, was trying insistently to push him. Thus, Pius had ripped Edgardo, the "bread" incarnate, from the jaws of the hungry Jews. Were these not, after all, those very "dogs" about whom Pius himself was to say, they "were barking throughout the city" and polluting it?

Fantastic hyperbole this scenario—perhaps not? Indeed; for in 1854, Pius IX had named St. Roche the patron saint of Montpellier. So very often, St. Roche's iconography includes a dog, which carries a loaf of bread in its mouth. The dog had stolen the bread from the table of a noble in order to nourish (the fourteenth-century) Roche, who was languishing in a cave, suffering from the plague.[60] St. Roche's intervention also wards off rabies and vicious dogs: "San Roque, San Roque," he is implored in South America and no doubt elsewhere, too, "may this dog not stare at me, nor may it touch me either" (que este perro no me mire ni me toque).[61] Is it not possible, then, that in Pius's mind, the symbols had become confused and rearranged? For Pius, Edgardo was the Jewish dog "domesticated." Yet, as counter-martyr, Edgardo was also the bread itself. Rather than purloining the "bread" as a Jew, therefore, the faithful Edgardo restored it, that is, himself, to its rightful possessor, Christ, in the form of Christ's Vicar on earth, the pope. In this way, Edgardo had succored the needy Christian, his Jewish bite and infection had been warded off. For Pius IX, so it may really have been. Under stress, minds do strange things.

Three Richard of Pontoise and Philip Augustus

We can only speculate about why the people of Oberwesel-Bacharach sought Werner's canonization in 1417.[1] It may have been out of sincere conviction, or perhaps the desire to glorify a local shrine, a motivation we have seen in the case of William of Norwich.[2] Whatever moved them, the testimonies they left behind furnished the Bollandists with the means to highlight some of the Catholic Reformation's most important doctrinal cruxes, not to mention its negative opinions and anxieties about Jews living in Catholicism's midst.

Avarice and the Martyr

The one major charge against Jews the Werner tale does not raise is that of usury. That of Richard of Pontoise does. Lending was a Bollandist concern, which in their own day and before posed a theological, no less than an economic challenge. Nowhere is this challenge clearer than in the diatribes of lending's most vociferous opponents, fifteenth-century Observantine Franciscans. Repeatedly, the Jews in these tirades are called "truly wild and thirsty dogs, who [through their lending activity] have sucked and go on sucking our blood." Such images, in their fullness, which the Franciscans also associated with ritual murder, no doubt affected the Bollandists, who must have also taken note of increasing papal negativity in their own day: amid protracted theological argument, Pope Innocent XI closed Rome's (so-called) Jewish "banks" definitively in 1682.[3] In the event, lending is central to the ritual murder story known as the *Passion of Richard of*

Pontoise, which word for word the Bollandists adopted into the *Acta Sanctorum* following an introduction that gives their own version of events. The *Passion of Richard*, actually a funeral oration according to Gérard Mathon, was composed in 1498 by Robert Gaguin, then minister general of the French Order of the Sacred Trinity of the Captives, which comforted the condemned on their way to the gallows. Richard allegedly died in 1179.[4]

According to Gaguin, Richard's martyrdom, during which the child proclaimed on high his undying Christian faith, persuaded King Philip Augustus to liberate France from the Jews and, in particular, from the great oppression of Jewish lending.[5] It is in this context that one should read the Bollandists' introduction to Gaguin's *Passion*, which opens with a discussion of Jewish avarice. Avarice, the Bollandists say, led the Jews to receive as pawns sacred vessels. This was sacrilege, the profanation of what should have been venerated, and they cite one of Jewish lending's implacable foes, the twelfth-century Peter the Venerable. They also know that Philip Augustus's biographer Rigord—the chief contemporary reporter of Philip's doings with the Jews, and the Bollandists' own prime source—himself attacked alleged Jewish financial abuses. Jewish avarice was also deemed infectious. It was avarice, the Bollandists say, that moved Philip Augustus, in 1198, to cancel the order of expulsion he had issued in 1182; Rigord says only that Philip flouted "the common opinion."

Jewish avarice—all avarice, Miri Rubin tells us—was identified with violence toward children and, indirectly, with the sacrament; but most of all, it was identified with the Virgin's saving intervention.[6] It was no accident that Gaguin's accusations of avarice and his assertions about the profanation of church vessels preface his declaration that as Richard died, he called out his passionate loyalty to the Virgin. One suspects that it was not Gaguin's story of itself, nor its motif of avarice that made this narrative so useful to the Bollandists, as important as both were. They were more interested in Gaguin's emphasis on loyalty to the Virgin. The contemporary chronicles of Rigord and Guillaume le Breton, which the Bollandists used to construct their introduction to the *Passion*, are sparse.[7] They lack in devotional pathos—except, perhaps, for Rigord's brief note that Richard died *feliciter*. For the Bollandists, Gaguin's "oration" was a "godsend."

Gaguin's text has its special twists. Beyond his account of Jewish "criminality," Gaguin wrote that in the wake of the Jewish expulsion, France was "liberated" from the English.[8] This was surely a(n unconscious) reprise of the Hundred Years' War, for since when was the Plantagenet duke of Normandy an "English(man)"—the so-called "liberation" at this time being Philip Augustus's confiscation of Normandy from John Lackland in 1204? Charges of ritual murder were clearly magnets to which any of the various ills afflicting the Christian body politic, or some part of it, might be attached. Yet more intriguing is Gaguin's linkage of events. Within the framework of his story, Gaguin notes the expulsion of 1182, the recall of 1198, and the so-called "liberation" from the English in 1204, lacing into a single, apparently continuous, skein events that took place during twenty-five years (1179–1204); like the Bollandists, he assigns Richard's death to 1179.[9]

This unity of action served the Bollandists well. Had they been asked whether the events that took place during this time were part of one whole, they would have answered yes, at least with respect to the Jews. They never say this in so many words, but in their introduction to Gaguin's *Passion*, they intentionally lump together all of Philip Augustus's principal actions concerning Jews. Richard's death is the springboard, the proverbial final straw convincing the young King Philip to act on already existing impulses. Carefully selecting from the chronicles of Guillaume le Breton and especially Rigord, the Bollandists offer their audience an integral drama that amalgamates events that took place between 1179 and 1198. This drama also includes the events at Blois in 1171, which they mention only briefly, but significantly, where thirty or more Jews, it will be recalled, were burned to death.[10]

The intent of this reconstruction is displayed in what today we might call an editorial tour de force. The single page that contains the full Bollandist reconstruction was culled from what otherwise is found on pages 15–16, 24–29, 118–19, and 141 of Delaborde's edition of Rigord's chronicle. When editing takes place within a single passage, it is signified by the now customary use of ellipsis dots (. . .).[11]

The Bollandists' editorial consciousness stands out more when noting that in other discussions of ritual murder, they invariably concentrate on the murder alone and its associated marvels. The narrative of Richard of Pontoise is the one instance where they indulge in extended historical discussion, including the background to the crime. By contrast, Werner's story was a parade of miracles.[12] The historicizing in the case of Richard was also purposeful. In Werner's story, martyrdom and its merits was the single issue; in Richard's, the Bollandists seized the "historiographical day" to provide, over and above an episode of saintly martyrdom—and that they certainly do provide—a recipe for correct royal action. Just as Philip Augustus persistently repressed the (Jewish) enemies of the Christian holy body, so Catholic monarchs should always be on guard. They were to intervene whenever the sanctity of the *corpus mysticum* was threatened. Philip himself, the Bollandists say, reversed his lapse of 1198 by sharply restricting lending after 1206 (as in fact he did). His example, by implication, is one that all kings should emulate, including those in the Bollandists' own seventeenth-century day.[13]

However, irrespective of whether this conjecture is correct or whether the Bollandists were speaking analogously about proper royal behavior, it is my principal contention that the Bollandist narrative about Richard of Pontoise provides a matchless tool for understanding something essential in the Christian spiritual past in its confrontation with Jews. The narrative of Richard masterfully relieves the range of reactions, emotions, and needs that charges of ritual murder might evoke. We are also speaking of a *longue durée*, of a past that reaches its apogee in the twelfth century, extends to the time of the Bollandists themselves, and culminates in the nineteenth and twentieth centuries. Moreover, the narrative of Richard had a special cogency. Its power went beyond Bollandist powers of collation, editing, and narration, to ensure its adoption by future generations of narrators and believers. For the Bollandist reconstruction, with its unification of late twelfth-century events and their underlying causes, is not simply a tale of their own creation or the repetition of a story told by predecessors like Gaguin, Rigord and Guillaume le Breton. What the Bollandists grasped, gave credence to, and bequeathed to future generations was a unity of action that was historically true—apart, of course, from the ritual murder itself.

However embellished and however faulty with respect to precise details, especially of dating, the Bollandists' reconstruction accurately mirrors the forces and motivations that shaped Jewish fate in late twelfth-century France. The best evidence pointing to the historicity of the Bollandists' account comes from contrasting their narrative and its modes of reexamining late twelfth-century happenings with the Hebrew parallels mentioned in the Preface. The reciprocity is striking. It is, I would go so far as to say, only by understanding the unity of late twelfth-century events as the Bollandists reconstructed them that we can at last understand what these Hebrew texts are about, which relate specifically to the burnings at Blois in 1171.[14] That is how decisive the motif of ritual murder had become in determining attitudes toward Jews, as well as in anchoring Christian soteriology.

Nonetheless, the road toward this understanding is tortuous. Any new interpretation of the Hebrew texts would be meaningless without a full exposition of the Bollandist case, whose presentation I now ask the reader patiently to follow. An analogy to the modus operandi of Hercule Poirot may not be out of place—pale as my skills at detection may be by contrast to those of Agatha Christie's master sleuth, not to mention to Agatha Christie's mastery of the written word: first the long buildup, the problems carefully arrayed, then Poirot confronting the assembled suspects and meticulously sorting out the clues.

The Unity of Events, 1179–1191

The events as the Bollandists present them are as follows. In 1179, on the Kalends of January (although his Saint's day was eventually translated to March 25, the Day of the Annunciation),[15] Richard of Pontoise was "martyred"; the Bollandists are absolutely firm on this date. Having heard of such acts since he was a child, Philip Augustus, whom the Bollandists call a *iustus vindex*, a just prosecutor, jumps into action. He arrests the Jews in their synagogues and fines them: "acting where his father had not," for Philip knew that every year, the Jews, *quasi pro sacrificio*, killed a Christian.[16] This all occurred *on a Sabbath*, XVI Kalends, March (1180). Philip had been crowned (as co-regent) on All Saints Day, November 1, 1179.

Armed with calendrical tables unavailable to the Bollandists, William Jordan has rightly queried the date of 1180, showing that in 1181, XVI Kalends, March fell on a Sabbath; in 1180, it did not.[17] This accuracy would have upset Bollandist intentions. For them, as for Rigord, it was essential to depict three distinct episodes. According to Rigord, there were, first, the arrests of 1180, second, a relaxation of debts owed Jews "at that time," which could be anytime between the arrests and the expulsion, and, third, the expulsion of 1182, including the confiscation of synagogues. To show that these episodes were truly distinct, following each other after an appropriate interval, the Bollandists emended Rigord's text. They changed "at that time," the phrase Rigord used to preface the events following the arrest of 1180, to the precise *anno deinde MCLXXXI:* "In the year *after* [that is, in] 1181," the king "heard other accusations" (alias . . . accusationes suscipiens). These accusations, the king heard from Rigord, just as his father had heard similar ones from Peter of Cluny.

This pithy statement condenses four full paragraphs in Rigord. Rigord dwells in detail on Jewish trespass, asserting that Jews had encouraged servants (illegally) employed in their homes to judaize (*judaizabant*). They were also abusing Eucharistic chalices held as pledges (again illegally), for in a profane mockery that veritably inverted the sacrament: "Jewish children were eating dough balls [*offas*] cooked in wine" (infantes eorum offas in vino factas comedebant) out of the chalices; Rigord's words verge on the Host libel.[18] As for the king, horrified—the theme of Jewish pollution is always at the surface or lying just below—he "consulted a hermit named Bernard" (consulvit quemdam eremitam nomine Bernardum), who advised him to cancel interest due.[19] Only after saying these things, which seem more to constitute a tale of Jewish contempt than one of ritual murder, does Rigord introduce the expulsion of 1182.

One would imagine the Bollandists would relish repeating these two charges, but they did not. They were so taken with the "other accusations" that they editorially eliminated Rigord's exposition. What were these "other accusations"? They were doubtfully Jewish lending, a topic the Bollandists had already, and conveniently, dealt with in their prologue, in addition to their condemning supposed Jewish contempt for Christian ritual objects. The vague generalization "other accusations" must, therefore, point to something else—and by that something the Bollandists meant a *second* charge of ritual murder.

The Bollandists' source for assuming Philip was reacting to a second accusation would likely have been the same as that used by the seventeenth-century Franciscan Antoine Pagi, commenting on events that supposedly occurred in the year 1181.[20] This source was the multi-authored Scottish annal known as the Melrose Chronicle,[21] on the basis of which Pagi wrote that in that year (1181), the Jews killed Robert of Bury St. Edmunds: "the Jews acted savagely in England [killing Robert], but were punished [by expulsion from] France [by Philip Augustus]" (Iudaei saeviunt in Anglia, sed puniuntur in Gallia). As Pagi saw it, what propelled King Philip to expel the Jews was an act of ritual murder, and the Bollandists clearly agreed. They specifically mention Robert of St. Bury and his death in their introduction to the story of Richard.

To emphasize the point, the Bollandists emended the text a second time. In the middle of Rigord's sentence, they inserted the three words "Not only that . . . " (Neque id tantum . . .) — the "that" being the canceling of interest owed to the Jews. The sentence now reads: *Not only that*, not only did he cancel interest, " . . . but [the king] decreed that they [the Jews] leave [the kingdom, specifically, the Île-de-France, in 1182]" (. . . sed exiit edictum).[22] With rhetorical aplomb, but mostly through overall context — treating arrests, confiscations, cancellation of debts, and, finally, the expulsion itself as the stages of an identifiable triennial sequence — 1180, 1181, and 1182 — the Bollandists have led readers to a logical climax. The expulsion of 1182 is Philip Augustus's royal response to accusations of ritual murder: first, that of Richard of Pontoise (which initiated the whole process and dominates it) and, second, that of Robert of Bury St. Edmunds. For good measure, and to ensure that the reader grasps the context, the Bollandists preface the entire Richard narrative by recalling the events at Blois in 1171, to which Rigord only alludes. The picture is rounded out by the introduction. There, the Bollandists summon up the stories of William of Norwich and Harold of Gloucester. All that the Bollandists say in their narrative regarding royal activity is therefore tied to ritual murder, which they perceived as an ongoing challenge, each recurrence a link in an unbroken chain of events.

Whether the Bollandist reconstruction is more accurate than Rigord's, or chronologically accurate at all, is beside the point. The real question is the Bollandists' perception of events and whether they correctly penetrated Philip's state of mind. How successful as well were they in transmitting their perception to readers in their own day and also in subsequent times? We must not forget that the Bollandists' purpose is to tell the story of a ritual murder; they are concerned primarily neither with Philip Augustus in his own right nor with overall Jewish fortunes under Philip's rule. Their principal interest is Richard, and, by definition, the story they tell and its details must all revolve around Richard and his *ritual* murder. That Richard's murder evoked—in fact, necessitated—a strong royal response is the Bollandist crux.[23] The emendation of Rigord's story to emphasize Philip's consistency says much about the Bollandists' historiographical skill and perspicacity.

Moreover, regardless of whether they used the Melrose Chronicle directly, as did Pagi, by linking the murders of Richard and Robert, the Bollandists were exploiting the Chronicle's principal motif: Jews murder Christians regularly; in fact, they commit serial murder. Indeed, immediately after naming Robert, the Melrose Chronicle reports the death of the boy Herbert of Huntingdon, whose father "lashes him to a pole and drowns him" (quam proprius pater ad stipitem impie ligavit et in aquam quae iuxta ipsam villam decurrit, miserabiliter extinxit). It is hard not to see this story as a modified, if somewhat disguised version—water substitutes for the oven—of the tale of the Jew of Bourges. It would have been superfluous for the Melrose Chronicle to have said the father was Jewish or that the son wanted to convert. By this time, the allusion was perfectly obvious. The Melrose story was a variation on a theme. Rather than being redeemed as a eucharistic surrogate, as in the original Bourges tale, Herbert was martyred and saved—through drowning—in baptismal waters.

Mary Minty has highlighted this drowning-salvation motif in a story originating in 1137. The culprit is a Jewish father, an avaricious lender; the son and victim is specially devoted to prayer to the Virgin. Redemption is signified by radiant light coming from the son's drowned body as it is pulled from the Danube at Regensburg. In the river's waters, the boy had undergone a martyr's baptism. During his lifetime, his father and an equally avaricious (implying Judaizing) archdeacon had prevented this from happening.[24] The reasoning in stories like this one is syllogistic: The Jews kill their own rather than allow conversion; the Jews are particularly avid to kill children on the verge of converting, or those who have just converted. This is tantamount to saying Jews gladly kill Christian children and thirst to kill any Christian child, especially if the child is noted for piety. Stories saying these things were being told and retold at this time, including, of course, stories of ritual murder itself. Chronicles like that of Melrose attest to this for the thirteenth century. But even much earlier, the stories moved around, as John McCulloh has recently shown. The tale of William of Norwich had reached the author of a German martyrological list by 1147, too early for the German author to have learned it from Thomas of Monmouth's account.[25]

What, in this light, the Bollandists wished to perpetuate, certainly as I see it, was their perception of the consistently murderous behavior of Jews. Why else would they have referred to four other such murders in their narrative of Richard of Pontoise: Robert, William, Harold, and the nameless (because wholly nonexistent) victim at Blois? Even more, why introduce into the story of Richard, as we shall now see, the tale of the purported Jewish perfidy at Brie in 1191?[26] The subtlety may be even greater. The Bollandist corpus contains about a dozen cases of ritual murder, far fewer than the real number of accusations made. Faithful to their tradition of winnowing the wheat from the chaff, the Bollandists recorded only "verifiable" ritual murders, those whose victims were true saints, thus immensely reinforcing (in their eyes) the credibility of the tales and the veracity of the accusation itself.

In the case of Richard of Pontoise, the Bollandists could also present readers with what they considered the proper royal response. With a brilliant editorial stroke they were able to demonstrate that Philip Augustus viewed vindicating ritual murder as his consummate kingly duty, the lynchpin of his policies toward the Jews.[27] This they accomplished by radically restructuring the order of Rigord's text. In the Bollandist version, the story of Richard of Pontoise and the expulsion of 1182 are tied directly to the episode at Brie in 1191, where eighty Jews were executed. Rigord's own discussion of Brie is tens of pages distant from his account of the events of the early 1180s. By emending Rigord a third time, by reconstructing and making the events of 1191 immediately follow those of 1180, 1181, and 1182, the Bollandists had converted the episode at Brie into a link in the ritual murder chain. Rigord verges on such a concatenation, but he never gets there. He writes only that Philip Augustus ordered eighty Jews burned for their role in having a Christian executed by the "corrupt countess." The Christian had allegedly been paraded with his hands tied and "crowned with thorns" (spinis coronatum), the Jews "whipping him the length of the town" (per totam villam fustigantes).[28] But whether Rigord considered this event ritual murder and the creation of a true martyr, he fails to say. By situating it in the context of the events of 1180–82, the Bollandists leave no doubt. For them, what happened at Brie was ritual murder indeed.

Fact, Fiction, or Something In-between

But was this expansive interpretation purely an imaginative synthesis? Or had the Bollandists properly read between the lines of Rigord's account to draw a conclusion that for some reason Rigord either failed to draw, did not care to draw, or simply felt was less important than the need to punish acts of Judaizing, exploitation, and contempt? Rigord did preface his remarks on Richard of Pontoise by saying that Philip Augustus had heard that every year the Jews killed a Christian as a sacrifice.[29]

In fact, the Bollandists seem to have intuited well. Charges of ritual murder did guide the twelfth-century mind with respect to Jews, especially that of royalty. The Bollandists repeat Rigord's report that Philip had heard about ritual murder from other "princes" (or better, youths) in the palace when he was young, actually a child; Philip was only fourteen or fifteen when he assumed the throne. As Rigord describes it, it was taken for granted in the late twelfth century that Jews committed ritual murder. If Rigord is also correctly representing the king's reaction to the death of Richard, as the Bollandists would argue, then Philip would surely have been flattered by their conclusion that "justly vindicating the whole of his people, [Philip] punished the Jews most severely, and deservedly" (qua ratione iustus vindex in totam nationem extenderit poenam infinitis iudaeorum flagitiis debitam).³⁰

Many others, too, would have shared this opinion, and not only in the later twelfth century. Bollandist references and cross-references indicate how deeply the idea of ritual murder had implanted itself in the consciousness of chroniclers and other writers. Rigord's idea of annual murder, the Bollandists note, appears already in Thomas of Monmouth's account of William of Norwich. It appears as well in Lillius's epitome of an anonymous 1235 Chronicle of the English Kings.³¹ Tales of ritual murder were also common enough to generate topoi that would endure over the centuries, sometimes with variations. The Melrose Chronicle, for example, refurbished the tale of the Jew of Bourges.

The telling of ritual murder accusations had become ritualized. The trope of the body being hidden in the woods is found in the William of Norwich tale, and it was restated as late as the seventeenth century by John Wilson writing about Hugh of Lincoln (1255); Hugh was also nourished (apparently as the fatted calf) for a year, as was a second child allegedly killed at Norwich in 1235.³² According to John Capgrave, whose sources go back to the thirteenth-century Matthew of Paris, the earth where Hugh was buried spat him up, shades of the resurrection. In a striking variation concerning a S. Ioannettus—known to us only through a 1598 narrative cited by the Bollandists—the corpse was tossed into "a thicket, . . . but pigs foraging with their snouts dug it out, as a swineherd told his mother" (cespitibus . . . sed rostris fodicando eruere[nt] porci, quod subulcus matri indicavit).³³ Capgrave again preserves traditional sources in writing that Hugh was "crowned with thorns" (spinis coronatum) by the Jews, precisely as was the—adult—victim at Brie, and, of course, legendarily, Christ. Child victims were innocent, hardworking, and often not locals, as at Winchester in 1190,³⁴ in the instance of the Good Werner, and (in a source the Bollandists likely did not know and do not cite) Adam of Bristol. Victims' bodies were disposed of in woods or, often, in rivers, as was the case with Harold of Gloucester,³⁵ Hugh,³⁶ and Werner.

These same topoi reappear in Jewish writings. Joseph HaKohen says that in 1475, Simonino was tossed into a pool near a Jew's house in Trent.³⁷ The (invented) child in Jewish accounts of the events at

Blois[38] was said to be hidden in a sack (actually a roll of leather), much as Thomas of Monmouth says of William of Norwich, and then secreted in the river Loire. This commonality, this sharing of motifs in Jewish, as well as Christian, narratives, reinforces on a wider scale John McCulloh's conclusion with respect to William of Norwich: that ritual murder was not only on people's minds—those who read about the libel, as well as the growing number who knew of it through word of mouth—but it was also being perceived uniformly. Whether we accept or reject Rigord's rhetoric about Philip Augustus, it seems only natural that the king knew and likely believed the ritual murder accusations he heard. Should we go beyond Rigord and accept the Bollandist framework, tying the events of 1179–91 into a progressively blossoming whole, we must conclude that ritual murder provoked the king far more, and far more constantly, than we have hitherto thought.[39]

We are also entitled to take a final step, to examine the words of Guillaume le Breton (Rigord's continuator). Rigord, we saw, wrote that Philip was told as a child that ritual murder was committed "as though a sacrifice" (quasi pro sacrificio). Guillaume le Breton writes that what the young Philip heard from his playmates was that "the Jews *sacrificed* a child and *took communion* [by eating] its heart" (immolabant, et eius corde se communicabant; which here, as in the Vulgate, means communion).[40]

A threshold had been crossed. Far more than ritual murder or crucifixion, this is the blood libel, precisely as Gavin Langmuir has defined it, where the essence is the blood (the heart, here, being its surrogate) and its sacramental (medicinal, or magical) use, not the act of murder alone. The ritual murder victim viewed as a blood sacrifice on the altar is also consumed, eaten, much as were sacrifices in the ancient Jewish Temple—or as is the Eucharist itself.[41] Moreover, Le Breton's words—"they take communion with the heart of a child" (se corde pueri communicabant)—reappear verbatim in a letter written by Innocent IV in 1247 denouncing a blood libel at Valreas in southern France.[42] Le Breton died in 1223. His variant on Rigord thus predates by more than a decade the libel at Fulda, the scene of the first known actual blood libel in 1235, which Emperor Frederick II rejected. It would be most illuminating to know when this concept took precise shape, as well as when Le Breton first wrote it down, although it was certainly prior to 1215, when he concluded his chronicle; and it may have been as early as 1179. To suggest that the phrase is a later interpolation copied into the chronicle from the letters of two popes is forced.[43]

The greatest significance lies in Le Breton's choice of words. The presence in the 1247 letter of Innocent IV of the words "consume"—in fact and in context meaning "took communion"—and, then, of the word "sacrifice" (*sacrificent*) in a later brief by Gregory X, which refers directly to drinking (Christian bodies and blood), bolsters the scholarly argument linking the blood libel with the Eucharist.[44] Neither letter, however, directly links sacrifice and consumption. Le Breton's text does, tying *communicabant* (took communion) to *immolabant* (sacrificed). The bond between the blood libel and (eucharistic) sacrifice has been perfectly demonstrated.[45] Only through this bond can we understand the tales in which the Eucharist becomes a child (the Christ child and the *agnus dei*) and is then devoured. Even more, Le Breton's text is moving toward the eventual rationale that facilitated the reciprocity between the *Corpus mysticum*, the *Corpus verum*, and the "real (physical) person of Christ" in the Good Werner tale. By picturing the ritual murder victim as truly a sacrifice, Guillaume had immensely shortened the step to reversing the image and picturing the true sacrifice, the Eucharist itself—the *Corpus verum*—as the ritual murder victim. This is to say that the final development of the Host Libel, which occurred only a few decades after the appearance of the full-blown blood libel, first required the perfection of the concept of the *ritual murder victim as sacrifice*. Only then could the Host Libel itself be realized. By the same token, without the full-blown Host Libel, the triple identification in the Werner story could never have been made.

The King

We can only speculate about Philip Augustus's actual perceptions beyond those visible through the dual filters of Rigord and the Bollandists. But there are solid grounds for thinking that he did believe Jews capable of consuming the *sacrificio* of Christian blood. Philip was only fifteen when he assumed the throne, and his susceptibility to tales of Jews cannibalizing the Eucharist or its real-life surrogates may have been especially great, shades of Guibert de Nogent's picture of sacrilegious Jewish eucharistic magic. There is also the question of whether Philip feared that his father had not sufficiently curbed the Jews, as Rigord implies and as scholars have usually agreed;[46] and this we shall examine below.

But there was something else besides. As part of their story of Richard of Pontoise, the Bollandists chose to cite Rigord to say that (out of character for secular rulers) Philip restored property in 1182 to those Jews who elected to convert and remain Christian. The Bollandists also seem to have known an anonymous chronicle claiming that in 1182, Philip forced all Jews who did not convert to leave.[47] They add, too—on what bases it is unclear, although the increasingly open presence of ex-conversos in (the Protestant parts of) the Low Countries in their own day may be one of them—that within ten years of the event, it was known which of these converts was sincere.

Converts were apostatizing in the twelfth century. Conversion and subsequent apostasy as a continuously disturbing fact of life had been an issue since 1096, following the violence of the First Crusade. The problem had previously existed in seventh-century Visigothic Spain; and, in 633, the Fourth Toledan Council had declared such apostasy canonically illegal, as no doubt it had always been.[48] It was also common knowledge that Jews were helping former Jews to return to Judaism, which, from the Christian perspective, was to apostatize.[49] The problem of apostasy and relapse appears in both Latin and Hebrew Crusade chronicles, the writings of the later twelfth-century Ephraim of Bonn, contemporary to Brie, the prologue to the polemic of Peter of Blois, also in the twelfth century, and the Letter of Maestro Andreas, a regretting thirteenth-century convert and likely an apostate himself, as well as in various Hebrew polemical writings.[50] It was against this background that the Bollandists painted Philip as perturbed; it should not be ruled out that they had read the Latin First Crusade chronicles and their portrait of defections, as well as the writings of Peter of Blois and others. When, therefore, and uniquely, they prefaced their account of Philip's savagery at Brie in 1191 by decrying the Jewish apostasy, which they said had occurred following false conversions in 1182 and by seemingly tying this apostasy to Philip's outburst, the Bollandists may have been intuiting Philip's motives precisely. Angered by both apostasy and the Jews' supposed role in the crucifixion-like death of a Christian, Philip initiated the savagery himself.[51]

The picture of royal initiative must also include Philip's well-documented dislike of Jewish lending. His decrees on the subject exceeded the demands of the popes, who, in fact, did not directly regulate Jewish interest-taking until 1198 (in what would be the eventual canon *Post miserabilem*). This was well after the forced restitution of interest Philip ordered in 1181.[52] Once again, the Bollandists (and, here, Gaguin, too) had correctly interpreted Philip. It is they who show us how lending integrates into an overall portrait in which the period 1179–91 emerges as a time of enormous upheaval. Equilibria that Philip's father, Louis VII, had reasonably upheld, if with exceptions now about to be discussed, his son discarded wholesale.[53] Conversion, apostasy, and lending at interest, but most of all ritual murder, if not the blood libel, could have, and very likely did, coalesce neatly in Philip's (the real Philip's) mind direly to affect the Jews.[54]

In emphasizing royal initiative independent of ecclesiastical prompting, the Bollandists were also reinforcing their (proposed) model of royal propriety. Yet once again they had intuited reality correctly. However, this time the intuition was paradoxical. It reflected the end of a process, not its beginning. The Premonstratensian chronicler Robert of Auxerre (d. 1214) reports that when, late in 1179 or early 1180, Archbishop Guido of Sens told Philip that he must enforce the decree of the recent Third Lateran Council (1179) that Jews dismiss Christian men and women serving in their homes, Philip responded testily that "the matters of this world" (secularium rerum causas) were the king's domain; ecclesiastical jurisdiction alone pertained to the Church. And when Guido refused to accept this, the "anger of the king flared up," and the enraged Philip forced Guido into temporary exile.[55]

Something is wrong here. Could Philip really *not* have known—or been told—that the call for Jews to dismiss Christian servants was not new in 1179; that it had been an ecclesiastical demand for centuries? More precisely, did Philip really not know that Guido's petition grew directly out of a letter sent by Pope Alexander III to Archbishop Guarin Gerard of Bourges rejecting what was actually a *second* royal petition by Louis VII, who had asked to be exempt from the conciliar decree? Finally, did Philip not know that Alexander's persistence signaled a Church that had become adamant about domestic service to Jews? From the end of the twelfth century and on, popes and the high clergy were going to demand—with eventual success—that rulers cancel the provisions in Jewish charters of privilege explicitly authorizing such service. Yet Philip seems to have paid no heed to this ecclesiastical turn.[56]

We should, therefore, hesitate before accepting at face value Rigord's indication that Philip—acting like a good son of the Church—proceeded against all the Jewish crimes his father had ignored. This includes allowing domestic service, which, as we have seen, Rigord singled out.[57] We know, too, that when Philip desired to act independently, he seems to have done precisely that. He was resolute as well, notwithstanding debates about his reliance on lay or clerical advisors. The initiatives about interest in 1181 and at Brie in 1191 were clearly Philip's alone; the initiative at Brie surprised even Rigord, and it also perplexed him.[58] Philip's initial rejection of the Third Lateran decree was his own no less. Explaining this rejection may allow a new perspective.

The explanation begins with Louis VII. Rigord and a second (anonymous) chronicler protest that Louis favored Jews, giving them "many privileges that went against God, kingdom, and his own best interest" (multa privilegia Deo et sibi et regno contraria). What were these privileges? It is unlikely that Rigord and the second chronicler were referring to lending. Rigord addressed lending separately—not to mention that the pope, as said, did not raise the question of Jewish lending directly until 1198. More important, Ephraim of Bonn minced no words in condemning Louis VII for canceling Jewish loan contracts at the time of the Second Crusade. On this subject, Louis seems to have been above criticism. In addition, in 1144, Louis issued a letter, which hitherto has gone unnoticed, threatening any Jew who had become a Christian and then relapsed (to Judaism) with capital punishment or mutilation.[59] Here, too, Louis was being ecclesiastically proper, if not more.

Writing from Lyons in 1247, Innocent IV castigated those in both Germany and France who "pressed [Jewish] children to be baptized against their parents' will" (filios invitos cogunt . . . baptizari) and "against [virtually binding legal] custom" (contra morem).⁶⁰ However, this same pope, a professor of canon law at that, would never have permitted violating the long-established practice forbidding those truly forced into Christianity to revert to Judaism. Innocent would no doubt have accepted the precedent of the anti-pope Wibert of Ravenna, who, following the massacres and forced conversions during the First Crusade in the Rhineland in 1096, forbade such returns. Yet Wibert's call had gone unheeded; Emperor Henry IV had allowed most forced converts in the Rhineland to return to Judaism. This means that in issuing his letter of 1144, Louis VII was not only following ecclesiastical practice, he was also willing to reject lay royal precedent. And Louis took this position even though, as he likely knew, some of the converts he was threatening may have been the children of Jews forced into Christianity in 1096, two generations before.

That Jews would see Louis's letter negatively was a foregone conclusion. Jews clearly hoped that kings would follow the lead of Henry IV, not Wibert. These hopes are summarized in the Hebrew letters examined below, which laud the archbishop of Sens for petitioning the king, with apparent success, to allow the return to Judaism (the "apostasy") of indisputably forced converts. Admittedly, in this letter, the king is presumably Louis VII. Yet in the light of Louis's actual severity, it seems that the real Louis VII disappointed the Jews. Rigord's implication that Louis improperly favored Jews, in contrast to Philip's determined disciplining, thus requires investigation.

Moreover, Rigord's opinion of Louis VII was not unanimous. Robert of Torigny reports that a certain William was killed in 1177, "by Parisian Jews, who were burned with fire" (occisus est Guillelmus a Judaeis Parisiis qui concremati sunt igne).⁶¹ The one who would have ordered the burning, could only have been Louis. It matters little that no known evidence supports this claim. The point is that for Torigny, Louis was anything but a "good king" for the Jews. Instead, Torigny's Louis acts correctly, strictly, even vindictively, which was as Ephraim of Bonn pictured him, not Rigord. We are left in a quandary. But there is a way out, and that is to propose that Rigord's reprimand of Louis for improperly bestowing *privilegia* referred not to Louis's overall record, rather to something particular. And that, most certainly, was Louis's consent to Jews employing Christian domestics.

Louis had petitioned Pope Alexander twice in this matter, for the Third Lateran decree had placed him in an awkward position. As just noted, despite centuries of canons to the contrary, Jewish charters through the twelfth century regularly specify the right to employ Christian domestics, or they imply this right by referring broadly to the preservation of the Jews' "good customs," meaning venerable practices. These no king could lightly overturn, as Louis VII clearly did not, nor did he want to do, which perturbed Rigord greatly.[62] Louis's selectivity may have perplexed Rigord, too. Once more not a "good king" for the Jews, Louis had apparently acquiesced to the Third Lateran's demand that no new synagogue be built. Yet by what, to Rigord, may have seemed arbitrary contrast, Louis balked at forbidding domestics. Initially, his son Philip did as well.

Angrily rejecting the appeal of Archbishop Guido of Sens, Philip insisted that the matter of Christian domestics pertained to him as king, not the Church. Philip also preferred to disregard, at least as the chronicle tells it, that Guido was conveying not his own wishes, but the demands of Pope Alexander III in reply to Louis VII's second petition. The existence of this second (!) petition suggests that Louis, even though he was still hoping to avoid capitulation (as Alexander's reply says he was), was nonetheless prepared to acquiesce; he would justify himself by pointing to papal insistence. Philip would have none of it.

How, then, in this light, are we to square Philip's stubbornness with Rigord's claims that unlike his father, Philip curbed the Jews' "other evil acts" (alia . . . nefanda), those acts being allowing Jews to employ Christian domestics? The reasonable explanation is that something fateful happened between 1179 and 1180-81, something that changed Philip's mind and led him resolutely to suppress the "evil acts," and for this, Rigord wished to give Philip full credit—which is also to say that for Rigord, in this matter, Louis and his actual policies were secondary.

The scenario, I believe, is straightforward. Philip had opened his reign by continuing the ways of his father. He was preserving, as it were, Jewish "good custom," following Louis's original policy, even though Louis himself seems to have been on the verge of giving in. Then, suddenly, as Jordan, too, observes, Philip reversed course. My sense is that it was during this short space of time that Philip heard about Richard of Pontoise; the story was certainly widespread. The vague claims Philip is said to have heard as a child were given substance; they were no longer just stories. Angered, or perhaps frightened, too, the young Philip—remember, in late 1179, he was in his impressionable and often mercurial mid-teens—decided to respond as only a king could. Louis VII, in this construction, appears to have exercised restraint upon hearing a ritual murder charge. In 1171, he did not follow his brother-in-law Theobold of Blois's lead and search out additional Jews to punish.[63] Philip would do otherwise, although he apparently refrained from outright violence until 1191, when, instructively, he had grown to adulthood.[64] Yet even in 1179, Philip resorted to effective force: arresting, confiscating, canceling loans, surely acceding to the Third Lateran decree on domestics, and, ultimately, expelling.[65] The charge of ritual murder had brought Philip to act.

Philip may also have decided to outdo his father with respect to conversion and apostasy, and not only, as we saw, in the case of Brie. We can only speculate, but Rigord's remark about Philip returning confiscated property to (presumably sincere) converts and the (anonymous) claim that Philip forced the exodus of Jews *refusing to be baptized* suggests that alongside the expulsion, the king exerted conversionary pressure in 1182. Had he also resurrected Louis's letter of 1144 decreeing death or mutilation for "apostates," which very likely had fallen into disuse? Apostasy threatened the health of the *Corpus Christi* no less than did ritual murder. Apostasy also (this, of course, would be the rallying point of the early modern Inquisition) introduced outsiders into the inner sanctum of the Christian altar, defiling its purity and breaking covenants, much in the way the dog was said to defile the Hittite Temple, and precisely as Paul and Ezekiel, not to mention Cyprian and Agobard, had said—and as Father Lambert would repeat in his eighteenth-century sermons against "false communion." Defending against apostasy would indeed have made Philip into the *christianissimus rex* that Rigord called him; the Bollandists have shown us just how justified this appellation was.

There was more. The Christian altar, as we have seen, was considered subject to contamination by "Jewish noise." Rulings prohibiting what was called loud, unseemly Jewish prayer had existed since the early centuries of the Church, and later they were inserted into papal letters and royal edicts. Jewish noise still preoccupied the early modern papal Inquisition in Italy.[66] The 1283 charter of King Philip III of France, too, took note of Jewish *strepiti*,[67] raucous noise, a din; and, not coincidentally, it prohibited Jews from employing Christian domestics. Rulings against Jewish "noise" were also an issue at the Third Lateran Council of 1179, alongside its determination to halt domestic service to Jews. The Council renewed the venerable proscription forbidding new places of Jewish prayer no doubt for just this reason. We are reminded that noise signified pollution by Pius IX's remark of 1871 decrying the Jews "barking" throughout the city of Rome, which rendered the city aurally impure, just as Pius thought Jewish meanderings polluted Rome's sanctified urban space.

However, most papal and even royal edicts from the time of Gregory the Great prohibiting "synagogal din" were accompanied by a clause permitting Jewish prayer in an alternative location; Jewish prayer itself was not forbidden. Gregory the Great had called it the Jews' rightful custom, supported by (Roman) law.[68] It is in this light perhaps that we should read the otherwise opaque reference in a letter of Innocent III to the "restraint of Jewish noise" (demissa voce) in Sens *even before* the 1182 expulsion.[69] In the years leading up to 1182, Philip Augustus—possibly following his father in accepting the Third Lateran prohibition on new synagogues—was apparently controlling Jewish prayer, especially its "noise." Philip was not closing synagogues, but he did insist that Jews pray as silently as possible.

In 1182, Philip confiscated the synagogues, which he then reconsecrated as churches.[70] Could it have been that one of Philip's motivations in ordering the expulsion was to silence Jewish prayer permanently? He had gone beyond the decree of the Third Lateran; the Council's ban on new synagogues did not anticipate violating Gregory the Great's injunction about providing alternative locations. By halting lending, then prayer, and, finally, what he believed were murderous assaults on the *corpus mysticum,* Philip appears to have initiated a uniquely stringent program of purification. By ostracizing the supposed Jewish "murderers," expelling them outright, he had done something the canons never even suggested.[71]

Whether Philip, especially at age fifteen, so conceptualized his actions is, of course, moot. That he was determined to repress Jewish actions he found offensive or threatening is certain, and Rigord would have exulted all the more in this had he known that Philip's actions set a precedent. In 1270 and again in 1283, Philip III prohibited not only the construction of new synagogues, in accord with the canons and the councils, but the repair of old ones, too, which the canons never forbade. Philip III was "out-poping" the pope, following in the footsteps of his father, Louis IX, whom the Jewish polemicist Meir ben Simeon had blamed for prohibiting just this.[72]

By closing synagogues, Philip Augustus was, of course, echoing deeply felt clerical feeling. When Rigord wrote that by reversing his initiatives and recalling the Jews in 1198, Philip offended "the common opinion," his words point to fire, not only smoke. But in his day, Rigord was no doubt referring principally to the will of rigorist clerics, people like himself, for whom the recall was reason for despair. Later on, people of the artisan class, too, laity, were infuriated, as we saw occur in Modena, in 1604. Raucous noises coming from a Jewish home situated adjacent to a church were said to disturb, if not mock, the divine office.[73] One protester, Barbara Rubbiano, also linked this noise to a charge of ritual murder.

However, Philip was a monarch, not a priest, nor, to be sure, an artisan, and, for kings, following "the common opinion" was an excessive luxury. The kingdom had terrestrial needs, not only spiritual ones. In 1198, Philip also realized that regardless of ecclesiastical criticisms, including those about noise coming from synagogues, his constancy was making him a fiscal fool.[74] Major barons, especially in Normandy and Champagne, had welcomed and profited from Jews fleeing the royal terror. Philip had also grown from an impressionable fifteen-year-old into thirty-three-year-old maturity.[75] In 1198, therefore, Philip veered away from Rigord's "common wisdom," succumbing temporarily to what the Bollandists suggestively named *avaritiam* (avarice). They were apparently implying that those who favored Jews, however briefly, acquired the despicable attributes of Jews themselves. This was precisely as Ratherius of Verona had once remonstrated with Emperor Otto III.[76]

It is hard to imagine that Philip Augustus had not seriously weighed avoiding the recall, and that he, too, would have preferred "a world without Jews." He very likely had been exposed visually to the demonization of Jews found in the near contemporary manuscript *Bibles moralisées,* of which Gerald Guest has perceptively written: "The figure of the Jew . . . emerges in [the pictorial representations in] these manuscripts as perhaps the ultimate threat to order in the medieval Christian world." It was to people like Philip Augustus, Sara Lipton has argued, that the *Bible moralisée* was directed—or certainly its prototype illustrations, which Philip may have seen. Its lessons he apparently absorbed.[77] He may also have been convinced of these lessons before they were given, as the tenor of the Bollandist narrative once again urges us to accept.[78] Philip's politics toward Jews, at least during the first decade of his reign, and likely afterward, were motivated by a sincere conviction of Jewish criminality and social threat. Moving him were emotions far stronger than those underlying anybody's realpolitik. Indeed, by 1206, he had overcome his temporary lapse of 1198, his so-called avarice, and he began to restrain Jewish lending anew.[79]

Yet in pursuing Jews, Philip would not remain alone. His convictions were eventually shared by other royal figures, including the kings of England, perhaps most notable among them Henry III. In 1255, Henry executed nineteen Jews charged with murdering Hugh of Lincoln.[80] Culturally, Henry, like Philip, was French, and like Philip, the young Henry may have heard from peers that every year, Jews murder a Christian boy, perhaps even that "they sacrificed a child and took communion [by eating] its heart" (immolabant, et eius corde se communicabant). We would like more information on Edward I, who expelled England's remaining Jews in 1290. On the subject of lending, at least, Edward fully admitted to Archbishop Pecham his royal responsibility to root the "nefarious" practice out.[81]

Besides, emotional conviction and realpolitik need not be mutually exclusive. Convinced as Philip was that charges of ritual murder were true, he must also have appreciated their political ramifications, which were weightier than simple monetary confiscations. In late twelfth-century France, ritual murder and the punitive reactions it evoked were a family affair, specifically, the family of Philip's mother, that of the counts of Champagne. At the start of his reign, Philip had rejected an alliance with this family, favoring one with the count of Flanders, which brought him to take steps against his own mother, the sister of the counts of Blois and Troyes and the archbishop of Rheims.[82] Perhaps motivating him in part was the memory of the events of 1171, when the count of Blois, married to Philip's half sister, had thirty or more Jews burned to death on a charge of ritual murder. Could it have been that one facet of spurning an alliance with the family of Blois was to take charge in matters of piety—matters of whose intrinsic merit Philip personally was convinced? In particular, Philip would be asserting himself in response to ritual murder where his father, Louis VII, as in fact happened in 1171, had not, all the better to entrench his rule.[83]

The scenario is one of inter- and intrafamilial competition played out through displays of piety—real piety, as we have seen—which were also viewed as instruments to demonstrate power, and to seize power as well. It was perhaps intentionally, in the context of Philip's rupture with the family of Blois, that Rigord reported the crime and executions for ritual murder *tempore patris* (Louis VII) without recalling Blois or its count by name or title. For completeness, it should be noted that in 1191, the countess of Brie, the scene of Philip's savagery, was the widow of Louis VII's brother, Philip's uncle.[84] Philip was being both consistent and thorough. So, at least, the evidence, however hard or circumstantial, makes us think. Real and political piety marched hand in hand.

Needless to add, the avidity of Philip, Rigord's *christianissimus rex*, to outstrip all others in his realms in piety earned him great praise from the Bollandists.[85] It was a value they greatly desired to instill. Kings must defend the faith. "In the name of clerical and church liberties" (pro defensione ecclesiarum et cleri libertate), Rigord says Philip attacked the counts of Charenton and Chalon during his first regnal year for violating ecclesiastical immunities.[86] The Bollandists, no doubt, were thinking of their own Counter-Reformation times, not the twelfth century alone, with an eye to (religiously and also politically) revolutionary events in France, Germany, and the Netherlands, and perhaps especially to the martyrdoms in England.

Yet it must never be forgotten that the Bollandists were writing on the basis of what they believed was real twelfth- and thirteenth-century precedent. Only the conviction that the events they recounted were true permitted such fervent retelling. In good Renaissance tradition, the Bollandists saw the past as a teacher of moral behavior, in this case, instructing kings how to behave. The reader will recall that the story of Richard of Pontoise and of Philip's reaction is the only ritual murder narrative in the *Acta Sanctorum* where the Bollandists introduce historical discussion. Did they realize that this was their sole opportunity to contextualize royal reactions to ritual murder as a unified chain of events?[87] One suspects they did.

Four   The Jewish Version
The Bollandist Reconstruction Vindicated

Enticing as the Bollandist reconstruction of Philip's actions may be, to demonstrate its historicity requires external corroboration. Apart from what is said in the always problematic Rigord, or Guillaume le Breton, the one solid piece of evidence revealing royal motivation is Philip's drastic change of course after he initially refused to accept Alexander III's reply to Louis VII's second petition. This is insufficient.

But there is better corroboration. It is found in a series of letters that are appended to the Hebrew account known as the Orléans Narrative, which is the principal source that records the burning to death of over thirty Jews at Blois in 1171 by order of Count Theobald of Champagne. Yet both the narrative and the letters are contained in a unique Hebrew manuscript that was copied in Treviso, Italy, in 1453, apparently from an earlier copy preserved at Speyer in the Rhineland.[1] So far removed in time and place from the events of 1171, the manuscript itself cannot help establish the letters' original date of composition. In theory, that could have been anytime between 1171 and decades afterward.[2]

This uncertainty is critical. If the letters were composed in 1171, they would have to be taken at face value, and their message would contradict much of what has just been said about Louis VII, for read literally, these letters are full of praise. The king is a protector.[3] He "honors" the Jews, denounces ritual murder, and orders the charge quashed. Ostensibly, this king is Louis VII. Moreover, the "king" in the letters complains to his wife about her brother's rashness in burning Jews. That brother would have been Louis VII's brother-in-law Theobald of Champagne, the villain of the Blois story; Theobald's sister was Louis's wife. The other characters in the letters, like Theobald, are also members of the ruling family of Champagne. The details seem to be in perfect order, and this has persuaded scholars to sustain the letters as historically reliable.[4]

I disagree. As I shall now argue, these letters were written years later, and what they are really saying (they may be read in full, in English translation with extensive annotation, in Appendix II) is the ironic contrapositive of their literal meaning. Their real message is stark: in their zeal for the faith, kings were dangerous, and their pious and punitive initiatives were threatening. It mattered little whether this zeal was pure or mixed with other motives. In particular, kings were capable of believing and acting on charges of ritual murder. Their motives in pressing the charge were far more hostile than the unrelieved avarice [*sic*] a letter of Pope Gregory X, issued in 1272, imputed to kings and other nobility.[5] Avarice signaled only a thirst for money. The highest bidder carried the day. Convinced believers in allegations of ritual murder could never be bought off.

This break with interpretative tradition demands a detailed explanation. How is it that rather than lauding the king, as they are normally interpreted, the Blois letters (as I shall call them for convenience) are actually damning him, offering not even "feint praise?"

Jewish Romance

The criticism of royalty in the Blois letters is not unique. Other texts criticize kings just as harshly. The brief but incisive narrative known as the "1007 Anonymous" takes sides neatly: the pope is a lawful ruler, the king is not.[6] We have long known that another Jewish writer, Meir ben Simeon, indirectly criticized Louis IX when he asked the archbishop of Narbonne why he followed the king rather than the pope in deciding how to govern lending.[7] But about Louis IX (possibly the king intended in the "1007 Anonymous"), it was, and is, easy to believe almost anything regarding Jews.

The king criticized by the Blois letters, I propose, is the youthful Philip Augustus. Possibly, though highly arguably, the letters are chiding Louis IX, too. Their subject is not Louis VII, the king in 1171, and this is regardless of the prima facie evidence that suggests otherwise. Intentionally, I believe, the letters never call the king by name. Perhaps concerned about a royal reaction should the letters be translated from Hebrew into Latin or the vernacular—such a thing was possible by the end of the twelfth century—the author alludes to one king but intends another, namely, the one reigning at the time of his writing, who is Philip. The criticism in the letters is harsh.

Something terrible happened at Blois in the late spring of 1171, a city in the Loire Valley, about an hour south, and slightly west, of Paris by rapid train. Count Theobald ordered the burning to death of between thirty-one and thirty-five Jews, who had been charged with ritual murder, even though no corpse was ever found. So strong was the memory of the event that about twenty years later, the Rhenish Ephraim of Bonn (d. 1196) reported the incident in great detail in his *Sefer Zekhirah*, *The Book of Remembrance*, a work that contains important memories of attacks on Jews during the twelfth century throughout northern Europe. No less important, not one, but two nearly identical lists of the Blois martyrs are found in the *Memorbüches*, the memorial lists composed in Ashkenazi communities and handed down for preservation. Normally, these lists, which were read on appropriate public and private memorial occasions, register martyrs by family grouping.[8] Women appear as mothers and wives. The Blois martyrs are registered as groupings of individual men and women. Men and women are also listed separately, and more women are named than men. Blois is also the sole instance where these lists memorialize Jews massacred outside of Germany. Why this great exception was made will remain for others to explain. In the event, our attention will focus less on events than on the *way* they are retold.

The prime source of information about Blois, as said, is the Orléans Narrative; Orléans itself is not far from Blois. The Orléans Narrative precedes chronologically that of Ephraim,[9] and as David Wachtel has demonstrated, it is the source of everything Ephraim knows, which Ephraim himself virtually admits.[10] The most recent investigation of these texts, and that of the Orléans Narrative, in particular,[11] has been by Susan Einbinder. Einbinder has been attracted to the literary and liturgical qualities of these texts, and she has concluded that they have much in common with the prose narratives, the Romances, that emerged in France at this time.[12] Whether in chronicles, letters, or poetry, Jews, too, "romanced" the past. These texts must not be read as purveyors of factual historical information,

For example, how shall we take literally the description of the condemned Jews who are said to have broken the bonds holding them and temporarily escaped the fire? Such an escape may be plausible. Nonetheless, the ending that "just their souls were burned, while the body endured" makes this story resemble the biblical tale of the three boys in the furnace (Daniel 3), combined with an inverted telling of the story of the Jew of Bourges.[13] Recently, Peter Schaefer has identified the Daniel furnace motif in the Jew of Bourges story itself.[14] The Jewish inversion comes in the image of flames that fail to consume and it is accentuated twice. The Jews place their trust in the God of Israel, contrary to the Bourges tale, which hinges on the Virgin's intervention.[15] In addition, the image of Jewish bodies that "endured intact" at Blois seems to anticipate the motif we saw in the Croxton play of a few centuries later in which a Eucharist sealed in an oven emerges as a bloodied (but intact) child when the oven bursts open.[16] Inversion motifs like this one—and there were many—were a two-way street,[17] emphasizing the kind of heuristic narrative the Blois sources set out to recount. Their existence also reminds us that these stories were being written, told, and read for polemical, aside from any other possible, motives; and this provided all the more reason to perfect their nature as *romance* (regardless of the cost to historical fidelity, which, in any case, is a modern historiographical lemma, and rarely, if ever, a medieval concern).

An additional sign of the literary quality of the texts is the discussion of the trial by ordeal to which the Jews' accuser is made to submit. Both the Orléans Narrative and (following it) Ephraim of Bonn say the innocent float. Normally, the innocent are supposed to sink—contrary to nature, which is the ordeal's essence. The ordeal's challenge to nature explains why Peter the Chanter led the assault that ended in the Fourth Lateran Council's prohibiting the ordeal in 1215: it seemed to bind God to magic.[18] The inverted ordeal image in the

Hebrew text is thus intentionally ironic. Ephraim of Bonn's irony goes still further. He says that because of the ordeal, Christians "have bad laws," which confound them. He is clearly playing on Paul in Romans, who used this concept (originating in Ezek. 20:25) to explain why the Torah hindered, rather than promoted salvation.[19] For Ephraim, need it be said, the truth is the reverse.

The Blois text contain other literary elements, too, especially those we have seen to be typical of ritual murder stories, to wit, the falling into water to commit suicide or the alleged hiding of a body in a leather pack, a parallel to the sack found in Robert of Torigny's narrative about Blois itself. Is this mimicry? Or is the Hebrew text perhaps copying the Latin, a usage not unknown?[20]

On another level, the texts contain potentially misleading pitfalls. Normally, it is said that the real fomenter of the burnings was an Augustinian friar. The text, however, says not "Augustinian," but that a "Gastinois" presided over the ordeal. The reference is to a local clergyman (of indeterminate, probably low, rank) from the Gastinais, or Gâtinais, near Orléans and Blois.[21] There was no monkish plot, although the warning about simple priests is direct—if not itself ironic. Here were the exalted count of Blois and his brother, an archbishop, as we shall see, allowing themselves to be misled by a mean country priest. More important, Susan Einbinder has shown that the expression in the Orléans account that "the count loved her" does not mean that the heroine-villainess of the Blois story, Pucellina, was Count Theobald's lover.[22] Rather, *ʾahavah* (love/loved) signifies feudal protection.[23] Pucellina was most probably an important lender, and it was for this reason that she (unwisely) relied on the count's *ʾahavah* to save the Jews. This interpretation of *ʾahavah* also makes the story believable. With Pucellina misperceived as the count's lover, a blunder I have made myself in the past, the story, at least in part, becomes absurd.

The Letters

It is against this setting of romance, irony, and textual pitfalls that we must fathom the series of letters, as many as six or, more probably, seven (depending on how one divides them), that are appended to the

Orléans Narrative in the Treviso manuscript.[24] And we should expect that the letters are much akin to this narrative in style and qualities. Yet at first blush, and regardless of their nature as "romance," it seems correct to prefer the simple and direct solution, to see the letters as telling a real story and to consider 1171 as the time of their composition. The letters ostensibly form a contiguous series revolving around the actions of Rabbi Jacob Tam, the paramount Jewish authority of the day, who died only two weeks after the Blois massacre. Read as such, the letters have been used to unravel Jacob Tam's imperious methods of decreeing new legislation, here, specifically, that establishing a new major fast day.

However, David Wachtel has shown that on the subject of Jacob Tam, the letters are not transparent. Jacob Tam's supposed centrality in all of them results from scholars following an error of Ephraim of Bonn.[25] Rather than ordaining a general fast, Wachtel explains, Jacob Tam, to whom some of the letters do seem to refer (as does Ephraim of Bonn directly),[26] opposed this innovation. In addition, if the letters are read as authentic reports of the events they recount, the results are too compact. Reactions and counterreactions to the massacre—both Jewish and royal, as well as episcopal—all take place within the two brief weeks that intervened between the burnings at Blois and Rabbenu Tam's death. One must also assume that Rabbi Tam was in full health and possession of his mental faculties till nearly the moment of his demise. The attribution of actions to Jacob Tam, whether in the appended letters or in the Orléans Narrative itself, may, therefore, be only a device. Its function would be much the same as the practice of invoking the name of Charlemagne to grant authenticity when charters and the like were contested, which certainly might have occurred when a new fast was authorized. In this case, however, we have all the more reason to suspect literary intervention, most likely after the fact, regardless of when the original letters were written.

Moreover, the subject of the letters (again as translated in Appendix Two) may be more or less uniform, and they may appear at first sight to grow out of the story of Blois. However, to argue that they were written at a single moment and that they represent a coordinated political effort, whatever its nature, is difficult.[27] The apparent unity rests on common themes, not origins, or even a common subject. No internal evidence such as intertextual references substantiates a nexus,[28] and the late date of the Treviso manuscript once again offers no help in determining the time of composition. The content also varies from letter to letter, sometimes greatly. Two brief letters report royal responses. In one, we learn what the king supposedly tells his wife; in the second, how the king (or possibly some other ruler) is upset that Jews may be cursing him. Two other letters describe appeals to the king in Paris and their apparently successful outcomes. A fifth letter reports the return of converts to Judaism, aided by the archbishop of Sens (in 1171, Guillaume, the brother of Theobald of Blois). A sixth tells of the fast and other penances decreed by the community of Troyes. Finally, a seventh (actually the first letter in the manuscript) concerns delation, or denunciation. Yet this letter is likely a composite, pieced together from distinctly incomplete segments drawn from at least two or even three earlier letters. Its contents pass from the story of a rejected suitor to informing, and to a vague report of people burned, with a possible hint at conversion. The scene of action is also not Blois. It is Loches, in the Touraine. And in 1171, the Touraine was in Angevin (English), not French Capetian, hands.

Politically and geographically, Loches had nothing to do with the county of Blois. Nor, in my opinion, does the letter.[29] What this letter does have in common with the other letters, and the Orléans Narrative is its report of a burning of Jews, including the motif of victims temporarily running out of the fire.[30] This motif, and ones like it would never appear in historical writing today, and, clearly, we have little expectation of extracting from the letter knowledge of what truly occurred at Loches. On the other hand, a medieval author might readily exploit the presence of such a motif to create a bridge, in this case, one linking the Orléans Narrative and the Loches letter together. The Loches letter could then provide a second bridge, to the other Blois letters, not because the letters and the Orléans Narrative have events, or at least motifs, in common, but because, as we shall now see, the "prince" or "ruler" mentioned in this letter is likely one and the same with the king intended by every one of the missives, and that is Philip Augustus. The letters' final editor (we shall never know whether the letters had one or more original authors) must have intuited that contemporary readers would understand that beaded onto a single strand, these letters offered an exceptional opportunity to say something essential about this king.

The evidence that Philip is the "ruler" intended by the Loches letter is substantive. Records preserved at the Cathedral of Chartres indicate that during the reign of Philip Augustus, a Jew converted at Loches and took as his baptismal name that of Philip Augustus. Whether for converting, assuming the king's name, or for both, Philip rewarded the neophyte with an annual stipend. Were we able definitively to link this neophyte with the hero/villain of the Loches letter, then its *terminus ante quem*, the time before which it could *not* have been written, would be resolved. In addition, the unity of royal identity in all of the letters would be the more easily proved (especially once the additional evidence now about to be adduced was weighed). Rarely, however, do historians benefit from such neat, convenient solutions.[31] Still, the possibility that the letter and the conversion of "Philip" refer to the same event cannot be disregarded.

What is certain is that the king in the letters could never have been Louis VII.[32] This is so, even though, the (unnamed) king mentioned in the two most central letters of the series, which report a meeting in Paris between the king and Jewish representatives, seems to be Louis VII. And this is so even if we perceive the letters as responding directly to the Blois events and within weeks of their happening, and even though the thrust of both letters is similar, albeit the second may have been copied from the first, from which it differs only in embellishing details. The two letters also contain common phrases urging greater respect (*kavod*) for Jews and their possessions, and in both, the Jews petition for redress, and the king answers uncompromisingly, even paternalistically, with the words of a true protector, declaring the charges made at Blois dastardly and forbidding their repetition.[33] Yet does this expansive behavior suit Louis?

Louis's actions, we know, were legally correct, most of the time. But there was also the Louis who aggressively voided Jewish loan contracts at the time of the Second Crusade, forbade reconversion, and accepted the Third Lateran decree prohibiting new synagogues.[34] With regard to Louis's repression of lending, which was reported by Ephraim of Bonn, Ephraim was writing at a great distance from the Île-de-France, Louis's royal domain. More than personal experience or knowledge, Ephraim was likely conveying widespread feelings: the real-life Louis alarmed French Jews, nor did he earn their trust. Though probably aware that Louis took no punitive steps against them in the wake of Theobald's butchery, this passivity was no basis for imagining royal denunciations of the count that no other source records. There was no justification either for the unlimited praise the king in the letters lavishes on the Jews. By contrast Philip's actions following libels of ritual murder were determined and consistently fierce. It was these actions that make the ironic inversions in the letters entirely plausible. The last thing anyone would conceive is Philip calling the sainthood of Richard of Pontoise "nonsense," as the king in the first Paris letter does. It would have been equally preposterous for Philip to order, as in the second letter, that "the Jews be honored far more [literally, twice] than they had been honored in the past."[35]

Something in the letters is awry. Like the Orléans Narrative itself, the appended letters clearly "romance the past"; and this romance postdates Louis. A difficult usage found in both Paris letters makes this very clear.

The first of the two Paris letters refers to what appear as separate accusations of ritual murder, one in *Kefar Pontiyeh* and the other in *P[o]ntiyeh-Rirt*. The second Paris letter mentions only *P[o]ntiyeh-Rirt*, and it associates this place-name directly with (the sainted) Richard (of Pontoise). *Pontiyeh* itself (in the first missive) is only one letter shy of *Pontiyeze*, the regular Hebrew spelling for Pontoise. However, the addition *Kefar*, town, is unique (in Hebrew).[36] *Rirt*, too, in *P[o]ntiyeh Rirt* appears nowhere else. Nor, *un*like *Pontiyeze*, do *Kefar Pontiyeh* or *P[o]ntiyeh-Rirt* have a neat Latin equivalent, *Pontoesia* or *Pontesia*. Alternate Latin names for Pontoise are *Briva Isarae*, *Brivisarae*, *Pons Isarae*, *Oesiensis Pons*, or *Isere pons*, and *Pontisara*. None fits. Both of the two Hebrew usages in the first Paris letter, therefore, conflate the Latin, and they give the impression of two separate events and locales. Yet the letter seems unaware of this conflation and the confusion of place names, which suggests detachment, whether in place, time, or both, from the events—and irrespective of the origin of the extant copy of the letter in the Rhineland.

This blunder aside, do not the sources—Rigord, Guillaume le Breton, Gaguin, and the Bollandists—say, in explaining Philip's motivations, that Richard died in 1179? The mention of Richard's death in the letters should thus provide an incontrovertible *terminus ante quem*, certainly one that is more defensible than that suggested by the existence of the neophyte Philip. It should be clear that the letters were written, or finished at the very least, during the reign of Philip Augustus, and we should be entitled to read and interpret them in the light of Philip's policies. However, that Philip heard of these events in 1179 or early 1180, or even 1181, does not (conveniently, to sustain our interpretation) mean they actually happened then. Not all of the sources, especially contemporary or near-contemporary ones, assign Richard's death to 1179. Two list it, respectively, in 1156 and 1163, and one of the authors, Lambertus of Waterloo, had died by 1170. It would seem that there has been manipulation, or some error, with respect to the date of 1179, although by whom it is not clear.

It might be expedient to resolve the issue by charging interpolation or to suggest confusion with the alleged murder of Robert of Bury St. Edmunds, which the Melrose Chronicle dates to about 1179. But neither of these possibilities is reassuring. Nor may it be said confidently that the Bollandists were unknowingly substituting Richard for a certain William, whose death, as noted above, is reported by Robert of Torigny, who writes that William was killed in 1177, "by Parisian Jews, who were burned with fire."[37] Accordingly, the date 1179 can be neither confirmed nor rejected. What is certain is that the Bollandists were anxious to place Richard's death in that year—they insist on it—for this date squared perfectly with everything they wanted to say about ritual murder and appropriate royal reaction. By the same token, the Bollandists with their enormous knowledge of textual history and manuscript traditions, regardless of errors or even distortions, may have been correct in accepting the 1179 date.[38] It would be precipitous to dismiss it out of hand; citing the Bollandists, the noted scholar of medieval sainthood André Vauchez affirms it.[39]

Moreover, in their reference to Richard, the letters speak about "[the allegedly murdered child] declared a saint in Paris." Richard had not been formally canonized, but even a popularly acclaimed saint took time to establish himself through miracles. Would the fifteen years between the earliest possible date for Richard's death, 1156, and the Blois incident, 1171, have been enough? The later possible dates for Richard's death make the squeeze even tighter. If the letters were written well after 1179, Richard's popular canonization presents no serious problem.

Yet, in the event, there is a piece of information that does permit a reasonably firm dating. The second Paris letter speaks of the Jews greeting the king when he "returned from Flanders." Louis VII, I am told,[40] if he ever journeyed to Flanders, returned no later than the spring of 1170—before the Blois massacre. Philip Augustus first visited Flanders in 1184. In the thirteen intervening years, apparently neither king was there.[41] This discrepancy creates substantial difficulty in accepting 1171 as the date of the letters' composition, let alone within two weeks of the Blois burnings. Even as romances, rather than chronicles, the letters would not refer to a royal journey, nor would their authors hasten to add specific, *corroborable*, yet *superfluous* information lacking a factual base; the second letter could have simply said "when the king came to Paris."[42] If one insists on saying that the reference to Flanders is a mistake, with the 1170 return erroneously advanced to 1171, this would only reinforce the conclusion that the author was well removed in time from the Blois events, writing considerably after 1171—in fact, well after 1184, too—when precise dates were no longer remembered.

The second Paris letter is equally persuasive. Of all people, Henri, count of Troyes, the brother of Theobald of Blois, is made to say, "I have not found in the Jews' Torah that it is permitted to kill a Christian." This statement reads like a paraphrase of the directive issued in 1236 by Emperor Frederick II, reacting to the blood libel at Fulda. Frederick denounced the libel, pointing out that *it is said in neither the Old nor the New Testament* that Jews need human blood; the Books of Moses and the Talmud prohibit blood's consumption entirely.[43] In 1247, Innocent IV repeated this denunciation and enlarged upon it. He rejected verbatim the idea—virtually identical to that which Guillaume le Breton had sustained during the reign of Philip Augustus— that Jews *se corde pueri communicabant* (take communion with the heart of a child).⁴⁴ By having Henri of Troyes repeat words so like those used by Frederick II, Innocent IV, and Guillaume le Breton, the second Paris letter betrays its chronological origins. Admittedly, Henry says "kill," not use or drink blood, but we must not press overly subtle distinctions and perceptions on Jews who were hearing the blood (as opposed to the ritual murder) libel for perhaps the first time. Besides, whatever the author of the letter understood, it stretches credibility to believe that he invented his words out of whole cloth; happenstance has its limits. He must have copied them from a Latin source, just as Shelomo bar Shimshon's First Crusade Chronicle borrowed directly from Albert of Aachen.⁴⁵ However, the Latin source, or sources, for the Paris letter originated in the thirteenth century, which was decades *after* Louis VII's reign. The Blois letters surely originated in the thirteenth century, too.

In the form it has survived, the second Paris letter represents the state of Jewish opinion during the reign of Philip Augustus, or later (but not before), as well as the state of Jewish knowledge about what Christians were saying. The same goes for the other letters, to some extent even that of Loches. Though disjointed in subject matter, the letters share a common outlook and logic, and this, too, may help explain why they were eventually gathered into a single packet, even though they were possibly written by different hands and at different times. Their texts were likely edited as well, although not so carefully, which may account for their sometimes hazy beginnings and endings, the repetition, and the difficulty in deciding their precise number. But they do share a common outlook, and that is one of paradox, parody, and irony.

This puts them in good company. *Sefer Yosef Hamekane*, for example, opens with extreme irony. Its author, Josef Official, tells us that as he rode on horseback one day, in the company of the archbishop of Sens (did he really?), the archbishop stopped to relieve himself on a bush. Official relieved himself, too, on a cross. The archbishop was livid. To this, Official responded: "You acted like a fool. God appeared in the bush to offer salvation, and there you urinated. The one you say is worthy of awe, but who erred and failed, deserves what he gets." That Jewish texts could be ironic is beyond doubt.⁴⁶

Irony

The irony of the Blois letters is scathing. Would even a Louis VII actually "favorable" to the Jews have called for "honoring," let alone "doubly honoring," them?[47] Reality was usually the opposite, or much, much less. The most expansive charters of privilege issued by the German emperors or the English kings, for example, decree protection and the observance of legal rights, never "honor."[48] Harder to believe is the statement of the king in the brief anonymous letter directed to a Rav Yom Tov, in which he tells his wife: "Your brother has laid hands on my crown and smashed it" (the brother being Theobald and the sister Adele, Louis VII's wife and Philip Augustus's mother). This is literary invention. How was the author privy to such information with its undertones of "pillow-talk?"[49] Political reality, moreover, dictated that Louis VII ally himself with Theobald, who was also his son-in-law (married to Louis's daughter Alix, who herself may have been commercially embroiled with Pucellina and a protagonist at Blois), not defame him.

Royal preoccupation with the state of "the crown" would also have been more appropriate to the thirteenth century and the propaganda the French kings were then issuing. In addition, as the king phrases it in the letter, "crown" presupposes a direct juridical bond between the Jews and the king: attacking Jews, the *tanquam* [royal] *servi*, is to attack the king. A royal-Jewish bond of this kind came into being during the thirteenth century, not before.[50] Besides, Louis VII was never the direct lord over Theobald's Jews, just as neither he nor Theobald was the lord of Loches and the town's Jews. In 1171, that was the English King Henry II.

However much, therefore, the letters appear to be enhancing and sweetening the royal image, readers were assumed to be more astute. By way of a description that used irony to invert reality, readers were to understand that the king intended was Philip. Even if one insists that the letters originated in 1171, the probability is great that they survived to be copied and heavily reworked for just this ironic purpose. They were copied into texts preserved at Speyer for this same purpose, too — and perhaps modified once more: Count Henri, *Henricus*, is called in

Hebrew by the German Heinrich. The ironically idealized image of royal behavior found in the letters, and their inversion of reality, was worth repeating, even in different circumstances, and even with a "new king."[51] Regardless of specific royal identities, these letters might offer encouragement—or perhaps consolation. For was not such encouragement needed when the German emperor Frederick declared—or was about to declare—the Jews his chamber serfs, notwithstanding his roughly contemporaneous denunciation of the blood libel? The Jews of his realm were exclusively his with respect to legal rights, and they were wholly dependent on his goodwill. They were also dependent on his ability to protect them, to whose failure (and that of his successors, too) the libels and massacres of 1241, 1298, and 1336 would soon attest.[52]

The irony of the letters is ever-present. Can you imagine, they seem to imply, our (present) sovereign, Philip, behaving in this way, exculpating the Jews, denying ritual murder, and pledging to support the lending that the real Philip Augustus suppressed. The letters have the king do all three.[53] The irony is compounded by the letter urging that converts be allowed to revert to Judaism and open Jewish practice. The principal actor is the brother of Count Theobald, Archbishop William of Sens, who is also Philip Augustus's uncle, close advisor, and the pivotal archbishop of Rheims during Philip's reign. Shalom Spiegel suggested that Archbishop William (1168–76 in Sens)[54] persuaded Theobald to offer the Jews at Blois a choice of death or baptism.[55] Yet for a late twelfth-century prelate openly to promote forced conversion, let alone a potential slaughter, would have been no less canonically illegal than a proposal favoring reconversion, which was apostasy. It is also most doubtful that the real William would have insulted his brother with such a proposal. Even more doubtful would have been the promise Count Theobald himself makes in this letter that he "would put it into writing that we could [safely] say that they would make no more false accusations." Doubtful, too, exceedingly so, is the image of the third brother, Henry of Champagne, preaching (in the second Paris letter) that ritual murder accusations were a canard. A declaration like this might have provoked an open rift with his brother Theobald, and that would have weakened the family's position before the king. The possibility that this might have truly happened was no greater than was the plausibility of the events in the pillow-talk letter, where Louis VII, politically allied with the Champenois, told his wife, Adele, that her brother (and his son-in-law) Theobald was a villain and a knave. By contrast, Philip Augustus may well have called Theobald a knave when he, Philip, repudiated the Champenois alliance and quarreled with Adele, his mother. On top of everything else, in 1144, had not Louis VII himself prohibited Jewish converts from returning to Judaism under pain of death? Twenty-seven years later, in 1171, could the archbishop, or anybody else, have opposed, in fact mocked, this prohibition? How consistently Louis's order had been applied is not the issue.[56]

The letters are a tour de force in irony, to which may be added purposeful inconsistency and revealing innuendo. Archbishop William's good deed of fostering "reconversion" is compromised. He ambiguously, if not deviously, fails to persuade his brother Theobald to allow converts reverting to Judaism to keep their goods and money; Theobald (in the letter) confiscates everything. And what is the meaning of the inscrutable addition to this letter about William (if it is not a separate missive) that begins: "Concerning the keys to the synagogue, they spoke lies and deceit?" Both letters, I suspect, refer to the actions of Philip Augustus, who Rigord says returned the property of those who converted in 1180/81—a highly unusual act (popes were continually berating kings for doing the opposite)[57]—but who also confiscated synagogues and consecrated (most of) them as churches.[58] This was far from "honoring" the Jews.

What, finally, is to be made of the seemingly undecipherable statement in both Paris letters that the Jews want to speak to the king in secret, to which, the king replies that it is unnecessary? Instead, the Jews should speak up before the assembled royal entourage. This is a sure allusion to Judges 3:15, the story of Ehud ben Gerah. This verse is also crucial in the text of the "1007 Anonymous," which cites the verse to invert the Ehud narrative. In the Book of Judges, Ehud kills King Eglon of Moab after enticing him away from his entourage to a distant attic, supposedly to reveal a secret. In the "1007," the hero, Jacob ben Yequtiel, takes the pope to an attic. But instead of killing the pontiff,

Jacob tells him he is God's Vicar, in whom the Jews trust. The pope responds by issuing the fundamental bull of guarantee, the constitution *Sicut iudaeis non*, which moves Jacob to declare the pope a "rightful authority."[59] By implication, the king, who in the "1007" is said to initiate a forced conversion, is "the wicked authority." No Jew who prayed daily, explicitly beseeching this "wicked authority's" demise, would miss the allusion.[60]

The two Paris letters replay this scene, altered and transposed. After telling the Jews there is no need to speak in secret, the king grants wide privileges that parallel the guarantees of *Sicut iudaeis non*. This pictures the king as "rightful authority." The letter, however, means the opposite. Indeed, the presence of the allusion to the Ehud story is explicable only as an intentional signifier, although it was strictly one for initiates. Jewish commentaries say that the Jews were known to the biblical Eglon to be "faithful servants," and, therefore, Eglon went freely to the attic.[61] In the letters, the king, who putatively, and in context, knows the Ehud story (he has to know it, or the scenario would fail) declines. He knows, too, that in accepting the invitation to speak in secret, Eglon sealed his fate, that the "faithful servants"—the Jews in the letter call him "Our Lord, the king"—were, instead, faithless. The king says as much. In the shortest of the seven letters, the one that opens with a hazy reference to the keys of the synagogue, and which likely refers to Philip's confiscations, the "ruler" says straight out: "the Jews curse me."[62] He was right.

Paradoxically, this royal exclamation of Jewish perfidy may be the most perfectly historistic element in the entire epistolary collection. Rigord—reporting Jewish reactions to the edict of expulsion in 1182— said that the Jews sought every avenue, every influence, to postpone their exodus, but to no avail. And when Philip held his ground, the Jews "in a state of shock and crying 'Hear O Israel,' began to sell all they had" (attoniti et quasi stupefacti, [and amid cries of] Scema Israel, id est Audi, Israel, agressi sunt vendere omnam suam supellectilem).[63] By contrast to this chilling ending—where Jewish curses were no doubt what Rigord was really recording—the Paris letters, with the mutually loving roles they assign respectively to king and Jews, are one big theatrical script, a burlesque, and a masquerade. The real Jews did not play the role of faithful servants. The real king was anything but generous and "rightful" in dealing with his Jewish flock.

Yet all of this could be told only through clever literary innuendo. French Jews were not likely to have admitted their distrust and fear of Philip openly. Philip was a king who believed ritual murder accusations and probably the blood libel, too. He expelled and despoiled his Jews, and, toward the end of his life, after the Jews had been allowed to return, he resumed his earlier stance by prohibiting lending and ordering a new seizure of Jewish wealth. *Gezelah di malkhutah gezelah*, the Jews may have responded: the law of the kingdom, *dina di-malkhutah*, may be the law (as the rabbinic dictum went), but so, too, theft, *gezelah*, was theft. And theft did not demand obsequiousness.

But in reality, the king was the one who dictated maneuvers. It was he who decided whether his "Jewish servants" would be "faithful," or what to do if they were not. One final time, therefore, we must understand the text as inversion, and what was inverted was the Jews' legal status. Sometime during Philip's reign, likely before the death of Guillaume le Breton in 1223, who himself employs the term,[64] French Jews began to be referred to as *tanquam servi*. From now on, Jews were legally "like *servi*," serfs or even slaves, and in the term's most pejorative sense, that of quasi "chattel," the parallel term found in English texts. The faithless "faithful" servants, who once enjoyed reasonable privileges, were in the process of losing them all. A vengeful king was blunting Jewish teeth.

The Jewish letters, then, convey enormous dissatisfaction, the contrary of Rigord's contentment upon seeing the Jews in a state of shock. For Rigord, the king was safeguarding the *societas fidei* by repressing the Jews. For the author (the final editor) of the Hebrew letters, the conclusion was sadly the same. Philip Augustus was King Eglon of Moab personified. But now there was no reliable means of defense. Not even the law could be invoked, especially the canons, as the hero of the tale of "1007 Anonymous" does when he confronts the pope. Unlike the pope, the king freely pursued his (arbitrary) will.

How, then, were the Jews to respond? In truth, there was precious little they could do. And nobody was realistically thinking of repeating Ehud's feat. The only possible response, but only sometimes, was flight, which, in Philip's day, might put a crimp in the king's purse.⁶⁵

However, Jews could take up their quills. They could write and describe their discomfort, resorting to bitter irony and black humor—and, of course, they could compose dirges in praise of martyrdom. Charges of ritual murder, alongside accusations of aiding and abetting converts' return to Judaism (which this time were correct), were turning rulers wholly against them, certainly the king of France. With clerical sanction and encouragement, such as that given by Rigord and the creators of the imagery in the *Bibles moralisées*, the royal initiatives of the late twelfth and early thirteenth century would only continue. No wonder the archbishop of Sens is mocked and pictured as doing the opposite of what he almost certainly would have done in reality.

Nor was there any true safe haven. The author of the "1007 Anonymous" praised the popes for observing the law, but he also obliquely admitted that the price of protection was unbearable. Jews had to concede to ecclesiastical authorities the right to censor Jewish texts. The author or authors of the Blois letters, too, camouflaged their message. From difficult start to disillusioned finish, it was one they delivered tongue in cheek. Telling the truth outright—could they have told it—would have been too painful for words, and perhaps too daring as well.

Yet, for a moment let us turn things upside down. Let us consider that the letters contain no irony, that they may be read at face value, and that their king is Louis, not his son Philip. The scene at Paris could make sense. Louis was aghast at what Theobald had done, which nobody had ever done before.⁶⁶ But more important, the king and other nobles had given privileges to Jews, which, apart from specific grants, guaranteed life and limb. And just as Louis was distraught with Alexander III for wanting him to cancel the clause in charters to the Jews allowing them Christian domestics, so he would have been beside himself with Theobald for having committed so gross a violation of fundamental, chartered rights. It was irrelevant that Theobald's Jews were not under Louis's direct jurisdiction. Theobald was his close ally, including through the two marriage beds of his wife and daughter. His ally's misbehavior—Theobold was also Louis's feudal vassal—reflected on Louis badly. So angry was King Louis that he told the Jews who approached him for relief that he would not paper it over in some back room but would express his wrath publicly and insist that judicial murder stop. The irony disappears.

This reconstruction, however, accounts for not one word of the way the letters retell the events, of why *instead* of simple exposition, the author or authors resort to one palpable exaggeration after another, to wit, the bombastic condemnations, or calling Richard's sainthood "nonsense." No king would have spoken of honoring the Jews *themselves*, but of their privileges alone. One could go on; it is enough to reread the preceding pages. But the point, I hope, is made. The letters—the reports, the only reports—we have are too full of irony to be retelling events "as they really were," regardless of any truth that may lie at their core. In the letters as we have received them anything historistic has been thoroughly ironized. Irony was the only way out. It alone enabled the safe expression of frustration and despair. This was especially true during the fearful reign of Philip II Augustus. Through irony and the language of inversion, Jews might even voice the worst truth of all, that the real Philip, the king who, in the letters, denies the libels, in actuality believed every one of them, from first to last.

The Bollandist reconstruction of Rigord and of the events between 1171 and 1198 is thus vindicated: the prime movers were ritual murder and a perceived Jewish social threat. Yet this reconstruction reflects more than royal motives and the designs of churchmen like Rigord. It also provides important understandings for the history of the Jews themselves. Individually, all of the royally initiated episodes after 1171 were—and have previously been called—traumatic. But thanks to the guiding hand of the Bollandists, and as substantiated by the Hebrew romances (the letters and other texts), we have no choice but to perceive these events as interlinked. Together, they define a crux in the history of northern French Jewry, if not all of Europe's Jews. More precisely, these events *explain* the crux. Christians had become convinced that Jews, whose real image had by now been so encrusted with myths like that of the rapacious Jewish dog, posed an ongoing danger to the Christian polity. Alleged Jewish usurious exploitation, attempts to overturn the right order of events, as at Brie (in 1191), and, most of all, the murder of Christian children were deemed a vital threat. All of these had to be stopped, and regardless, it seems, of the means employed.

Moreover, beginning with Philip Augustus, episodes of supposed Jewish malfeasance were increasingly cloaked in an aura of eucharistic piety and mysticism. The status quo, if not the very continuity, of French Jewry was being put to the test. Kings like Philip Augustus appear even to have feared their Jews. In 1062, Pope Alexander II had said Jews lived peaceably among Christians, "always prepared to obey" (semper parati servire). Philip and those who followed him seem to have thought the opposite. Rather than "serve," Jews "were always prepared to kill" (semper parati trucidare).[67] This message spread quickly, and the response was often homicidal. It was very much intentionally that the author(s) of the Blois letters put ritual murder at center stage. Yet more than the events, what he (or they) were seeking to publicize were royal, noble, and clerical reactions, which could be retold safely only through resort to satiric inversion. In real life, ostensible royal and episcopal promises to protect, the ones the letters ironically laud, too easily dissolved into commitments to punish and avenge. This is the satire's message, which is also what we set out to observe. Thus, the inestimable historical value of the Blois letters, which are indeed the "flip"—and hence validating—"side" of the story told by Rigord and Guillaume le Breton, the very story—believed, however, as incontrovertibly true—that the seventeenth-century Bollandists preserved, and then passed on to future generations.

Five A Usable Past

Continuity and Challenge

However consciously, the early Bollandists perpetuated the medieval vision of a constant Jewish threat. Their avowed intention was to advance the glory of martyrs; in fact, they perpetuated the idea that martyrdom and Jewish machinations often went hand in hand. Moreover, if believers, martyrs, and their "passions" reaffirmed Catholicism's resilience, which Protestantism had specially challenged in the Bollandists' own day, martyrdom at Jewish hands had unique, even beneficial, qualities. Indeed, so reassuring were the accounts of such martyrdoms, that the Bollandists felt compelled to retell them in a world that was virtually "one without Jews;"[1] the constellation of anxieties that challenged the existence of thirteenth-century northern European Jewry had remained alive even without a Jewish presence. Yet the reassurance the seventeenth-century Bollandists sought was the same as that which the Jews' twentieth-century accusers, too, so ardently desired. The unflagging capacity of tales of Jewish assault to restore confidence and confer spiritual and emotional gratification, whatever the circumstances, gave urgency to their constant repetition.

In some circles, the need to repeat these tales still exists, and it provides the impetus that makes the charge of ritual murder so impervious to logic. Did not W. H. Hart, the editor of the chronicles and charters of Gloucester, suggest this neatly that: "the frequency [of the charges] . . . is sufficient to demand our attention?" Was it possible, he was intimating, that not all the charges were false.

Fortunately, gullibility has its limits, probity its exponents. Was the Christian polity to be defined through its phobias and anxieties, the need to prove itself invincible in times of imagined challenge, the ship braving the stormy sea, as perhaps first Justin Martyr and then other apologists after him pictured the Church? Or was a confident Christian polity to be founded on the grounds of justice, principle, *and* scholarship,[2] as was asserted by Vernet and Vacandard, and demanded by others, including those modern (and "modernist") continuators of the original Bollandists, Delehaye and Halkin, not to mention Browe and especially Döllinger, as well as Gigot in the 1910–12 *Catholic Encyclopedia*? All of them called the charge of ritual murder nonsense.

This, as we said at the start, is the marvelous paradox of our story. The seventeenth-century Bollandist legacy was strikingly dual. Its creators touted the truth of ritual murder, but they also willed to their heirs the scholarly tools of reasoned analysis. Taking advantage of these tools, twentieth-century Bollandists debunked unsubstantiable myth, whether benign or pernicious, and refuted the libel of ritual murder. It is this reasoned method that underlies Delehaye's 1903 *Les Légendes hagiographiques* and his 1912 *Les Origines du culte des martyrs*.

The Bollandist emphasis on rigorous scholarship was also infectious. The Jesuit Peter Browe, whose final word on the Host accusation is a simple *nein*, systematically discounts the tales of its transmission. The accusation itself he calls "limitless and un-Christian" (maßlos und unchristlich). The libels, he writes, are too overburdened with miracles to be believable, and told so much later that the record is worthless; some are accounts of Christian crimes transformed and projected onto Jews.[3] Browe's analysis might have silenced the skeptical Hart. The frequent repetition, which Hart had seen as a possible sign of historicity, justified nothing. The original fable was being simply retold.[4]

The stance of people like Delehaye and Browe might further be defined. It was that of churchmen *not* afraid to confront the novelty of their times. Jacques Kornberg's argument is compelling that Ignaz von Döllinger spoke out primarily not to defend Jews — although his defense of Jews was intentional — but to preserve the rights of those within the Church to be critical, to propound scholarly and rigorous theories diverging from received integralism, and to insist on the right to individual conscience and thought. These were, of course, the very rights that the integralist movement had done all in its power to quash during the decades prior to Ignaz Döllinger's 1881 lecture *Die Juden in Europa* (The Jews in Europe) — so obsessed were Catholic integralists with their need for fortresslike conformity and theological stasis.[5]

How greatly the modernist stance contrasts with the determined belief in ritual murder of the seventeenth-century Bollandists! Their opening to the story of Werner verges on the credulous: "Through the centuries, the Jews' hate of Christ and the Christians was so enormous that they cursed Christians daily and atrociously persecuted them, stealing Christian children in secret and cruelly killing them, especially at the season of the passion when Christ was venerated." Bollandist standards of measuring a text's authenticity, but not the reliability of its contents, preordained their outlook. What pious authors truly wrote was truly to be believed.

It is notable that the early Bollandists never mention that even in the later Middle Ages, there were those who reacted to ritual murder charges without prejudicial passion. Beset by challenges from within and without in the seventeenth century, the Church needed uncompromising reassurance. And just that is what the Bollandists derived from collating what they believed were authentic testimonies. They seemed to have been unequipped to differentiate right from left. Innocent III's apparent acceptance that Jews killed Christians clearly convinced them more than did Innocent IV's and Gregory X's denials that Jews used Christian blood or intentionally committed murder.[6] This Bollandist refusal to accept the papal lead anticipated the efforts of their Jesuit successors in Italy during the pontificate of Leo XIII (at the turn of the twentieth century), who sought to conceal past papal denunciations of the blood libel, including Innocent IV's very words to that effect.[7] These clerics had also forgotten that some in the Middle Ages, including lay people, denied that Jews used Christian (or any human) blood; they also protested wrongful executions. Johann von Winterthur of Swabia, about 1332, was outraged "that wholly innocent Jews [accused of abusing a Host] had been killed" (iudaei immunes et alieni a prefato reatum . . . deleti sunt).[8] At least once, Christian judges acquitted Jews of a blood libel in open court, which happened in Savoy in 1329. They did convict one Jew, but *not* for murder. Deathly afraid of torture, he had falsely accused innocent others (as he was innocent himself). Fortunately—for him—he died in jail before the verdict was rendered.

The Bollandists never mention this trial; the reason seems patent. In 1329, there was no corpse, no martyr, no passion, no life of a saint for the Bollandists to perpetuate, not even the history of a ritual murder itself. The Savoyard verdict assured that no memory of even an anonymous martyrdom could be created. Without a corpse the Savoyard judges would not be swayed. This was the contrary to what had happened at Blois one hundred sixty years earlier. We would like very much to know whether the Bollandists had heard this story. But would hearing it have affected their thoughts? Would it have changed their mode of presentation when they wrote about Werner, Richard, and Simon? I doubt it. Their need for martyrdom was too great.

The charge in 1329 was particularly threatening. Jews, it was said, used the heads and intestines of Christian children to make *haroseth*, the mixture of fruits, nuts, and wine eaten at the Passover Seder meal in memory of the bricks the Jews were forced to make in Egypt. This *haroseth*, the text goes on, was eaten on matzoh or with lettuce (as it normally is), and eating it was said to grant salvation. The combination of *haroseth* and matzoh was a complete eucharistic surrogate, both body and Host, in the eyes of the accusers, and its ingestion was said to function as did receiving the real Host—eating it fulfilled the Eucharist's redemptive ends. After all, had not the Jewish matzoh, made of pure wheat, been replaced by Christ himself? The Jews were thus being accused of satanically inverting that which Christianity called holiest; the imagery of the blood libel, indeed, a blood and Host libel as one, had attained maximum development.

The accusation at Savoy was not unique: the fourteenth-century Flemish poet who had written in verse the story of the Good Werner, saying, "the dirty, stinking Jewish dogs" (Les sales Juifs, les chiens puants), had gone on to say that the Jews had drained Werner's blood, "since with this blood, they wished to make *their* sacrament" (Parce qu'avec ce sang, je le sais,/ Ils voulaient faire leur sacrement).[9] This amazing accusation endured. It was repeated almost verbatim, in 1840, in connection with the death of one Father Thomas in Damascus, for which local Jews were accused of ritual murder.[10]

Providentially, fantasies like this were not universal. The charge was too much for the Savoyard judges, perhaps the same Savoyards who were trying and condemning witches at this same time.[11] Through due process, the Savoyards declared the accused innocent. Justice, which medieval people considered a divine virtue, was affirmed.[12] The concept of justice had also moved Innocent IV, who had invoked it in questioning whether burning the Talmud violated recognized Jewish privilege.[13] Pope Innocent again spoke of justice in his 1247 bull *Lachrymabilem*, which impugns the blood libel. While still a professor of canon law, Innocent (Sinibaldo Fieschi) had declared that the pope might judge and punish Jews who erred theologically against Judaism yet remained unpunished by their rabbinic masters. But he was not deflected from preserving judicial principle, which the careful definition of "the permissible" in his declaration reinforced to the hilt; Innocent provides no example of a (so-called) "favorable" pope.[14] Guiding him was his preference for carefully defined justice over arbitrariness. The author of the *1007* narrative saw this clearly, leading him to insert at least one clause of Innocent's declaration into his argument that popes observe the law, while kings do not.

Six hundred and sixty years later, the Jesuit Bollandist François van Ortroy once again took a stand in defense of principled legal behavior, in fact, specifically as the bull *Lachrymabilem* had spelled it out. Van Ortroy cited its text in his 1904 review of G. Divina's *Storia del beato Simone*; this review we first met in Chapter 1. Van Ortroy of course knew that Innocent IV was not the only pope to issue a bull denouncing the blood libel. But *Lachrymabilem* was the first to do so, and its wording is pellucid.[15] It was also the bull whose possible republication had been the source of contention just five years earlier, in 1899, under Leo XIII. And the fight had been public knowledge. Van Ortroy was displaying great determination, therefore, when he cited *Lachrymabilem* to underpin his refutation of Divina's belief in the truth of Simonino's murder at Jewish hands in 1475.[16] He had chosen to root his modernist position in the words of a magisterial voice from the past, the same voice that contemporary integralists were doing their best to conceal.

It was apt and specially suited to van Ortroy's purposes that in *Lachrymabilem*, Innocent IV had emphasized that Jews charged with murder were being executed without formal legal accusation, proper trial (Innocent said "confession," but he meant trial as the term was then understood), or even a public verdict. Over two hundred years later, the specific protest of Bishop Battista de' Giudici, whom Pope Sixtus IV had sent to investigate the proceedings (shortly after the Jews of Trent were executed), was that Simon's trial had been canonically corrupt.[17]

This episode brings us full circle. It leaves no doubt about the constant presence of ritual murder along a path that has led from the modernist crisis back to medieval accusations and now once again to modernist expression, as found in van Ortroy's review. The continuities in attitudes toward Jews, and the imagery with which they were depicted—beginning even before the Middle Ages with the interpreted words of St. Paul and reaching to the time of Leo XIII and beyond—have made it inevitable that we return to where we began.

Yet this is only one half of the story. Holding the parts of this chronologically diffuse study together has been the theological glue that cemented fierce hostility to Jews to rigorist Catholic integralism. This bond was already there in the writings of Chrysostom, and it continues even today in openly derogatory web sites like Holywar.org, which has made charges of ritual murder part and parcel of its struggle against what it calls Catholic theological perversion.[18] It is in this light that we should examine in some detail van Ortroy's review and the sharp responses it evoked in integralist circles. Armed now with an intimate understanding of the medieval story and its legacy, we can properly appreciate the furor van Ortroy's review so defiantly raised.

Notable of itself, the review is twice notable in its *contexte événementiel*. Scandalized, Rome instantly intervened to censure (and censor) van Ortroy. The orchestrator was the integralist papal secretary of state Cardinal Merry del Val, who had also orchestrated the forces refusing to republish *Lachrymabilem* in response to a libel made in Bohemian Polna in 1899. With respect to Trent, it was asked whether van Ortroy was unaware that Sixtus IV had issued a bull approving the legality of the trial in which the Jews were condemned. This was provocative, since van Ortroy had already referred to this text in his review. It must have irked his opponents that van Ortroy had understood Pope Sixtus's intent correctly, while they were misconstruing it, as they likely knew from Sixtus's text itself.

Sixtus had issued no blank check favoring persecution. His bull admits that only those Jews who act against Christianity are to be called before the bar of justice. Following the opinion of the papal representative at Trent, Bishop de' Giudici, the bull strongly implies that this principle had been violated. Politically savvy, Sixtus IV knew that he had to concede the *prima facie* legitimacy of the 1475 trial, and this his bull does. Yet he also knew from de' Giudici that the trial had been a railroading and that, worse, it had made a farce of papal "prerogative," on which point, the bull stands its ground. So much for the position of Sixtus IV, a Franciscan, and Battista de' Giudici, a Dominican, in the matter of Trent.[19] The Dominican drive to censor rabbinic texts[20] and Franciscan rage against Jews taking interest[21] had definite limits.

Through the medium of the Jesuit van Ortroy's review, Sixtus IV's fifteenth-century demand for proper legal procedure had been made again, and, in one sense, more openly than it had been at Trent. There, the mendicant pope and bishop had to resort to carefully chosen language, faced as they were by a bevy of humanist clergy, led by the bishop of Trent, Johannes Hinderbach; intraclerical competition played a pronounced role in the events. In 1904, the protagonists on both sides were Jesuits, Bollandists in Antwerp opposing Jesuit curialists in Rome, and nobody was mincing words. In addition, aside from appealing to legal justice, van Ortroy had insisted on moral probity. First naming "rapacity" as the source of ritual murder libels, he laid the primary blame on "racial hatreds" (les haines de races). Even remembering that in 1904, the term "race" carried far fewer pejorative connotations than it does today, more often than not meaning simply "a people," this accusation should stop us "dead in our tracks."[22]

The censor was aghast. So radical did the integralists consider contemporary Bollandist expression that shortly before van Ortroy's review appeared, Merry del Val had decided to have Bollandist writings censored.[23] The censor he chose was clearly living in a world of medieval canons, which, among other things, disallow nearly all Jewish testimony against Christians. How exercised this censor must have been when he saw that van Ortroy had drawn his conclusions about

Lachrymabilem on the basis of what Innocent IV himself admitted (in the bull) was the testimony of *Jews* (the emphasis is the censor's, not mine). Besides, the censor went on—he was writing in Latin; the review appears in French: "there was no clear reason why full faith should *not* be placed in the transcript of the trial [on which Divina had relied], which had been certified. The trial's verdict [*and* the guilt of the Jews] should *not* be repudiated solely through conjecture" (my emphasis [neque ulla ratione positiva demonstratur fidem ei adiungi non posse. Ad eius auctoritatem repudianam haud sufficiunt coniecturae]). As for van Ortroy's reference to a "highly equivocal state of affairs, in which racial hatreds played a preponderant role" (situation fort équivoque, où *les haines de races* ont joué un rôle . . . prépondérant [p. 28, ll. 20ff.]), the censor responded that "the conclusion that the situation was most precarious and that the 'hate of the races' played . . . a major role . . . ought to be [read: has to be] modified [to say] . . . a difficult, two-edged affair, in which the 'hate of the races' perhaps had *great* influence" (Ipsam vero conclusionem hoc vel alio simili modo mutare oportet. . . . "situation" difficilem, ancipitem, in quam "les haines de races" forsitan *magnum* influxum habuere; censor's emphasis). This hate, the censor wrote, was on both sides, "ancipitem," meaning, there is no problem in believing that the Jews killed Simonino. Van Ortroy's "audacity" had to be crushed.

The censor lost. The printed version of van Ortroy's review in the *Analecta Bollandiana* reads: "Tout cela trahit une situation très perplexe, où les haines de race ont peut-être exercé une funeste influence" (All this reveals a very perplexing situation, in which hatreds of race perhaps had a baneful influence). Van Ortroy's concessions were at once clever, and insignificant. For the original plural, "haines de races," by which he intended abstract "racial hatreds," he substituted "haines de race," singular, and instead of the censor's proposed "*magnum*," he wrote "funeste," which is to say, "baneful," "disastrous," or even "deadly." The result, as the text now reads, is that the one race that was hated was the Jews, regardless of whether that hatred's influence was "funeste," or "magnum," or even just "peut-être" (perhaps). It was the hatred itself that was to be condemned. At Trent, it had led to judicial murder.

Once again, therefore, we see anti-modernism and modernism locked in conflict over ritual murder. Yet the terms in which this conflict was played out were the meanings of the past and their legacy. The question asked was how and why are past examples pertinent for "today." Both modernists and anti-modernists had chosen to quarrel through the medium of textual debates, point by interpretative point; establishing the true meaning of time-honored texts and commentary stood in for ideological pronouncements. What precisely had Innocent IV intended in *Lachrymabilem*, and Sixtus IV in his *Facit nos pietas* of 1478?[24] For the debaters, these meanings were as valid in 1904 as they had been hundreds of years before. Anxieties, too, were the same: where was justice, how was it best to be preserved, and how was the Church to be protected? To these questions, each side provided radically opposing answers. The answers themselves, however, never changed.

The Legacy and Fruits of Scholarly Rigor

There was one signal difference. In pursuing the truth about sainthood, the proponents of modernism tread where their scholarly predecessors had not. Their insistence on scholarly reasoning and critical analysis brought them to cross what others considered dangerous lines, and this was so whether they pursued their investigations in Belgium, Germany, France, or, apparently, England as well.[25] Dedication to scholarly truth led to intellectual openness, as the reader may already have imagined. Discovering this openness gave me special pleasure. Delehaye, for one, entered into a rigorous and mutually respectful dialogue with the Jewish savant Solomon Reinach; and for doing so, Merry del Val criticized him severely. Christian savants in the past had studied with Jews to learn their texts and especially Hebrew, and the early Bollandists report consulting rabbis in Amsterdam about the date of Passover. Delehaye saw Reinach as a partner in learning.[26]

Delehaye had to face even sharper opposition from Emmanuel Barbier, an arch-defender of integralism and author of many essays in the integralist *La Critique du libéralisme*. For Barbier, Reinach was *unfit* to spar with. In an essay of July 15, 1912, Barbier referred to Reinach as "peu recommandable" and "de mauvais renom," ready to impugn Catholicism at every chance. Reinach, for his part, had spoken of Delehaye as a person of "un courage scientifique." Delehaye returned the compliment. Reinach, Delehaye wrote, was the consummate scholar, a person of "loyauté" (honesty) with respect to scholarly truth. Delehaye's admiration for Reinach was also personal, even to the point of playful exaggeration. Should Reinach, said Delehaye, find (in his reading of essays in the *Analecta Bollandiana*) even a kernel of truth to support the legend of the Neapolitan St. Januarius (S. Gennaro)—whose sainthood disturbed Delehaye no end, and, even more, the belief in the annual liquification of the saint's blood—then Rheinach would willingly "'give up the opportunity of being disagreeable to Catholics'" (perdrait ... l'occasion d'être désagréable aux catholiques) and, by implication, proclaim St. Januarius a true saint. [27] Delehaye was being especially sardonic. Rome had laid it on him hot and heavy for tearing down St. Janarius's image. By contrast, Reinach loved polemic and debate. But defining the limits, as Delehaye so clearly intimated, was scholarship, not the kind of passion that motivated people like Barbier. Delehaye had referred to Reinach to make precisely this point.

Delehaye never mentions that Reinach was a Jew, which would have had no place in their ongoing scholarly exchange. Volume 10, page 59 of the *Analecta Bollandiana* (1891) first reports a finding of Reinach, whose scholarship about early Christianity the *Analecta* considered perfectly correct to publish. Nor was Reinach alone in being so respected. On the same page, the *Analecta* also published the précis of a rebuttal offered by Mgr. Louis Duschesne, the head of the École française de Rome, to an address Joseph Halévy had first delivered before the French Academy and then published in the *Revue des études juives*.[28] The rebuttal's subject was the early sixth-century massacre of Arian Christians in Nedjram, in Yemenite Himyar. It was Jews, wrote Duschesne, not Gentile Judaizers, as Halévy had argued, who led the attack; Halévy had gone too far, overemending the text in order to remove the blame from the Jewish king of Himyar, Dhu Nuwas.[29] Duschesne's tone was scholarly, as were the terms of the debate. Partisan theological issues were nowhere in sight.

Nor could they have been. The full text of Duchesne's rebuttal, as even the *Analecta* signals, was published in volume 20 of the *Revue des études juives* (1890).[30] Its contents were the edited transcript of an oral presentation Duschesne had delivered before the French Société des études juives. Duschesne had spoken following "a warm invitation from his honored colleague M. Joseph Derenbourg" (à l'aimable invitation de mon vénérable confrère M. J. Derenbourg). This society and its publication, the *Revue des études juives,* were (and in many ways still are) the principal seat of French Jewish scholarship. Ten years earlier, in 1881, Duschesne's own warmth had been anticipated by the noted Isidore Loeb. Emphasizing the openness of the dialogue, Loeb had no hesitation to summarize an essay by Duschesne that had first appeared in the *Revue des questions historiques*. The topic was the date of Easter as it was debated at the Council of Nicaea in 325. This essay, Loeb said, "should be summarized for our readers" (mérite d'être résumé pour les lecteurs de notre recueil). And to his summary, Loeb added his own comments stressing the importance of Duschesne's views: they were essential for understanding the course of early Christian Jewish relations, especially in the city of Antioch.[31]

As for Halévy, he responded suggesting that Duschesne had too readily taken the word of two known "fanatic Monophysite rhetors, distinguished for speaking badly of Jews."[32] Other, more reliable texts, in Halévy's opinion, did not support the case. Here again, the tone was scholarly. One suspects Duschesne was avid to support the texts found in the Bollandist *Acta Sanctorum* on the subject (*ActaSS*, 24 October [10]: 721–59), but he certainly was not saying that Jews made a habit of massacring Christians. Had Duchesne ever been suspect of harboring beliefs like that, Loeb's summary of Duschesne's essay would never have been written.

The dialogue between Christian and Jewish scholars was ongoing, and it transcended confessional allegiance. In this spirit, Delehaye recounts a tale of a student Reinach had sent him for advice.[33] At Rome, such a dialogue would have been impossible. Was not Giovanni Oreglia just then warning of the corruption produced by Jews and Christians studying in the same school, pressed into familiarity and dangerous proximity, occupying the same school bench? In fact, was not publishing in the *Revue des études juives* of itself effectively to Judaize, keeping company with the likes of those whom Barbier called "peu recommandable" and "de mauvais renom?" In Barbier's terms, the censure was proper.

Proximity to Jews, even intellectual proximity, reading and reflecting on their scholarly works, had caused Jesuit priests (the modern Bollandists) to say what for anti-modernists was the unacceptable. Dismissing the ritual murder charge raised in 1921 by one Vincenzo Legè with respect to the death of the young Giovannino Costa in 1468, François Halkin wrote in 1925 of the inanity of the accusation (l'inanité de cette accusation). Halkin emphasized his meaning by referring to Delehaye, who, barely a year earlier, had spoken of "this murderous and absurd calumny" (cette calomnie absurde et meurtrière) in his review in the *Analecta* (where Halkin was writing, too) of Solomon Reinach's 1923 *Cultes, mythes, et religions*.[34] No wonder people like Barbier believed the Jewish danger was ubiquitous.

Yet such criticism did not deflect these modern Bollandists. They continued to hold fast to their ideal goal of critical scholarship, the Bollandist touchstone in all periods. At one point, Delehaye's scholarly bent seems to have brought him even to ignore the doctrine of supersession. Was he aware of this; it would be so important could we know? At the start of his *Les Origines du culte des martyrs* (referring wholly to martyrs, not to Jews), Delehaye praised the Maccabean martyrs, calling them "glorious models [for] those who embraced the new faith in abandoning Judaism [and suffered martyrdom]" (si glorieux modèles [pour] ceux qui embrassaient la nouvelle foi en abandonnant le judaisme). The praise of the Maccabees is not the point; in the event, the Maccabees are Saints of the Church, the only figures from the Hebrew Bible so exalted. The point is the wonderfully neutral idea of "those who embraced the new faith in abandoning Judaism." They *abandoned* Judaism; they did not "see the truth." Supersessionist hierarchies seem left behind. Is Delehaye proposing that there are non-hierarchical alternatives in religion? One chose Judaism or Christianity following the dictates of conscience? Perhaps. It is unimaginable to picture Delehaye not supporting the idea of freedom of conscience, precisely as Döllinger had before him. This was the very freedom of conscience that Gregory XVI and Pius IX had so shortly before denounced as a "delirium."[35]

Delehaye and his companions also questioned some of Catholicism's most enduring myths. They queried the authenticity of the Shroud of Turin, the sheet said to bear the impression of Christ's body, and they doubted the story of the House of Loretto, called the house of the Virgin, transported miraculously from Nazareth to Loretto. They cast doubt, too, on other objects of staple belief, such as St. Januarius, as we saw, and St. Expeditus. No wonder that Bollandist inquiries aroused enormous ire among Rome's highest echelons and led to the kind of "extraordinary censorship" that was applied to van Ortroy's review.

The censor, an outsider, not a member of the Jesuit Order, and whose identity was known only to the Spanish Jesuit Father General Luis Martín, was instructed to use a heavy hand, which, indeed, he did.[36] His arrogance only reinforced Bollandist resolve, as well as that of like-minded others. It was to be expected that Bollandists would continue, as they did, to denounce accusations of ritual murder. Confident in their faith and its compatibility with modern thinking, they needed neither myth nor false martyrs to overcome anxiety. In the framework of their authorial present, it was devotion to *true* saints and *untainted* belief that perpetuated Catholic salvation. Transparent martyrdom demonstrated Catholic virtue. "Calumny" and "inanity" did the reverse. Nor did Catholicism need to turn inward. Fear of competition and contemporary challenge could be left to the integralists.

Yet, just as the twentieth-century Bollandists were insisting that Catholicism could hold its own in the arena of modern scholarly tools and methods, the Bollandists of the seventeenth century had said the same. These compilers of the *Acta Sanctorum* had set out to combat their opponents by adopting the standards of critical scholarship espoused by the most advanced exponents of textual study in their day, especially in France and the Low Countries, not all of whose Catholic orthodoxy was above suspicion, and not all of whom were Catholics. The early Bollandists, to apply to them Anthony Grafton's expression, were "defenders of the text." They were also advocates of the *mos gallicus*, the attempt to understand legal texts in their original as opposed to contemporary meaning, which Donald Kelley has called the initiation of modern historical study.[37] If only by implication, the early Bollandists were arguing that even the most erudite challengers could not topple Catholicism's *scholarly* claim to truth.

Delehaye perceived his forebears and their achievement in just these terms.[38] They were analytical scholars, whose ways were synchronic with his own. However, the faithfulness to scholarly rigor of both Bollandist generations—as each understood this concept—led in opposite directions. As we said above, the Bollandist heritage was dual. The first Bollandists used critical skills "to prove" the myth of ritual murder, later ones to lay its fallacies bare. Alas, there are some who still prefer the earlier reading. To understand this tenacity, we must proceed one step further down.

Six   Purity and Its Discontents

Paul's fear of compromising the body of Christ (1 Cor. 10:1–20), I have argued, is rooted in the admonitions of Ezekiel (44:7), who was agitated lest impure adepts defile the Temple altar and who insisted that only the pure might partake of the *bread* of God that was the fat and the blood. These preoccupations correspond to the Hittite rule of the second millennium B.C.E. prohibiting dogs and pigs from entering and polluting temples, and they may somehow derive from it. Evolved into Christian discourse, this prohibition took on the specific guise of distancing the filthy, promiscuous "Jewish dog" or the clerical *lapsus* from the (sacrificial) Eucharistic "bread." The touch of either—that is, real bodily touch—contaminated. Jews, for their part, were told to steer clear of excessive contact with Christians.

This brings us back to what was intimated in the Preface and Introduction: that despite teachings to the contrary, which go back to the time of Christian origins, the competition between Jews and Christians is not, nor has it ever truly been, one between exponents of Paul's "spiritual" Christianity confronting a "carnal Israel." Rather, it has been a competition between two mutually exclusive systems, both devoted to *bodily* purity and pollution's avoidance. It was not that Jews were feared only to pollute Christian spirituality as they attempted to devour the "bread" of the *Corpus Christi*. They were feared also, if not more so, to pollute that *corpus* in its literally physical embodiment. It is for this reason that maintaining purity required shunning "excessive" physical proximity, especially that created by improperly sharing (highly symbolic) food or fluids or through wrongful physical contact. Those who became impure were to be segregated to preclude impurity's transmission. Pollution itself was sometimes perceived literally, as infection or contagion.[1]

At stake for Christians was the purity of the "body" in its multiple and intertwined definitions, especially those propounded by Christian theology. Realizing the existence of this continuous fear of bodily pollution goes a long way, I believe, toward explaining how in all periods, including the modern one, disdain for Jewish belief has so consistently gone hand in hand with a disdain that is political, social, and racial. Disdain for the physical Jew, alongside that for the "Jew of Judaism," began in Christianity's earliest times. Hate-filled web sites reveal that it still continues today. To sharpen this point, let me briefly recapitulate, but taking the opportunity to recast the argument. The emphasis now falls on how Christians, and Jews, too, not only feared pollution—this we have seen—but on how they cast their fears in bodily terms, and why.

The fear of impure contact is extensive in the Hebrew Bible and even more so in rabbinic literature. Most particular is the need to avoid the menstruating woman. Contact with her blood (and by extension any physical contact) confers (temporary) ritual impurity, with the impure disqualified from participating in sacrifice at the altar. A bath of purification—the *mikveh*—is then obligatory. No less important is avoiding contact with the dead, which creates the pollution that so troubled Hosea, among others. The table, too, Judaism admonishes, may defile and itself be defiled, which is tantamount to polluting the altar; for the rabbis, the table and altar are interchangeable.[2] Christian discussions treat impurity through touch in much the same way. Did not Cyprian stress that the impurity of *lapsi* was transmittable to the altar itself, if not the Eucharist? He was taken with Haggai's caution that the polluted transfer their defilement to all they touch: "sacrificial flesh . . . bread, stew, wine, oil" (2:12).

Agobard applied Haggai's cautions to contacts with Jews. It seems clear that fears of pollution underlie the canons prohibiting "anybody defiled by a banquet of Jews [from] eat[ing] bread with any cleric of ours."[3] The polluted priest would transfer his imperfection to the eucharistic communicants, just as would the *lapsus*.[4] In either case, Christian contact with Jewish food, not unlike Jewish contact with a menstruating woman, impaired the perfection of the priestly sacrifice, whether in the Jerusalem Temple or on the eucharistic altar. Pollution through sexual touch was feared no less,[5] and it was commonly prohibited.[6] Sicard of Cremona thus forbade a Jewish husband converted to Christianity to have marital relations with his still unconverted wife, however firm were her intentions to follow her husband's religious choice. She remained physically impure until baptized. Sexual relations with her corrupted her husband ritually.

Sicard may have also been taken with issues of menstrual blood; in Christianity, as in Judaism, menstruation was grounds to prohibit sexual intercourse.[7] Whether some believed impurity might pass to the actual sacrament is moot. Theoretically impossible, for how could God be corruptible or corrupted, and theologically denied, Guibert of Nogent's tale of the monk who—at Jewish magical urging—spilled his seed on a Host makes one wonder what people really thought. Joseph Lambert's eighteenth-century fears of eucharistic "magicians" who physically assault the host should make us wonder again.[8] Guibert also seems to be crediting Jewish magic with the power to subvert the virtue of sexual continence the Eucharist is said to bestow.[9]

Jews, in turn, conferred a magical and idolatrous cast on the Eucharist, especially the eucharistic "blood," which was to be meticulously avoided. Innocent III and the dominant thirteenth-century canonist Hostiensis were no doubt justified in censuring Jewish mothers whom they charged with making (actually illegal) Christian wet nurses "pour their milk into the latrine" for three days after they had received communion.[10] Medieval people thought mother's milk was a by-product of the nurse's own blood. Jews must have been convinced that were their children to drink this milk following communion, they would become eucharistically tainted and idolatrously infested.[11] No Jewish mother or father would take this chance.

This Jewish example also shows how contrasting definitions of bodily pollution were more than mechanisms of protection. They were ways to define the self, at least to define what the self was *not*.[12] Christians, in particular, indulged in this kind of self-definition. The teachings on (physical) purity of Cyprian, Chrysostom, Agobard, Johannes

Theutonicus, and Sicard are unambiguous. The true and qualified Christian is one who, in his or her bodily purity, neither corrupts the altar nor allows it to be corrupted. Cyprian may even have called for the polluted to be rebaptized.[13]

The issue was not sin. To atone, as Burchard said in his *Corrector*, speaking of those who dined with Jews, *penance* more than confession and priestly absolution, was required. Similarly, Rabanus Maurus declared that the impurity acquired through dining with Jews required the Christian *emundari*, to be (physically) cleansed.[14] Ironically, therefore, in striving to shun what it called corrupting and polluting Judaizing, Christianity itself was "Judaizing," imitating Jewish ideals of bodily purity and their maintenance. Moreover, because purity was so central, especially to the Pauline vision of Christian-eucharistic unity, what Catholic Christianity was Judaizing was its entire self. Catholicism's inheritance from Judaism of the very ancient pursuit of bodily purity could not be shaken off.[15]

Catholic Christianity, therefore—certainly medieval Catholicism, but also the Catholicism of the twentieth-century circles of *La civiltà cattolica*—did not reject a carnal Judaism in favor of a spiritualized faith so to become Paul's asserted new and spiritualized *Verus Israel*. Rather, Catholicism rejected one system of contact-impurity, one system of "carnality," and, in its place, substituted another. It was, I believe, precisely to this exchange of "carnalities" that Martin Luther was alluding when, commenting on Galatians 4:30, he said that the Pope is Esau, the child of Hagar, the bondwoman under law and works. Not the Jew, as Paul had made of him, Esau for Luther was the Catholic. This explains why Luther questioned, in *That Jesus Christ Was Born a Jew*, why Jews should have converted when they heard Catholic teaching.[16] Though verbalizing the implications was likely beyond his ken, Luther had sensed that Catholicism and Judaism were "two peas in a pod." In the mold of Esau, as he saw it, both were "slaves" of ritual bodily purity, far from the carnal-spiritual antinomy Paul had envisioned. The responsum of the fifteenth-century legist Angelo di Castro on buying Jewish meat, discussed below, draws exactly this same conclusion.

There was also the matter of Catholic holy space. Exactly as the precincts of the Jews' Jerusalem Temple were to remain inviolate, so

Catholic holy space had to be defended from physical incursion; this included the sites of epiphanies or significant events, areas and borders marked through processional rogations, and other places that had been declared holy.[17] That incursion might originate in sensory disturbance: of touch, smell, sight, and hearing. Synagogues had to be removed from proximity to churches, and the "barking" of Rome's Jews that so immensely disturbed Pius IX had likewise to be silenced. Or so Pius IX wished. Here the olfactory sense of ordure, the Jew's imputed "stench," like that of an unwashed dog, no doubt came into imagination's play. Pius must have believed that Rome should be populated only by members of "the [Christian] holy seed," living on what Ezekiel (20:40) called the "holy mountain."[18] This is precisely what the biblical books of Ezra, Nehemiah, and Chronicles prescribe for Jerusalem. It was Rome's physical purity that Pius was defending, perhaps even its genealogical purity, the kind that prevented descendants of Jews from occupying high places in the Jesuit order, or the doubt so often expressed about converts in general.[19]

With regard to Jews, such thinking was fraught with special danger. In the Middle Ages, it promoted segregation and possibly massacres as well. In modern times, the problem deepened. Medieval concepts of protection from sensory and contact pollution were combining with contemporary ideas of political and racial purity. The result was Giovanni Oreglia's fear of "dangerous proximity." A menacing kinship was slowly being forged between Catholic teachings and ideas like those underpinning *la difesa della razza*, "racial defense," the term used in propagating Mussolini's 1938 racial laws.[20]

As the Jews Saw It

At least one medieval Jew, the late thirteenth- or early fourteenth-century author of the *Nizzahon Yashan*, understood medieval Catholicism's preoccupation with physical purity, and with that of its holy places in particular. He also knew that to support teachings about the transfer of impurities, churchmen, perhaps beginning with Cyprian, had made frequent reference to the words of Hosea (9:4) and Numbers

(19:13) prohibiting impure contact with the dead. How, then, the puzzled author of the *Nizzahon* queried, "could it be that Christians knew and cared that a dead man is impure and defiles all who carry or touch the body and everything 'in the tent where it is found' (Num. 19:13),[21] yet priests constantly defile themselves by bringing [dead bodies] into their houses of idolatry [the churches], which makes of Christians . . . corrupt in all your words and deeds, and your affairs vain and exceedingly evil?" The author of the *Nizzahon* must have known that his readers would easily grasp the mockery, which was especially biting, since for Jews, avoiding contact with the dead was fundamental. Moreover, he was far from being alone in spotting contradictions between proclaimed and actual Christian behavior.

Jewish writings reveal an exquisite awareness of how fixated Christian ritual was on the purity of objects—objects that Jews viewed as polluting. Eucharistic rites, said Rabbi Yosef Official, were pernicious.[22] With their impure rituals, Christians have become impure. By partaking of the (idolatrous) table of Christ, Official said, they have truck with idolatry itself. The (eucharistic) sacrifice pollutes communicants like the "bread of mourning" (once again citing Hosea 9:4). This is an exact, and surely intentional, inversion of Christian teachings about sharing the table of the Jews. It was not, as Christians said, the Jewish altar, or ritual, that might be likened to the polluting touch of the dead, but the altar and ritual of Christians. Citing Hosea verbatim, Yosef Official, like the author of the *Nizzahon*, must have known that his was a response to the Christian understanding of this passage; Official was particularly well versed in Christian teachings.

Figuratively speaking, Official's interpretation also answers the satiric query of the (slightly later) *Nizzahon Yashan*. The reason the dead do not pollute the Church, the *toʿevah* (the abomination), as church buildings are so often called, is because of the polluted rituals that take place in them. The buildings themselves are polluted, from the start, idolatrous in nature, and they perpetually pollute all who enter, whether dead or alive. They cannot be contaminated any more than they already are. In the same spirit, the mid eleventh-century Italian Scroll of Ahimaaz refers to the Church of Hagia Sofia in Constantinople as *binyan ha-tumʾah* (the house of impurity).[23]

Beyond the polemical scorn, Christian practice itself might encourage Jews to picture Christian ritual as neither spiritual nor transcendental. The physical eucharistic wafer is carefully guarded and prepared of the wheat to which Christ had compared himself.[24] This is much as the purity of the wheat from which the Passover matzoh is baked is rigorously controlled and the baking perfectly supervised, lest the matzoh be rendered unfit by *leavening*. These two breads, therefore, both ritually prepared, are nevertheless *real*. The wafer and the matzoh, so alike in appearance and so often contrasted, became figuratively the standards of two opposing camps.

By the same token, the specific prohibition on Christians eating Jewish matzoh, viewed as a countersacrifice, must have brought some Jews to ask, as some Christians did, too, how the essence (in the Eucharist) could become accident and the accident substance. In simple terms, how could bread and wine become God, as though the bread and wine had physically ceased to exist?[25] For Jews, the idea was preposterous. The irony is that the episodes of Host desecration foisted onto Jews in order to prove the Eucharist's efficacy attributed them with subscribing to a belief they totally rejected. Perhaps in response, Jews, like the *Nizzahon Yashan* and Yosef Official, made this belief into the butt of ironic satire. At their most generous, Jews in the Middle Ages might credit Christianity with being a mundane sacrificial system that did its best to make life miserable for Jews. They unquestionably resented its attempt—through supersession and doctrines of ritual bodily purity—to compete with Judaism on Judaism's own terms.

These were two systems of contact purity battling it out with each other, yet hardly as equals. As the author of *Nizzahon Yashan* once more demonstrates, it was really competing claims to the ritual purity of the physical this-worldly altar, not its (possibly) transcendental counterpart, that were at stake. Christians must have been specially bothered by Jewish remarks that brought the Eucharist "down to earth" and stripped the sacrament of all spiritual content—and legitimacy: "They abuse us," the *Nizzahon* says, "by saying that they do not have sacrifices and burnt offerings of the kind that once existed among Jews [saying their sacrifice, as all their faith, is spiritual]. But they do have sacrifices and burnt offerings in that *they sacrifice the flesh of the hanged one and eat it*. Respond [too] by pointing out that sacrifices and burnt offerings should not be brought here [in France] but only in Jerusalem. So it is written in Deuteronomy (12:1–14)."[26] In Deuteronomic terms, this is to say that what Christians do is (virtually, if not actually) idolatrous, the term "Deuteronomy" applies to any sacrifice performed outside the *Jerusalem* Temple.

It was strictly flesh, real flesh, moreover, that Christians consumed at their altars. The sacrifice Christians performed was human, cannibalistic, and pagan. It was also to the Molekh (again in the context of Deuteronomy), the most rapacious of the Bible's despised pagan deities, who also demanded *human* sacrifice. Did not Christians, according to their own interpretation of the Eucharist, consume the blood, whose consumption Deuteronomy 12:16 strictly forbids? All Jews heard this verse read annually in the synagogue, and none would have missed the *Nizzahon*'s implied allusion to the continuation of the previous verses 12:1–14. Deuteronomy 12:16 is also the verse Frederick II and Innocent IV cited to say Jews did not use Christian blood. This the *Nizzahon* likely would have known; Jews themselves had petitioned both pope and emperor to issue protective texts.[27] Was the *Nizzahon* then accusing Christians of foisting their own blood-guilt onto Jews through propagating the blood libel? We are left to wonder.

As though to complete the *Nizzahon Yashan*'s claim that the true eucharistic essence was carnal, although changing the tone notably, Yosef Official chided: "Do you not know that all that man puts in his mouth enters the stomach, and from there it descends [to the drain]; so what you eat on Easter goes down to the drain?"[28] But Official did not invent this response out of whole cloth. The first half (up to my semicolon) is an enormously clever citation of Matthew 15:17, verbatim, which is the prelude, although it is not directly connected, to the story, in Matthew 15:26, of the Canaanite woman, the children, their food, and the dogs. The food your children get, Official is tacitly asking, their "bread," is it God? No, it is ordure.[29] Regrettably (for us), Official does not comment on the so-called "bread" section of Matthew 15 itself, verses 2–29. Perhaps he realized he had said more than enough, that the conclusion I have just drawn, other readers in his day might draw too, including Christians. It was already scandalous enough, perhaps too dangerous to say out loud.

The *Nizzahon Yashan* does refer to Matthew's story of the Canaanite woman, and with some aplomb. His approach, as it was with his reference to proper Jerusalemite sacrifice, rests on a penchant for *peshat*, the simple meaning of the text, which destroys all transferred or allegorical meaning. For Christian exegetes, allegory was indispensable. The *Nizzahon* simply retells Matthew's story, adding but a single comment: "It is not right, he says, "to steal the kindness which I have come to perform for the Jews *and give it to other nations*. He means to the Canaanite, whom Matthew calls a dog." It is as though the *Nizzahon* is sustaining Christ, saying that Christ, the speaker in the story, was correct. It was, and still is "this Canaanite who is called a dog"; nobody else, no allegories allowed. Had the author of the *Nizzahon* been able to read the Greek-speaking Chrysostom, who said: "We, who *were* dogs, received the strength, [while] the [Jews] fell to kinship with dogs," he would have replied, "You have *received* nothing." The Jews remain God's elect.

That by "Canaanites" the *Nizzahon* understands Christians we learn a bit further on, when, for once, the *Nizzahon* indulges in a bit of midrash; he himself may have considered it *peshat*. "They [the Christians]," he says, "*bark* their assertion that it is improper for the uncircumcised and impure to serve Jews. Tell them: On the contrary. . . . that the Torah [commands us to give the meat we will not eat to the 'stranger in the gates' (always a positive image, especially in the prophetical books, referring to one who deserves compassion), and that we] sell such meat to Gentiles, *because they will serve us*, and God does not withhold the reward of any creature."[30]

Read all together, the *Nizzahon Yashan* has flipped on its head the entire Christian theological structure. He has upended the Christian view of supersessionism, resolved the question of divine choice, and clarified who is the elder serving the younger (Gen. 25:23 and Rom. 9:12, a verse he also cites here). The Christians, the Canaanites, are still the dogs. The generosity of the "true children," the Jews, also requires mention, for the Jews feed the Christian "dogs." In turn, and as is proper with dogs, the Christians should faithfully serve their (Jewish) masters. Perhaps it was in this same vein that the thirteenth-century Moshe of Coucy noted that "we are obligated to feed dogs and Christians [but not pigs, which we may not raise]; the obligation is out of propriety [literally, the 'ways of peace'], which demands that we care for the poor goy as we care for the poor of Israel."[31]

By implication, moreover, the eucharistic sacrifice is bread that fails to nourish. It leaves even the dogs hungry, whining for the "true meat" (graciously given them by the Jewish "children"). Disparagingly, but revealing a complete understanding that only enhances the dig, Yosef Official calls the Eucharist the "redemption of the Christian soul."[32] This was much—and I suspect he knew it—as the twelfth-century Rupert of Deutz called the Eucharist the single road to salvation. Except that for Official, Rupert's "redemption" was damnation. For Official, as for the *Nizzahon Yahan*, the Eucharist redeems nothing at all.

Inversions like this one are again the key to interpreting *Midrash Tannaim to Deuteronomy* 12:31, which Official and the *Nizzahon Yashan* indubitably knew well. The midrash queries what the word *beneihem* (their offspring) means in the context of a verse warning against human sacrifice.[33] This midrash dates from a time (about the mid third century at the earliest) when eucharistic ideas were being refined. "Their offspring," says the midrash, means sons, daughters, fathers, and mothers. And it continues: Did not "Rabbi Akiva[second century] say: 'I saw a goy who tied up his father and stuck him before his [the goy's] dog, and the dog ate him.'" It is hard to escape wondering whether it is not Matthew 15:26 that this midrash reflects. Jews, we have seen in the *Nizzahon Yashan*, were aware of the eucharistic meaning imputed to Matthew; and the context of both Deuteronomy 12:31 and *Midrash Tannaim* is human sacrifice. The father (in the midrash) thus is God (incarnate), the goy and the dog rapacious Christians, who devour the Father (the bread, the Christian God, the *corpus verum*). In addition to presuming to claim God from the Jews, therefore, the Christians have also anthropomorphized and cannibalized Him. The Eucharist is idolatry at its worst.

However speculative, perhaps far-fetched, something in this reading rings true. Jews saw Christianity and Christians—the goyim—as earthly, if not brutal, their nature worldly and spiritually wanting, and their ritual akin to the worst kind of paganism. Jewish commentaries, including the commentary of the all-important eleventh-century Rashi on Deuteronomy 18:9, which also forbids sacrificing children to pagan gods, say that the human sacrifice this verse forbids is the way of the *nokhrim*, the Christians. To which, Rashi adds: "learn not to do" these things. For Rashi, Christians sacrifice and eat their (idolatrous) God. This no Jew should ever think of doing.

Rashi also represented the norm, and Jews took him at his word. To avoid anything even remotely linked to the Eucharist, Jews (most Jews, anyway) put special emphasis on the age-old halachic precept to avoid wine simply touched by non-Jews. And, as we have seen, Jewish mothers made Christian wet nurses pour their milk into the latrine for three days following the Eucharist's reception. Though a chimera in their eyes, nonetheless, Jews ascribed a magical aura to the Eucharist. Certainly it smacked (literally, had the "dust") of idolatry, against which rabbinical literature constantly rails. One kept the Eucharist as distant as possible. Even commerce with Christians was permitted with the proviso that nothing be bought or sold that might be used in the "idolatrous sacrifice."[34] All unnecessary contact with the goy was to be avoided—at least in principle.

Between the goy and the dog, moreover, there was little, if any, distinction. Eleazar the Rokeah, an important figure in early thirteenth-century German Jewish Pietism is explicit. A "boy," he said, "should be covered so that he will not see a goy or a dog on the day he is consecrated, *mehankhim 'ot 'o*, to the study of the holy letters."[35] Describing this same consecration ceremony, a slightly later, anonymous German text phrased it in reverse: The child is to be covered and brought home following the ceremony, so that it should not "be seen by a 'dog, pig, ass, or goy.'"[36] Just as the Eucharist seen by a Jew might somehow be slighted, or worse,[37] being seen by the goy = dog would do the same for the consecrated Jewish child. And such concerns endured beyond the Middle Ages. The mystical *Shnei Luhot ha-brit* of Isaiah Hurvitz, from the early seventeenth century, warned not to frighten a child by invoking the impure, namely, by threatening that "a cat, or a dog, or a goy might come to take the child away."[38]

The metaphor of the "Christian dog" could be particularly unkind. Shades of Sicard of Cremona's prohibition of sexual relations between a baptized husband and his not yet baptized Jewish wife, Eleazar the Rokeah writes that a post-menstruant Jewish woman who has purified herself in the ritual bath must avoid contact with a dog. By implication, the ritual impurity from which the bath had just cleansed her would be renewed. "Should she have relations with her husband [without repurifying herself], her children would be ugly, and their faces would resemble those of a dog." The Rokeah was citing an ancient text.[39] But considering his remark about protecting the child in the consecration ceremony, when this time, too, the Rokeah wrote dog, he surely heard "goy." This was one system of physical purity avoiding pollution by the other.

Purity and Society

Jews thus accused Christianity of the same kind of impurity that Christians said typified the Jews, and there was more truth here than Christianity would wish to admit. The writings of Mary Douglas make this clear. Her analyses of the relationship between body and society provide the tools to contextualize culturally Christianity's fears of bodily pollution, fears that should *not* have been present in a noumenal system that proclaims the defeat of carnality and the triumph of spirit.

We are not reading Douglas into Paul. Rather, what we read in Douglas, whose education at London's Sacred Heart Convent informs her every word,[40] is Paul transposed and anthropologized. Pauline thinking is basic to Douglas's social anthropology. By contrasting Douglas and Paul, it becomes clear that Paul's pursuit of spirituality ended in carnality's embrace, even for Paul himself.[41]

"The social body," Douglas writes, "constrains the way the physical body is perceived." But this constraint is reciprocal. People conceive a (correct, or necessary) "correlation between social and bodily forms." Paul would have agreed. Should the physical body be blemished by circumcision, Paul wrote, the (Christian) social body loses spiritual perfection. Its purity and wholeness are compromised. The problem, he said, is that "flesh lusts against the spirit, the spirit against the flesh [in crimes of lust, murder, impurity, and filthiness]" (Gal. 5: 1–24). More simply: "a little leaven spoils the whole lump [of dough]." People, therefore—returning to Douglas—create structures of constraint, an idea that Paul, again, puts succinctly: "touch nothing unclean" (2 Cor. 6:17).

Paul explained himself more fully in 1 Corinthians. "Your body," he wrote, "is a shrine of the indwelling Holy Spirit . . . the fornicator [with the literal or figurative harlot] sins against his whole [in Paul's terms, his individual and collectively eucharistic] body" (1 Cor. 6:19) "Anyone who eats the bread or drinks the cup of the Lord unworthily will [therefore] be guilty of desecrating the body and blood of the Lord [which, for Paul, is equivalent to the body and blood of the collective Christian fellowship]" (1 Cor. 11: 27) Paul makes the relationship between individual body and that of the collective explicit: "there is one loaf, [and] we, many as we are, are one body . . . the body of Christ [in which] we share" (1 Cor. 10:17). The bodily transgression of one leads to the bodily imperfection of all. The danger of the "little leaven" is everywhere.

Though some of the wording has been reversed to suit the grammatical structure, this is all Paul. It is the same epistle, all eucharistic, and all resting on the purity of the unified one that is at once spiritual *and* physical. Paul may have tried to flee the latter, but his doctrine of union in 1 Corinthians 10:1–17 doomed to failure from the start his attempt to transcend the physical through faith. His struggle to escape the commandments, which he said dealt (spiritual) death, since they were impossible to fulfill in their wholeness, could not succeed. The melding of spiritual and physical in the verses just cited is as inescapable as it is reciprocal.[42]

Had he been asked, Cyprian might have reluctantly agreed. To support the rubric: "That the Eucharist is to be received with fear and honor," in his *Three Books of Testimonies Against the Jews*, Cyprian cites 1 Corinthians 11:27. The subject is unworthily receiving the Eucharist, which Cyprian parsed as identical with the warning in Leviticus 7:20: "Whatever soul shall eat of the flesh of the sacrifice of salvation, which is the Lord's, and his uncleanness is still upon him, that soul shall perish from his people."[43] This is the same verse Cyprian used in writing of "lapsed" priests, and it was there that he cited Hosea 9:4, "Such sacrifices shall be like the bread of mourning; all who eat of it shall be defiled."[44] What Cyprian has preached, therefore, as we have already once observed, is a Levitical doctrine of personal defilement. It is a doctrine of physical purity and impurity, however spiritual this doctrine's pretended ends were—and however uniquely spiritually some might still attempt to interpret it.

This Levitical doctrine, as expanded in Ezekiel and Hosea, had subtly entered into the teachings of the Church. It was absorbed first by Paul, whose ideas percolated down into those of Cyprian, then Chrysostom, and then Agobard. By the early sixteenth century, the English John Colet, commenting on 1 Corinthians 6, phrased it without reserve:

> Beware of misusing your own body, which is no longer your own, but a member of Christ. For in dishonoring your own body, you violate the body of Christ and the Temple of the Holy Spirit; you sacrilegiously take what is for holiness and belongs to Christ to give it to a harlot for shameful dishonoring, besmirching and debasing your own body—indeed Christ's body in yours—since in that union it is made all one and a harlot with the body of the harlot, as that ancient testimony teaches: "They shall be two in one flesh" [Matt. 19:5].[45]

Violate your *fleshly* body, Colet is saying, and you have violated the (collective) body of Christ. Others expressed the same anxiety by transferring the harlot's attributes to the Jew. Contact with Jews, like that with the harlot, "besmirched and debased." This was the fear of Giovanni Oreglia and also Pius IX. Yet perhaps nobody put it more clearly than did the author of the *Schwabenspiegel* of 1275, in his statement that: "If a Christian lies with a Jewess, or a Jew with a Christian woman, they are both guilty of superharlotry [*überhure*]," and they must be burned, "for the Christian has denied the Christian faith [by joining his limbs to harlotry and so alienating himself from Christ's body]."[46] In Levitical terms, or those of Numbers, the bodily Jewish source of physical impurity was to be "cut off." As Mary Douglas would put it: "the *social* [my emphasis] experience of disorder [whether real or the product of ungrounded anxiety alone] is expressed [and acted out] by powerfully efficacious symbols of purity and danger."[47]

However, in this instance, that social experience is intrinsically this-worldly. Only by projection into symbolology does it pretend to be transcendental and spiritual. By projection, too, the fear of personal failings was (and for some still is) constantly transferred onto the Jew in the hope of assuaging disillusion. The desire is to avert attention from the futile Christian attempt to flee "carnality," the same futility that Paul himself reluctantly concedes in his figure of union with the harlot.

This reconstruction can be taken a step further to enhance the earlier argument about the martyr's iconographic salvific function. Douglas reminds us (in this same discussion) of Arnold van Gennep's concept of *rites de passage*, which requires a "preliminary separation and reintegration into the community" in order to change or ascend to a higher social level.[48] With respect to relations between Christians and Jews, this does not correspond to Paul's idea of Jewish separation followed by the Jews' engrafting onto Christianity, which is what one might at first think. Rather—albeit in a somewhat unorthodox application of van Gennep—it reflects society's need to test its mettle and move forward toward fulfillment through martyrdom, the need to have martyrs created for it, or actually to create them, in order to reenact a social drama.[49]

Acts of martyrdom, as we have seen, whether in their own day or long afterward, have long served to reintegrate a purportedly threatened *Corpus Christi*. It has mattered little whether the perceived threat was to the *corpus politicum*, the *corpus mysticum*, or even the *corpus verum* of the Eucharist itself. Martyrs, like the waxen image of Toledo, stand simultaneously for the individual and the whole. Yet, as in a rite of passage, the narrative of the martyr so often begins with kidnapping or theft, hence, the rite's radical separation. The martyr moves out of the group to experience danger (in anticipation of the eventual martyr's crown), and, at length, is reintegrated through postmortem transfiguration or through miraculous escape, as in the tale of the boy of Bourges, assisted by the perennially healing and reintegrating powers of the Virgin. The reintegration goes beyond the martyr him- or herself to embrace the group as a whole.

Viewing martyrdom as a rite of passage brings into especially sharp relief the Christian martyr's eucharistic efficacy and his or her role in eucharistic renewal. This is true not only with respect to that concept's narrower (ritual) sense but in its wider social ones as well, exactly as was said of the Good Werner.[50] The pure social union of those rightfully associated with the altar is reinvigorated and the goal of eucharistic redemption advanced. Enemies who wrongfully seek access to the Eucharist or who seek to work mayhem receive their just deserts. The Christian altar, understood as the *corpus* of the Christian fellowship, remains pure; the Eucharist and its adepts are protected from contact with the "bread of mourning." To return to the start: through the body of the martyr, tried by separation, yet now restored to the group, the food, the "bread," goes to the rightful "children." The attempted theft by the socially disintegrative "dogs" is thwarted. Salvation for one, and all, is promoted.

Nonetheless—and it is here that relating martyrdom to the rite of passage adds a new dimension to our earlier perspective—no matter how much the martyr is spiritualized, it is still his or her physical body alone that is—or can be—reintegrated. The rite of passage is one undergone by living individuals. Even associated with a mythical figure of the past or present, that figure is a surrogate for the flesh-and-blood person vicariously experiencing the rite. Once again it shows that in Catholic Christianity, the confines between "things of the flesh" and "things of the spirit" may be wholly diaphanous, as in fact they often are. The two realms insistently affect each other. The drama is as carnal as it is spiritual, and sometimes even more.

Theory and Practice

To test these assertions, we need only return one last time to Philip Augustus and Rigord, and to ask why Rigord was so laudatory of Philip in 1182, yet so discouraged by the reversal of 1198. The answer emerges from juxtaposing the legislative demands of the Third and Fourth Lateran Councils, demands, which, contrary to what is normally said, were not new, but centuries old. These were: first, the prohibition of Christians, especially women, serving in Jewish homes and the construction of new synagogues (Third Lateran), and, second, the forbidding of sexuality between Jews and Christians expressed as the (indeed new) insistence on special Jewish clothing (Fourth Lateran). We should concern ourselves only with this legislation's intent to prevent illicit contacts, not with its patently faulty, if explicit, expectations about what special dress might achieve; the history of sumptuary laws is generally a history of failure. Nonetheless, despite the lack of real legislative innovation, scholars have felt that these councils mark a major change of course.[51]

In saying that there was a certain novelty in the ecumenism of the conciliar decrees, these scholars are correct; the Third and Fourth Lateran Councils were indeed ecumenical, their decisions meant to apply to the entire Church. However, prohibitions on domestics and mixed sexuality appear multiple times in Gratian's universally studied *Decretum* of the mid twelfth century, which made them ecumenical in fact decades before the Lateran councils made them ecumenical *de iure*. The intent to protect Christians from "ritual stain" was also not new. Did not the *Summa Coloniensis*, compiled in about 1169 from earlier teachings, speak explicitly of domestics becoming *maculati* through service to Jews?[52] What differed this time was the determination to give the restrictions teeth. We have seen Alexander III ready to go to the barricades to have his Third Lateran decree on domestic service enforced. And special dress was being demanded in some places within just a few years of 1215.[53] The reasoning—and here lies the true novelty—was eucharistic.

The legislation concerning Jews promulgated at both the Third and Fourth Lateran Councils reflects the critical decision, maturing at the time of the Third Lateran and put into effect at the Fourth, to obligate all Christians to partake annually of the Eucharist. In preparation for this event, both participants and celebrants had to be ritually pure. Impure contact prior to communion had to be avoided. This included wrongful contact with Jews, even eye contact. Were not Jews long prohibited from being present at eucharistic processions, where they might view the Host? And at least once—our example is from later, but no doubt there were earlier instances—Jews were forbidden to hear the divine office sung. Pius II wrote to the city of Frankfurt am

Main in 1462 complaining bitterly that Jews had long lived near the city's main church, St. Bartholomew's:

> circumcirca eius cymiterium, *unde quasi continue viderunt et videre potuerunt cerimonias religionis christianae* tam in sepulturis mortuorum et delatione sacramenti eucharistiae quam reliquiarum et aquae benedictae, *audiendo etiam divinum officium*, quod in eadem ecclesia . . . quotidie decantatur. Quo cum cedat in *vilipendium et opprobrium* ipsius religionis ac divini cultus et ad perniciosum exemplum et scandalum christifidelis populi, vos [Emperor Frederick, to whom the Jews are subject] pio zelo et cultu . . . ad tollendum huiusmodi abusum et confusionem ipsos cum eorum sinagoga ad alium locum dicti opidi secretum . . . poterunt transferre.[54]

> They live near the cemetery, where they constantly see Christian religious ceremony, the burial of the dead, and the processions of the Eucharist, relics, and holy water. They hear the divine office sung, as it is daily in that church. This is opprobrious and brings infamy to the Christian religion and the divine cult. It sets a pernicious example and is scandalous for the Christian populace. [Emperor Frederick] moved by pious zeal [should act] to remove this abuse and source of confusion, enabling the Jews to move their synagogue to an unobtrusive place in the city, hidden from view.

Sight, hearing, and, by implication, even what the Jews thought might be scandalous and injurious to the sacrament and its recipients.

It was against this backdrop that Rigord stressed the horror of Jews employing Christian domestics and the alleged misuse of the eucharistic chalice. To Rigord the resulting pollution was no less acceptable than ritual murder, regardless of the latter's extra gravity—as opposed to the Bollandists' greater preoccupation with ritual murder and martyrdom's eucharistic validation, which led them to syncopate Rigord's text.

But, then, the number of visible Jews in the Bollandists' day, certainly in northern Europe, were few.[55] By contrast, Jews in Paris at the time of Rigord were many and highly visible. They also lived in the city's heart. Late twelfth-century piety, as Rigord saw it, *had* to "defend" itself against Jews daily, as much as when ritual murder was suspected. The most effective defense was through expulsion. For ordering expulsion, but only for so long as the expulsion lasted, Philip Augustus earned Rigord's encomiums. Its reversal in 1198 created danger anew, and Rigord boldly denounced Philip's "avarice." Troubling Rigord no less must have been the fear of contact between Jews returning in 1198 and those who had converted in 1182. The opportunities for corruption, pollution, and apostasy were endless.

Rigord's preoccupation with pollution added a new wrinkle to the dangers of domestic service in a Jewish home. Not only—to recall the phrasing of the *Summa Coloniensis,* might the domestic be *maculata/us,* stained—which Rigord no doubt feared, but there was the additional concern that Jews might manipulate and exploit the domestic to the Host's detriment. An anonymous fifteenth-century commentary on the *Summula Raymundi* of the fourteenth century explains it well:

> Quicunque morantur cum iudeis, illis non debes dare corpus Domini . . . quia forte tales inducerentur a iudeis, ita quod possent illus corpus domini observare et iudeis praesentare, et ipsi postea cum isto sacrmento possent nephas perpetrare, sicut sepius expertum est.[56]

> Whoever lives with Jews should not be offered [in communion] the body of the Lord . . . since the Jews might induce them to keep this body of the Lord [to slip it into their clothing or the like] and give it to the Jews, so that they might perpetrate nefarious deeds with the sacrament, as *frequently* has happened. [emphasis added]

The Christian servant, shades of Guibert de Nogent's monk, becomes an agent of corruption and pollution. Moreover, for the *Summula*'s author, this was the truth, not a fantastic vision. Did he not have the testimony of the various libels made between 1290 and his own day? He needed to go no further than the letter *Operante illo,* which Innocent III sent in 1213 to the archbishop of Sens; it should not surprise us that the events occur near Paris.

This letter tells the tale of a Jewish serving maid who Judaized and blasphemed in disrespect of the Eucharist, captivated as she was by Jewish blasphemy. She repeated their error herself, saying that the Host was bread like any other, or that "ordinary bread . . . is just as efficacious." And "she pressed on to the church along with the other Christians on the Feast of Resurrection, then at hand, where she received the

Eucharist, and hid it in her mouth. Then, she gave it into the hands of the [Jewish] father . . . who unwittingly . . . placed it into a box in which there were seven Parisian livres."⁵⁷ Surprisingly, the Jew is not accused of avariciousness. But in the event, he lost the coveted money, since all the coins in the box turned into consecrated Hosts. The tale ends with the conversion of the Jew and his entire family, for which the pope rewards the converts with a stipend.

This story obviously anticipates the Host libel; it was written decades before the first actual libel was made. But we must note that in its concentration on the miracle and its conversionary effects, it ignores the Jews' possible sinister motives. It even seems to go out of its way to emphasize that the Jews do not initiate purloining the Host, although it is their "error"—and the violation of the insufficiently enforced canon prohibiting domestic service—that provokes the maid to act.

Nonetheless, this concentration on eucharistic perils does allow us to refine our insights, which we may refine even more by revisiting Innocent's other letter, *Etsi Iudaeos*, where the pope fumes about wet nurses having to spilling milk into the latrine. His prescription is to insist that these—illegal—wet nurses be dismissed. The offense itself must be halted. Yet Innocent's motivation was not, as is so frequently said, "anti-Jewish," whatever that term may mean. Rather, he was bent on limiting "infection," which he sought to achieve by limiting Jewish-Christian contacts. Even where the Jew is not criminal, as in *Operante illo*, his intrinsic "error" was believed capable of rubbing off onto others, who would be led into polluting perversion. *Operante illo*'s subtext, therefore (its actual subject is the stipend), is the need to safeguard the sacrament and, principally, its recipients through segregation. In *Etsi Iudaeos*, this is patent. The popes, moreover, knew that restriction for its own sake might be dangerous. Its imposition should correspond to demonstrable need. Accordingly, sometime in late 1215 or early 1216, Innocent III wrote to the French ecclesiastical hierarchy that "distinguishing clothing" was *not* intended "to force [Jews] to wear such as would lay them open to the danger of loss of life."⁵⁸

Like Rigord and, a century later, the author of the *Summula Raymundi*, Innocent was focused on the sacrament. And it is this focus that *Operante illo* reinforces by recounting the ability of the purloined

Host to convert coins into additional Hosts, as though to overcome nefarious plots.[59] People must have been asking whether the Host was truly incorruptible and immune to attack. Had there been no one wondering whether, as God, the wine and wafer of the Eucharist were wholly immune, there would have been no need to portray the Eucharist practicing magic, as *Operante illo* does—which, by monotheistic definition, God is above.[60] The truth seems to be that people did doubt the Eucharist's incorruptibility.[61] But if this was so, if Jewish contact somehow endangered not only persons but the sacrament too, there is no escaping the import. In expressing horror at the potentially damaging effects of Jewish contact, Christianity was exposing itself as a virtually inverted "carnal" Judaism. The Christian sacrifice was no less vulnerable to physical pollution than was that offered at the altar of the Jews. And to avoid this pollution—because both Jews and Christians saw its origins in mutual encroachment—the two religions locked in mortal combat, each calling the devotees of the other thieving, contaminating "dogs," each demanding that the other's devotees be kept at the safest possible remove.

Di Castro's Protest

Christian pretensions to a spiritual essence thus turn out to be flawed. And it was precisely this flaw that the fifteenth-century legist Angelo di Castro sensed, and which he expressed in a *consilium* on whether Christians might purchase those portions of ritually slaughtered meat that dietary regulations prohibited Jews to eat. That his arguments are a product of forensic logic, in which legal deduction and real fact do not always correspond, is irrelevant. Giovanni di Capistrano took di Castro seriously enough to pen a damning response.

Di Castro insisted that to refrain from buying and consuming Jewish meat—as previous tradition forbade—is *ridiculum*, "nonsense; . . . in fact, it is to Judaize and sin" (sic Iudaizare et peccare). Did not, he argued, "the Apostle say that Christians should not discriminate concerning food?" Christians who discriminate place themselves under a law no less binding than that of the Jews. We might say that di Castro was accusing normative Christian practice of adhering to what eventually Ludwig Feuerbach would call a Jewish "alimentary (materialistic) theology," which is much as Luther accused the pope of being Esau. Possibly, di Castro was thinking of (the hopeful side of) Galatians 5:1–24: " . . . if you are led by the Spirit, you are not under law . . . those who belong to Christ have crucified the lower nature with its passions and desires." This verse may easily be read as a mandate to end discrimination about anything one ate.

By contrast, Cyprian cited verbatim this very passage in Galatians as the content of book 3, paragraph 64 of his *Three Testimonies Against the Jews*, whose rubric is: "Carnal things that beget death."[62] Contrary to di Castro, and as the rubric gives away, Cyprian was thinking of these verses' negative side, Paul's warning of the dangers of the flesh and Cyprian's own concern that flesh would emerge victorious. One therefore, extrapolating from Cyprian, avoided all things "carnal," especially the dangers of Judaizing, particularly mixed commensality. It was even more pernicious to consume the Jews' ritually unfit meat. No wonder that di Castro's opinion raised hackles.

The Franciscan Giovanni di Capistrano responded passionately. Countering di Castro in a *reprobatio*, Capistrano fell back unreflectively on the old canonical prohibitions. If, he wrote, "Jews consider the meats we handle as filthy, why should Christians eat the meat the criminal and putrid hands of Jews and other infidels treat as refuse."[63] We become their inferiors, Capistrano continued, and as though their slaves (subverting the Pauline order). He had entirely misconstrued di Castro's argument. It was precisely by eating Jewish meat, di Castro was saying, "that one becomes superior" (faciendo non facit se inferiorem Iudeo, sed maiorem potius) and free—declaring him- or herself to be rid of the carnal law—to seek salvation in the realm of the spirit alone, exactly as Paul had wanted (even if Paul, as we saw, traduced himself in 1 Corinthians [6:12–19] by insistently linking spiritual to bodily purity). For di Castro, by *not* distinguishing foods, whatever their origin and whoever prepared them, the Christian was liberated. To distinguish, as did the Jews, was inferior—and carnal.

It was clearly easier to judge and impugn Jews, than to judge one's self, the *iudicio alienum* (judging the other) that was typical of the

Middle Ages.⁶⁴ It was easier for Capistrano to accuse Jews of being carnal than to confront Christian "carnality"—the truth that di Castro's argument had insightfully unmasked.⁶⁵ It was this same projection onto Jews of Christian "carnality" and the fear of its effects that led Innocent III in his 1208 letter to the count of Nevers to lump together laments about the meat Jews sold to Christians with anger at the rancid wine he said Jews were selling Christians, too. The wine, in particular, he feared might end up in the communion chalice.⁶⁶ Innocent's additional condemnation of Jewish women buying the choicest milk fits this pattern well.⁶⁷

Concerns like these were leading Innocent III ineluctably to his fateful decision of seven years later to order Jews, otherwise unrecognizable in his own Roman milieu, to wear special clothing. Roman Jews—permanent residents of Rome for centuries before anybody had ever heard the name pope—looked, talked, ate, and dressed just as did Innocent, a Roman himself.⁶⁸ The rule of clothing was so innovative (in Europe—under Islam it had been in force for centuries) that Innocent himself never quite specified, or decided, what garb he precisely meant. The best he could do was to root the novelty in the biblical precept that Jews must put fringes on the four corners of their garb.⁶⁹ The pope was preoccupied with keeping Jews and Christians physically apart.

One wonders what Innocent might have said about Johannes Buxtorf's statement in 1603 that whatever else the reason not to buy the meat Jews rejected, Christians should take note that "Jews had their children, boys and girls alike, befoul it with urine" (illos hanc carnem primum inquinare, ab illorum filiis et filiabus urina conspurcari).⁷⁰ The fear of contamination through contact, physical contact, direct or indirect, generating bodily and carnal impurity, was extraordinary and, in Buxtorf's case, literal. That in fearing Jewish carnality so greatly Christians were sublimating a carnality and a fear of pollution of their own was something most Christians preferred not to recognize.

Buxtorf himself strangely avoided the implications that are so obvious in his linkage of Leviticus 22:8 to Exodus 22:31 in the same chapter of his *Synagoga Judaica* in which he spoke of Jews "polluting" meat sold to Christians. Consuming the meat unfit for Temple sacrifice, these two verses say, pollutes, and it should be thrown to the dogs (and it is this unfit meat that Jews were selling to Christians, at least its equivalent in Jewish ritual terms).[71] Hermeneutically, Christians eating discarded Jewish meat themselves turned into dogs. Perhaps understanding these unflattering implications, Buxtorf refrained from making them explicit. His central concern was possible Jewish insult. Had somebody pointed out to di Castro the implications of citing these two verses to justify *not* consuming Jewish meat, he would instantly have retorted in good Italian: *Appunto*! Precisely, and indeed! The minute you restrict what we can eat for canonical reasons, you have said that even as Christians, we are "under the carnal law," susceptible of being turned into "dogs." This was a "carnal" approach to Christianity, and it was exactly this approach to which di Castro was objecting—and to which Luther, as noted, objected too.

For Christians to rid themselves of even the veneer of carnality, it was necessary to subscribe to di Castro's logic; it was discrimination, not disregard, that made one carnal. But di Castro had no audience. Christian protagonists like Capistrano invariably preferred sublimation and denying carnality. They chose to hide behind the frequently given rationale of both canons and commentators that to purchase Jewish meat was a sign of inferiority, turning the faithful into the "son of the slave woman." In di Castro's terms, this rationale was self-defeating, just as it thwarted Paul's raison d'être for Christian belief.[72] As Angelo di Castro so acutely observed, to refuse meat discarded by Jews was to Judaize (alas, di Castro does not comment on actually dining at the Jewish table), and it was also to sin: "Iudaizzare et peccare." It was to neglect the freedom from law the apostle had proclaimed to be the Christian lot, the true sign of "spirituality"—unless the goal was the unintended and unconscious one of establishing a new carnality in place of the old. This was not at all Paul's hoped for liberation of the spirit. Yet this is exactly what came into being.[73]

The "new carnality" of Christianity also competed with the "old." Is not Innocent's letter of 1208, forbidding Christians to purchase Jewish wine a perfect mirror of Jewish rules about contact with wine produced by Christians, which Jews were dead set against consuming? Jews even stipulated when Christians might press Jewish grapes, lest the oven, it asks. The "Jewish dog" is the answer. But we know ahead of time that the thief is a dog; Matthew (15:26) told us that long ago. What remains unanswered in the refrain is the dog's identity. Is the dog a Canaanite, a Gentile in Matthew's original sense, or is the dog, as Chrysostom interpreted it, a Jew? Or, as in the construction of the *Nizzahon Yashan*, is the dog a Christian—which is to say that Christianity has not inherited the Jew? These anxieties about the dog's identity, so deeply rooted in early Christianity, still darkened the schoolchildren's faces nearly two millennia later. Is it any wonder that with Marjorie, a real Jew, in the middle, the borders between play and real life, between feigned and real fear, in a game whose underlying meaning and iconography the players most surely did not know, dissolved into true and, for Marjorie, terrifying emotion?

The complex paths this iconography took until it was transformed into this children's refrain, much as André Vauchez has argued for the interplay of clerical and popular religion in promoting the cult of saints or pseudo-saints like Werner, is not my immediate interest, important as revealing these paths may be. My concern is with the iconography's survival, its embeddedness in the Christian imagination, and its integration into Christian/Catholic culture. In the event, and regardless of their ignorance of the precise overtones, the children did understand that their words were grave. Their confrontational game left Jew and Christian on opposing sides of the "fence." The play formation, the circle and the child inside, unmasks the words' heavy social charge.

The measure of that charge comes out clearly in another myth of borders; only this one is exceedingly old: the apocryphal, and probably early medieval, *Apocalypse of the Virgin*:

> And the all holy one [the Virgin], when she saw the angels humbled on account of the sinners, lamented and said: Woe to sinners and their neighbours. And the all holy one said: Let us see the sinners. And the highly favoured one's voice said: Lord have mercy. And after the making of the prayer earnestly, the wave of the river rested and the fiery waves grew calm, and the sinners appeared as a grain of mustard-seed: and seeing them the all holy one lamented and said: What is this river, and what are its waves? *And the commander-in-chief*

said: This river is the outer fire, and those who are being tortured are the Jews who crucified our Lord Jesus Christ the Son of God, and who refused holy baptism, and [they are also] *those who commit fornication and sin against the sweet and passionless perfume of marriage, and he who debauches mother and daughter, and the poisoners and those who slay with the sword, and the women who strangle their offspring. And the all holy one said: According to their faith so be it unto them.* And straightway the waves rose over the sinners and the darkness covered them. And the commander-in-chief said: Hearken, thou highly favoured one: if anyone shall be cast into this darkness, his remembrance shall never be in the sight of God. And the all holy Mother of God said: Woe to sinners, because the flame of the fire is everlasting.[7]

It is not that murderers, poisoners, and violators of the marital sacrament are as guilty *as* Jews. Rather, all are guilty equally, of the same crime and of espousing the same "faith"—which is faith in its total absence. Assassins, adulterers, and the perpetrators of incest have, in common, crucified Christ anew, just as the Jews crucified him the first time on the Cross. They have traduced the faith and joined themselves with the harlot, polluting "the bread" and forgetting that through its ingestion, they had become one in Christ: *unus panis unum corpus multi sumus*, to again cite 1 Corinthians 10:17, but this time, in the Latin of the Vulgate, whose expression of oneness is exceedingly powerful: "One loaf, one body, though we are many." They had traduced the Christ in themselves. And like those original traducers, the Jews, they were guilty of lacking faith, reason, and humanity. They were the Judaizing sons of Hagar, rightly cast into the "outer fire" and washed over by "fiery waves" and "darkness." By transference, they had become Jews themselves.

We are forcefully reminded of Augustine, writing to St. Jerome, that "whoever has observed Jewish rites, whether truly or in their spirit [*veraciter . . . etiam simulate*], and [embracing, especially as time went on, supposed Jewish murderousness], merits eternal damnation [*barathrum diaboli devolutum*]."[8] In this way, the "bread in the oven" is protected—just as in the Chilean game, decisive action identifies the "thief," isolates him to protect "the faithful," and ends by striking him down. The Chilean children save "the bread," which is the collective Christ in themselves, from disaster.

The need for protecting the collective is paramount. It is, indeed, capable of eclipsing too much, perhaps all else. A letter sent in 1938 by German bishops to ecclesiastical colleagues in Rome makes this disturbingly clear: "As we German Catholic bishops write a collective letter to you from the tomb of St. Boniface, we wish first to affirm . . . *our spiritual union* [with you] *in Christ, whose mystical body* [the Church] *represents the most intimate unity of its members*" (Cari diocesani, se noi, Vescovi cattolici tedeschi, ci rivolgiamo a voi dalla tomba di S. Bonifazio con una Lettera collettiva, vogliamo anzitutto affermare *la nostra unità spirituale in Cristo, il cui Corpo mistico rappresenta pure la più intima unità dei suoi membri* [emphasis added]).[9] So thorough is the letter's concentration on the travails of the Church, not only here, but in its continuation, that its concern for the "mystical body" ignores the menace then so enormously threatening "those without" (qui foris sunt, the medieval legists' way of referring to Jews and other non-Christians). I mean, of course, the Gypsies, Jews, and so many other Nazi victims, whose daily sufferings the bishops surely witnessed.

The realm of the faithful, as in the *Apocalypse*, is exclusive. Is it the bishops' terror, or is it something more that creates this myopia? One must wonder whether at the root of their exclusivity, was a fear of Jews that surpassed even apprehension about Nazis. For were not the Jews allies of the Bolsheviks, whom, in the 1930s, the Catholic Church viewed as its deadliest enemy?[10] This is speculation. But I am hesitant to discard it. For the letter continues by evoking the spirit of martyrdom: "This is not the first tempest. . . . The more we are persecuted, the closer we are to God. . . . We take joy in tribulation, for it produces staying power, virtue, and hope [of salvation through unity in Christ]" (Non è la prima tempesta. . . . Quanto più siamo perseguitati tanto più vicino è Dio a noi.. . . . Ci vantiamo anche nelle tribolazioni, sapendo che la tribolazione produce tolleranza, la tolleranza produce virtù provata, la virtù provata speranza). The bishops picture themselves reliving the saga of Ignatius, daring the beasts to "grind" them into the "wheat" of God. We are reminded once again of the Chilean game.

The children revel in repeatedly singing their refrain. Will the "dog" in the middle pounce, will it lunge at the "faithful"—stealing the (eucharistic) bread that is also the martyr—or will the game end by their striking the dog a blow that preserves the *unus panis*, one powerful enough to reintegrate the "threatened" children's fellowship? This is, is it not, a game about those within and "those outside"? One would like to believe that the bishops wished Germany's Jews no ill. But their concentration on those within the *unus panis*, alongside the ingrained and centuries-old identification of Jews and enemies, now revitalized in perceptions of Bolshevism, seems to have led them to turn only inward. Calls to help Jews were not forthcoming.[11] When these bishops spoke of the unity of believers in dire need, they spoke only of themselves.

Catholic Teaching Today

Few would follow this precedent today. But how many are there who would be willing to turn the vision of both the game and the *Apocalypse*, that of the Jew threatening the body of Christ, upside down? How many would say that should a Christian kill a Jew—united as he or she is in the *unus panis* of Christ, alongside all other Christians—it is as though the Jew has been killed by Christ himself? The idea is not mine. Its authors, if my reading is correct, are senior clerics who clearly understand that Pauline theology allows this reading. They also admit that it applies to acts committed during the Shoah. The admission is highly masked, actually denied, but it is there nevertheless. I am referring to the 1998 Vatican teaching document "We Remember: A Reflection on the Shoah."

The admission is made with ingenious subtlety. In their hearts, the authors knew how deeply "We Remember" is otherwise flawed. How facile is the *stated* distinction between anti-Judaism and twentieth-century racial anti-Semitism, from which they entirely distance the Church. The document's *actio* clause, the clause that prescribes actions to be taken, calls for an end to all Holocausts, yet it never mentions the Shoah of the Jews.[12] The deeper meaning of "We Remember" reveals these flaws to be ones of words, not conviction.

In fact, the authors of "We Remember" deftly "atoned" for the document's verbal shortcomings—*teshuvah*, atonement, as Bishop Eugene Fisher puts it in the context of his "Update on Catholic Education on Jews and Judaism."[13] All that was necessary was a change of subject. "The Church," the text says, "desires to express deep sorrow for the failures of her sons and daughters in every age. This is an act of repentance (*teshuva*), since as *members of the Church, we* are linked to the sins as well as the merits of all her children. *The Church* approaches with deep respect and great compassion the experience of extermination, the Shoah [emphases added]." The critical phrase is "since as *members, we* are linked." For in the following sentence, where "we" is again the expected subject, its place is taken by "*The Church,*" which substitutes for, and is interchangeable with, both "we" and "members" in the previous sentence. That sentence may now be read as "the Church [the whole, and the unity of its parts, not merely we the individual Christians] is linked to the sins . . . of her children," who are its "members"—and who are also *identical* with "the Church," including (by obvious implication) those Nazis, who, like Hitler himself, were baptized Catholics.

This change has enormous resonance in a document that otherwise speaks of long-standing sentiments of mistrust and hostility that are called "anti-Judaism, of which, unfortunately, Christians have also been guilty"—Christians, but not the overall and collective Church and its teachings. The change of subject from "we" to "Church" makes it clear that the authors of "We Remember" knew such a distinction was false. There can rightfully be no distinction between "we," "members," "Church," and "the children [and their] sins." There cannot be, because the doctrine of *unus panis, multi sumus*, does not allow it. The Church can neither exculpate nor dissociate itself from what "certain Christians" did. We have been brought back one final time to 1 Corinthians 10:17, hence, to where we started. So much of this study has been an extended historical exegesis of this verse.

This thought also invites us to revisit the 1938 letter of the German bishops calling the Church, the "the most intimate unity of its members" (più intima unità dei suoi membri). The meaning here is the unity binding each of the parts into one. But did being a part of this the unity confer only belonging and privilege, or did it (and does it) also mean responsibility? "We Remember" affirms that it does.

Exegetically, this is not my private hermeneutic. It is that of Pope John Paul II in his major encyclical *Ecclesia de eucharistia* of April 2003 that places great weight on the "eucharistic life" dedicated to moral responsibility.¹⁴ One who flees that responsibility, as did the German bishops or, perhaps worse, the German archbishop who, in the closing days of the war, proposed a memorial mass for Hitler, would, it seems, have cut him- or herself off from not only the eucharistic life but the collective eucharistic *unus panis*. He or she would figuratively have consigned himself to the fiery river that the *Apocalypse of the Virgin* describes in such fearful detail. In which case (this time wholly without supersessionist, but with unabashedly moral, overtones—and, once more) as asked by the author of the *Nizzahon Yashon*: who were the true children and who the (murderous) dogs? In their hearts—and in their redeeming rhetoric—the authors of "We Remember" had made it very clear. Some of them may also have read the tenth-century Regino of Prum, who said that "to murder a Jew is to destroy the image of God."¹⁵ To carry my metaphor to its extreme, and to explicate it in Catholic terms, the Shoah, inasmuch as many of its primary perpetrators were Catholics, was the "one loaf" killing its "image." It was Christ killing Christ, surely the greatest of all imaginable theological horrors.

Perhaps it is this realization, or certainly one like it, that has aroused the very deep awareness within the formal bodies of today's Catholic Church that the past in the Catholic-Jewish encounter must be revised. The religious teachings of purity, unity, and anxiety, which combined so facilely and perniciously with social—and even racial—doctrines of the same tenor must be expunged. Pope John Paul II's memories of the loss of immediate Jewish neighbors and childhood companions during the Shoah certainly aided him in taking a courageous stance. Today, no papal secretary of state would approve an analysis of papal policy toward the Jews like that proposed by a certain Mgr. Jouin in 1919. The then Secretary Cardinal Gasparri did just that. Jouin wrote:

> There is no doubt that all these measures, even those concerning race and commerce, were aimed to protect the Christian faith from the destructive Jewish influence. *But the popes well understood that it is impossible to dissociate the Faith from the entirety of social life* [emphasis added], and it was for this reason that they entered into such detail, legislating not only in religious matters, but in all that touched the

life of the family, the professions and civic life. They also acted in Rome as temporal sovereigns, concerned to protect their people from the clever enterprise of those whom they constantly spoke of under the name of "perfidious Jews"—hence these severe limitations of their economic and financial power.[16]

No such approval would now be given, even were the restrictive legislation justified as protecting the faith alone and the fears of pernicious social effects (like those that motivated Lorenzelli, Oreglia, and de Pol) abandoned. The Catholic Church as such has formally renounced the teaching, whose roots run so old and deep, of the Jew as agent of corruption. Sorrowfully, this teaching—alongside unrelenting supersessionism!—is alive and well on the Internet, where, with illustration and cross-referenced documentary support, it is more formidable than ever.[17]

It is also alive in putatively more sophisticated formats, to wit, the transposed and inverted Marxism in the recent book *La guerra* by Alberto Asor-Rosa, a noted Italian historian.[18] If asked, Asor-Rosa would vigorously deny being an anti-Semite. *La guerra,* nevertheless, contains passages that are highly anti-Semitic. Much like the early—as opposed to the repentant, later—Ignaz von Döllinger on Jewish xenophobia,[19] Asor-Rosa tells us that Jews for centuries were unassimilable. This was thanks, principally, to their ingrained opposition to the "Imperium" of the West, which made them resist, as Thomas or Rupert of Deutz would have put it, integration into rational (Christian) mankind. Attacks on Jews stemmed from anger at this resistance. Then, to make amends for the excessive burst of violent acting-out that was the Shoah, Jews were co-opted into the Western power matrix. At long last, they were "assimilated" into the West, rewarded with a state, but at Muslim expense in the Middle East (a gross error, since so many of the Arabs in the Land of Israel-Palestine are Christians, but Asor-Rosa needs a martyred victim). They now rule through oppression. The people of thinkers and a religion have been reembodied politically in a nation-state, in all that term's pejorative senses.

This argument co-opts and inverts Marx. In *The Jewish Question*, Marx blames the world's ills on finance capital, whose essence lies in Judaism. Christianity, too, was infected with this evil, but to remove the infection, it was necessary, first, to remove Judaism from the Jews;

Marx's soteriology, like that of Paul, anticipates an ultimately harmonious parousia. The converse of Marx, Asor-Rosa writes that the infection moves not from the Jews outward, but from the imperialistic Christian West to the Jews. In either version, however, the Jews are "on the outside." For Asor-Rosa, contemporary Jews also misrepresent their "real" identity, which is that of a victim; in St. Augustine's words "witnesses [in degradation] of their own iniquity and *our* truth."[20] Jews, by nature, are not—nor do they have a right to be—a nation. Jewish nationhood (apparently) ended with the Temple's destruction, as Christianity classically has taught, "the elder serving the younger."

Rather than accept its properly submissive role, Judaism, presented in these terms, has emerged in the post-Shoah period as the perennial aggressor. Jews are still out to steal the "children's bread"; it is inconsequential that Asor-Rosa does not directly invoke Matthew's image. The Jews' victim is all mankind, not Muslims alone. Regardless of the merits or demerits of any particular Jewish political policy, Jews, as embodied in Israel's existence, stand ready to pounce and perturb the purity and oneness of (Marxist) truth. The inventiveness with which the Jewish–non-Jewish relationship is articulated, even where traditional Christian teachings have been wholly transmogrified, seems to have no limits. In appreciating the Jews, Asor Rosa and others like him—for he is not alone in his views—have lagged far behind the Catholic establishment.

Within the Church itself, and among its hierarchy, there has been a turn, and not only on the part of the late Pope John Paul. In 1965, the German Jesuit Cardinal Bea made the first breach in the wall of the charge of deicide, and alongside Pope John XXIII, he was instrumental in having the decree *Nostra aetate* issued at the II Vatican Council. The effects of this decree in denying Jewish culpability in Christ's death have been notable. In the *Forward* of January 31, 2003, a Jewish weekly that appears in New York, Michael Berenbaum writes that in fifteen years teaching at Jesuit Georgetown he found that the words of this decree *were* being applied. "None of his students [many the products of American Roman Catholic parochial education] had been taught to see Jews as Christ-killers." What John McCulloh's friends once heard in school today is heard no more, not certainly (if Berenbaum is correct) in Catholic schools in the United States.[21] Bishop Eugene Fisher's statement on "a firm resolve to change from the former path by turning toward righteousness and truth," made in his "Update on Catholic Education on Jews and Judaism" of 1994, has left no doubt that many in the Church think even this important advance is not enough. Bishop Fisher is director for Catholic-Jewish Relations in the National Conference of Catholic Bishops.

Nonetheless, the challenge portended in Matthew's parable of the children and the dogs, the challenge of supersessionism, has yet fully to be overcome. In the words of Kurt Hruby, written in 1975, when he was director of the Judaism Section of the Paris Ecumenical Institute and a professor of Rabbinic Hebrew and Judaism at the Catholic University of Paris, "The essential condition for fruitful contact which could then lead to a further phase of understanding is *full and unreserved recognition of the other party's legitimate theological and existential autonomy*" (emphasis in the original). In unadorned terms, Hruby was asking whether supersessionism could be rejected, which he then said in just so many words. I cite him at length. Paraphrase would not do justice to his text:

> In fact any real meeting with Judaism is impossible without a clarification of theological premises on the Christian side. This is a difficult and delicate matter, but one thing at least is clear—the question is the significance for the Christian Church of *Judaism today*, not the Judaism of the past, whose significance no one, presumably, would dispute. In practice this means the questioning of the whole of the "traditional" [Catholic] theology of Israel or, better, an admission and recognition that . . . traditional theses . . . have been much more the product of historical conditions than an expression of real theological data.
>
> If the whole significance of Judaism for the Christian community is really contained in Augustine's remark that the Jews are *testes iniquitatis suae et veritatis nostrae* (In *Ps. 58 Enarr.* 1, 2–22; *PL* 2–37, 765), "witnesses of their own iniquity and *our* truth,"[22] then it is totally unnecessary to argue for a theological reappraisal and look for a meeting with Judaism. If this is the position, we must simply accept once and for all—as it was for centuries accepted—that, to adapt

Aquinas, *antiquum testamentum novo cedat ritui*. That is to say, the "old" Jewish order has given way to a new Christian one. Christianity has suceeded totally to the spiritual position of Judaism and so made it theologically superfluous. [It is thus necessary to test the "traditional teaching" against critical examination, whether it can give way yet nonetheless be "theologically defensible."] If it is not, Jewish-Christian relations will remain in a state of more or less peaceful coexistence, but with the ever-present danger that external circumstances . . . will seriously disrupt them. . . .

Most theologicans today feel that the "classical" description of the relationship between Judaism and Christianity has become untenable and indefensible. But when it comes to withdrawing from it and working for a new approach, they all too often do nothing and become seized by a "prudence" for which the weight of history must be largely responsible. It is hard to escape the impression . . . that people fear that the whole structure of Christian doctrine will be made unsafe if attempts are made to do justice to Judaism and recognize it as a theological factor and a valid form of spirituality in the present.[23]

This, as said, was in 1975. The then Cardinal Ratzinger's recent denunciation of religious relativism, cited at the outset of this study—let alone those of Catholic individuals and groups to his right, who admittedly speak mostly for themselves—suggests very strongly that Hruby's reservations about movement are still correct, even thirty years later. A true testing of "traditional teaching" has yet to occur. The voyage begun in 1965 by *Nostra aetate* remains unfinished.

Yet despite Ratzinger's importance as the chief officer for doctrine within the Church (until his election in April 2005 as Pope Benedict XVI), he did not, nor does he today, represent the whole. The statement made on August 12, 2002, by the Bishops' Committee for Ecumentical and Interreligious Affairs of the United States Council of Catholic Bishops, entitled "Reflections on Covenant and Mission" (made in conjunction with a similar statement by rabbis who work with this committee), points to significant movement.[24] It cites "John Paul II [who] has explicitly taught that Jews are 'the people of God of the Old Covenant, never revoked by God.'" St. Paul would have agreed; he said this in Romans 11. But cited in the context of Pope John Paul's further statement: "urg[ing] Christians to remember 'how the permanence of Israel is accompanied by a *continuous* [my emphasis] spiritual fecundity, *in the rabbinical period*, in the Middle Ages, and in modern times . . . ,'" the implications are revolutionary. The words go straight to the charge, repeated explicitly from the thirteenth through the twentieth century, that talmudic, rabbinic, Judaism corrupted the biblical Judaism that presages Christ and, therefore, has no validity.[25]

The pope had affirmed that the original Jewish Covenant need not be understood in a Christian context. It "continues" to be valid unto itself and even after Christ. It is not the "Old Covenant, [which has been superseded]." Rather, as the pope continued, the "Rabbinic Judaism that developed *after the destruction of the Temple*, must also be 'of God.'" For centuries the "destruction of the Temple" in Jerusalem in 70 C.E. was seen as the end point of a valid Judaism; the rabbinic Judaism that followed was considered sterile. Pope John Paul had said that post-destruction Judaism was *continuously* "fecund" and "of God."

Only one more thing needed to be said—and it was, in May 2003. Addressing a delegation of the American Jewish Congress in Rome on May 22, John Paul said: "God's word is a lamp and a light to our path. . . . This word is given to our Jewish brothers and sisters especially in the Torah. *To Christians* [my emphasis] this word finds its fulfillment in Jesus Christ." Paul himself had said similar things, but he had interposed the reservation that salvation was out of reach through the Torah.[26] Pope John Paul had rejected this idea, saying that God's "word" travels along two independent and equally valid paths. More important, the "word[s] . . . fulfillment in Jesus Christ" refers to Christians alone.[27] The pope had initiated major theological emendation.

Cardinal Walter Kasper, who has been so active in promoting Jewish-Catholic rapprochement, then took the last step, saying that "the Church believes that Judaism . . . is *salvific for them* [the Jews], because God is faithful to his promises." Kasper, like the pope, was being cited in "Reflections on Covenant and Missions." With this statement, Hruby's hope for Jewish "theological and existential autonomy" seems to have been realized. Kasper also went farther, to say that "the Catholic church . . . acknowledges that Jews [to be read: "Jews, as Jews," not as potential Christians] already dwell in a saving covenant with God." Paul said the same, but he did so as part of his vision (Romans 11) of

Jews being regrafted onto the tree of salvation. Kasper had rejected Paul's expectations. "Reflections on Covenant and Mission" adds to this that the Church "respects . . . freedom of conscience." The bishops were coming firmly down on the side of modernism. Had not this principle been a casus belli in the modernist–anti-modernist debate, and is it not still a bone of angry contention on web sites like Holy war.org, which call Pope John Paul II a heretic for preaching just this?

The predicate is that all mission must be renounced. The Bishop's Council did so explicitly:

> the Church must bear witness in the world to the Good News of Christ [the Gospel] so as to prepare the world for the *fulness* of the kingdom of God. However, this evangelizing task no longer includes the wish to absorb the Jewish faith into Christianity and so end the distinctive witness of Jews to God in human history. Thus, while the Catholic Church regards the saving act of Christ as central to the process of human salvation for all, it also acknowledges that Jews already dwell in a saving covenant with God.

Nonetheless, in the text's *immediate* continuation, a disturbing addendum intimates that something is still awry:

> The Catholic Church must always evangelize and will always witness to its faith [*sic*] in the presence of God's kingdom in Jesus Christ to Jews and to all other people. In so doing, the Catholic Church respects fully the principles of religious freedom and freedom of conscience, so that sincere individual converts from any tradition or people, including the Jewish people, will be welcomed and accepted.

To speak of converts, even those who come of their own initiative, in the same paragraph that anticipates the "fulness of the kingdom of God," refers us inescapably to Romans, chapter 11, and to Paul's insistence that the anticipated "fulness of time" depends on the "ingathering" of the Jews. This reference also harks back to *Nostra aetate* of nearly forty years earlier, which proclaims God's expectation "of the day when all peoples will address Him with a single voice."[28]

A certain haze hangs over this otherwise optimistic text. Paul's vision has been weakly, yet unmistakably, kept alive by tying it to the "welcoming," if not really the "desire" for converts. "Reflections on Convenant and Mission" has renounced the essence of supersessionism, but its authors have not abandoned their hope and belief that Catholic truths will eventually prevail. For a believing Catholic, this may be reasonable. However, this also means that the conundrum continues to exist. "The fear," as Hruby put it, has not been put to rest once and for all that in "questioning of the whole of the 'traditional' [Catholic] theology of Israel [principally the teaching supersession] . . . the whole structure of Christian doctrine will be made unsafe."

We have returned to the ambivalence with which we began, less open, more aware of its pitfalls, but there nonetheless. To witness Jews and Christians, jointly "the children" of Matthew, yet individually enjoying the "bread" of the sacrifice, remains a wish—regardless of whether that bread be the Eucharist or the Jewish prayer that for two thousand years has substituted for the sacrificial Temple rites. Should the authors of "Reflections on Covenant and Mission" refute this reading, I shall be pleased. To me, however, it seems that the vision of Agobard of Lyon is still seductive. The siren call of a society "where there is neither barbarian nor Scythian, Aquitanian nor Lombard, Burgundian nor Alemanni, slave nor free, but all are one in Christ," in the "fulness" and calling upon him "with one voice," clearly beckons. It attracts even those—some of those, anyway—whose sincerity in seeking to bury all enmity is otherwise unimpeachable.[29]

Perhaps one day the tide of these attractions will ebb. One must hope that "this too will pass." Yet the weight of so long and complex a historical past says that this will not happen easily, certainly not on its own. The vision of protecting the children and their bread has been too central. Hruby's concern that true change will be impeded by a "'prudence' for which the weight of history must be largely responsible" was not only prescient, it struck at the matter's crux. What I hope to have accomplished here is to show how great the force of that "historical weight" is, as well as the implications of its real nature. The prescriptive conclusion that I said would end this study is one that measured historical research has virtually constrained me to reach.

The fight is uphill, and none other than Cervantes may have explained its nature best. In his farcical dramatic *intermezzo*, *El retablo de las maravillas*, people claiming to be Old Christians (by law the offspring of Spaniards who were Christians before 1391) fear so greatly having their vaunted purity challenged, that they play the fool. Convinced by a troop of travelling actors that only Old Christians will see the "wonders" about to be enacted on stage, the pretendant Old Christians outdo one another in pointing these wonders out. Until a visitor arrives, a quartermaster by profession, who, much like the child in the tale of the "Emperor's New Clothes," tells the townsmen that nothing is being performed at all, to which they react in total denial. The quartermaster, they say, is surely a New Christian, infected with the mixed *converso* blood (of Jews converted after 1391). He is "ex illis," Cervantes's words, "one of them."[30] He is *not* "one" with the Old Christian *unus panis*; his challenge is an attempt to steal the Old Christians' identity—and, of course, to purloin their "bread"—by calling it nought. Blinded by pride and having substituted the artificial for the real, false Christian virtue in place of the true, the Old Christians are driven to assert their presumed unicity, and they keep on doing so to the point of absurdity. So be it.

Reference Matter

Appendix One   Bollandist and Parallel Texts

A. Richard of Pontoise

The Bollandist Text

The reader should note especially the second paragraph on page 181. The Bollandist text, in Italics, and Rigord's, in Roman type, is unchanged from the original; the lettering in brackets is the titles found in the margins of the volumes of the *Acta Sanctorum*, again part of the original. In this paragraph, the Bollandist interjection: *anno deinde*, "the following year, 1181," emends Rigord. The purpose is to create continuity and, more, causal linkage, much as the more forceful second interjection: *Neque id tantum*, "not only that." Further, whereas Rigord (see below) goes on about Judaizing, Christian servants of Jews, and more, the Bollandists are brusque, just noting "other accusations." The story of Brie the Bollandists attach to their tale of Richard; Rigord tells the tale many pages later, in chronological order. The reference of the Bollandists to "other accusations" is thus indeed to other libels, and "not only that" implies that the expulsion, too, is recompense for ritual murder. The entire Bollandist context is ritual murder. The Bollandists tie their story neatly together by opening with the expulsion from France in 635, with references to Jewish avarice, apostasy after conversion, and to the events of 1171.

Special attention should be paid, both here and in the text of the Good Werner narrative, to the thorough Bollandist discussion of sources. The Bollandists took great care in choosing sources. They were seeking textual legitimacy and were rarely guilty of fideistic credulity. It goes without saying that historians today would read medieval chronicles more critically.

*

The seventeenth-century *Acta Sanctorum* (*ActaSS* in common citation), *a Ioanne Bollando S.I. colli feliciter coepta. A Godefrido Henschenio et Daniele Papebrochio, S.I., aucta.* . . . (Antwerp 1668, for the volume most used in this study), March III, with saints listed by their day; *Acta Sanctorum,* ed. Socii Bollandiani, 69 vols. (Paris, 1863–1940), has also been reproduced electronically by Chadwyk and Healy and is available for consultation and downloading in subscribing libraries only. The electronic version is identical to the original. The printed tomes, though weighty, are easy to consult. Microfiche versions are available.

Mar. III
XXV MARTII.
DE S. RICHARDO PVERO MARTYRE PARISIIS IN FRANCIA.

[Praefatio]

Richardus puer, Martyr Parisiis in Francia (S.)
[Col. 0591B]

Ex Anglia transitum in Gallias facimus, Christiano sanguine saepius cruentatas per eos, quorum maiores Christi sanguinem fundentes in Cruce, [Sub Dagoberto pulsi ex Gallijs Iudaei,] *eiusdem sitim velut haereditariam traduxerunt in posteros. Quamuis enim iam olim magnis ibidem slorentes opibus Dagobertus* I, *Heraclij Imperatoris consilio exemploque inductus, anno sui regni* VIII, *qui fuit aerae Christianae* DCXXXV, *omnes ex imperij sui finibus pelli iußisset, nisi qui sacrum baptisma consensissent recipere; ijsdem tamen partim reuersis postliminio partim ad auitam perfidiam relapsis, ita inualuit execratae stirpis propago, vt totius regni opes penes* [Col. 0591C] *Iudaeos ferme essent, & quae diuitias consequitur quidlibet audendi agendique impunita libertas. Sub hac cum Gallicanae ecclesiae gemerent;* [XII seculo rursum inualescunt,] *qui tamen de remedio sollicitus esset magnopere, nemo fuit. Certe, si quis esset, parum aut nihil proficiebat, propter summam Regum ipsis indulgentium socordiam: vnde ad Ludouicum Iuniorem scribens Petrus Abbas Cluniacensis conqueritur, quod vt Iudaeorum sacrilega commercia tutiora essent,* lex iam vetusta,

Appendix One 179

sed vere diabolica, ab ipsis Christianis Principibus processit, vt si res ecclesiastica, vel, quod deterius, aliquod sacrum vas apud Iudaeum repertum fuerit, nec rem sacrilego furto possessam reddere, nec nequam furem Iudaeus prodere compellatur.

Cum autem auaritiae accesserit crudelitas, & vtrique impunitas accedit scelerum, [& varios pueros ibi atque in Anglia mactant:] *quid non audebit praefidens impietas? Congerit exempla aliquot Robertus de Turreneio ex monacho Beccensi S. Michaelis de monte Abbas in Appendice ad Sigebertum anno MCLXXI hisce verbis:* Theobaldus Comes Carnotensis plures Iudaeorum, qui Blesis habitabant, igni tradidit: siquidem cum infantem quemdam in solennitate paschali crucifixissent ad opprobrium Christianorum, postea in sacco positum in fluuium Ligeris proiecerunt: quo inuento, eos conuictos de scelere igni tradidit, exceptis illis qui fidem Christianam receperunt. Hoc etiam fecerunt de S. Wilhelmo in Anglia apud Norwic tempore Stephani Regis: quo [Col. 0591E] sepulto in ecclesia Episcopali multa miracula fiunt ad sepulcrû eius. Similiter factum est de alio apud Glouecestriâ tempore Henrici II Regis. Sed & in Francia castello, quod dicitur Pons-Isarae, de S Richardo impij Iudaei similiter fecerunt, qui delatus Parisios in ecclesia sepultus, multis miraculis coruscat. Et frequenter, vt dicitur, faciunt hoc in tempore Paschali, si opportunitatem inuenerint.

Hactenus Robertus, de Monte vulgo cognominatus, ipso illo pene, quo Richardus est occisus, anno scriptionem suam finiens, [in quibus S. Richardus] *vtpote in anno MCLXXX desinentem: cum ante anni praecedentis Pascha martyriû ille passus probetur inferius ex supparis* [Col. 0591F] *aeui scriptore Rigordo: quod côfirmatur ex Guilielmo Armorico in gestis Philippi Augusti Regis Francorum ad annû illius primû sic loquente*: In diebus illis S. Richardus a Iudaeis crucifixus fuit, & martyriû passus: cuius corpus requiescit in ecclesia S. Innocentij Parisius, in loco qui Campellus dicitur, & fiunt ibi per orationes eius mirabilia vsq; in hodiernû diem. *Id est post annum MCCXX,* [occisus Pontisarae.] *in quo historiam suam concludit ipse Regis praedicti Capellanus, & accuratissimus annorum ac pene dierum supputator. Habemus igitur a testibus pene oculatis annum, secundum Francos eius temporis MCLXXVIII exeuntem, secundum hodiernum morem nostrum* MCLXXIX *a Kalendis Ianuarij inchoatum. Habemus locum passionis Pontisaram, cultus vero Parisios vrbem regiam. Modum carnificinae ex Martyrologio Gallicano Saussaij possemus attexere, nisi hic accepisset ex Roberto Gaguino, Ministro Generali Ordinis Sanctißimae Trinitatis de redemptione captiuorum*; [Acta descripta a Gaguino.] *qui tractatum hac de re vulgauit & populo Parisino inscripsit anno* MCCC-CXCVIII XVII *Kal. Octobris. Hunc tractatum, ex antiquißimae impreßionis libro bibliothecae nostrae Claromontanae Parisijs, eruditißimus noster Gabriel Cossartius curauit transcribendum, prout illum hic edimus, simulque lectorem admonemus, ambiguis Rigordi mox citandi verbis persuasum eidem Gaguino fuisse, quod Parisijs occisus esset S. Richardus.*

Extat ettiam nunc Parisijs iuxta Crucem coemeterij supra dicti tumba eleuata seu grandis lapis, . . .

Ceterum e coemeterio in templum translatum fuisse corpus sanctum, [Rex Philippus (vt Rigordus testatur)] *postquam coepit miraculis clarescere, videntur indicare auctores praecitati, quando dicunt illud in ecclesia quiescere: nisi ampliandam aliquis putet huius locutionis significationem: de qua cum vlterius nihil certi habeamus, potius* [Col. 0592B] *videamus qua ratione iustus vindex in totam nationem extenderit poenam, infinitis Iudaeorum flagitijs debitam. Tractauit argumentum istud amplißime Rigordus, Philippi Augusti chronographus, ea scribens quae proprijs oculis vidit, aut ab alijs diligentius exquisiuit, vt profitetur in prologo ad eiusdem Regis gesta.* . . .

Reuolutis autem quam paucis diebus, ex quo nouus Rex post sacram inunctionem Parisius redijt; [hoc alijsque Iudaeorum sceleribus commotus,] opus quod longo tempore mente agitauerat, sed pro nimia reuerentia, quam Christianissimo patri suo exhibebat, perficere formidabat, aggressus est. Audierat enim multoties a Principibus, qui cum ipso pariter in palatio fuerant nutriti, & hoc sine obliteratione memoriae [Col. 0592C] commendauerat, quod Iudaei qui Parisius manebant, singulis annis Christianum vnum, in opprobrium Christianae religionis, quasi pro sacrificio, in cryptis subterraneis latentes, in die coenae vel in illa sacra hebdomada poenosa iugulabant. Et in huiusmodi nequitia diabolicae fraudis diu perseuerantes, tempore patris sui multoties deprehensi fuerant & igne consumpti. S. Richardus, cuius corpus requiescit in ecclesia S. Innocentij in Campellis Parisius, sic interfectus a Iudaeis & crucifixus feliciter per martyrium migrauit ad Dominum: vbi ad honorem Domini per preces & intercessiones S. Richardi, multa miracula ipso Domino operante facta fuisse audiuimus. [eos bonis primum spoliari praecepit,] Et quia Christianissimus Rex Philippus diligenti inquisitione a maioribus haec & alia quamplurima de Iudaeis plenius didicerat; ideo zelo Dei inflammatus ad mandatum ipsius eodem anno, quo Remis sacra regni Francorum suscepit gubernacula, XVI Kalendas Martij in Sabbato, capti sunt Iudaei per totum Franciam in Synagogis suis. Et tunc expoliati sunt auro & argento & vestibus, sicut & ipsi Iudaei in exitu de Aegypto Aegyptios spoliauerant.

Anno deinde MCLXXXI *alias atque alias contra eosdem Iudaeos accusationes suscipiens idem Rex (quas praedictus Rigordus fuse prosequitur*, [deinde ab eorû debitis Christianos absoluit,] *& iam pridem ad patrem Regis scribens Petrus Cluniacensis pathetice exposuerat)* consuluit [Col. 0592D] quemdam eremitam, nomine Bernardum, virum sanctum & religiosum, qui eo tempore in nemore Vicenarum degebat, quid facto opus esset. De consilio cuius relaxauit omnes Christianos de regno suo a debitis Iudaeorum, quinta parte totius summae sibi retenta. *Neque id tantum [Bollandist comment; italics in original; my extra emphasis with larger font]*; sed anno Dominicae Incarnationis MCLXXXII exijt edictum a Serenissimo Rege, [ac denique e regno expulit:] quod omnes Iudaei de regno suo vsque ad sequens festum S. Ioannis Baptistae ad exeundum parati essent. Et tunc data est licentia a Rege quod omnem suam supellectilem venderent. . . . reseruatis sibi & Francorum Regibus successoribus suis possessionibus. . . . Quo audito perfidi Iudaei, quidam ex ipsis regenerati ex aqua & Spiritu sancto conuersi sunt ad Dominum, quibus Rex intuitu Christianae religionis omnes possessiones eorum in integrum restituit, & perpetua libertate eosdem donauit. *Ceteri autem diuenditae suppellectilis suae* pretium habentes pro viatico, egressi sunt cum vxoribus & filijs & vniuerso comitatu, mense Iulij.

Verum vel simulatam fuisse multorum qui remansere, [Col. 0592E] *conuersionem, vel eos qui egreßi fuerant clam iterum regressos, non tantum ad ea quae prius incoluerant loca,* [iterumque deprehensos in simili delicto] *sed etiam ad vsitata scelera, intra decenniû patuit. Siquidem* reuolutis aliquot mensibus (*post natalem Domini anno* MCXCI *apud fontem Eblaudi celebratum*) eiusdem anni, *more Francico vsque ad Pascha protracti,* XV Kalendas Aprilis, Philippus Rex existens apud S. Germanum de Laia, audita cuiusdam Christiani morte ignominiosa a Iudaeis perpetrata, fidei & religioni Christianae compatiens, subito, nescientibus suis familiaribus quo pergebat, iter arripuit; & gressu velocissimo ad castrum quod Braiam vocant (*in Campania scilicet ad Sequanam fluuium, Gallicanis leucis quindecim ab vrbe Parisina, a Sancto Germano autem fere viginti distans*; [Braiae comburi iubet:] *cum alterum eiusdem nominis in Picardia ad Somonam duplo distet interuallo*) Braiam, *inquam,* velociter venit, positis in portis ipsius castri custodibus: & comprehensis Iudaeis octoginta & eo amplius, fecit comburi. Comitissa enim ipsius castri, magnis Iudaeorum muneribus corrupta, tradiderat eis quemdam Christianum, cui falso imponebant furtum & homicidium. Quem Iudaei antiquo odio commoti, manibus a tergo ligatis, spinis coronatum, per totam villam fustigantes duxerunt, & postea patibulo suspenderunt: cum ipsi tempore Dominicae Passionis dicerent; Nobis non licet interficere quemquam.

[Col. 0592F] *His ita gestis prorsus admirabile est, Regem a tam laudatis initijs orsum,* [patitur tamen eos reuerti Parisios.] *auaritia & adulatorum suasionibus eo potuisse adduci, vt anno* MCXCVIII *mense Iulio,* contra omnium hominum opinionem suumque ipsius edictum, Iudaeos Parisius reduceret, & Ecclesias Dei grauiter persequeretur. *Cuius vtriusque criminis quas poenas dederit, Rigordus prosequitur. Reductis autem isto modo Iudaeis eorumque posteris poena non minima fuit miraculorum frequentia, quae suum ipsis facinus diuinitus exprobrabant, & apud Claudium Malingraeum in Antiquitatibus Parisinis describuntur, verbis ex Roberto Guaguino mutuatis, quibus suam ad Parisinos epistolam hic concludit num.* 8, *quaeque eadem fere transcribit Saussaius, continentia sancti corporis auectionem, factam antequam Angli Parisijs eijcerentur anno* MCCCCXXXVII, III *Aprilis.*

Quibus idem Saussaius in suo Gallicano Martyrologio, probabili potius coniectura quam certi alicuius testimonij fide, videtur addidisse, quod in Angliam S. Richardus translatus ibidem signis diuinis radiauit; [Angli corpus B Richardi auferunt,] donec tandem ab haereticis, in hac insula tremendo Dei iudicio praeualentibus, cum ceteris Beatorum pignoribus exustum, nouam ab infida gente persecutionem sustinuit, ex qua nouam etiam retulit victoriae coronam.

Rigord's Account

The text to follow includes English translations of those parts of Rigord's Latin text that the Bollandists cited. In Rigord's text, the three events concerning Jews appear as distinct incidents: 1. the arrest, 2. the cancellation of loans, and 3. the expulsion. Paul Hyams, the translator, suggests rightly that Rigord himself saw the events, those of the 1180s, at least, as connected. Hyams makes this point by inserting headings. Rigord never makes the point outright. The Bollandists, we saw, carefully tied the three events togther, and their account is integral to the narrative of Richard of Pontoise. Hyams's numeration shows the gap between the expulsion and the Brie tale in Rigord's strictly chronological account. Selections from Rigord's translated text are reproduced here with Paul Hyams's kind permission; the added emphases are mine.The source is *Oeuvres de Rigord et de Guillaume le Breton, historiens de Philippe-Auguste, publiées pour la Société de l'histoire de France par H. François Delaborde* (Paris: Librairie Renouard, 1882), vol. 1. Translation © Paul R. Hyams 1998.

6. A few days after the holy anointing, the new king returned to Paris. He started the job which he had long borne in mind but had feared to complete, because of the great reverence which he showed to his most Christian father. For he had heard many times from the boys who were fostered with him in the palace—and commended to memory without ever forgetting it—that the Jews who lived in Paris every year slit the throat of one Christian in the hidden underground caverns on Maundy Thursday or during the Holy Week of penitence, as a kind of sacrifice in contempt of the Christian religion, and that many who

long persevered in this kind of wickedness by diabolical seduction, had been burned at the stake in his father's time. St. Richard, whose body rests in the Church of the Holy Innocents in the Little Field of Paris (petit champ?), after being killed in this way by the Jews and fixed to a cross, happily migrated to the Lord in martyrdom, a fact which we heard when God worked many miracles to the Lord's honor and by the intercessions of St. Richard. And because the most Christian king Phillip learnt by careful investigation of the older people (majoribus) these and many other scurrilous things about the Jews, which inflamed him with the zeal of God, the Jews were arrested in their synagogues all over France at his order on the fourteenth of February [1180] and despoiled of their gold, silver and vestments, just as the Jews themselves had despoiled the Egyptians on their exodus from Egypt. By this was signified their coming expulsion, which followed in time by God's disposition. [http://falcon.arts.cornell.edu/prh3/408/texts/Rigord1.html (accessed May 20, 2005)]

Here Is Placed the First Reason Why the Most
Christian King Phillip Expelled (Exterminavit)
the Jews From the Whole of France

At that time, there lived in France a very great multitude of Jews who had gathered there over a long period from the various parts of the world on account of the lasting peace and the generosity (liberalitatem) of the French. For the Jews heard that the kings of the kingdom of the Franks were strong against their enemies and kind (pietatem) towards their subjects. [The Jews grew] so rich that they claimed almost half of the whole city and—which is against God's decree and the Church's regulations—had in their houses as servants Christian men and women, who manifestly moving away from the Christian faith judaized with the Jews themselves.... When the most Christian king Phillip heard this [and of Jewish excesses concerning lending], he was moved by benevolence (pietate) and asked a certain hermit named Bernard [de Bré] a holy and religious man . . . for advice on what to do. At his suggestion, he released all Christians in his realm from debts to the Jews, keeping for himself a fifth part of the whole sum.

A Second Reason Is Placed Here

13. Church ornaments dedicated to God, gold and silver crosses bearing the image of the crucified Lord Jesus Christ and chalices were deposited with them by way of pawn because of the pressing needs of the churches. To further increase their damnation, they treated these so vilely in censure and reproach to the Christian religion, that their children ate their eggs[1] cooked in wine and drank from chalices that had contained the body and blood of our Lord Jesus Christ, [This was much as] the Lord was angered against Balthazar [when he and his court drank from the vessels of the despoiled Jerusalem Temple] and showed him the sign of his destruction, that is the hand writing against him on the wall "Mane, Techel, Phares" [Daniel, v]. That same night Babylon was captured by Cyrus and Darius and Balthazar was killed....

The Third Reason for the Ejection of the Jews Is Placed Here

14. At that time therefore when the Jews were afraid that their houses might be searched by the king's officials, it happened that a certain Jew who was then living in Paris and had some church ornaments, a gold cross augmented with gems and a Gospel book wonderfully decorated with precious stones, as well as silver goblets and other vases, put these in a sack and most vilely threw it down into a deep pit in which he was (alas!) accustomed to empty his bowels. All of this was soon afterwards revealed.

Deeds of the Third Year of the Reign of Phillip Augustus, King of the Franks

15. In the year of the Lord's incarnation 1182, during the month of April which is called by the Jews Nisan, an edict came out from the most serene king Phillip Augustus that all Jews of his realm should prepare to leave by the feast of St. John the Baptist following. They were then given license by the king to sell all their household effects in the intervening time, that is before the feast of St. John's, with their

possessions in the sense of houses, fields, vineyards, barns, (wine?)-presses and that kind of thing being reserved to himself and the future kings of the Franks. When they heard this, some of the perfidious Jews were reborn from the water with the Holy Spirit, and once converted to the Lord persevered in the faith of our Lord Jesus Christ. To these the king out of respect for the Christian religion restored and granted them in perpetual liberty all their possessions complete. Others blinded by their ancient error persisted in their perfidy and sought to entice the princes of the land, counts, barons, archbishops and bishops among them, with gifts and great promises, to see if they could by their advice and suggestions and the promise of an infinite amount of money call the king's mind back from so firm a decision. But the compassionate and merciful Lord . . . so strengthened with the Holy Spirit the enlightened mind of the king . . . , that neither prayers nor promises of temporal goods could soften it.

On the Princes' Setback

16. When the infidel Jews saw that the princes, through whom they were accustomed to bend the will of other, previous kings easily to do their will, had suffered a setback, they wondered at king Phillip's magnanimity and firm constancy in the Lord. Stunned and almost stupefied by wonder, they cried out "Shema Yisrael," that is "Hear O Israel" and hurried to sell their furniture. For the time was approaching when they were bound by the king's command to get out of all France (de tota Francia), and this could on no grounds be put off longer. The Jews then had all they could do to fulfill the king's orders and sold off their movable property with amazing speed, for all their (landed) possessions devolved to the royal fisc. So having sold their things, the Jews had the expenses for the journey and left with their wives and sons and their whole following in the aforesaid year 1182, in the month of July, which the Jews call Tamuz, the third year of king Phillip Augustus' reign with the 17th year of his age having begun the previous August.

That Phillip the King "Semper Augustus" Had the Jews' Synagogues Dedicated to God as Churches

17. Once the infidel Jews had been ejected and dispersed throughout the whole world, king Phillip "semper Augustus" quite aware of what he was doing completed with God's help the work begun in glory in even more glory. For he ordered that all the synagogues of the Jews be cleaned up and, against the will of all the princes, had the same synagogues dedicated to God as churches, with altars consecrated in them to the honor of our Lord Jesus Christ and to the blessed mother of God and virgin Mary. These same "synagogues" were called schools by them, and the Jews gathered there daily for the sake of counterfeit prayer in the name of the fabricated religion.

By a Great Release of Debts Made by the Most Christian King, the Christians Dwelling in the Kingdom of France Achieved Perpetual Liberty

[Note the skip in paragraph numbers in Rigord at this point—KS.]

84. Some months later, on the 15th kalends of April [March 18, 1192], while king Phillip was at Saint-Germain-de-Laie, he heard about the ignominious death of a certain Christian perpetrated by the Jews and at once, moved by compassion for the Christian faith and religion, took off, leaving his intimates with no idea of where he was headed and swiftly reached the castle which they call "Braia." He placed guards at the castle gates and had the Jews he caught there, 80 and more, burnt. The countess whose castle it was, corrupted by the Jews with great gifts, had handed over to them a certain Christian, whom they falsely accused of theft and homicide. The Jews motivated by their ancient hatred tied his hands behind him, crowned him with thorns, beat him through the town and then hanged him from a gallows, though they had said at the time of the Lord's Passion: "We are not permitted to kill anyone."

B. The Good Werner

The Werner Story in the Gesta Trevorum

One notes the absence of the overtones to be seen in the version of the Bollandists, who cite the *Gesta*'s account only on col. 702, well into their exposition. In their introduction, the Bollandists say they prefer other accounts, no doubt because these other accounts portray Werner as a substitute *Corpus Christi*. We should note the *Gesta*'s concern (emphasized by me) that episodes of ritual murder led to great destruction of Jews, even of women and children. The displeasure, at least the empathy, of the *Gesta* is evident. Why the Bollandists, who are otherwise so condemnatory of Jewish actions and motives, retained the *Gesta*'s references to the Jewish plight in citing the *Gesta* is not fully clear. But, then, the Latin crusade chroniclers, too, make much of Jewish suffering, despite their negativity toward Jews otherwise. Besides, and perhaps deciding the issue, the Bollandists were "defenders of the text," not bowdlerizers.

The source is *Gesta Boemundi archiepiscopi Treverensis*, chapter 10, edited by G. Waitz, Monumenta Germaniae Historica, Scriptores, vol. 24 (Hannover, 1879), 470.

Anno Domini 1287, domino Boemundo adhuc in Romana curia existente, puer quidam christianus et mendicus Wernerus nomine, cum apud Wesaliam villam Treverensis dyocesis de celario cuiusdam Iudei cum cophino terrram exportaret, hora quadam, dum facultas se optulit oportuna, inito consilio, perfidi Iudei, christiani nominis inimici, irruerunt in eum, qui diversis plagis innocentem puerum afficientes, membratim laniabant et tandem crudeli morte perimerunt, corpusque exanime et exangue longius a villa in dumis et vepribus absconderunt. Deus autem corpus sui martyris a bestiis et avibus conservans intactum, inventum est a quodam rustico, qui ibi iuxta terram arabat. Et ad hoc spectaculum vicinis convocatis, exortum est murmur in populo, quod impii Iudei hoc facinus perpetrassent; sicut etiam ancilla quedam christiana Iudeis serviens testabatur, que asseruit, se per rimam parietis premissa conspexisse. Quam ob rem homines illius terre longe vel prope positi furore repleti, in miseros Iudeos crudeliter exarserunt, quosdam suffocantes, alios cum uxoribus et parvulis concremantes, alios submergentes ac plures gladio perimentes. Tantum illi qui se in castris et municionibus nobilium recipere poterant ab huiusmodi peste vix tuebantur. Corpusque venerabile martyris translatum est Bacharacum, et statim ibi ad honorem Dei et sui martyris capella construitur opere sumptuoso. Cuius mortem preciosam in conspectu suo Dominus pie creditur multis miraculis declarasse. Ad cuius tumulum spe venie peregrinorum turbe de propinquis et longinquis regionibus catervatim cucurrerunt.

Selections from the Werner Story in the Acta Sanctorum

The central texts pertinent to our discussion have been presented in Chapter 2, above. Here, these texts are placed in a broader setting. Much of the testimony derives from the canonization trial that was the Bollandists' principal source. Many testimonies are nearly identical, which would raise a modern researcher's suspicions. The Bollandists judged the transcript legitimate, hence, its contents, too. In fact, their discussion of sources is punctilious, especially about the actual date of Werner's passion. It is a window into Bollandist method, justifying its presentation here at some length. What repeats is the theme of Werner as the three bodies of Christ, true, mystical, and real. At one point Werner is warned that the Jews will "eat" him, *comedent*, recalling the text in Guillaume le Breton.

Apr. II
XIX APRILIS.
DE S. VVERNHERO PVERO VVESALAE A IVDAEIS OCCISO, BACHERACI DEPOSITO, AD RHENVM IN DIOECESI TREVIRENSI,

[Praefatio]

Wernherus puer, Wesaliae occisus, Bacheraci depositus, ad Rhenum in dioecesi Trevirensi (S.)
[Col. 0697C]

Immane seculis omnibus in Christum & Christianos Iudaeorum odium fuit, qui illos quotidie devovent, & atrociter persequuntur, eorum pueros furtim abducunt & crudeliter mactant; [A Iudaeis plurimi pueri occisi,] *potißimum illis diebus, quibus vel suum ipsi Pascha agunt, vel Ecclesiae Catholica paßionem & mortem Christi Salvatoris pie solet venerari. Ita S. Simon puer Tridenti, & S. Ioannettus puer in dioecesi Coloniensi, impie a Iudaeis occisi, proponuntur in hoc opere nostro ad diem* XXIV *Martii; item S. VVilhelmus puer, Norwici in Anglia; & S. Richardus, Parisiis ab eisdem Iudaeis interempti referuntur* XXV *Martii: ubi etiam agitur de aliis pueris simili perfidae gentis rabie interfectis. Eodem modo a crudelißimis illis occisus Rudolphus puer*, [& S. Wernherus Wesaliae in dioecesi Trevirensi.] *colitur* XVII *Aprilis; & S. VVernherus puer, de quo hic agimus, trucidatus est VVesaliae, dioecesis Trevirensis oppido, in laeva Rheni ripa, inter Bacheracum (ubi corpus occisi fuit depositum)*. ...

[tum ex Processu ad canonizationê] *Ceterum nulla res magis nos iuvit ad gloriam sancti pueri illustrandam, quam insignis Collegii nostri Trevirensis Codex membraneus, sub fide Notariorum septem fidelißime descriptus anno* MCCCCXXIX, *studio VVinandi Pastoris Bacheracensis, ad B. VVernheri cultum promovendum & solennem ejusdem canonizationem impetrandam, zelosißime satagentis: cujus voti compotem factum persuaderet Legenda recentior, Vesontione post annum* MDXLVIII *scripta (ubi dicitur VVernherus, sive ut ibi scribitur Vernerius, a Martino V Pontifice maximo in Divorum catalogum relatus) si vel minimum hujusmodi assertionis fundamentum appareret in aliquo vetustiori auctore Tunc* [Col. 0698A] *autem id factum esse debuisset ultimo anno Martini, qui fuit post mortem Sancti, non* CXX *annus, ut dicit Legenda illa, sed* CXLIV. *Dabimus ex ea historiam translati Vesontionem digiti, cujus occasione assumptus ibidem est in Patronum Viticolarum,* [datur, ante ultimam inventionem] *erecta sub ejusdem nomine Sodalitate: & huic gratificari volens Fr. Eusebius Capucinus Legendam praedictam Gallicae reddidit, vulgavitque anno* MDCXXI.

Porro Treverensis, quam dixi, Codex, aliud non est quam Processus, juridice formatus, auctoritate Apostolici Legati, Iordani Cardinalis Vrsini; anno MCCCCXXVIII, *praedicti Papae Martini anno* XI; *cui verbotenus in-*

seruntur omnia de S. Wernhero monumenta, usque ad illum annum jam inde ab ipsius paßionis tempore, publicis privatisve litteris consignata; ex quibus hoc loco post Historiam paßionis ejusque Epitomen jam indicatam, dabimus primo [Col. 0698B] *Synopsim miraculorum nonaginta, intra primos duos a martyrio menses patratorum.* . . .

His ita deductis, quid attinet rei gestae testimonium ab Annalium scriptoribus petere? Dabimus tamen ex Boemundi Archiepiscopi Trevirensis gestis Mss. illustre compenpendium Paßionis istius: de qua etiam agunt Henricus Stero Altahensis in Bavaria monachus, in Annalibus a Marquardo [Col. 0698C] *Frehero tomo 1 scriptorum Germanicorum editis, tunc cum res gesta est vivens; & Steronis aequalis Siffridus Presbyter, lib. 2, Epitomes inter scriptores editos a Ioanne Pistorio; & Trithemius in Chronico Hirzaugiensi. Accuratißimus inter eos Siffridus ad annum* MCCLXXXVII, Hoc anno, *inquit*, felix adolescens Wernherus excruciatus est a Judaeis, & occisus in die Parasceves, ad littus Rheni fluminis, in civitate Wesalia, & in oppido Bacherach sepultus: cujus sanctitatem miracula ibidem protestantur. *Trithemius ad eumdem annunt* Abbatis Crafftonis anno quinto, Judaei quemdam puerum Christianum, ex villa Wamraid oriundum, furtive rapientes, ad oppidum Wesaliense juxta Rhenum secum abducunt, eumque pro recipiendo sanguine ejus, XIII Kalendas Maji, acubus & cultris pungentes, post longum martyrium crudeliter occidunt. *Erravit tamen in eo quod furtim raptum Wesaliamque adductum credidit, qui ultro eo venit suamque operam Ludaeis pro mercede locavit: cetera verius, ubi ait:* cujus corpusculum in oppido Bacherach humatum usque in praesentem diem, . . . *Stero eamdem* [Col. 0698D] *miraculorum famam pro suo tempore verbis fere similibus expreßit, sed erravit cum* Pacherat *adscripsit* dioecesi Herbipolensi; *magis autem cum signavit annum* MCCLXXXVIII.

[occisi anno 1287,] *Etenim annus martyrii certißimus, nec in dubium revocandus, est millesimus ducentesimus octogesimus septimus, quo Pascha celebratum fuit* VI *die Aprilis: & consequenter (quod valde notandum est) festum Ascensionis incidit in* XV *Maji, & festum Pentecostes in* XXV *ejusdem: qui dies aliique plurimi, cum suis Dominicis & Feriis, accuratißime signantur in Synopsi miraculorum, quae mox ob obitu ejus sunt patrata, incipiendo a Vigilia Apostolorum Philippi & Iacobi idest ab ultima die Aprilis, quando credimus corpus cum solenni pompa juxta Bacheracum in ecclesia S. Cuniberti depositum fuisse.* . . . *Verum difficultas est quomodo cum hoc consistat, quod in iisdem Actis dicitur idem S. Wernherus, cum in Coena Domini corpus Christi sumpsisset captus a Iudaeis; quodque exinde deductum* [Col. 0698E] *velut consequens, post annos centum quadraginta, Winandus Pastor Bacheracensis inseruit novae historiae seu Officio a se composito, objisse Wernerum* ipsa die mortis Christi aut sepulturae. *Miraeus, scriptor alias accuratus, nullam hic difficultatem animadvertens, in fastis Belgicis atque Burgundicis scripsit, quod Iudaei* anno MCCLXXXVII die Parasceves, qui tunc erat XIX mensis Aprilis, in Vesalia superiore Wernerum adolescentem forcipibus & cultro dilaniarunt. *Difficultas autem in eo est quod dicto anno Pascha fuerit celebratum a Christianis die* VI *Aprilis, atque adeo Coenae Domini die ejusdem mensis* III. [cum fere ab initio mensis fuisset in manibus Iudaeorum,] *Observo igitur Iudaicum Pascha, quod dicto anno* MCCLXXXVI *celebratum fuerat die* XXV *Martii Feria* III, *juxta resolutionem Rabbinorum Amstelodamensium de hac re consultorum, impiis fuisse praeteritum, quando in manus ipsorum sanguinolentas venit innocens Wernherus; adeoque eosdem nihil causa habuisse, quo minus destinatam caedem differrent in aliud quodvis sibi opportunum tempus. Distulisse autem illam ad dies saltem quatuordecim, credibile mihi facit, monitus ancillae indicio Scultetus, & ad eam in qua Wernherus detinebatur domum accedens: qui licet pecunia delinitus in suorum tortorum manibus dereliquerit adolescentem, nequidquam obtestantem ut ejus jussu dimitteretur: non credo tamen id fuisse facturum, si ipsi crudeli carnificinae* [Col. 0698F] *superveniens tam immani in scelere deprehendisset Iudaeos, a quibus quantamlibet pecuniae summam potuisset extorquere, ob manifeste designatum licet non consummatum facinus; ipsumque Wernerum metu gravioris mali obligare ad tacendam injuriam sibi irrogatam. Neque vero magnus hic error fuerit, si initium finemque paßionis conjunxerint ii qui rei gestae seriem, non ex ipsa Iudaeorum confeßione, sed ex indiciis panum distinctis cognovere: ipsius autem hanc puto fuisse seriem. Primo redeuntem a sumpta Communione Wernherum (quod utrum ipsa die coenae Domini an alia intra Paschale tempus fecerit, puto ex relatione tam parum accurata haud satis constare) conati fuerint eamdem extorquere, suspensum in caput retitinendo aliquamdiu:*

cum autem id non succederet, servatum adolescentem ad consilia alia postea sumenda: quae cum ancillae Christianae suboluissent, merito formidanti ne primis deteriora succederent, adierit illa Scultetum & significarit quomodo herili in domo Christianus quidam habitus fuisset atq; etiamnunc teneretur, verosimiliter occidendus: [securitatem peragendi sceleris praestolantium.] *Iudaei autem ingressum ad se Schultetum praeoccuparint, aliam quamvis detentionis causam mentiendo, & sic efficiendo ut ipse externi & pauperis adolescentis, praetensas rationes refellentis, defensionem non satis aequus audierit; ejusque adversariis, periculum excusantibus turbarum si publice a Sculteto educeretur,* [Col. 0699A] *ac promittentibus illum clam educere, consensum praebuerit, nihil ultra solicitus. Tunc vero dies aliquot expectaverint Iudaei, si forte interim requireretur a consanguineis aut notis: cumque nihil a quoquam moveri viderent, tutumque crederent quidvis audere, rursus convenerint ad eum excruciandum die* XVII *Aprilis, illaque & sequenti feria* VI *habuerint in tormentis, sub quibus tandem spiritum beatum efflarit die Et tunc quidem nihil egerint circa cadaver, ne sacrosanctum suum scilicet Sabbatum violarent, postera autem Dominica die extulerint atque inter vepres abdiderint; ubi prodigiosis noctium aliquot luminibus indicatum vicinis, & Bacheraci in praetorio expositum fuit, donec in sacello S. Cuniberti deponeretur: ad quae omnia sufficiunt decem illi dies, qui usque ad finem mensis restabant, unde sumitur initium narrandorum miraculorum.*

Historia Passionis
Ex Ms. Antverpiensi Societatis Iesu.

Wernherus puer, Wesaliae occisus, Bacheraci depositus, ad Rhenum in dioecesi Trevirensi (S.)

[Col. 0699C]

Prologus I

Wernherus dicitur, secundum quod sonat Teutonicum, [Nominis etymon & mystica ratio:] Abactor vel Praemonitus, quia a se tres abegit inimicos, & vita sua docet abigendos, vanitatem videlicet mundi, invidiam diaboli, & desideria carnis. Primo a se abegit vanitatem mundi, per virtuosam simplicitatem, & manuum suarum operationem; secundo suggestiones diaboli, per vitae innocentiam, tertio desideria carnis, per virginalem puritatem: vel quia abegit a se infidelitatem, per fidei integritatem & veram religionis Christianae confessionem; ambitiosam hujus mundi vanitatem, per sui contemptum & amaram passionem; carnales delicias, per virginalis continentiae integritatem.

[triplex praerogativa,] Et propter haec tria promeruit praerogativum triplex, videlicet Martyrum, Virginum, & Confessorum. Primum promeruit per amarissimam martyrii [Col. 0699D] palmam, [Martyrii,] non quidem subito ut multi Martyres, quia triduum puer pius & Catholicus suum continuavit martyrium, martyrium utique novum, stupendum, & singulare. Primo namque iste Martyr inclytus, loco Christi passus est: quia dum Judaei ipsum corpus Christi verum habere non poterant, exarserunt in ipsum corpus mysticum. Secundo in ipso Christus passus est: videntes namque Judaei quod corpus Christi verum ex ipso extorquere non possent, illud tamen venerabile Sacramentum, cui contumeliam inferre intendebant, affecerunt tormentorum contumeliis in ipso puero. Tertio in Christo passus est, quia per illud venerabile Sacramentum fuit ille benedictus puer Christo incorporatus, in Christo manens, & Christus cum eo. Quarto Martyr Christi passus est cum Christo, quia eodem tempore, & eodem die, quibus illud mysterium ab Ecclesia frequentatur; vel quia realiter per passionem secutus est servus Dominum suum. Quinto pro Christo, quia dum perfidi Christum regnantem in caelis persequi non possunt, persequuntur pro eo Christianum ejus cultorem. Sexto pro Christo, quia sicut Christus passus est, ut fieret & salvaretur Christianus, sic Christianus patitur propter Christum, ut exaltetur fides [Col. 0699E] Christiana, & glorificetur Deus. Beatus ergo qui persecutionem patitur propter Christum.

Prologus II

Justum enim & dignum est, illum piis commendare memoriis Christifidelium, in quo Christus, & cum quo Christus, & pro quo Christus passus est; & cujus patientia exemplariter ad aeternam vitam erudimur.

Post hoc veniens ad Imperiale oppidum Trevericam Wesaliam, [Wesaliae operam suam Iudaeis locat,] in ea laborem, quem quaesivit, invenit. Hunc itaque juvenem perfidi Judaei, in eodem oppido commorantes, callide ad laborem inducunt; ad quem se promptum reddit: sicque ad [Col. 0700D] profundum ergastulum pro portando terram puerum induxerunt. Instante autem solennitate Paschali, dixit puero hospita sua, apud quam hospitabatur: Certe, Wernhere, cave te a perfidis Judaeis: quia instat dies parasceves. Sine dubio te comedent. Respondit puer columbina simplicitate perfectionis verbulum, & verae spei in Christo expressivum; Hoc, inquit, committo Deo. [The Jews of course capture Werner.] Nam primo apprehendentes puerum, obstruxerunt vocem ejus, per globum plumbeum ejus ori impressum, ne vociferaretur. Deinde ligaverunt sive suspenderunt ad statuam ligneam, ad hoc paratam, per pedes sursum & caput deorsum, ut haberent *corpus Christi verum*, quod eodem die benedictus puer acceperat.

Sed frustrato eorum studio, se penitus dederunt [Col. 0700E] *ad martyrizandum corpus ipsum mysticum*, & ad tollendum ejus vitam & sanguinem; & sic cum flagellis varia & profunda in corpus ejus inflixerunt vulnera. Accipientes nihilominus cultrum, [vacuatur sanguine:] quod usque hodie penes ipsum continetur, inciderunt venas ejus per omnem partem corporis; nec non cum forcipibus, in poenam etiam amarissimam, *de venis sanguinem expresserunt* in pedibus, manibus, collo & capite, sic quod nulla apparuerat in eo sanitas. Sic perfidi Judaei illum sanctum puerum triduo tenuere suspensum in illa statua lignea donec cruentare desiit, versando saepe corpus, modo caput sursum, modo deorsum.

In hac domo Judaei famulam habuerunt Christianam, [who is corrupted by the Jews with money, and when the boy calls out for help, he says:]: *Si tu mihi non subveneris, subveniat mihi misericors Deus, & dilecta ejus Mater*.

[corpus, quod avehi longius non potuit,] Sicque sancto puero a Sculteto derelicto, & a Judaeis interfecto, mox cum dies abscesserat, & se coeca nox adduxerat, acceperunt sancti Martyris corpus, suo rubricatum sanguine: [The Jews then want to be rid of the body, which they try to sink in the river. However,] nam artem invenire nequibant, [inter vepres abjicitur:] quomodo illud corpus in aquis submergerent: sed in valle prope Bacharacum parvula cryptula apparuit, septa spinis atque vepribus, ubi nunc S. Wilhelmi Ordinis [Col. 0701A] claustrum, dictum Wyndesbach, est situm; ibi sancti Martyris corpus projecerunt, & mox inde recesserunt.

Additional testimony repeats the central charges:

Col. 0717

Item, quod idem venerabilis puerilis adolescens ab eisdem Judaeis fuerit suspensus ad statuam deorsum, [a Iudeis suspensus triduo,] ut Judaei haberent Christi corpus verum. Quo frustrato studio, se penitus dederunt ad martyrizandum corpus ipsum mysticum, & ad tollendum ejus vitam & sanguinem. Item quod iidem perfidi Judaei istum sanctum puerum triduo tenuere suspensum in lignea statua, ejus sanguinem per omnem partem corporis sitienter incidentes, hodie testibus statua in loco suae passionis, & cultro, sudario, [sanguine copioso extracto,] ac cereo lineo, sanguinolentis, in Bacheraco in loco sepulturae ejus. Item quod medio tempore passionis ejus, per ancillam Judaeorum Christianam, sancti pueri passio fuerit prodita, & ad [Col. 0717E] Eberhardum, Scultetum tunc Wesaliensem, deducta. Item quod idem Eberhardus Scultetus venerit ad locum certaminis, & a S. Wernhero exultationis voce fuerit inclinatus pro sui liberatione, [a Sculieto derelictus sit,] scilicet temporali. Item quod *idem Scultetus Eberhardus, capta iniquitatis mercede a Judaeis, puero in tormentis adjutorium negaverit,* & quod sanctus puer neganti responderit: si mihi non subveneris, subveniat mihi misericors Deus, & dilecta mater ejus. Item quod de praemissis omnibus, & singulis sit publica vox, & fama historiae, ac diversa cantica.

[Primut testatur] Et primo Dominus Joannes Fudersack *Testis* CLXXXI, juratus, receptus, admissus & examinatus, sexaginta annorum, non excommunicatus, aut crimine irretitus famoso, satis abundans in têporalibus, nihil lucri seu emolumenti sperans, at solum Deum & ejus gloriam prae manibus retinens; primo dixit, . . . : quodque ipsa die coenae Domini in Wesalia fuit communicatus, [S. Wernheri nativitatem] *& ab impiis Judaeis crudeliter martyrizatus, in eo quaerentibus Christi Corpus: verum quod dum habere non poterant, suam saevitiam converterunt in Corpus Christi mysticum, scilicet puerum sanctum, & ipsum suspenderunt ad statuam, quae hodie in Wesalia [Col. 0730F] Treverensis dioecesis, in capella sancti Spiritus, [martyrium] a cunctis in non modica habetur reverentia: & ibi eumdem sanctum puerum occiderunt, prout haec in Legenda antiqua ejusdem Sancti.* . . .

Appendix Two   Translation of the Blois Letters

The Letter from Loches

My translation. See Chapter 4, above, for a discussion of this letter's significance. A variant translation by Robert Chazan appears in id., *Church, State, and Jew in the Middle Ages* (New York: Behrman House, 1980), 115–17.

The community of Loches reported that before the "trouble,"[1] they [the principals in the story] had escaped in peace. Only the delator was imprisoned. I, Baruch b. Meir, will now tell you the story. A young man of Loches desired a maiden, and he asked her hand from her father and her other relatives.[2] To which they answered: We would drown her before letting you have her. The youth then secretly betrothed the young woman before witnesses.[3] He went to her father, and said: We have been united [as a married couple]; your opposition was for naught. The father replied: This abomination will not work.[4] [But his threat was empty]; the youth approached the prince (*ha-sar*).[5] He informed on them,[6] and they [the father and his relatives] were imprisoned.[7] They were released; praise be the Lord. But he [the delator!] is still in custody. We also have not discovered whether, heaven forbid, this trouble has embarrassed them.

And because of our many sins, the [bodies] have not been released for burial. The bonfire was [set] in a low place [a ravine of some sort]. And the ruler [*ha-shilton*] ordered the bodies to be covered with ashes, dirt, and stones. We heard that the ruler was furious at the goyim who [threw] wood and staves aplenty on those who came out of the fire and killed them.[8]

After I finished what I had to say, I was reminded of one *kedoshah*, a holy woman, who was forgotten.[9] Praised be they who are numbered among those [lit., whose number is] with God, whom we have not found, and who[se charred bodies] are perhaps as one with the two maidens and the young man who were not wrapped [as the halachah requires] in a shroud and have been set onto the byways of Creation. Blessed are they who underwent this trial.

The First Letter from Paris

This is the letter from the [Jewish] leaders of Paris: This is a day of good news for God's people, Israel, from the great king who turned his humanity toward us for the better. We went to the king in the village of Poissy, to prostrate ourselves before him regarding the following matter. When we saw that he welcomed us with peaceful [good] intentions, we said to him, that we would prefer to speak to him in secret.[10] He responded: No, speak in a clear and loud voice [saying what you have to say publicly]. He then summoned all his retinue [lit., his servers], those who were in the compound [*migdol*: the large area],[11] and instructed them: Hear now what Count Theobald did [*shilton*]—may he and his all be sterile this coming year—and [judge] whether he acted uprightly, and all is well, or whether he violated the law, for which he should pay, even with his person. Even I am horrified about what he did. But now the Jews in my lands have no need to fear what this evil one did in his realms. For about those in the town of Pontiyeh [Pontoise][12] and about those in the city of Janville it has also been said by the throngs (lit., peoples of the world, ʾ*umot ha-ʿolom*)[13] that the Jews have done such a thing [ritual murder]. Yet when this charge was brought before me, it was found baseless. The king also spoke to the Jews of events in Ponterirt [also Pontoise],[14] about how [the people there had the allegedly murdered child] declared a saint in Paris, which was nonsense. The same applied here [to Blois]. So let all the Jews in my land know that I do not suspect [them of doing] this. Even if the goyim find a goy who has been killed, whether in a city or in an open field, I shall not hold it up to the Jews [lit., say nothing to them]. Hence, do not be apprehensive about this [Blois]. [Still], we cannot yet go there. But the king has sent a patent seal [a sealed message] throughout his land, saying that the Jews should be left in peace and quiet. All his officials are to do honor to the Jews and to all Israel, to protect their persons and their possessions even more than they have done in the past. He said much more, too, which we have not written. Praise and thanks to the great king.

Letter to Rabbi Yom Tov

What is revealed [or known] I shall now send on to Rabbi Yom Tov. He, in turn, may transmit it to the holy rabbi [(implying) Jacob Tam]¹⁵ as a true record, to give thanks to the Rock of our Salvation, who turned the heart of the king [putatively Louis VII] in our favor. For when he heard this evil thing, he jumped up in shock and froze in his tracks [lit., for one, or a full hour]. And he said to the queen: "Today, your brother has struck at my crown and shattered it. The saints have warned us to preserve their [the Jews'] persons, and their belongings, too, like the pupil of our eye."¹⁶ The king was beside himself about what [Theobald] had done, and he did not cavil about making his displeasure known. And his princes [or courtiers, *sarim*] asked whether they should avenge us.¹⁷ To which he answered: "No, that is wrong. Not that. My intention is to honor and protect them twice as much as we have in the past."¹⁸ And he sent his seal throughout his land to his officials, to protect the Jews' persons and their goods as the apple of their [the courtiers'] eye.¹⁹

About the Bishop of Sens

Yesterday, I approached the bishop of Sens²⁰ to discuss the release of the prisoners who had been jailed by his brother, the evil count, as well as the forcibly converted *(ha-ʾanusim,* the sons of righteousness.²¹ I paid [lit., bribed him with]²² 102 pounds and 100 more for the count. I also gave guarantees.²³ And he issued a sealed rescript to have them removed from jail, including the youths who had been "forced," whom he asked [whether they wanted; or just "requested" of them] to return to the Lord [to Judaism].[24] They came proudly;[25] and all the prisoners were freed from the grip of the evil one [the count], but only with what they had on their backs, no more. He [the count] retained all their goods, including their bonds [*hovot*] and possessions.[26] He [also promised that he][27] would put it into writing that we could [safely] speak out, that they would make no more false accusations against the Jews, for whatever reason. All this was done for us through the hand of God.

The Keys to the Synagogue

And about the keys to the synagogue, they spoke lies and deceit. There was simply nothing. It was true that the ruler [*ha-shilton*][28] said to Joseph ha-Kohen: "I hear the Jews curse me." To which Joseph answered: "My lord, do not believe this. Nobody entertained such an idea. And who would think to do such a thing? My lord should dismiss the idea." His [the ruler's] anger subsided. May our Rock guard us from the hand of the plotters and the [grip] of all our enemies, and [may He] bring us into the light of day. Amen, may God do so.[29]

The Second Letter from Paris

And this is what our brothers in Paris wrote us, although we do not have the actual letter in our possession, because it was sent elsewhere. But I did set down a memorandum:[30] When the king returned from Flanders, the heads [lit., officers] of Paris [Jewry] and from other [Jewish] locales appeared and petitioned the king's vassals [lit., servants], asking to speak to the king. And they were told to come along. When they saw that the king gave them his peace, to which they responded in kind, they were deeply pleased. They said: Our lord the king, we wish to speak to you in secret.[31] The king answered that he would not treat with them privately, in secret, but he would say what he had to so openly, that Theobald has committed a mortal sin [lit., he sinned in his soul].³² I have taken this badly indeed, and I am dismayed. Nor do I believe that the [Jews] killed any Gentile, ever, not in Ponte Rirt [Pontoise],³³ where they made him into a saint, nor this time in the case of Theobald. Do not be afraid, for I shall add honor to your honor. He then had it proclaimed³⁴ throughout his kingdom to honor the Jews twice as much as in the past and to protect their persons and their possessions more than previously. And the *haver*³⁵ Mr.³⁶ Natan ben Meshullam is going about with 220 pounds, trying to ransom³⁷ those who had been imprisoned and [hoping] to have those who died interred [halachically]; oh, might he succeed!³⁸ [To complete matters,] Count Heinrich [*sic*],³⁹ the brother of the evil [Theobald], expressed his sorrow over the affair, and he said: We have not found in the Jew's Torah that it is licit to kill a Christian. Just yesterday, on the eve of Easter, a rumor was heard in Épernay, which I did not believe. In any case [notes the author of the memorandum] money was given to still the rumor.⁴⁰

Letter from Troyes

We the insignificant ones of Troyes have decreed upon ourselves and our community not to summon to the *huppah* [any] except those of the city itself.⁴¹ And if a *minyan* [quorum of ten men] is not to be found there, it will be completed [by people] from somewhere else.⁴² We have also bound ourselves not to wear cloaks of fine silk for a three-year period, neither man nor woman. We, the men [or residents], have also determined to fast every Monday and Thursday until the New Year (Rosh haShannah). This [we say] should be the rule in all of the land of Lotharingia. Perhaps God will hear your voices⁴³ and bestow his wonders upon us, so that all should know [He has acted to avenge, or requite] the blood of those *hasidim* [the martyrs, presumably of Blois].⁴⁴ However, this last, you should erase from my letter, lest converts and informers see it.⁴⁵ May the Rock of Israel give you only good tidings and words of peace, love of justice, and the hatred of evil, desire of truth, freedom from lies, a straight tongue, adherence to propriety, and distance from rage.

Notes

Preface

1. *Acta Sanctorum a Ioanne Bollando S.I. colli feliciter coepta. A Godefrido Henschenio et Daniele Papebrochio, S.I., aucta* . . . (Antwerp 1668, for the volume most used in this study, March III) is the great Bollandist work, with saints listed by their day; reprinted under the editorship of the Socii Bollandiani, 69 vols. (Paris, 1863–40). Cited hereafter as *ActaSS*.

2. For an earlier important revisionist reading of one aspect of these texts, see David Wachtel, "The Ritual and Liturgical Commemoration of Two Medieval Persecutions" (MA thesis, Columbia University, 1995), which Wachtel has most graciously shown me; see also Chapter 4 on Wachtel. The letters appear in Abraham Haberman, *Sefer gezerot ashkenaz ve-zarfat* (Jerusalem, 1945), 142–46.

3. Félix Vernet, "Juifs et Chrétiens," in *Dictionnaire apologétique de la foi catholique II* (Paris, 1910–12), cols. 1651–1764.

4. Gabrielle Spiegel, *Romancing the Past: The Rise of Vernacular Prose Historiography in Thirteenth-Century France* (Berkeley, 1993).

5. Karl F. Morrison, *History as a Visual Art in the Twelfth-Century Renaissance* (Princeton, 1990), and see esp. xix, 36, 67, 85, an extraordinarily ambitious attempt to grasp the essence of medieval historiography, especially that with a spiritual bent.

6. Jean-Claude Schmitt, *La Conversion d'Hermann le Juif: Autobiographie, histoire et fiction* (Paris, 2003), 56–58.

7. We might note this last idea expressed in terms of changing concepts of memory and commemoration by Pierre Nora, "The Era of Commemoration," in *Realms of Memory*, ed. id., trans. Arthur Goldhammer (New York, 1998), 3: 609–38.

8. Bernard Joassart, *Hippolyte Delehaye: Hagiographie critique et modernisme*, 2 vols. (Brussels: Société des Bollandistes, 2000).

9. Most recently, Kathleen Biddick, *The Typology of the Imaginary: Circumcision, Technology, History* (Philadelphia, 2003), has also undertaken to place supersession at the center of the centuries-long Jewish-Christian encounter, seeking out continuous imagery as I do here. Her focus is on what she calls "graphic technologies";

mine is on persevering images of impurity. Nonetheless, her conclusion, stated on page 1, that "the purported 'secularization' of modernity ... has never overtaken this core Christian conception of supersession," is one that also informs this present study. Both of us, needless to add, have worked independently.

10. This was the main point of a paper delivered at the University of Haifa on March 26, 2003, by Ada Tagger-Cohen, who kindly provided me with the following two references: James C. Moyer, "Hittite and Israelite Cultic Practices: A Selected Comparison," in *Scripture in Context II: More Essays on the Comparative Method*, ed. William Hallo, James Moyer, and Leo Perdue (Winona Lake, Ind., 1983), 29–32, citing an ancient Hittite text, as here, and the reference to Isa. 66:3–4a; and, too, David P. Wright, *The Disposal of Impurity: Elimination Rites in the Bible and in Hittite and Mesopotamian Literature* (Atlanta, 1987), 106: "Since a dog approached the [altar] table and consumed the daily [sacrificial offering of] bread, they 'consume' [destroy] the table." Wright places this under the heading: "cultic pollution by a dog." See also Simo Parpola, *Assyrian Prophecies*, State Archives of Assyria, vol. 9 (Helsinki, 1997), passim, for general affinities between ancient religious perceptions and later ones, including the concept that God has a son, xxxvi–xxxviii (I thank Gershon Galil for this reference).

11. I thank Devorah Dimant for this point. Though implying more a state of filth than impurity, the idea carried on. In his great poem "In the City of Slaughter," on the massacre of Jews at Kishinev in 1903, the Hebrew poet Hayim Nahman Bialik wrote that the Jews "died like dogs." English by A. M. Klein in Alan Mintz, *Responses to Catastrophe in Hebrew Literature* (New York, 1984): 132–41. In the Babylonian Talmud, *Abodah zarah* 54b, one finds "You call the idol a dog," which resonates with issues like those discussed here but is clearly not as condemnatory.

12. Not everyone would agree with my belief. A clear attempt to persuade audiences that there have been distinct epochs and fundamental qualitative change with respect to thought about Jews and Judaism is the 1998 Vatican teaching document "We Remember: A Reflection on the Shoah." To make this distinction, the authors invoke the well-worn terms "anti-Judaism" and "anti-Semitism." But their attempt fails, as the document's authors themselves acknowledge, and as we shall see just prior to this study's end. In any case, historical discourse as a whole would profit by discarding the distinction between anti-Semitism and anti-Judaism from its lexicon. Too often, these two "anti's" serve as escape hatches to open and slip through rather than to delve fully into phenomena that require careful exposition. Anti-Judaism and anti-Semitism are named "causes," rather than the "effects" that they really are. In this book, neither term appears (except on two carefully chosen occasions). Besides, the neat detachment between anti-Judaism and anti-Semitism has always seemed to me more historiographical than historical. Modern racial theories adopted and perfected by the political anti-Semites of the nineteenth and twentieth centuries, who formed "anti-Semitic" (their own term) political parties,

are essentially one more expression of the centuries-old fear of Jewish pollution.

13. Cited in Kenneth Stow, *Catholic Thought and Papal Jewry Policy, 1555–1593* (New York, 1977), 42: "nilhil profecto est tam voluntarium quam religio"; David de Pomis, *Enarratio brevis, de senum affectibus praecavendis, atque curandis . . .* (Venice, 1588), 80.

Introduction

1. The papal prayer of March 26, 2000, reads: "God of our fathers, you chose Abraham and his descendants to bring your Name to the Nations; we are deeply saddened by the behaviour of those who in the course of history have caused these children of yours to suffer, and asking your forgiveness we wish to commit ourselves to genuine brotherhood with the people of the Covenant." At the same time, one might accuse the pope of double-talk, noting that *Nostra aetate*, the "Declaration on the Relationship of the Church to non-Christian Religions," of October 28, 1965, at the Second Vatican Council, states in its paragraph 4 that "all Christ's faithful, who as people of faith are daughters and sons of Abraham (see Gal. 3:7)," which supports the notion that the children of Abraham are only those who believe in Christ. Hence, the pope would mean only Christians, perhaps Catholics alone. Yet, I believe the pope was being purposefully ambivalent, allowing all listeners to hear the text as they preferred. However, in the context of the locale, as I go on to explain above, he certainly meant Jews as Jews, too, therefore tacitly emending the statement of Vatican II. See Chapter 7 for further clarification.

2. Some might say the pope was preempting the Jewish holy site for the Church; the claims of the Church to Jerusalem—and well into the twentieth century—are well documented; most recently, see Sergio Minerbi, *Vatican and Zionism: Conflict in the Holy Land, 1895–1925* (New York, 1990). However, I would not attribute intentional deception to the pope. At the most, he may have been saying this is a holy site for three peoples, hence, it should—politically—be internationalized, long the Church's policy. But this would not take away from the main point: the legitimately autonomous validity of the site as a holy site of Jews. I thank Magda Teter for the observation about the ambivalence of the site's identity, as well as that of the prayer's intended "children."

3. See Congregation for the Doctrine of the Faith, "Declaration '*Dominus Iesus*' on the Unicity and Salvific Universality of Jesus Christ and the Church," www.vatican.va/roman_curia/congregations/cfaith/documents/rc_con_cfaith_doc_20000806_dominus-iesus_en.html (accessed May 7, 2005). On January 17, 2003, the then Cardinal Ratzinger reiterated a position he had taken already in October 1987 against religious relativity.

4. Some tout it even more than Ratzinger and call *Dominus Iesus* heretical. See, e.g., "A Critical Analysis of Ratzinger's Dominus Jesus by Rev. Donald J.

Sanborn, 4th April 2001," www.geocities.com/orthopapism/ahrs.html (accessed May 7, 2005), Sanborn writes:

> Text no. 1 "This Church, constituted and organized as a society in the present world, subsists in [*subsistit in*] the Catholic Church, governed by the Successor of Saint Peter and by the Bishops in communion with him."
> Qualification: HERETICAL
> The quotation is directly lifted from *Lumen Gentium* at Vatican II, and represents the fundamental heresy of Vatican II concerning the Church. Fr. Curzio Nitoglia, of the Institute of Our Mother of Good Counsel, explained the error of this text in an article that appeared in their journal *Sodalitium*:
> "What does this formula actually mean? It was chosen deliberately in order to deny that the Church of Christ is only the Catholic Church. '*Subsistit in*' means, in fact, that the Church of Christ is found *in* the Catholic Church, but is not exclusively *identified with* the Catholic Church."
> "The change of *est* (Pius XII) to *subsistit* [16] (*Gaudium et Spes*) took place for ecumenical reasons," explains Fr. Mucci, S.J. in *Civiltà cattolica* (December 5, 1988). And Fr. Louis Bouyer writes that thanks to the '*subsistit*' introduced by the Council, one has sought to "propose again the idea of the one Church, even if it is presently divided among the diverse Christian Churches, as if among many branches." [17] This idea was taken up again by John Paul II in Canterbury.

We get from Sanborn a clear measure of how strongly supersessionism, presented as the need of the Catholic Church to be the sole beneficiary of God's choice, as alone identical with the "Church of Christ," may be deemed cardinal. Perhaps it was in reflecting on thinking like Sanborn's that David Berger, a well-known scholar of Jewish-Christian polemic, tried in an essay addressed to a forum of Orthodox rabbis to distinguish levels of supersessionism, saying that Ratzinger was within acceptable bounds with respect to Jewish-Catholic dialogue in *Dominus Iesus*, and that Ratzinger was turning inward, not outward, missionarily. Berger writes:

> At this point, we need to confront the real question, to wit, is there anything objectionable about this position? In a dialogical environment in which the term "supersessionism" has been turned into an epithet by both Jews and Christians, this may appear to be a puzzling question. We need to distinguish, however, between two forms of supersessionism, and in my view Jews have absolutely no right to object to the form endorsed by Cardinal Ratzinger. There is nothing in the core beliefs of Christianity that requires the sort of supersessionism that sees Judaism as spiritually arid, as an expression of narrow, petty legalism pursued in the service of a vengeful God and eventually replaced by a vital religion of universal love. Such a depiction is anti-Jewish, even antise-

mitic. But Cardinal Ratzinger never describes Judaism in such a fashion. On the contrary, he sees believing Jews as witnesses through their observance of Torah to the commitment to God's will, to the establishment of his kingdom even in the pre-messianic world, and to faith in a wholly just world after the ultimate redemption. ([*Dominus Iesus*] pp. 104–105) This understanding of Jews as a witness people is very different from the original Augustinian version in which Jews testified to Christian truth through their validation of the Hebrew Bible and their interminable suffering in exile.

For Jews to denounce this sort of supersessionism as morally wrong and disqualifying in the context of dialogue is to turn dialogue into a novel form of religious intimidation. As Rabbi Joseph B. Soloveitchik understood very well, such a position is pragmatically dangerous for Jews, who become vulnerable to reciprocal demands for theological reform of Judaism, and it is even morally wrong.

Dr. David Berger, Rabbinical Council of America, "On *Dominus Iesus* and the Jews" (delivered at the 17th meeting of the International Catholic-Jewish Liaison Committee, New York, May 1, 2001), www.bc.edu/bc_org/research/cjl/articles/berger.htm (accessed July 17, 2005).

One would like to share Berger's optimism, but, as put by Kurt Hruby, who will be cited just before the end of this study, supersessionism, however presented, never stops being precisely that, hierarchic succession, and as such it is always problematic. Hruby also anticipates people, like Peter Herbeck, who say *Dominus Iesus* reaffirms unity and mission: "The goal of *Dominus Jesus* is to clear up the confusion caused by this kind of thinking. They stated their concern succinctly: 'the Church's constant missionary proclamation is endangered today by relativistic theories which seek to justify religious pluralism'" (www.renewalministries.net/booklets/WWF.htm [accessed July 17, 2005]).

5. In an interview to the Italian Catholic journal *Il sabato*, Ratzinger insisted that "Il Papa ha offerto rispetto ma anche una linea teologica: Cristo è il compimento di Abramo" (The Pope [then John Paul] has offered respect but also a clear theology: Christ is the complement of Abraham). More recently, he said: "in the Old Testament [the people of God] was the people of Israel, from Christ onwards the new people is that of his disciples" (*Il tempo*, February 27, 2004, p. 7). Finally, in his inaugural address as Pope Benedict XVI of April 24, 2005, he said: "With great affection I also greet all those who have been reborn in the sacrament of Baptism but are not yet in full communion with us; and you, my brothers and sisters of the Jewish people, to whom we are joined by a great shared spiritual heritage, one rooted in God's irrevocable promises." Yet what are those promises? We might think of Paul in Romans, speaking of the Jews ingathering (into Christianity). And the pope leaves no room for doubt, continuing further on: "Here I want to add something: both the image of the shepherd and that of the fisherman issue

an explicit call to unity. 'I have other sheep that are not of this fold; I must lead them too, and they will heed my voice. So there shall be one flock, one shepherd' (*Jn* 10:16)." This is a locus classicus calling for the union of all in Christ. In the sixteenth century, the import was messianic, and the verse John 10:16 was invoked frequently by those seeking to convert Jews; see Kenneth Stow, *Catholic Thought and Papal Jewry Policy, 1555-1593* (New York, 1977), chap. 11. The discourse of Pope Benedict is found at www.vatican.va/holy_father/benedict_xvi/homilies/documents/hf_ben-xvi_hom_20050424_inizio-pontificato_en.html (accessed May 25, 2005). By way of balance, Cardinal Walter Kasper, "The Jewish-Christian Dialogue: Foundations, Progress, Difficulties and Perspectives" (speech at the Israel Museum, Jerusalem, November 21, 2001), emphasizes "the permanent and actual salvific significance of Jewish religion for its believers." However, Kasper defended *Dominus Iesus*, claiming that it has been decontextualized. We should note that the official Vatican web site, when searched for the word "Jews," revealed papal letters issued over the past century and more—none of which concern Jews directly—but which at least once cite Colossians to the effect that there will "be no distinction between Jew, Gentile, Scythian. . . . For Christ is all and all are in Christ." This citation, as we shall see, was used by the early ninth-century Florus of Lyon to promote Agobard of Lyon's vision of a unified Society of the Faithful; see here also Gary Lease, "The Modernist Drama Revisited: Ratzinger and Kuss: Two Types," in id., *"Odd Fellows" in the Politics of Religion: Modernism, National Socialism, and German Judaism* (New York, 1995).

6. On attempts to quash all deviation from doctrinal rigidity, even in the twentieth century, see Lease, "Merry del Val and Tyrell: A Modernist Struggle," and "Merry del Val and the American Church," in id., *"Odd Fellows,"* 55–93. Lester R. Kurtz, *The Politics of Heresy: The Modernist Crisis in Roman Catholicism* (Berkeley, 1986); and Marvin R. O'Connell, *Critics on Trial: An Introduction to the Catholic Modernist Crisis* (Washington, D.C., 1994), are good introductions to the problems and nature of this crisis.

7. See esp. Jacques Kornberg, "Ignaz von Döllinger's *Die Juden in Europa*: A Catholic Polemic Against Antisemitism," *Journal for the History of Modern Theology* 6 (1999): 223–45; Giovanni Miccoli, "Santa Sede: Questione ebraica e antisemitismo fra Otto e Novecento," in *Gli ebrei di Italia*, ed. C. Vivanti (Turin, 1996), 2: 1371–1574; id., "L'Italia cattolica e il fascismo," *Rassegna mensile di Israel* 69 (2003); David I. Kertzer, *The Popes Against the Jews: The Vatican's Rome in the Rise of Modern Anti-Semitism* (New York, 2001); id., *The Kidnapping of Edgardo Mortara* (New York, 1997); and Sheryl Kroen, *Politics and Theater: The Crisis of Legitimacy in Restoration France* (Berkeley, 2000).

8. Holywar.org also regales "visitors" with the infamous *Protocols of the Elders of Zion*, virulent anti-Zionism, and the blood libel. George Bush, Dick Cheney, and Colin Powell are called "racist Jews." The site has a Norwegian address but is probably run by Italians, Italian being the language most extensively represented.

The issue here is not whether the site is representative, but its existence. Some sites like this one reproduce a vast body of relevant material by known theologians, for instance, the site that calls itself St. Michael's Cyberspace Scriptorium, much of whose material consists of articles from the 1910–12 *Catholic Encyclopedia*, papal letters, or essays by priests, principally Jesuits, and prelates like Cardinal Ratzinger/Benedict XVI. Though offbeat, from Roscoe, South Dakota, and not above suspicion on subjects like the Shoah, this site is liberal. A parallel from the Islamic world was cited in the Israeli daily *Haaretz* on September 9, 2003, speaking of the Barbie doll as a "Jewish toy . . . offensive to Islam. . . . The Committee for the Propagation of Virtue and Prevention of Vice, as the religious police [of Saudi Arabia] are officially known, lists the dolls on a section of its Web site devoted to items deemed offensive to the conservative Saudi interpretation of Islam: 'Jewish Barbie dolls, with their revealing clothes and shameful postures, accessories and tools are a symbol of decadence to the perverted West [note the assimilation of all things Western to Judaism, a pattern that follows, as we shall see below, the identification of Judaism and all things modern in Europe at the turn of the twentieth century]. Let us beware of her dangers and be careful.' A spokesman . . . speaking to The Associated Press [from Medina] claimed that Barbie was modeled after a real-life Jewish woman [the real and mythical wholly blended]." Needless to say, there are Protestant-driven anti-Semitic web sites, too. Finally, I would mention the signposts sitting at the entrance to southern towns like Holman, Mississippi, even in the 1950s: "No Niggers, No Jews, No Dogs." All three clearly polluted.

9. Pius IX, in *Quanta cura Syllabus* of December 8, 1864—citing Gregory XVI—said it was a "delirio, [especially to say that] la libertà di coscienza e dei culti essere un diritto proprio di ciascun uomo" (It is a delirium to say that every individual has the right to liberty of conscience and cult).

10. Marjorie Agosín and Emma Sepúlveda, *Amigas: Letters of Friendship and Exile* (Austin, Tex., 2001), 13.

11. Jacob Neusner and Bruce Chilton, *Jewish and Christian Doctrines: The Classics Compared* (New York, 2000), write that "intentionality of practice and observation of the integrity of one's body are together held to define an ambit of purity" (84) and stress the incorporation of all into the one body through the Eucharist (93–99). They note that 1 Cor. 12:12–13 stresses unity too, but through baptism, not the Eucharist. I thank Jeffrey Chajes for the reference to Neusner and Chilton, which reached me as this study neared completion.

12. Likewise Mark 7:24–30, esp. 27, "Let the children be fed first, for it is not fair to take the children's food and throw it to the dogs"; and, similarly, but without reference to dogs, John 6:26, 27, 35: "I am the bread of life."

13. Also recently on Paul, see John Gager, *Reinventing Paul* (New York, 2000), and Daniel Boyarin, *A Radical Jew: Paul and the Politics of Identity* (Berkeley, 1997). One should not omit the classic by W. D. Davies, *Paul and Rabbinic Judaism* (London, 1960).

14. St. John Chrysostom, *Homilies Against the Jews* 1.11.1–2, trans. Wayne Meeks and Robert Wilken in *Jews and Christians in Antioch in the First Four Centuries of the Common Era* (Missoula, Mont., 1978); and also in the Internet Medieval Sourcebook, ed. Paul Halsal, www.fordham.edu/halsall/source/chrysostom-jews6.html (accessed May 13, 2005). See Robert Wilken, *John Chrysostom and the Jews, Rhetoric and Reality in the Late Fourth Century* (Berkeley, 1983), 122, who warns that rhetoric was to be taken as just that, not literally, but then adds that problems arose when Jewish issues were involved (123, and see 122 for other examples of Chrysostom likening his adversaries to dogs: e.g., those who "live only for their bellies, dogs, dumb and raging mad"). In these cases, says Wilken, Chrysostom meant pagan philosophers and the emperor Julian the Apostate. Yet rather than spreading the onus to encompass others beside Jews, what these citations mean, in fact, is that Jews are one with the most despised of all groups and people.

15. Matthew Henry Bible Commentary, www.gospelcom.net/eword/comments/matthew/mh/matthew15.htm (accessed May 7, 2005). As for Paul, the author of Philippians, he meant Judaizers, as he would in Galatians, not Jews themselves, as subsequent exegesis in both cases reads it.

16. The ongoing interaction between clerical and popular religious mentalities often prevents popular concepts from being distinguished from canonical or theological ones (or even, I would add, from literary ones), André Vauchez notes in "Antisemitismo e canonizzazione popolare: San Werner o Vernier (+1287) bambino martire e patrono dei vignaioli," in *Culto dei santi, istituzioni e classi sociali in età preindustriale,* ed. Sofia Boesch Gajano and Lucia Sebastiani (L'Aquila, Rome, 1981), 492. The fact that Vauchez chooses the Good Werner of Oberwesel, a pretended ritual murder victim, to illustrate his case is significant. At one point or another, Vauchez explains, clergy, including members of the hierarchy, either supported or attacked the Werner cult. Eventually, however, Werner's "martyrdom" was either accepted—his cult was not fully suppressed until 1963—or legitimated in a wholly different setting, that of the saint, or protector, of vine growers.

17. Cited in Shlomo Simonsohn, *The Apostolic See and the Jews* (Toronto, 1990), 1: 4–5; cf. Prov. 26:11 and 2 Peter 2:22. Gregory does not add like a dog, but nobody would have misunderstood him. These verses were often cited in full by Church Fathers.

18. I thank Tom Cohen for this reference, which is taken from Thomas V. Cohen, *Love and Death in Renaissance Italy* (Chicago, 2004), 138.

19. For Herman, see Schmitt, *Conversion d'Hermann le Juif,* 255. William Shakespeare, *The Merchant of Venice* 2.8.14, "dog Jew"; 4.1.292, "currish Jew."

20. For Bede on synagogue, *grex,* and sheep, see Marta Cristiani, *Tempo rituale e tempo storico, Communione Cristiana e sacrificio: Le controversie eucaristiche nell'alto medioevo* (Spoleto, 1997), 65; but see also Jeremy Cohen, *Living Letters of the Law: Ideas of the Jew in Medieval Christianity* (Berkeley, 1999), 143, which requires elaboration. On 1 Cor. 10:16–17, see John Chrysostom, "Homily XXIV,

Homilies on First Corinthians," *Nicean and Post-Nicean Fathers,* ser. 1, vol. 12, where he links the Jewish altar to idolatry and demands segregation from it; Chrysostom also stresses the unity of all Christians in Christ. See also on Corinthians the interpretation of Boyarin, *Radical Jew,* 73–75; also 33–34 on Galatians. See Introduction nn. 56 and 111, below, and Chapter 2, n. 52, on other legislative echoes of Corinthians and Galatians in the Council of Carthage and Regino of Prum. See also above and the reference in the text to Cardinal Ratzinger (Pope Benedict XVI), whose remarks reflect this kind of Pauline thought and interpretation; Ratzinger is not, of course, being accused of supporting ritual murder charges. He has consistently denounced hatred of Jews and the events of the Shoah (see, e.g., *L'osservatore romano,* December 29, 2000), and he plans to visit a German synagogue to promote dialogue, although his understanding of that term is still unknown. Most recently, see Raúl González Salinero, *El antijudaísmo cristiano occidental, siglos iv y v* (Madrid, 2000), 81–104, discussing the active fight specifically against Judaizing in the fourth and fifth centuries throughout the Empire—a Judaization that was at this point considered a real threat to Christianity's victory. See also on this theme Robert Wilken, *Judaism and the Early Christian Mind: A Study of Cyril of Alexandria's Exegesis and Theology* (New Haven, 1971), 37. Those looking for an unencumbered Pauline-Augustinian solution to explain the problem of the Church and medieval Judaism do not pay sufficient attention to these passages; see Jeremy Cohen, *Living Letters of the Law,* and compare my review of *The Jews in Legal Sources of the Early Middle Ages,* trans. and ed. Amnon Linder (Detroit and Jerusalem, 1997), *Jewish Quarterly Review* 89 (1999): 460–65. In addition, see Anna Sapir Abulafia, *Christians and Jews in the Twelfth-Century Renaissance* (London, 1995).

21. Yet were not Jews possibly a part of this one body? Ernst H. Kantorowicz, *The King's Two Bodies: A Study in Mediaeval Political Theology* (Princeton, 1957), 308, argues, following Aquinas, that Jews and Muslims are part of the overall *corpus,* being potential members, since the *corpus* is coterminous with all men. The real distinction is between Jewish membership in the *ecclesia militans,* the Church of this world, and membership in the *ecclesia triumphans,* open only to believers. No doubt, the vast majority, not splitting scholastic theological or legal hairs, would make no such nice distinctions. One was either in or out. Further, the distinctions between the two *ecclesiae,* defining the actual and potential members of the *corpus,* really follow Paul in Romans, first, on the notion of the Jews' entry (into the *corpus*) in the fullness of days, and, second, the idea that Jews are still dear to God because of their fathers, while they are enemies of the Gospel. In the event, Paul explicitly makes Jews part of the *corpus* in Eph. 2:14–16, "Gentiles and Jews, he [Christ] has made the two one . . . so as to create out of the two a single new humanity in himself . . . to reconcile the two in a single body to God through the cross." However, Paul means the ultimate future, not the unrealized ingathering of his own time.

22. Linder, trans. and ed., *Jews in the Legal Sources*, e.g., nos. 121, 124.

23. See the texts cited in n. 14 above.

24. See Peter Brown, *The Body and Society: Men, Women, and Sexual Renunciation in Early Christianity* (New York, 1988), 35, who cites this text with the intention of passing from Jewish to Christian images of the body. Of course, even the Mishnah, let alone the much later Gemarrah, was posterior to Paul by over a century. Nonetheless, much of its material is far earlier in origin, whether in its finally edited or inchoate original form—not to mention that Paul himself was a pupil of the Pharisees, from whom the mishnaic rabbis intellectually descended. Whether, therefore, the saying as we have it preceded Paul, or somehow derived from him directly, in either case, it originated in the same conceptual melting pot. It should be noted that there are Jewish counterparts to the Christian concern with impurity derived from Jews that will be a consistent theme here. *Avodah Zarah* 36a warns against consuming bread and wine of Gentiles, as well as mixing with their daughters, lest one become "unclean." On the full implications, as well as a deep analysis of Gentile impurity in rabbinic eyes, see Christine E. Hayes, *Gentile Impurities and Christian Identities: Intermarriage and Conversion from the Bible to the Talmud* (Oxford, 2002), esp. chaps. 6 and 7. Hayes discusses 1 Cor. 6:14–19 in chap. 5, on which see my Chapter 6. Hayes has hesitations about the effect of these restrictions on Jews. I suspect they gained greater importance, at least a greater ideological importance, as the ancient period moved into the Middle Ages, where Jews had to distinguish most carefully about when to keep their distance from Christians, and when they could, or needed to, drop their defenses, for instance, in business affairs or in partaking of non-Jewish culture, which they did.

25. Abraham Melamed, *The Image of the Black in Jewish Culture: A History of the Other* (New York, 2003), 79–81.

26. See, again, n. 14 above.

27. St. Thomas Aquinas, *Summa Theologica*, IIa, IIae, 10. Similarly, Aquinas invoked Paul's image of the Jewish "elder brother" as the paradigm of the absence of faith and its (dire) consequences. See Abulafia, *Christians and Jews in the Twelfth-Century Renaissance*, passim. Amalric of Metz, citing Bede, anticipated Thomas by calling the synagogue a pen for sheep; see Cristiani, *Tempo rituale*.

28. Martin Luther, *That Jesus Christ Was Born a Jew*, in *Luther's Works*, trans. W. I. Brandt (Philadelphia, 1971), 45: 195–229, 195 (I thank Magda Teter for this reference). There will be occasional references to Protestantism, but Protestants are not the issue in this book. Luther's reference to the sow is possibly intended to recall 2 Pet. 2:22: "'The dog returns to its own vomit,' and 'The sow after a wash rolls in the mud again,'" the former originating in Prov. 26:11. Luther's rejection of the blood libel here, compared to later in his career, is striking. In his *On the Jews and Their Lies* (1543), he also used the dog image: "They are real liars and bloodhounds . . . who [also] imagine that they are God's people who have been commissioned and commanded to murder and to slay the Gentiles." And again:

"They have been blood thirsty bloodhounds and murderers of all Christendom for more than fourteen hundred years in their intentions, and would undoubtedly prefer to be such with their deeds. Thus they have been accused of poisoning water and wells, of kidnaping children, of piercing them through with an awl, of hacking them in pieces, and in that way secretly cooling their wrath with the blood of Christians, for all of which they have often been condemned to death by fire" (trans. Martin H. Bertram and reproduced in the Internet Medieval Sourcebook, ed. Paul Halsall www.fordham.edu/halsall/basis/1543-Luther-JewsandLies-full.html [accessed May 13, 2005]).

29. The pairing would be automatic for those with Pet. 2:22 in mind. The pope is Ishmael in Luther's commentary to Gal. 4:30. Hence he applies to Catholicism a verse long applied to Jews, making these two identical, with all the implications. On the exchange of the symbolism of Israel = Jews for Israel = Christians, and the Jews as Esau, see also Gerson D. Cohen, "Esau as Symbol," in *Jewish Medieval and Renaissance Studies,* ed. Alexander Altmann (Cambridge, Mass., 1967). The New England preacher Cotton Mather said "without the grace of faith, 'we should every one of us be a *dog* and a *witch* too,'" which in some ways extends Luther's extrapolation. Cited in Phyllis Mack, *Visionary Women: Ecstatic Prophecy in Seventeenth-Century England* (Berkeley, 1992), 258. Faith has substituted for bread, and one may read that all those without faith—especially those who trust in popery, namely, in such uses as the Eucharist—are dogs.

30. See Stow, *Catholic Thought and Papal Jewry Policy,* 231–32, on Luther and conversion. Luther was not really seeking conversion—he would not reject it, of course—his concern was with what he called bad Catholic exegesis. By saying no wonder Jews have not converted, he was attacking Catholic teaching rather than proselytizing.

31. Neusner and Chilton, *Jewish and Christian Doctrines,* 90, say Paul "set aside usual restrictions on fellowship at meals," but this did not include the meal of the Eucharist, as their later discussion, noted above, of the body of Christ and the Eucharist would surely lead them to agree.

32. See also Matthew Henry (cited above) on 1 Cor. 10:17: "By partaking of one broken loaf, the emblem of our Saviour's broken body, who is the only true bread that came down from heaven, *we coalesce into one body*, become members of him and one another." The idea of the body with its united membership thus continues into Protestantism.

33. The precise translation of Ezekiel here is mine, but note: the crucial identification of bread as the sacrifice that is fat and blood is common to all translations, and see esp. *The Prophets: A New Translation* (Philadelphia, 1978), 751–52, which emphasizes the identity. For Pauline definitions, see Robert Stacey, "From Ritual Crucifixion to Host Desecration: Jews and the Body of Christ," *Jewish History* 12, no. 1 (1998): 12. The link to Ezekiel in 1 Cor. 10:18 is verbal, not only conceptual. Paul says: "Look at the Israel of the flesh (the Jews). Are not those who

partake of the sacrifices [who also are those who offer them] adepts of the altar?"—insiders, therefore, Jews, not the outsiders, against whose sacrificial participation Ezekiel warns.

34. Cristiani, *Tempo rituale*, 45–46.

35. Directly or indirectly, Agobard of Lyon and Chrysostom extend Cyprian's meaning to embrace Jews and those who have contact with them. Cyprian, Epistle 67, reads at greater length: "Nor let the people flatter themselves that they can be free from the contagion of sin, while communicating with a priest who is a sinner, and yielding their consent to the unjust and unlawful episcopacy of their overseer, when the divine reproof by Hosea the prophet threatens, and says, 'Their sacrifices shall be as the bread of mourning; all that eat thereof shall be polluted'; teaching manifestly and showing that all are absolutely bound to the sin who have been contaminated by the sacrifice of a profane and unrighteous priest. Which, moreover, we find to be manifested also in Numbers, when Korah, and Dathan, and Abiram claimed for themselves the power of sacrificing in opposition to Aaron the priest. There also the Lord commanded by Moses that the people should be separated from them, lest, being associated with the wicked, themselves also should be bound closely in the same wickedness. . . . Since they, says he, who do such things are worthy of death, he makes manifest and proves that not only they are worthy of death, and come into punishment who do evil things, but also those who consent unto those who do such things—who, while they are mingled in unlawful communion with the evil and sinners, and the unrepenting, are polluted by the contact of the guilty, and, being joined in the fault, are thus not separated in its penalty." *Ante-Nicene Fathers*, vol. 5, www.ccel.org/fathers2/ANF-05/anf05-92.htm#P6106_1928147 (accessed May 13, 2005).

36. *The Ante-Nicene Fathers*, vol. 5, Cyprian, Treatise III, *De lapsis*, 15 (http://ccel.org/fathers2/ANF-05/anf05-113.htm#P7009_2277176 [accessed June 29, 2005]. See also ibid., 16. "All these warnings being scorned and contemned . . . before the offence of an angry and threatening Lord has been appeased, violence is done to His body and blood; and they sin now against their Lord more with their hand and mouth than when they denied their Lord [the priests,] who joined in pagan sacrifice," not the Jews condemning Jesus to the Cross, with whom the priests are ominously being identified. Most recently on Cyprian, see James Patout Burns Jr., *Cyprian the Bishop* (London, 2002).

37. As the rabbis explained in *Mishnah Ohalot* (following Hosea and Leviticus), a corpse pollutes not only all those who touch it but also the dwelling of the dead person, its inmates, and all uncovered utensils. See also *Jewish Encyclopedia* (Philadelphia, 1901), 4: 278, s.v. "corpse."

38. If we are to believe Eusebius, Cyprian saw even ideas as concretely, or physically, polluting, and, therefore, in Eusebius's words, "Cyprian . . . was the first man of his time to maintain that only when cleansed by baptism ought they [those who 'had abandoned a heresy of any kind'] to be readmitted." Eusebius,

The History of the Church from Christ to Constantine, trans. G. A. Williamson (New York, 1966), bk. 7.3, 288. That Cyprian was thinking in terms of the cleansing Jewish ritual bath, which removes ritual impurity, hardly need be said.

39. Cyprian, *De lapsis* 15. On the problem, the difficulty, of physical matter dissolving in the sacred spiritual, see Miri Rubin, *Corpus Christi: The Eucharist in Late Medieval Culture* (Cambridge, 1992), 14, including her citation from Aquinas, and see also 35–42, on eucharistic purity. Nonetheless, the problem of eucharistic contamination per se was there, as may be seen in a text Friedrich Lotter cites from Abbot Adam of Perseigne, a Cistercian, at the end of the twelfth century. In the context of discouraging what the abbot saw as fruitless debate with Jews, he remarks that it would be better to debate, for their correction, with those "who make themselves companions of the Jews by crucifying Christ a second time. . . . Whoever assumes guilt by unworthily receiving Christ's body and blood could not defeat the unbelief of the Jews or convince them of their crime of having murdered the Lord" (Cum his potius de fide disserendum est qui Dei filium habentes ostentui, Iudaeorum facti participes Christum iterum crucifigunt. . . . Quomo de ergo qui talis est, Iudaeorum infidelitatem redarguit et de reatu Dominicae mortis convincit qui sacramenta indigne accipiens eiusdem se culpa reatus involvit?). The point here is that behaving like a Jew, which is equated with taking the Eucharist unworthily, is to kill Christ anew—implying, in the context of unworthily accepting the sacrament, that such acts defile the Eucharist itself. Lotter, "The Position of the Jews in Early Cistercian Exegesis and Preaching," in *From Witness to Witchcraft: Jews and Judaism in Medieval Christian Thought*, ed. Jeremy Cohen (Wiesbaden, 1996).

40. On early eucharistic theology, see Gary Macy, *The Theologies of the Eucharist in the Early Scholastic Period: A Study of the Salvific Function of the Sacrament According to the Theologians c. 1080–c. 1220* (Oxford, 1984).

41. Cyprian cites the verses in bk. 3, para. 62 of his *Twelfth Treatise: Three Books of Testimonies Against the Jews*, 1.41–42.

42. Cyprian's *Three Books of Testimonies Against the Jews* are a compilation of headings and verses intended to illustrate standard theology, enumerate Christian principles of belief, and define Christian moral behavior. They are not a real polemic against Jews. Pope Stephen is cited in Bernhard Blumenkranz, *Les Auteurs chrétiens latins du Moyen Age sur les juifs et le judaisme* (Paris, 1963), 142, and Simonsohn, *Apostolic See and the Jews*, 1: 25–26.

43. St. John Chrysostom, Homily 24 on 1 Cor., in *Nicean and Post-Nicean Fathers*, ser. 1, vol. 12, on-line edition: "But do thou, I pray, consider, how with regard to the Jews he said not, 'they are partakers with God,' but, 'they have communion with the altar'; for what was placed thereon was burnt: but in respect to the Body of Christ, not so. But how? It is 'a Communion of the Lord's Body.' For not with the altar, but with Christ Himself, do we have communion. But having said that they have 'communion with the altar,' afterwards fearing lest he should

seem to discourse as if the idols had any power and could do some injury, see again how he overthrows them, saying, Ver. 19. 'What say I then? That an idol is any thing? or that a thing sacrificed to idols is any thing?'" The "they have 'communion'" can be read as Jews or pagans, or the two as the same, as Chrysostom likely intended, exploiting his rhetorical skills to elide the slightest trace of difference between the two.

44. Linder, trans. and ed., *Jews in the Legal Sources*, no. 502.

45. *Patrologia Latina,* 8: 1255—late first, early second century.

46. St. John Chrysostom, *Eight Homilies Against the Jews* 2.3.5, Internet Medieval Sourcebook, ed. Paul Halsall, www.fordham.edu/halsall/source/chrysostom-jews6.html (accessed May 13, 2005); see also the translation of Meeks and Wilken cited above.

47. See Brown, *Body and Society,* 195, on vigilance to protect the body, which is also Paul's concern here, although it is only indirectly Ratherius's worry.

48. Blumenkranz, *Auteurs chrétiens*, 230.

49. Jewish concerns about impurity acquired through contact with Christians most often yielded to exigencies of the need for commercial contact and, eventually, to the acceptance that Christianity was not idolatry. With supervision, Christians could prepare various Jewish foods, although not wine, or dine at a Jew's table. To the best of my knowledge, Jewish discourse does not attribute Christians with the intention of corrupting Jewish food, nor does it hold Christians responsible for any after-effect of corruption; see Babylonian Talmud, *Abodah zarah*, 37b, 39b. In the event, moreover, the food rendered unkosher by improper Christian contact would be the locus of the corruption, not the Jew him- or herself, who might/would pass this corruption on to others. This is the opposite of Agobard's teachings, which are modeled on Cyprian—not to mention that contact with impure food and the like did not disqualify the Jew from participation in Jewish rites (at least those outside the now destroyed Jerusalem Temple), nor is there any rite in Judaism equivalent to taking the Eucharist. See Haym Soloveitchik, *Principles and Pressures: Jewish Trade in Gentile Wine in the Middle Ages* (Tel Aviv, 2003; in Hebrew).

50. Saint Agobard, *Agobardi Lugdunensis Archiepiscopi Epistolae contra Iudaeos,* ed. and trans. A. Gilboa (Jerusalem, 1964; Latin text with Hebrew translation), 24, 26, 32, 36, 38, 40, 44, 49, from *Agobardi Lugdunensis Archiepiscopi Epistolae,* Monumenta Germaniae Historica, *Epistolae Karolini Aevi*, vol. 3, ed. E. Dümmler (Berlin, 1899); and Linder, trans. and ed., *Jews in the Legal Sources,* no. 866, esp. p. 542.

51. Agobard, *Epistolae contra Iudaeos,* ed. and trans. Gilboa, 32.

52. On the *societas fidei,* see n. 74, below. On food and impurity, see, among others, Leopold Lucas, *The Conflict Between Christianity and Judaism: A Contribution to the History of the Jews in the Fourth Century* (Warminster, Eng., 1993), 30; see also Linder, trans. and ed., *Jews in the Legal Sources*. The force of these teachings about ritual pollution may also explain a hitherto unnoted dimension of the

legislation issued at the Third and Fourth Lateran Councils of 1179 and 1215; see the discussion in Chapter 6. Why, in particular, does the Third Lateran stress servitude and the Fourth establish special clothing, if not to avoid the impurity of sexual mixing? Yet would not an emphasis on impurity at this time correspond to the contemporary perfection and implementation of Eucharistic doctrine, with the priest at the center (see Rubin, *Corpus Christi*, 14)? Eviatar Zerubavel, *The Fine Line: Making Distinctions in Everyday Life* (New York, 1991), 38, renders these anxieties about miscegenation into modern sociological-cultural theory. "Sexual intercourse," he writes, "threatens the image of an insular self . . . 'intercourse reveals the individual to be not the closed contained, but rather an open sieve, liable to contamination.'"

53. Lev. 22:4–7: "And whoever touches any one that is unclean by the dead; or from whomsoever the flow of seed goes out; [5] or whosoever touches any swarming thing, whereby he may be made unclean, or a man of whom he may take uncleanness, whatsoever uncleanness he hath; [6] the soul that touches any such shall be unclean until the even, and shall not eat of the holy things, unless he bathe his flesh in water. [7] And when the sun is down, he shall be clean; and afterward he may eat of the holy things, because it is his bread." Buxtorf writes of the unkosher hindquarters sold to Christians by Jews (much to ecclesiastical rancor): "The animal is *asur* [forbidden] and no Jew may eat from it, as it is written Ex. 22.31; Lev. 22.8. You shall not eat carrion that was torn in the field, but you shall throw it to the dogs." Surprisingly, he does not cite these texts as reasons why Christians should refrain from purchasing this meat, although he does suggest, as will be discussed further, that Jews urinated on these portions before selling them. Johannes Buxtorf, *Synagoga Judaica* (Basel, 1603), trans. Alan Corre, chap. 27, www.uwm.edu/People/corre/buxdorf/chp27.html (accessed May 14, 2005).

54. Linder, trans. and ed., *Jews in the Legal Sources*, no. 1163.

55. In *Patrologiae cursus completus: series latina*, ed. J.-P. Migne (Paris, 1844–1902), 110: 490.

56. Linder, trans. and ed., *Jews in the Legal Sources*, esp. pp. 544, 569, 576, and 597.

57. Raymundus of Peñaforte, *Summa de poenitentia et matrimoniae* (Rome, 1603), 32–38.

58. On Sicard, see James Brundage, "Intermarriage Between Christians and Jews in Medieval Canon Law," *Jewish History* 3, no. 1 (1988): 31–32. Most recently, see David Nirenberg, "Conversion, Sex, and Segregation: Jews and Christians in Medieval Spain," *American Historical Review* 107 (2002): 1065–93. Penetratingly, and following Brundage, Nirenberg links laws forbidding sexual miscegenation to fears of pollution. However, in doing so, he expressly divorces them from the "corporatist" (as he calls them) teachings of the Church, speaking instead of boundaries for individuals that reflect on the community and its identity. This is an important and valid point. Still, it is not clear to me why Nirenberg does not

want to see this drama in terms of the (eucharistic) Christian fellowship as the term is used here, and why he divorces sexual purity from the "corporatist." He, indeed, adduces a perfect example of this pairing, a painting in which the Eucharist (!) slits the throat of a Christian woman communicant who has just left her Muslim lover; see Nirenberg at n. 19. This is identical to the fear of Cyprian and Agobard for the communicant who is harmed by being polluted through improper contact, whether with a *lapsus* or a Jew. And what they fear is for the safety of the eucharistic Christian fellowship. I argue here that it is precisely the "corporatist" essence that sex with a Jew pollutes. Nirenberg's distinction in some way detracts from this point, especially since, in medieval Catholicism, all sexuality has a burden of impurity. Sexual miscegenation, when the sexuality is not within the limits the canons allow (for the sake of faith and procreation, and the unity of the Church, the same goals symbolized by the marital sacrament), affects the purity, the eucharistic, hence "corporatist/corporeal," unity of the Christian fellowship. We shall see an example in Chapter 7 apropos of the early medieval *Apocalypse of the Virgin*. All of this notwithstanding, it must be said that Nirenberg is concerned with the implications of borders created by prohibited sexuality in the concrete context of events in Spain between 1391 and 1418, when thousands of conversions took place, and how St. Vincent Ferrer's preaching of sexual separation between Christians and others established ways of distinguishing Christians from Jews at a time of great uncertainty. In this context, his emphasis on community and boundaries is important.

59. Marquardus de Susannis, *De Iudaeis et aliis infidelibus* (Venice, 1558), 2.3.1 and 15. That this is the reverse of a Christian being sullied through union with a harlot, as in 1 Cor. 6:15–16, should give us reason for some pause, although one may not be overly speculative either.

60. Both refer to marrying an infidel as harlotry (de Susannis, *De Iudaeis et aliis infidelibus,* cites Augustine, *De adulterinis coniugiis et de fidelibus puellis*, bk. 1, and Cyprian, *De lapsis*); but, in fact, the distinction between pagan and Jew once again fades, in the same way it did in Ratherius's and Chrysostom's citations of Paul. On Jewish views, see Hayes, *Gentile Impurities and Jewish Identities*, 92–94, but note again her doubts about Jewish application.

61. Cited by Guido Kisch, *The Jews in Medieval Germany* (New York, 1949), 205.

62. Esther Cohen, "Symbols and Culpability and the Universal Language of Justice: The Ritual of Public Executions in Late Medieval Europe," *History of European Ideas* 11 (1989): 411; Salo W. Baron, *A Social and Religious History of the Jews* (Philadelphia, 1952–69), vols. 11 and 14, esp. 11: 90.

63. Katherine Aron Beller, "The Inquisition and the Jews in Modena in the Seventeenth Century" (Ph.D. diss., Haifa, 2003), chap. 5.

64. Gérard Fransen and Stephan Kuttner, *Summa "Elegantius in iure divino" seu Coloniensis* (New York, 1969–90), 106–8; cited also by Brundage "Intermarriage Between Christians and Jews"; de Susannis, *De Iudaeis et aliis infidelibus* 1.4.14.

65. See Chapters 3 and 6 on the Fourth Lateran decrees.

66. Simonsohn, *Apostolic See and the Jews*, nos. 24 and 25: "Quid enim sunt Christiani omnes nisi membra Christi? Quorum videlicet membrorum caput cuncti novimus, quia fideliter honoratis. Sed quam diversum sit, excellentia vestra perpendat, caput honorare et membra ipsius hostibus calcanda permittere." On Gregory in general on purity and impurity, see Rob Meens, "Ritual Purity and the Influence of Gregory the Great in the Early Middle Ages," in *Unity and Diversity in the Church*, ed. R. N. Swanson (Oxford, 1996), 31–43. Gregory preferred a spiritual understanding of biblical laws of purity, but his attitude was not adopted, particularly in Gaul through the ninth century and especially with respect to menstrual impurity, and sometimes even discrimination in foods. The general clerical view, even in the literature of the penitentials, was that physical purity and its protection counts. Eventually, clerical interpreters, especially of the biblical text, tried to run from this position through allegory, especially of books like Leviticus, where the touch of the dead is said to mean to be touched by sin, and so forth; on which, see John Van Engen, "Ralph of Flaix: The Book of Leviticus Interpreted as Christian Community," in *Jews and Christians in Twelfth-Century Europe*, ed. Michael Signer and John Van Engen (Notre Dame, Ind., 2001). Van Engen's useful suggestion in this same essay that the opposition was between one legal community and another (the community of those who followed Christian law and the community observing Jewish law) struggling to determine which is the rightful law of God would still leave us with the notion of communities in conflict, which is essential to our argument. Moreover, these laws did include rules of physical purity, writers like Ralph of Flaix aside. In so many areas, as we shall see, especially the touch of Jews, concepts of ritual purity and impurity acquired through wrongful contact did not disappear.

67. Agobard, *Epistolae contra Iudaeos*, ed. and trans. Gilboa, 18, and 46, citing Rom 11:25–26.

68. This addition, in my opinion, is an interpolation in a real letter on a wholly different subject concerning diocesan affairs, not Jews at all; see Kenneth Stow, *Alienated Minority: The Jews of Medieval Latin Europe* (Cambridge, Mass., 1992, 1994), 30, 31, 96, and the literature cited there.

69. Citation of Matt. 7:6 to justify expulsion seems not to have been repeated. However, the fourteenth-century Avignonese jurist Oldradus da Ponte said that (in theory) Jews might legally be expelled on the basis of Paul's saying in Gal. 4:30 that the son of the bondwoman Hagar should be expelled (although Paul meant excising Judaizing by Christians, not expelling Jews themselves). Oldradus da Ponte, *Consilia* (1478), Cons. 51, c. 42vA–B.

70. Diane Owen Hughes, "Distinguishing Signs: Ear-Rings, Jews and Franciscan Rhetoric in the Italian Renaissance City," *Past and Present* 112 (1986): 33–34; Maurice Kriegel, "Un Trait de psychologie sociale dans les pays Méditerranéens du Bas Moyen Age: Le Juif comme intouchable," *Annales ESC* 31 (1976): 326–30.

The precise origins of these rules about touching food may, however, be Shiite. They continued in force in Shiite countries until recently, as immigrants to Israel from places like Iran recount. Whether the Shiite rules themselves were transferred to the West, or whether the parallel is happenstance, requires study, just as do the other parallels of special clothing required in all Muslim lands by the Pact of Omar, as it is called, from about the tenth century. Finally, Innocent III's addition to the *Sicut iudaeis non* text, which soon disappeared (to reappear briefly in the later fifteenth century), that the bull's protection extended only to those who do not plot against Christianity is also found in the Pact of Omar. It seems more than a simple replacement of the clause found in various medieval charters indicating that Jews must remain *fideles*, which translates more as subjects bound by something akin to fealty. This is not the opposite of "Jews who hatch plots."

71. *Codex diplomaticus Majoris Poloniae* (Poznan, 1877–1989), 1: 563–66: "Item statuimus etiam, ut iudaei vendant omnia libere et ement, et panem tangant, similiter ut christiani prohibentes vero poenam nobis pro eo solvere tenebuntur." Grand Duke Witold Alexander's text was published by Mathias Bersohn in Warsaw in 1910 (I thank Magda Teter for this reference).

72. Battista de' Giudici, *Apologia Iudaeorum*, ed. Diego Quaglioni (Rome, 1987), 54–55. Never once in his life, it was said, did Giudici break bread or drink with a Jew ("nunquam in omni vita sua vel semel cum aliquo Iudeo aut comedit aut bibit"). He was evidently suspicious of child martyrs and also wrote a tract titled *De Canonizatione beati Bonaventurae*, reprinted in Étienne Baluze, *Stephani Baluzii Tutelensis miscellanea* . . . (Lucca, 1764), 471–87, in which he says that a martyr is one who wills it, and this cannot be the case with young children, "[whom] non voluntas, sed necessitas [eos] fecit martyres." Cited by André Vauchez, *Sainthood in the Later Middle Ages*, trans. Jean Birrell (Cambridge, 1997), 155. In the sixteenth century, de Susannis linked common dining with forbidden sexual relations between Jews and Christians under the rubric of endangering the faith (de Susannis, *De Iudaeis et aliis infidelibus* 1.3, 1.4, and 1.13); and see also Kenneth Stow, "Papal Mendicants or Mendicant Popes: Continuity and Change in Papal Policies Toward the Jews at the End of the Fifteenth Century," in *The Friars and the Jews in the Middle Ages and the Renaissance,* ed. Stephen McMichael and Susan Myers (Leiden, 2004).

73. Brundage, "Intermarriage," and Nirenberg, "Conversion, Sex, and Segregation."

74. For more detail on this problem of "the society of faith," including discussion of ancient and early medieval developments, see Stow, *Alienated Minority*, 28–36, preceded by Stow, "Agobard of Lyons and the Medieval Concept of the Jew," *Conservative Judaism* 29 (1964): 68–75; now taken up again, following similar lines, by Jeremy Cohen, *Living Letters of the Law*, 143; and see also, Bernard Blumenkranz, "Deux compilations canoniques de Florus de Lyon et l'action antijuive de Agobard," *Revue historique de droit français et etranger* 33 (1955): 227–54, 560–82. See further Stow, "Conversion, Apostasy, and Apprehensiveness: Emicho

of Flonheim and the Fear of Jews in the Twelfth Century," *Speculum* 76 (2001): 911–33. The earliest explicit identification of Judaizing with endangering the state may be the 1492 edict of expulsion from Spain. As legal pretext, it is said that just as a *collegium* or *universitas* is disbanded and declared illegal for damaging the *republica* (admittedly a still imperfectly formed term in the fifteenth century), so, because of Judaizing, by way of seducing *conversos* back to Judaism, the Jews are being expelled. Christian and statal integrity were perceived as identical. Many remained of this opinion even in the modern era; see esp. Chapter 1 on the papal nuncio in France during the Dreyfus affair, Monsignor Lorenzelli, who, based on 1 Corinthians' doctrine of the inviolability of the social body of Christ, had no difficulty seeing Judaism as a threat to the body's integrity, as was modernity itself.

75. Miri Rubin, *Gentile Tales: The Narrative Assault on Late Medieval Jews* (New Haven, 1999); *The Jewish-Christian Debate in the High Middle Ages: A Critical Edition of the Nizzahon vetus,* ed. David Berger (Philadelphia, 1979); and Rabbi Yosef Official, *Sepher Joseph Hamekane of R. Joseph b. R. Nathan Official,* ed. Judah Rosenthal (Jerusalem, 1970; in Hebrew), par. 91. Commenting on par. 89, Rosenthal refers to Cyprian on Jews; in 91, Official cites Hosea 9:4 twice and says the Eucharist creates *tum'ah*, impurity, and cannot be brought into the Temple (lest it pollute it). See Chapter 6 for a fuller discussion.

76. Solomon Grayzel, *The Church and the Jews in the Thirteenth Century* (New York, 1966), 1: 128–29: "quod vendemiarum tempore uvas calcat, Iudaeus lineis caligis calceatus et puriori mero iuxta ritum Iudaeorum extracto, pro beneplacito suo retinent ex eodem, residuum quasi foedatum ab ipsis relinquentes fidelibus Christianis; ex quo interdum sanguinis Christi conficitur sacramentum."

77. "Ne aliquis Christianus retineat apus se marcum vindemiarum, quem Judaei calcant aliquo modo, propter illam horribilem immunditiam quam in contemptum sacramenti altaris faciunt; et si remanserit, detur porcis vel expandant ad opus pro fimo." Cited by Grayzel, *Church and the Jews,* 1: 300–301, who translates slightly differently "because of the horribly filthy practices which they commit"; however, if Odo's text is compared with Innocent's reference to a foul residuum, meaning wine of second or worse quality, my reading, I believe, becomes the more correct one. Grayzel (following earlier scholars, going back to Buxtorf) says the "wine" in question was a kind of fresh grappa or eau-de-vie, which was diluted. If Grayzel is correct, however, and Odo literally meant the marc, or what is also called pomace, there is something of the fantastic in his prohibition. Grappa is hard alcohol: the marc, the sticks, seeds, and skins of the grapes, are its beginning. Refined grappa can be far more sophisticated and expensive than fine brandy. Nor would it be confused with wine, transparent in color as it regularly is. Was there hearsay in the legislative process; or we are simply speaking as Innocent does, of a second pressing, likely mixed with residues, not grappa at all? For Jewish attitudes toward commerce with Gentiles involving wine, Jewish wine in particular, see Soloveitchik, *Principles and Pressures*.

78. Hippolyte Delehaye, *Les Origines du culte des martyrs* (1912; Brussels, 1933), 6. On Campion, see also Brad S. Gregory, *Salvation at Stake: Christian Martyrdom in Early Modern Europe* (Cambridge, Mass., 1999).

79. Brown, *Body and Society*, 195.

80. Rupert of Deutz in Abulafia, *Christians and Jews in the Twelfth-Century Renaissance*, 119; see also James Patout Burns Jr., "The Eucharist as the Foundation of Christian Unity in North African Theology," *Augustinian Studies* 32 (2001): 1–24.

81. Morrison, *History as Visual Art*, 145–46; where Morrison adds, as though echoing Campion, "Modern heroes of the faith also offered themselves as sacrifices and oblations."

82. Vauchez, *Sainthood in the Later Middle Ages*, 150, explains Werner's case as the fruit of a popular mentality with a high regard for childhood "innocence . . . and a virulent anti-Semitism which found its justification in the accusation of ritual murder" and the Host libel. I hope to show the roots of this "virulent anti-Semitism" in precisely the melding of the images of martyr and the body of Christ. On Werner and on the relationship between martyrs "created" by Jews and the attributes of the martyr in general, see here also Miri Rubin, "Choosing Death? Experiences of Martyrdom in Late Medieval Europe," in *Martyrs and Martyrologies*, ed. Diana Wood, 153–84 (Oxford, 1993), esp. 164–68.

83. Peter Biller, "Views of Jews from Paris Around 1300: Christian or Scientific," in *Christianity and Judaism*, ed. Diana Wood (Oxford, 1992), discusses this most clearly.

84. Quoted by Dean P. Bell, *Sacred Communities: Jewish and Christian Identities in Fifteenth-Century Germany* (Leiden, 2002), 108, citing Rochus von Liliencron, *Die historischen Volkslieder der Deutschen vom 13. bis 16. Jahrhundert*, 5 vols. (Leipzig, 1865–69), 3: 339.

85. Willis Johnson, "Before the Blood Libel: Jews in Christian Exegesis After the Massacres of 1096" (MA thesis, Cambridge University, 1994 [typescript]). The Cistercian Abbot William of St. Thierry, Rupert's contemporary, basing himself largely on Romans and, hence, not on the Galatians' and Corinthians' anxieties, nonetheless saw fit to cite Matt. 15:26 in the context of discussing Jewish rejection of Christ. He qualifies his words, however, by noting that the disgraced (Jewish) dogs may accede to the crumbs ("canes humiliati . . . ad colligendas micas . . . ad ipsam mensam mererentur accedere"). What William's statement shows, especially in its context lacking hostility, is how common the contrast between Jews and dogs had really become. On William, see Lotter, "Position of the Jews."

86. Johnson, "Before the Blood Libel," citing Cambridge University Library Ii. 4, 26 (xii. e, English), f. 9v. Alfonso de Espina also mentions the lamia in his *Fortalitium Fidei* (Lyon, 1487), 119, with no reference to Rupert.

87. Lisa Lampert, "The Once and Future Jew: The Croxton *Play of the Sacrament*, Little Robert of Bury and Historical Memory," *Jewish History* 15, no. 3 (2001), and id., *Gender and Jewish Difference from Paul to Shakespeare* (Philadelphia,

2004). On the Virgin as healer, see Denise Despres, "Mary of the Eucharist: Cultic Anti-Judaism in Some Fourteenth-Century English Devotional Manuscripts," in *From Witness to Witchcraft*, ed. Jeremy Cohen, 375–402; and see Blumenkranz, *Auteurs chrétiens*, 136, Pseudo-Bede I, 8thc.

88. See David Nirenberg, *Communities of Violence: Persecution of Minorities in the Middle Ages* (Princeton, 1996), 220 (I thank Katherine Beller for this reference).

89. As reported by Bell, *Sacred Communities*, 106.

90. Gonzalo de Berceo, *Los milagros de nuestra señora*, ed. Brian Dutton (London, 1971), 140–41.

91. Abulafia, *Christians and Jews in the Twelfth-Century Renaissance*, 130.

92. Abbot Clement of St. Andrew's Benedictine Abbey in Cleveland, July 2002, http://csnmail.net/bocohio/07-01-02.htm (accessed June 29, 2005).

93. In this sense of individual identification with Christ and the anxiety that Jews might be bent on killing every individual Christian, one might venture that the Christ in Mel Gibson's movie *The Passion of the Christ* is an inverted ritual murder victim, the murdered child projected back onto Christ, which is why so many viewers identified so strongly with the scourged and endlessly suffering figure on the screen.

94. Gavin Langmuir, *History, Religion, and Antisemitism* (Berkeley, 1990), 238; Stow, *Alienated Minority*, 238.

95. See Claudine Fabre-Vassas, *The Singular Beast: Jews, Christians and the Pig*, trans. Carol Volk (New York, 1997), who also speaks of the total draining and consumption of blood itself in foods like blood pudding as somehow associated with Jews.

96. Robert Bonfil, *The Jews in Renaissance Italy* (Berkeley, 1992), 23.

97. Ariel Toaff, *The Jews in Medieval Assisi, 1305–1487* (Florence, 1979), 61.

98. Cited by Bell, *Sacred Communities*, 113.

99. On holiness in the town, see the work of Edward Muir, Elizabeth Cruzet-Pavan, and Guido Ruggiero, cited in Kenneth Stow, *Theater of Acculturation* (Seattle, 2001), 152; and esp. Natalie Zemon Davis, "The Sacred and the Social Body in Sixteenth-Century Lyons," *Past and Present* 90 (1981): 40–70.

100. On the centrality of private property in legal developments, alongside social implications, see Donald R. Kelley, *The Human Measure: Social Thought in the Western Legal Tradition* (Cambridge, Mass., 1990). Apostolic Poverty, declared heretical in 1322, yet apparently relegitimized by the fifteenth century, was the teaching that Jesus and the Apostles not only held all in common, but they actually owned nothing at all. Early Franciscans emulated this ideal. Pope John XXII condemned it, perceiving that it threatened the material fabric of the Church; see Ernst Benz, *Ecclesia Spiritualis: Kirchenidee und Geschichtstheologie der franziskanischen Reformation* (Stuttgart, 1934).

101. Ronnie Po-chia Hsia, *Trent 1475: Stories of a Ritual Murder Trial* (New Haven, 1992), 54.

102. Esther Cohen has called my attention to James Marrow, "*Circumdederunt me canes multi*: Christ's Tormentors in Northern European Art of the Late Middle Ages and Early Renaissance," *Art Bulletin* 59, no. 2 (1977): 167–81, and id., *Passion Iconography in Northern European Art of the Late Middle Ages and the Early Renaissance* (Kortrijk, Netherlands, 1979). The imagery Marrow brings extends from the ninth century onward. Marrow also shows textual parallels, especially in the account of Arent Willemsz, a sixteenth-century Dutch pilgrim to Jerusalem, who speaks of the Jews who arrest Jesus as "raging around the garden like fierce dogs," clearly the same image as that of the Psalmist. Additional material, both textual and pictorial, has been added by Debra Strickland, *Saracens, Demons, and Jews: Making Monsters in Medieval Art* (Princeton, 2003), esp. 159–160, 190, who traces the appearance of dog imagery to antiquity and demonstrates the prevalence of cynocephalic, dog-headed, figures in plastic art. Her overall thesis that the enemy is made a monster has merits, and I hope to see it fully elaborated. See also Debra Hassig [= Strickland], "Iconography of Rejection: Jews and Other Monstrous Races," in *Image and Belief: Studies in Celebration of the Eightieth Anniversary of the Index of Christian Art*, ed. Colum Hourihane (Princeton, 1999), 35, 37.

103. For this reference, I once again thank Magda Teter, who tells me that in the written legend, the dog not only consumes the dismembered child but vomits it out. As an undergraduate student at the University of Massachusetts, Amherst, pointed out to me, in the original colors, one notes the dominance of red and blue, the colors of the Virgin. Is the artist implying that the Virgin always savingly intervenes, as in the tales of Gonzalo de Berceo and the Jew of Bourges? The painting is one of a group known as the *Martyriologium Romanum*, which show Catholics being martyred by Protestants, Cossacks, and Tatars. The series was commissioned by Stefan Zuchowski, a local priest, and was executed by Carol de Prevot, an Italian, although of French origin, who worked on it from 1708 until his death in 1737, after which it was completed by Jan Sroczyn'ski of Lvov. In 1710, Zuchowski instigated trials against Jews whom he charged with ritual murder. Vivian Mann pointed out to me the child in a crucifixion pose.

104. The problem in all these cases, which go back to Gregory the Great, was conflicting noises, those of the Church apparently drowned out by those of the synagogue, and they were all resolved by removing the synagogue, as did Philip V. Gregory's text is in Simonsohn, *Apostolic See and the Jews*, vol. 8, and Petrus Browe cites all the other texts in "Die religiöse Duldung der Juden im Mittelalter," *Archiv für katholisches Kirchenrecht* 118 (1938): 29–30. The concept of *strepitum* occurs in Modena in the seventeenth century at the center of an inquistional trial, on which see Beller, "The Inquisition and the Jews in Modena."

105. See Miccoli, "Santa Sede," a book-length study, esp. 1404–5, where the pope says: "per la loro durezza e incredulità divennero cani. Di questi cani ce n'ha pur troppi oggidì in Roma, e li sentiamo latrare per tutte le vie, e ci vanno molestando per tutti i luoghi" (We have too many of these dogs in Rome these days,

whom we hear barking up and down the streets, annoying everyone everywhere). Some months later, the pope added: "Non conoscono Dio questi ebrei che scivono bestemmie e oscenità nei giornali" (These Jews do not know God, who fill the papers with blasphemies and obscenity). This material is now also discussed by Augusto Sartorelli, "Ebrei e società cristiana ne pensiero tradizionalista cattolico," *Rassegna mensile di Israel* 69 (2003): 139. Was Pius thinking of something along the lines of what Matthew Henry said: "The prophet calls the false prophets dumb dogs (Isa. 56:10), to which the apostle [Paul] here Phil. 3.2 seems to refer. *Dogs*, for their malice against the faithful professors of the gospel of Christ, barking at them and biting them" (Internet edition)? Quite possibly. Henry's Protestantism was not the issue here. See, too, further mentions of Jews and animals in Stow, *Alienated Minority*, chap. 11. An ironic upside-down version of this image is noted in Schmitt, *Conversion d'Hermann le Juif*, esp. 20, which discusses "lingua canum contra inimicos . . . latrantes" (The tongues of the dogs who bark at their enemies) as cited in the anonymous "Vie de Godfried de Cappenberg" (c. 1150), commenting on Ps. 68:24. Here the dogs bark against the enemies of God, but the dogs are converts from Judaism, and the enemies remain the Jews. Is this a racial-like taint in the twelfth century? And see the texts cited by Lotter, "Position of the Jews," which also make one wonder whether the converted Jews are to be understood as *humiliati*, eating crumbs, somehow second-class. This suggestion has the air of midrash about it, yet somehow the two texts seem connectable.

106. Ramón Martí [Raymundus Martinus], *Pugio fidei adversus Mauros et Judaeous* . . . ed. J. Carpzov (Leipzig, 1687), pt. 3, distinction 3, chap. 22, par. 15, and also 16, "foetet adhuc doctrina scribarum," and again 19, "foetida facta sit doctrina" (their stinking doctrine).

107. On the Roman Ghetto, its background, history, and social structures, see Stow, *Theater of Acculturation*, passim.

108. Simonsohn, *Apostolic See and the Jews*, no. 5.

109. Gregory of Tours, discussed in Stow, *Alienated Minority*, 55–56, and the citation there.

110. Simonsohn, *Apostolic See and the Jews*, no. 8: "Praedictos vero Hebraeos gravari vel affligi contra rationis ordinem prohibemus. Sed sicut Romanis vivere legibus permittuntur [Jews should not be burdened against the rule of reason. They should be allowed to live by the Roman law], annuente iustitia actosque suos ut norunt nullo inpediente disponant. Eis tamen Christiana mancipia habere non liceat."

111. For some initial references to this issue, see n. 20 above. Too often, the Augustinian influence is posited, not demonstrated. Try as I may, I simply find no direct citation of Augustine in books like Linder, trans. and ed., *Jews in the Legal Sources*, and Blumenkranz, *Auteurs chrétiens*. When Bernard of Clairvaux berated the monk Rudolf for agitating against Jews on the eve of the Second Crusade, he cited Paul, Rom. 11:25–26, linked to Ps. 146/7:2, "Aedificans Jerusalem Dominus,

dispersiones Israelis congregabit?" From Ps 58:12, Bernard cited only the three words "ne occidas eos?" not Augustine, and certainly not the verse's continuation, "lest my people forget," which supposedly "explains" the Augustinian theory of witness. Bernard does speak of Jews as living words of Scripture, but immediately adds: because they recall for us Christ's passion. This does not mean they preserve Scripture or are witnesses of pre-Christian truth. Bernard of Clairvaux, *Epistolae*, no. 365, in *Patrologiae cursus completus: series latina*, ed. Migne, vol. 182. Otto of Freising, too, in his *Gesta Friderici I. imperatoris*, ed. Waitz and von Simson (Hannover, 1912), 1: 37–38, cites only the three words from Psalm 58, "Do not kill them," and attributes them to Bernard. Again, the complement is not the immediate continuation of "Lest my people forget," but the succeeding verse: "Scatter them by your power," as though avoiding the questions of memory and witness and saying that it is enough they are scattered and subservient; we must not add to this by massacre. For a citation of the full verse of Ps. 58:12 (Heb. 59:12), we must wait for, of all places, the very late twelfth-century *Sefer Zekhirah* of Ephraim of Bonn, who attributes the full verse to Bernard—well after the fact, of course—and has Bernard say that to harm a Jew is the same as to harm Christ himself (Haberman, *Sefer gezerot*, 116), recalling an image invoked by Regino of Prum (Linder, trans. and ed., *Jews in the Legal Sources*, no. 620). We can only guess at Ephraim's source. It is puzzling that if that source was Augustine, and perhaps it was for Bernard as well, Augustine was not cited directly. Was Bernard specifically reviving Augustine, therefore, or an idea that had filtered its way through time but had exceeded its original context? The same would apply to others, should they be found, who may have cited the verse the way Bernard did. Whatever their intention, it was not to sustain a preexisting doctrine of "Jewish witness."

As for papal texts, there is no evocation of Jewish witness until the *Sicut iudaeis non* of Innocent III; the identical bulls of Alexander III and Clement III have no such reference (Grayzel, *Church and the Jews*, no. 18; Simonsohn, *Apostolic See and the Jews*, 1: nos. 49 and 63). Nor does this mean that Innocent finally made the implicit explicit or that Augustine's text and supposed "doctrine" had at last been discovered. More likely, the text was known but had neither been used nor was deemed of much value. There were too many solid reasons for tolerating Jews, including Pauline-dictated necessity and the heritage of Roman law. By the time of Innocent, however, the papal Church began to appreciate how difficult maintaining Jewish status had become and was casting about to reinforce it, preferably with a biblical citation, much as Gregory the Great had once denounced forced conversion precisely because no biblical verse sustained it. The idea was to balance subservience with protection. We should not make light of Innocent III's letter warning that a special habit for Jews must not be allowed to endanger them (Grayzel, *Church and the Jews*, 1: no. 31). Put otherwise, the time when Regino of Prum could say Jews should not be harmed, since they are created in the image of God, had passed (Linder, trans. and ed., *Jews in the Legal Sources*, no. 620); yet

Regino himself favored strict regulation. It was not one or the other, mildness versus severity, as traditional historiography has preferred to view it.

A letter of John XXII, issued to protect Jews from the devastating attacks of the Shepherds, does speak of "defensione Iudaeos, quo specialius sunt in testimonium Catholice fidei reservati" (protection of the Jews, who have been especially maintained in testimony of the Christian faith) (July 9, 1320, Simonsohn, *Apostolic See and the Jews,* no. 306). Yet one must ask what stimulated the introduction here of the idea of witness, which may also be the testimony offered by the Jews' punishment, as Augustine himself would say (on which see n. 118 below)? Was it reading Augustine directly, despite the long gap in time during which he was *not* cited, or, more likely, a reference to Ps. 58:12 in the *Summa Theologica* of Aquinas or in the mid thirteenth-century *Summa* by Alexander of Hales? In the event, the Augustinian idea of witness, or the use of Ps. 58:12 as a proof text, seems to be a later construct rather than an earlier one, and it stretches the imagination to attribute the fully articulated idea of Jewish witness as it is invoked today to Augustine himself. The implications for those who wish to divide the Middle Ages of the Jews vis-à-vis the Church into Augustinian and post-Augustinian periods of tolerance followed by heavy restriction or even represssion clearly need serious rethinking. A continuous textual tradition substantiating this old vision does not exist. In fact, the texts suggest the contrary.

112. De Susannis, *De Iudaeis et aliis infidelibus,* 1.7.4, *iure optimo expellendos;* on the Udine episode, see Kenneth Stow, "The Jew as Alien and the Diffusion of Restriction: An Expulsion Text from Udine, 1556," in *Jews in Italy: Studies Dedicated to the Memory of U. Cassuto,* ed. Haim Beinart (Jerusalem, 1988). It is noteworthy that de Susannis did have a text to lean on here, the *Sicut Iudaeis non* of Innocent III, whose clause threatening the cessation of protection should Jews hatch plots had been revived one or two times in fifteenth-century papal letters. Clearly, though, this text was too extreme to be cited as legal precedent. Even Oldradus da Ponte steered clear of it, on whom and the other texts cited here, see nn. 69 and 70 above.

113. Mary Douglas, "Deciphering a Meal," *Daedalus* 101 (1972): 61–82. See Chapter 6 on Douglas's interpretations as they reflect on issues of purity. The pig is "half-kosher," since it has a cloven hoof, the first of the two requirements for a kosher mammal, but it does not ruminate, the second requirement; cows, of course, do both.

114. Augustine, *Adversus Iudaeos,* in *Treatises on Marriage and Other Subjects* . . . trans. Charles T. Wilcox et al., ed. Roy J. Deferrari (Washington, D.C., 1969), 391–416; Agobard, *Epistolae contra Iudaeos,* ed. and trans. Gilboa, 18 and 46, with Agobard citing Rom. 11:25–26.

115. Cited, along with the French original, in Maureen Boulton, "Anti-Jewish Attitudes in French Literature," in *Jews and Christians,* ed. Signer and Van Engen, 242. Superfluous to say, this is really Paul in Romans 11, turning Paul's question

about ultimate Jewish rejection into "whom we should kill as dogs," paraphrasing in a nutshell the distance attitudes toward Jews had traversed since Paul's own day.

116. Agobard is, after all, otherwise known as St. Agobard, for his defense of the Church.

117. See Gerson Cohen, "Esau as Symbol."

118. Jeremy Cohen, *Living Letters of the Law*, table on 41. For Augustine, Jews also witnessed something else. In his direct analysis of Psalm 58, Augustine wrote that Jews bore "witness to their iniquity and our truth" (testes iniquitatis suae et veritatis nostrae [*In Ps. 58 Enarr.* 1, 21–22; *PL* 26–37, 765]), and see this verse again in Chapter 7, as discussed and cited by Kurt Hruby. Jews thus bear witness to (theological) criminality, hardly a reason for gentle toleration. See, moreover, Innocent IV's bull *Lachrymabilem*, July 5, 1247 (Grayzel, *Church and the Jews*, 1: 268, no. 116), where to fend off unwarranted assaults the pope says "quasi ex archivio eorum Christiane fidei testimonia prodierunt" (. . . as though their past testifies to the Christian faith). But could Innocent, who fully appreciated the charge of blasphemy leveled at Jewish books in his day, even though he was cautious about whether they all were blasphemous, have meant "the testimony of their books"? No, I believe he meant the testimony of their past, their actions. Just as did Augustine.

119. See, too, Augustine, *Contra Faustum* 12.12–13, as cited and trans. in Jeremy Cohen, *Living Letters of the Law*, 28: "Every Emperor or King . . . having discovered them with the mark [of Cain], has not made them cease to live as Jews, distinct . . . by this blatant and appropriate sign of their observance."

120. Augustine, *Adversus Judaeos*, final chapter.

121. On this episode and its various interpretations, see Stow, *Alienated Minority*, 35–36.

Chapter One. Ambivalence and Continuity

1. The entry on Simone di Trento in the *Enciclopedia cattolica* (Rome, 1949–54) is 13: 640. In the *New Catholic Encyclopedia* (Washington, D.C., 1967), Edward Flannery, whose strong stance against anti-Semitism is well known, speaks of "delusions" (1: 635), while Kurt Hruby writes of the "calumny of ritual murder" (8: 1331), a position he had already taken in the *Lexikon für Theologie und Kirche* (Fribourg, 1963); see Chapter 7 for more on Hruby. F. D. Lazenby, a professor of classics at Notre Dame University, is ambivalent on Simon of Trent in the *New Catholic Encyclopedia* (13: 226), referring neither to the sharp denunciation of the trial by the Dominican Bishop de' Giudici nor to the great reserve of Pope Sixtus IV: his entry raises questions. Simon's cult had already been repressed in 1965. It was unfortunately decided not to include a revised entry on the medieval papacy and the Jews in the revision of the *New Catholic Encyclopedia* that appeared in 2003 (http://cuapress.cua.edu/NCE/NCEDescription.htm [accessed June 29, 2005]). I myself was commissioned to write this entry, a draft of which was positively vetted,

only to be rejected afterward as unwanted; this decision possibly reflects reaction to Kertzer, *Popes Against the Jews*.

2. Gérard Mathon, "Richard of Pontoise," *Bibliotheca Sanctorum* (Rome, 1968), 11: 170; see Lazenby cited in the preceding note. As of the year 2000, Mathon was co-editor of the important encyclopedic series published under the patronage of the Institut catholique de Lille, *Catholicisme*; it has no entry on Richard of Pontoise. We must, however, soon return to Mathon, whose real meaning was the opposite of first appearances.

3. Most remarkable in this vein in the *Catholic Encyclopedia* are the paired essays on "Jews: History," and "Judaism," both by François Gigot, who wrote many essays for this encyclopedia but who is otherwise unknown to me. The essay on Judaism is compassionate, but supersessionist, including some sharp comments about Jewish attitudes. But even it does not accuse all Jews of the death of Christ, and it notes that "it is said [in the Gospels] that Jews are guilty." The "Jews: History" essay should be compared with what the nearly contemporary *Jewish Encyclopedia* has to say on the subject. The two have very much in common, including scholarly rigor and choice of subject. Gigot avoids theology entirely and speaks of both persecution and papal defense of Jews. He also republishes Innocent IV's letter of 1247 about the falsity of the blood libel, the very same letter Leo XIII had refused to publish about a decade prior to Gigot's essay. The record, however, is not perfect: on Hugh of Lincoln the *Catholic Encyclopedia* says: "Whether there was any basis of truth in the accusation against the Jews there is now no means of ascertaining." These entries were transcribed in 1999, on the web site NewAdvent.org. Further ambivalence appears on the Internet in Catholic-Forum.com, which lists Simon of Trent under patron saints (despite the suppression of the cult and absence of formal canonization), saying: "Child reported murdered by Jews during Easter time out of hatred for Christ; libel of the day claimed they needed his blood to make matzoh bread. Seventeen Jews were tortured into confessions. Miracles were reported through Simon's intercession, but the incident is a matter of anti-Semitism rather than sanctity." Catholic-Forum boasts of thousands of "hits" a day; for other sites, see Chapter 5, at n. 18, below, and also those mentioned above.

4. Alban Butler, *Lives of the Saints*, ed. Herbert Thurston and Donald Attwater (New York, 1956). In fact, with respect to Hugh, Attwater is a bit imprecise, saying (for August 27): "It is impossible to tell now whether the Jews were innocent or guilty of the crime attributed to them; the widespread anti-Semitism of the Middle Ages encouraged the conviction that Hugh suffered in *odium fidei*." However, this is to be read within the context of (March 25, on William of Norwich): "It is to the credit of Butler's sober judgement that even while he accepts without question that the various child victims were really put to death by Jews in hatred of the Christian faith, he adds that 'it is a notorious slander of some authors, who, from these singular and extraordinary instances, infer this to have been at any

time the custom or maxim of that people." Attwater also points to Thurston's vigorous rejection of the accusations at the turn of the twentieth century in the Jesuit journal *The Month* 90 (1898): 561–74, and again in 122 (1913): 502–13, which regrettably I have been unable to consult directly.

5. Donald Attwater, *The Penguin Dictionary of Saints* (New York, 1965), 342.

6. *Historia et cartularium monasterii Sancti Petri Gloucestriae,* ed. William Henry Hart, Rerum Britannicarum medii aevi scriptores, 33 (London, 1863–67), 1: xl and li. However, see Gavin Langmuir, "Historiographic Crucifixion," in id., *Toward a Definition of Antisemitism* (Berkeley, 1990), 288, who feels that Hart's ambivalence toward ritual murder tales should not be judged harshly. Israel Jacob Yuval, *Two Nations in Your Womb* (in Hebrew) (Jerusalem, 2000), 185, adduces evidence from Ephraim of Bonn that in Ephraim's own words, "a crazy Jew" killed a Christian woman. Such things may have, perhaps really did, happen, but they were not ritual murders. It is perhaps with this thought in mind that Yuval disagrees with Langmuir about episodes like that at Blois, where no victim or body was ever found. Langmuir claims that such cases should not be classed as ritual murders. The distinction should not be taken lightly. Yuval (apart from his difficult argument that Jewish actions stimulated ritual murder narratives) responds that the essence of the accusation is the narrative, not the specific act or its nature. Murder fantasies by themselves count no less than an accusation when a body has been discovered. Narrative and event have the same potential effect: at Blois, thirty Jews were burned to death without a corpse ever being found. This argument makes enormous sense.

7. Paul Guerin, *Les Petits Bollandistes: Vies des Saints* (Paris, 1888), 3: 617–18, Simon of Trent, and 3: 619, William of Norwich; Richard of Pontoise, 3: 634–36. As for the title, the Jesuit Bollandist of the early twentieth century Hippolyte Delehaye, whom we are about to meet, was indignant. He listed this work as a "pseudo-Bollandist" production in his book on Bollandist history, *À travers trois siècles: L'Oeuvre des Bollandistes, 1615–1915* (1920), trans. as *The Works of the Bollandists Through Three Centuries, 1615–1915* (Princeton, 1922), 267.

8. Sabine Baring-Gould, *Lives of the Saints,* rev. ed (Edinburgh, 1914), viii.

9. See here Miccoli, "Santa Sede," and Kertzer, *Popes Against the Jews*. And see also Hillel Kieval, "Representation and Knowledge in Medieval and Modern Accounts of Jewish Ritual Murder," *Jewish Social Studies,* n.s., 1 (1994): 52–72, and id., *Languages of Community, The Jewish Experience in the Czech Lands* (Berkeley, 2000), 181–97, which appeared in an earlier form in *Jewish History* 10, no. 1 (1996): 75–91.

10. Elphège Vacandard, "La Question du meurtre rituel chez les Juifs," in *Études de critique et d'histoire religieuse,* 2d ed., 3d. ser., 311–77 (Paris, 1912); Langmuir mentions Vacandard in "Historiographic Crucifixion," 288.

11. Leopold Lipschitz, ed., *Christliche Zeugnisse gegen die Blutbeschuldigung* (Berlin, 1882), 12–18. Delitzsch did criticize certain Jewish attitudes toward Christianity. He also engaged in missionizing. This work is an extraordinary collection

of statements made by both Catholic and Protestant professors of theology, various academics, and two Catholic bishops. Delitzsch himself may have been the editor. The unambiguous criticism stands in sharp relief to the ambivalence of later times just noted.

12. Henri Desportes, *Le Mystère du sang chez les juifs* (Paris, 1889, 1890), is discussed in Vacandard, "Question du meurtre rituel," as is the *Osservatore cattolico*. Vacandard also discusses Rohling and Delitzsch, on whom, see also Vernet's magisterial essay "Juifs et Chrétiens," esp. col. 1706, where Vernet lists sixteen variations on the ritual murder-blood libel theme.

13. On *La civiltà cattolica,* see the succinct and valuable entry by Emmanuel Beeri in the *Encyclopedia Judaica* (Jerusalem, 1971), 5: 599–600, which makes the principal points detailed in subsequent discussions of this journal.

14. Innocent III did speak of "a certain poor scholar who had been found murdered in their latrine," suggesting that the pope accepted the by then common belief that Jews did murder Christians; see Grayzel, *Church and the Jews,* 1: 109. But to the contrary, Innocent IV categorically denied that Jews "shared [take communion with] the heart of a murdered child" (se corde pueri communicant interfecti) during Passover solemnities (ibid., 268–71, no. 116; though Grayzel is correct to translate *communicare* as share, as will be seen in Chapter 3, at n. 40, in this instance the sacramental sense of the term is preferable, "to take communion," as Jerome already uses *communicare* in the Vulgate, in particular, in the determinant I Corinthians 10: 16, *communicatio* sanguinis Christi; and see, too, J. F. Niermeyer, *Mediae Latinitatis Lexicon Minus* [Leiden, 1976], 222-223). Innocent IV also condemned the habit that "wherever a dead body is found, their persecutors wickedly throw it up to them" (ac eis malitiose obiciunt hominis cadaver mortui, si contigerit illud alicubi reperiri), which is really a condemnation of the claims in many of the ritual murder narratives (to be seen below) that Jewish murderers hid their victims buried in the ground or in pools of water.

15. Lipschitz, ed., *Christliche Zeugnisse*, 9.

16. Ibid., 25, and passim.

17. Peter Browe, *Die eucharistischen Wunder des Mittelalters* (Breslau, 1938), and see Browe against the Host Accusation, "Die Hostienschändungen der Juden im Mittelalter," *Romische Quartalschrift* 34 (1926): 167–97.

18. It is difficult to imagine there is no link between the Jesuit attachment to the ritual murder accusation and the Order's persistence, as late as 1923, and even afterward, in limiting membership for those whose ancestors were Jewish, a veritable continuation of the *limpieza de sangre* laws of the sixteenth century and the source of disputes in the Order at that time; see Anna Foa, "The Religious Orders and Conversion," in *The Friars and the Jews,* ed. Stephen McMichael and Susan Myers (Leiden, 2004), for the sixteenth century, and James Carroll, *Constantine's Sword: The Church and the Jews: A History* (New York, 2000), 383, for more modern issues.

19. Browe, who lived in Switzerland and Italy, beside Germany, was thus speaking out more directly, certainly more publicly, than was the Catholic hierarchy, including the popes, of the time. On Browe's essays on Jews, see the introduction of Bernard Blumenkranz to the reprint of Browe's *Judenmission* (Rome, 1973; originally 1942), and Kenneth Stow, "The Church and the Jews, From St. Paul to Paul IV," in *Bibliographical Essays in Medieval Jewish Studies*, vol. 2 (New York, 1976), 129, 145. In a review of Browe's "Die Judenbekämpfung im Mittelalter," a copy of which I found attached to Grayzel's personal copy of Browe's essay, but with no reference to its provenance—probably the *Jewish Quarterly Review*, no. 122 or 123 (1939–40): 210, 212n5, Solomon Grayzel questioned Browe's assertion that Christians were not as bitter in their attacks on Judaism as were Jews in their attacks on Christianity. Yet, emotionally, Browe must have needed to say something like this. We might ask how Browe's generally sympathetic picture, except perhaps on lending and its ills, came to be published in Nazi Leipzig in 1938. Was the censor on vacation, or did somebody display true courage? In drawing his conclusions, Browe surely knew that self-abnegating (Christian) love is rarely practiced. We should concentrate, in any case, on the ability of people like Browe to distinguish scholarly study from their personal anxieties and desires; the same applies to François Gigot, the author of the rigorously scholarly essay on Jewish history in the 1910 *Catholic Encyclopedia*, mentioned above. Browe also tries to distinguish "legal" from "illegal" persecution. In a handwritten note, Grayzel remarked to the effect of "What difference does it make?"—correctly, to be sure. Yet this same distinction, toned down, informs the Vatican's 1998 document "We Remember: A Reflection on the Shoah" (www.vatican.va/roman_curia/pontifical_councils/chrstuni/documents/rc_pc_chrstuni_doc_16031998_shoah_en.html [accessed May 17, 2005]), which tries to distinguish anti-Judaism from anti-Semitism. Were Grayzel, a man of true generosity and blessed memory, still alive, he would, no doubt, upon reading "We Remember," have repeated what he said about Browe's (similar) distinction. We shall return to "We Remember" in Chapter 7.

20. Kurtz, *Politics of Heresy*, 72.

21. As Gavin Langmuir pointed out in his classic "Majority History and Postbiblical Jews," reprinted in his *Toward a Definition of Antisemitism*, once again, seeking out its Jewish aspects often reveals otherwise hidden dimensions of a subject usually studied only from the angle of non-Jewish history. In this case, we see how irrational the anti-modernist party had become.

22. Joassart, *Hippolyte Delehaye*, 109–10. Its frankness and condemnation of fundamentalism in the Church at the start of the twentieth century make Joassart's book, published by the Bollandist press in 2000, the best discussion of the modern Bollandists and Catholic modernism (Joassart himself is a leading contemporary Bollandist). None of Delehaye's anger had to do with attitudes toward Jews. Delehaye and Halkin were writing from Leuven (Louvain) in the *Analecta Bollandiana* 43 (1925): 211 and 44 (1926): 183, of which Delehaye was an editor (I thank Tomasso Caliò for the references to the *Analecta*).

23. Vauchez, *Sainthood in the Later Middle Ages*, 155, noting specifically the twelve-year-old Maria Goretti, whom Pius XII canonized in 1950; Vauchez himself mentions de' Giudici and Pius XII in the same sentence. See also Introduction n. 72, above.

24. Delehaye, *Work of the Bollandists Through Three Centuries*, 87–116, outlines the Bollandist method, emphasizing analysis and criticism of sources, together with outspokenness about myth.

25. Delehaye's *Les Légendes hagiographiques* (Brussels, 1903, 1905, 1927) and *Origines du culte des martyrs* are perhaps the classic works of modern scientific, scholarly hagiography, and one is not surprised to hear his name mentioned among modernism's proponents.

26. Ignaz von Döllinger, *Die Juden in Europa: Rede, gehalten in der Festsitzung der Münchener Akademie am 25. Juli 1881* (Berlin, 1921), 11; and see Kornberg, "Ignaz von Döllinger's *Die Juden in Europa*," 230, 233.

27. Kornberg, "Ignaz von Döllinger's *Die Juden in Europa*," recognizes that ultramontanism and integralism promoted anti-Semitism—he cites, in particular, the study of Olaf Blaschke, *Katholizismus und Antisemitismus im Deutschen Kaiserreich* (Göttingen, 1997). I am suggesting, beyond affinity, that responses like that of Döllinger to attacks on Judaism were endemic to modernism, wherever modernism appeared, regardless of whether the link was intentional, as in Döllinger's case, or parallel, as in Delehaye's.

28. Döllinger, *Juden in Europa*, p. 766. See also L. Erler, "Die Juden des Mittelalters," "Die Päpste und die Juden," and "Die Judenverfolgungen des Mittelalters," *Archiv für katholisches Kirchenrecht* 42 (1879): 3–80, and the continuation in vols. 43, 44, 48, 50, and 53.

29. James Carroll, in *Constantine's Sword*, is, by his own eloquent admission, following a similar path, which may explain Döllinger's attractiveness for Carroll, regardless of how aware Carroll was of Döllinger's early writing.

30. On this entry, see n. 3 above.

31. See n. 1 above on Lazenby.

32. The full title is *Martyrologium Romanum ad formam editionis typicae scholiis historicis instructum*, which is also known more commonly by its other title, *Propylaeum ad Acta Sanctorum Decembris* (Brussels, 1940) (I thank John McCulloh for this reference).

33. Delehaye, *Work of the Bollandists Through Three Centuries*, 116–56.

34. Domenichino del Val, c. 1250. The story of this commission is found in Miccoli, "Santa Sede," 1525–44, 1540.

35. Apparently Father Herbert Thurston, the reviser of Butler, was part of this group, on whom, see n. 4 above.

36. Kertzer, *Popes Against the Jews*, 230–35. Oddly, there was no Host libel revival—or perhaps not so oddly, since as the libel is normally told, it rests on miraculous fantasy and would not, in modern terms, evoke credence the way the

murder libel does, not to mention that, as we shall see, the ritual murder, blood, and Host libels had been wholly integrated by the fifteenth century, if not earlier.

37. "Gli ebrei simbolo della modernità" is a subheading in Miccoli's "Santa Sede," a broad study of the Church and the Jews at the turn of the twentieth century, 1394–1401. See also the bull *Quanta cura*, discussed in Kertzer, *Kidnapping of Edgardo Mortara*, 257, and the references cited there.

38. On this theme's contemporary resonance, see Ernesto Galli della Logia in the Italian newspaper *Corriere della sera*, March 25, 2000; and most recently, Kertzer, *Popes Against the Jews*.

39. On this event, see Anna Foa, *Giordano Bruno* (Bologna, 1998), 7–12.

40. Kornberg, "Ignaz von Döllinger's *Die Juden in Europa*," 235, 239. Kornberg's translation.

41. Miccoli, "Santa Sede," 1394–1401. On medieval Christian reaction to Jewish prayer, see William C. Jordan, *The French Monarchy and the Jews* (Philadelphia, 1989), 17. On Pius IX, see Miccoli, "Santa Sede."

42. On sacred space and Jews in Italian cities, see Elizabeth Crouzet-Pavan, "Venice Between Jerusalem, Byzantium, and Divine Retribution: The Origins of the Ghetto," *Mediterranean Historical Review* 6 (1991): 164; Edward Muir, "The Virgin on the Street Corner: The Place of the Sacred in Italian Cities," in *Religion and Culture in the Renaissance and Reformation*, ed. S. Ozment (Kirksville, Mo., 1989), 28.

43. Simonsohn, *Apostolic See and the Jews*, no. 8; see also Chapter 3, at nn. 62–67, recalling that it was considered imperative that the sounds of Jewish prayer should not disturb Christian liturgies.

44. *La civiltà cattolica*, 3d ser., 8–10 (1881).

45. Thomasso Caliò, "Antisemitismo e culto dei santi in età contemporanea: Il caso del beato Lorenzino da Marostica," in *Il pubblico dei santi: Forme e livelli di ricezione dei messaggi agiografici*, ed. Paolo Golinelli (Rome, 2000), 421, 427, 412, in that order.

46. See Chapter 5 for this accusation made in Savoy in 1329. Roger Gougenot des Mousseaux, *Le Juif, le judaïsme et la judaïsation des peuples chrétiens* (1869; 2d ed., Paris, 1886), xxxiii, is cited here and in further references from Vernet, "Juifs et Chrétiens," inasmuch as I have been unable to consult Gougenot directly. The anonymous 1840 citation is found in Maria Teresa Pichetto, "L'antisemitismo di mons: Umberto Benigni e l'accusa di omicidio rituale," in *Italia Judaica IV*, ed. Ministero per i beni culturali (Rome, 1993), 435.

47. Vulgate, 1 Cor. 10:16–17: "calicem benedictionis cui benedicimus nonne communicatio sanguinis Christi est et panis quem frangimus nonne participatio corporis Domini est quoniam unus panis unum corpus multi sumus omnes quidem de uno pane participamur."

48. On *patria communis*, see Kantorowicz, *King's Two Bodies*, 195–96; in general, Kantorowicz persuasively demonstrates the medieval transfer of theological

terminology to the state and to the (lay) concept of sovereignty. The *patria communis*, which was originally a denomination of the Church, gradually became the state. Competition was implicit, and the French Revolution brought it to a climax by establishing the secular sacred mystical body. On the role of Christ's actual body in this process, see Stacey, "From Ritual Crucifixion to Host Desecration," 12, who adds the dimension of the historical body of Christ, which will be important in the fusion of all three elements so explicit in the story of the Good Werner of Oberwesel.

Pierre Birnbaum has noted that in destroying "collective identities," the postrevolutionary French state left a void, whose existence was denoted, on the one hand, by those deprived of these "identities" (sustainers of the previous corporate or religious bodies), who focused attention on Jews as the symbol of this change, and, on the other, by the rapid insinuation of Jews into positions of leadership in state offices. A new world had been created, wholly displacing the old. More, the state, as a state, put the weight of its political, judicial, and even police apparatus at the service of Jews, in the sense that it rigorously defended them against attacks, which did break out (note that already Agobard had complained to Louis the Pious about the king's defending Jews). What Birnbaum describes, then, is the tangible aspect, and direct reaction to it, of the structural replacement of the prerevolutionary *corpus mysticum* by the new one of the postrevolutionary epoch; see Pierre Birnbaum, "Un Antisémitisme à la française," in *L'Antisémitisme éclairé: Inclusion et exclusion depuis l'époque des Lumières jusqu'à l'affaire Dreyfus*, ed. Ilana Zinguer and Sam Bloom (Leiden, 2003).

49. On theological politics in nineteenth-century France, see Kroen, *Politics and Theater*, 76–108. The importance of Kroen's thesis for this study is, first, that the promoters of this political vision were in large part Jesuits; second, it makes it clear that, even after the Revolution, and for Catholic integralists, if the state is the *Corpus Christi*, and the king who unifies it (metaphorically) is Christ himself—the real presence, both humanly and eucharistically—then any attack on the state is an attack on Christ. Anyone who harms the body of Christ ipso facto attacks the state. But he who attacks the body of Christ is also, and by definition (at least until Vatican II), always a Jew, following the logic of: if the Jews killed Christ, then all who kill/ed Christ must be Jews. Hence, to depict the monarchs as Christ is also to turn the revolutionaries into Christ-killing Jews, ritual murderers, tramplers on the Host, and all the other related accusations, which, as Miccoli so well explains, are bundled together under the heading of modernity. That Jews would come to symbolize modernity was almost a given. With respect to the total expropriation of Corinthians, an idea that probably would have surprised the revolutionary theorists themselves, is this not the final stage in the long process of expropriation of theological terminology described by Kantorowicz? Nobody today, I believe, would argue that historical processes are necessarily conscious ones.

50. Jean Delumeau, *Sin and Fear: The Emergence of a Western Guilt Culture*, trans. E. Nicholson (New York, 1990), 437.

51. However, to all rules, there are exceptions, and the following words of A. Messinio, S.J., in "Gli elementi costitutivi della nazione e la razza," *Civiltà cattolica* (Rome) 89, 3, no. 2115 (August 6, 1938): 209–23, speak for themselves: "La teoria, che riduce la nazione alla razza, è rappresentata oggi e difesa, con una ostinatezza e un fanatismo ideologico degno di migliore causa e con una povertà di argomenti pseudo-storici, e pseudo-scientifici, che fanno poco onore alla scienza, da tutti gli scrittori che traggono ispirazione dal mito razzista della nuova Germania. . . . Sembra, dunque, necessario concludere, dopo quanto si è detto, che *né la razza, né la lingua, né la religione; né il territorio costituiscono l'essenza della nazione, e che pertanto questa debba essere ricercata in qualche altro elemento* [emphasis added], che riduca ad unità gli individui contrassegnati da tutti questi caratteri distintivi." Although Messinio took the idea of race seriously, especially after the racial laws were promulgated in Italy in 1938, he nonetheless presents a theory of what constitutes a nation that in its wording seems to deny not only racial but even religious criteria for establishing a modern state, as well as ethnic and linguistic ones: "The theory that reduces the nation to race is presented and defended today with a fanatic and ideological obstinacy worthy of a better cause, and with a pseudo-historical and pseudo-scientific poverty of argument that does little credit to scholarship, [and is] . . . inspired by the racial myth of the new Germany. . . . [Rather] *neither race, nor language, nor religion, nor even territory constitutes the essence of the nation.*" Messinio sounds more like a scion of the French Revolution than one of its opponents, as other Italian Jesuits so firmly were. Having renounced even *religione* as a unifier, Messinio then offers a justification of the modern, might I even add "nation," state. How this essay got into print, and where it did, should be pursued.

52. On the matter of Judaizing as a social threat in nineteenth-century Germany, especially its theorization, with an awareness of continuities going back to Paul, see Steven E. Aschheim's penetrating essay "'The Jew Within': The Myth of 'Judaization' in Germany," in *The Jewish Response to German Culture*, ed. Jehuda Reinharz and Walter Schatzberg (Hanover, N.H., 1985), esp. 212–14.

53. Stacey, "From Ritual Crucifixion to Host Desecration," 15. Feuerbach is cited, translated, and discussed by Kalman Bland, *The Artless Jews: Medieval and Modern Affirmations and Denials of the Visual* (Princeton, 2000), 25.

54. As we shall see in Chapter 7, the identification of the Jews with "modernity" and, for that matter, racism, however developed and secularized, ultimately reverts to issues of ritual purity and supersession.

Chapter Two. The Bollandists and Their Work

1. See David Knowles, "The Bollandists," in *Problems in Monastic History* (London, 1963) for the best work on the early Bollandists to date; and see also Delehaye, *Works of the Bollandists Through Three Centuries*, and Joassart, *Hippolyte Delehaye*, which also discusses the early Bollandists, albeit briefly. Although all modern

scholarship on saints is deeply indebted to the Bollandists, nobody beyond Delehaye and Knowles has paid them serious attention as scholars. Even Vauchez rarely mentions the Bollandists directly in his landmark *Sainthood in the Later Middle Ages,* except to say that they established, studied, or rejected one sainthood or another; and even these references are principally in brief footnotes. The Bollandists as investigators, their methods, and their goals are never touched on—in which sense, this present study is a step, however rudimentary, in that direction. With respect to the Bollandists' devotion to textual authenticity—as they understood it—see Chapter 5 preceding n. 35, comparing the Bollandists to those Anthony Grafton has called *Defenders of the Text.*

2. Vernet, "Juifs et Chrétiens," col. 1707.

3. On Delehaye's principles, about which he was strikingly frank at times, saying that a mountain of tales might be no more valid than the stories in the *Arabian Nights,* see Joassart, *Hippolyte Delehaye,* 1: 110–30, and Delehaye, *Légendes hagiographiques,* passim.

4. See Delehaye, *Works of the Bollandists Through Three Centuries,* 11, on Roswyde, the real founder of the Bollandists.

5. Du Sollier, of Herseaux in West Flanders; active as a Bollandist, 1702–40; Delehaye, *Works of the Bollandists Through Three Centuries,* 40–43.

6. Hinschius is known to have been responsible for much of the work for March, the month in which the saints' days of many of the ritual murder victims fall, but Delehaye says he asked to remain anonymous; ibid., 30.

7. Joassart, *Hippolyte Delehaye,* 1: 121. Delehaye himself is a bit more restrained on this point in *Works of the Bollandists Through Three Centuries.*

8. Hugh of Lincoln, *ActaSS,* July, 6: 494–95. Jordan, *French Monarchy,* 18, has noted this dating carefully.

9. On the importance of the Eucharist in the Counter-Reformation, see Ronnie Po-chia Hsia, *The Myth of Ritual Murder* (New Haven, 1988), and also the comment of Rubin, *Gentile Tales,* 188. On the continuity of the Catholic world as a *corpo organico* even through the twentieth century, see Giovanni Miccoli, "L'Italia cattolica e il fascismo," *Rassegna mensile di Israel* 69 (2003): 167.

10. On the possible ritual murder charge that preceded and may have played a role in the establishment of the Roman Ghetto, see Anna Foa, "Il gioco del proselitismo: Politica delle conversioni e controllo della violenza nella Roma del Cinquecento," in *Ebrei e Cristiani nell'Italia medievale e moderna: Conversioni, scambi, contrasti,* ed. M. Luzzati, M. Olivari, and A. Veronese (Rome, 1988), 155–70; Joseph HaKohen, *ʿEmeq haBakhʾa,* ed. Meir Letteris (Kraków, 1895), 132; and the chronicle of Benjamin ben Elnatan in Isaiah Sonne, *Mi-Pavolo ha-Reviʾi ʿad Pius ha-Hamishi* (Jerusalem, 1954), 27–28; even the future Paul IV was avid to get his hands on a book of Jewish divination, as appears in *Archivio di Stato, Roma, Tribunale del Governatore, Criminali, Costituti,* 37, 38.

11. The 1066 incident is reported by the *Gesta Treverorum,* for whose text, see Julius Aronius, *Regesten zur Geschichte der Juden im Fränkischen and Deutschen Reiche*

bis zum Jahre 1273 (Berlin, 1902), no. 160. Rubin, *Gentile Tales*, 25–26, stresses the "leap in gravity" between the two charges. Yuval, *Two Nations*, 185, also points to this story as a prototype and notes its possible relationship to a Hebrew tale of events in Limoges or Le Mans (supposedly) in 992; on both of which stories and this relationship, see the Introduction at nn. 87–90 above. On waxen images in general, see nn. 12–14 and 28 below. On Jews and sorcery, the pseudo-chapters/laws concerning Jews named after Charlemagne threaten with burning or drowning any "Jew who should do sorcery against the Christian law or against any Christian" (Linder, trans. and ed., *Jews in the Legal Sources*, 586).

12. See, too, Joshua Trachtenberg's discussion of the poems (c. 1250) of Gonzalo de Berceo in *The Devil and the Jews* (New Haven, 1943), 121. Trachtenberg, great pioneer that he was, refers to many of the incidents or stories noted here, albeit in different contexts. See the text of Gonzalo de Berceo, *Los milagros de nuestra señora*, 140–41. On August 15 (Assumption Day) in Toledo, Gonzalo writes, the Virgin announces to the crowd in the cathedral that the Jews "Once again are crucifying my dear son" (Otra vez cruçifican al mi caro fijuelo), at which news, the crowd and the clergy rush to the *judería*, where in the house of the most noble rabbi, they discover a great body of wax that looks like Christ crucified—a complete melding of images. This same "miracle" is noted in the *Cantigas de Santa María* of Gonzalo's contemporary Alfonso el Sabio (Schmitt, *Conversion d'Hermann le Juif*, 193 and the literature cited in n. 37 there), and it also appears in the *Chronica Slavorum* of Arnold of Lübeck, which transposes it to Cologne.

13. On the *Corpus Christi* as symbol of the body politic, see Kroen, *Politics and Theater*, 25–26, for a precise and concise summary of Kantorowicz's lengthy argument in *King's Two Bodies*. This symbolism, which embraces king, kingdom, body politic, *Corpus Christi*, and even the Eucharist as embodied in the waxen funeral effigy of kings, is shown in Ralph E. Giesey, *The Royal Funeral Ceremony in Renaissance France* (Geneva, 1960), 89. Giesey warns us not to confuse this royal image with that of the *envoûtement*, the French term for sticking pins and other objects into an image to cause harm. However, if the waxen image is truly intended to personify the continuously alive royal political body until the funeral, one must believe it really lives, which can be done by pointing to the reality of the effects of *envoûtement*. Extrapolating from the symbolism, if Jews "murder" waxen images, they are capable of "murdering" the king(dom), too. Moreover, if the waxen image stands for the Eucharist, Jewish actions against it are tantamount to killing Christ and desecrating the Host. All the elements here are interchangeable. This is the iron logic of the irrational; one can but speculate about the possible associations medieval people may have made.

14. The use of blood in image magic was certainly not unknown in this period; see, e.g., Juris Lidaka, "The Book of Angles, Rings, Characters and Images of the Planets Attributed to Osbern Bokenham," in *Conjuring Spirits: Texts and Traditions of Medieval Ritual Magic*, ed. Claire Fanger (University Park, Pa., 1998),

55, on a magic text of the thirteenth century that talks about anointing the image with cock's blood (an element easily transferred and reworked into a blood or Host libel), saying, "daub [the waxen image] with the blood of a black cock on the brow, breast, and feet" (I thank Jeffrey Chajes for this reference). Cf. Minucius Felix, *Octavius*, trans. and ed. Jean Beaujeu (Paris, 1964), 47–48: 28, 2: "quasi Christiani monstra colerunt, infantes vorarent, convivia incesta miscerent, . . . 5. de incestis stupris, de inpiatis sacris, de infantibus immolatis faterentur."

15. John Capgrave et al., *Nova legenda angliae*, ed. Carl Horstman (Oxford, 1901), 2: 39: "ad artes magicas exercendas . . . corpus insontis augurio, ad hoc enim eviscerabatur." Capgrave drew heavily on John of Tynmouth, who died in 1366. On Capgrave, see Langmuir, "Historiographic Crucifixion," in id., *Toward a Definition of Antisemitism*, 286–87, and also 283–89, where Langmuir mentions a number of the works cited above, including Hart, Butler, Flannery, and Vacandard, but not the French sources. Hugh in *ActaSS* is July, 6: 494–95; and see Georg Caro, *Sozial- und Wirtschaftsgeschichte der Juden im Mittelalter und der Neuzeit* (Frankfurt a/M, 1924), 1: 357–61, and 504 for sources.

16. Richard in *ActaSS* is March, 3: 591–92, for the Bollandists' text, including their citations of Rigord, and 593–94, for the *Passio* of Gaguin, where they also cite John Wilson.

17. *ActaSS*, March, 3: 591, referring to crypto-Jews as part of the discussion of the 1182 expulsion, in which the Bollandists effectively display a preference for a society without Jews. On these crypto-Jews, see esp. Yosef Kaplan, *An Alternative Path to Modernity: The Sephardi Diaspora in Western Europe* (Leiden, 2000).

18. On these themes, see especially Adriano Prosperi, "L'inquisitore come confessore," in *Disciplina dell'anima, disciplina del corpo e disciplina della società tra medioevo ed età moderna*, ed. Paolo Prodi and Adriano Prosperi (Bologna, 1994), 187–224, and more widely, Prosperi's *Tribunali di coscienza: Inquisitori, confessori, missionari* (Turin, 1976).

19. On piety of this sort, combining these images, see Despres, "Mary of the Eucharist," 386–88. The Bollandists did not have the long account about William of Norwich we now have by Thomas of Monmouth (I thank Johannes Heil for pointing this out). Nonetheless, no version of the William story contains the kind of materials the Bollandists could draw on with respect to other victims, Werner most particularly.

20. See again Vauchez, "Antisemitismo e canonizzazione popolare." The texts are *ActaSS*, April, 2: 699–730.

21. Hayden White, *The Content of the Form: Narrative Discourse and Historical Representation* (Baltimore, 1987), 58–72. In the full Werner text, the Bollandists explain their reasoning about which source they prefer, explanations that today would be deemed insufficient, but that in their day bespoke the height of scholarly investigation. And see Appendix Two for their text.

22. For this, see the account of Richard of Pontoise in Chapter 3.

23. On this concept in the context of attitudes toward Jews, see Peter Biller, "Views of Jews from Paris Around 1300: Christian or Scientific," in *Christianity and Judaism,* ed. Diana Wood (Oxford, 1992), in which also see Miri Rubin, "Desecration of the Host: The Birth of an Accusation." See also Appendix One for the text of the *Gesta Treverorum*, which tells the Werner story with none of the overtones of the Bollandists' principal sources.

24. Rubin, *Gentile Tales,* 25–26, discusses this symbolism in detail, and see, too, her "Choosing Death?" in *Martyrs and Martyrologies,* ed. Wood, 163–68; and see below the references to Mary Minty, "Kiddush HaShem in Christian Eyes in Medieval Germany," *Zion* 59 (1994): 235–40 (in Hebrew), who also emphasizes the link between this story and eucharistic imagery. On the concatenation of imagery concerning the Jews, see Stow, *Alienated Minority,* 231–42. Most recently, see Peter Schaefer, *Mirror of His Beauty: Feminine Images of God from the Bible to the Early Kabbalah* (Princeton, 2002), esp. 207, "the Jewish boy thrown into the oven and almost baked like a Host." Schaefer, 206, argues that the Bourges story is not one of Jewish threat but of the possibility for all to be saved. In effect, the two elements are not wholly distinct. There is threat, but it is overcome through the saving powers of the Virgin, which induce union into Christianity. The threat is also sought out, if only because the child relates the tale to his father. Arguments now to be made here will try to carry this line of thought a step further.

25. *ActaSS,* April, 2: 699–700. Note that when the Jews try to dispose of the corpse, they throw it into the Rhine, but it will not sink. On this water motif, see Yuval, *Two Nations,* 188–98. The issue of Bollandist editing will be especially important in discussing their editing of the text of Rigord on Philip Augustus and the Jews.

26. *ActaSS,* April, 2: 700E; this testimony is repeated slightly changed by three or four witnesses. The essential terms "mystical" or "true" body appear in all the testimonies. Rubin, *Gentile Tales,* 25–26, reports this testimony in the mouths of two witnesses, citing it from a 1981 essay of André Vauchez, *La Sainteté en occident* (Rome, 1981), 107–8 (I have otherwise cited the English translation here). Vauchez is citing a version from the *Trier Stadtarchiv*, MS 1139, fols. 66r and 89v; this latter text is found almost verbatim in the *ActaSS,* April, 2: 730, par. 93. The Bollandists refer to this as one of their sources, calling it the Codex of Trier. The wording as reported by Vauchez varies slightly from the text cited below, but in the full version from the *ActaSS,* one sees, as Rubin notes, the identity between the true Body of Christ and the mystical body: "et credit eum pro sacramento xristi ymmo ipsum in xristo ut historia cavit occisum"; "verumque dum habere non poterant suam seviciam converterunt in co[r]pus xristi misticum scilicet puerum sanctum et ipsum suspenderunt." The version of the *ActaSS*: "& ab impiis Judæis crudeliter martyrizatus, in eo quaerentibus Christi Corpus: *verum quod dum habere non poterant*, suam sævitiam converterunt in *Corpus Christi mysticum*, scilicet puerum sanctum, & ipsum suspenderunt ad statuam, quae hodie in Wesalia Treverensis dioecesis, in

capella sancti Spiritus, a cunctis in non modica habetur reverentia: & ibi eumdem sanctum puerum occiderunt, prout haec in Legenda antiqua." In truth, the Bollandists repeat varying versions, all separate testimonies that differ only slightly in wording. They all concur on the images and symbolism, perhaps too repeatedly for this to be real testimony.

27. On Adam of Bristol, see Stacey, "From Ritual Crucifixion to Host Desecration," 15, 22, and 27, and esp. 12, citing Alger of Liège speaking about "the body of Christ in human form, the body of Christ in the Sacrament, and the body of Christ in the Church," all three of which Werner was said to incarnate; and see also Yuval, *Two Nations*, 203–18. On such "symbol clusters," as she calls them, which emphasize child images in particular, see Despres, "Mary of the Eucharist," esp. 387. What the literary characters whom Despres discusses intuit or envision becomes explicit in figures like Adam and, even more, Werner.

28. "Through Aristorius, a corrupt Christian merchant, Jonathas and a group of his fellow Jews procure a Host for 100 gold ducats. Once they have the Host they put it through a series of gruesome tortures designed to test the efficacy of Christian belief in 'a cake.' They stab the Host and it bleeds. Then they prepare to throw it into a cauldron of boiling oil, but it sticks to the hand of Jonathas, whose arm ends up severed from his body, but still attached to the Host. Then the Host is thrust into an oven and sealed within. The oven bursts asunder and the image of a bloody child appears" (Lampert, "Once and Future Jew," 235–36, lines 57–60). The Croxton *Play of the Sacrament* is found in *Non-Cycle Plays and Fragments*, ed. Norman Davis, Early English Text Society, suppl. ser. 1 (London, 1970), 58–89. Lampert notes that the oven in which the Eucharist is baked is sealed with clay, much as the oven is sealed with stones and cement in one version of the Bourges story. The exchange of the Host for the boy in the Croxton play is thus intentional. Host, ritual murder, and blood accusations, Lampert says, form a "constellation." Elements of the Bourges host libel and ritual murder accusation once again meld with a variation on the story of waxen images (as in the text of Gonzalo de Berceo; see n. 12 above) in Sogorb, Spain, at Passover time, in 1322, when Jews were accused of molding the crucified Jesus out of bread dough and burning him in an oven (David Nirenberg, *Communities of Violence*, 220). Rubin, "Desecration of the Host," 178, reports a similar story, in which a rich widow steals a Host to sell it to Jews, although there is a strange intermediate stage in which the Host becomes a frog.

29. Odo cited in Abulafia, *Christians and Jews in the Twelfth-Century Renaissance*, 130. And see also *John Colet's Commentary on First Corinthians*, trans. and ed. Bernard O'Kelley and Catherine Jarrott (Binghamton, N.Y., 1985), 213, and its direct continuation: "Nor do they transform the nourishment into themselves, but they are themselves transformed by the nourishment, as by a stronger thing, into itself. For from this comes the conformity and unity of all."

30. Delehaye, *Origines*, 3–4.

31. Gregory, *Salvation at Stake*, 280, 285, 289. "Common good," *communis utilitas*, was a term being used politically as early as the thirteenth century. The king acted for the *communis utilitas* of the body politic. This is to say that Geninges's phrase especially emphasizes the theme of unity of the body, this time, a eucharistic unity.

32. Ibid., 256, 279.

33. Ibid., 277.

34. Ignatius *Ad Roman.* 4.1.2, quoted by Delehaye in *Origines*, 6.

35. See Introduction at n. 91.

36. On the notion of Werner's incorporation into Christ, and on its continuity to today, see not only the decrees of the Council of Trent and similar texts on the Eucharist but what Abbot Clement of St. Andrew's Benedictine Abbey, Cleveland, wrote as recently as July 1, 2002: "The Eucharist doesn't turn into us, but we turn into Jesus" (quoted in the Introduction). In this light, of union with Christ, one might think all charges of ritual murder must involve males, surrogates for Christ, but not so. The ritual murder charge of Valreas in 1247 concerns a young girl (Grayzel, *Church and the Jews*, 1: 265), as does the Polna charge of the late nineteenth century (Kieval, "Representation and Knowledge"). The Bollandists do not bring up the Valreas case, probably because no sainthood was involved, which, we should not forget, was their direct interest.

37. Gavin Langmuir, "Thomas of Monmouth: Detector of Ritual Murder," in id., *Toward a Definition of Antisemitism*, 235.

38. See esp. Langmuir, "Doubt in Christendom," in id., *Toward a Definition of Antisemitism*, but also Rubin, "Desecration of the Host."

39. Macy, *The Theologies of the Eucharist*, 87, who notes that Browe in his *Die eucharistischen Wunder* brings up over one hundred such stories, and Browe of all people knew how and where to distinguish between Host miracle stories that did or did not refer to Jews.

40. See Stow, *Alienated Minority*, 236–40, which also emphasizes transfer and projection of insecurity onto Jews.

41. Aquinas, *Summa Theologica* III: 80: 10 (Cambridge, 1964–1981); see the essays under "Eucharist" in the 1911 *Catholic Encyclopedia* (on-line at Advent.org). The precept of the yearly paschal Communion was solemnly reiterated by the Council of Trent (Session XIII, canon ix).

42. For Barbara Rubbiano, a housewife, see Beller, "The Inquisition and the Jews in Modena," chap. 5, citing *Archivio di Stato, Modena, Fondo inquisitoriale*, b. 4, fol. 21; and also see Giovan Battista Spaccini, *Cronaca di Modena*, ed. Albano Biondi, Rolando Bussi, and Carlo Giovannini, vol. 1: *Anni 1588–1602* (Modena, 1993), 584. The custom of hanging Jews upside down alongside dogs should not go unmentioned.

43. This would also account for the diffusion of ritual murder stories beyond their original venue, on which, see esp. John McCulloh, "Jewish Ritual Murder: William of Norwich, Thomas of Monmouth, and the Early Dissemination of the

Myth," *Speculum* 72: 3 (1997): 698–740. The diffusion reinforces Rubin's theory of legitimacy conferred by stories being told and retold.

44. For Cyprian in the Middle Ages, see Gregory, *Salvation at Stake*: "Lay martyrs also yearned to die for Christ. . . . In exalting martyrdom Catholic writers drew freely on patristic authors, especially Cyprian, Augustine, and Tertullian. Hide's Consolatory Epistle and Southwell's Epistle referred to them repeatedly. Henry Garnet in his Treatise of Christian Renunciation, let them speak for themselves. His final chapter . . . consisted entirely of translated excerpts from Cyprian, Augustine, Ambrose, and Bernard [closing with the story of Hannah and her seven sons in Maccabees]" (280); "If martyrdom, then it was surpassingly valuable. . . . martyrdom was eminently desirable (not as with Protestants [something] that one did for lack of choice)" (279).

45. John Gallen, S.J., "Eucharist: The Mystical Body," Millennium Monthly (on-line publication), July 2000, www.americancatholic.org/Newsletters/MM/ap0600.asp (accessed May 9, 2005). See the similar statement made in 2002 by Abbot Clement of Cleveland, cited in the Introduction and in n. 36 above. Gallen's "Jesus that we are" emphasizes more the points made here, the imminently divine in the martyr.

46. Apart from the work of McCulloh, Langmuir, and Rubin, cited above, see especially Mary Minty, "Kiddush HaShem," and also Israel Jacob Yuval, "Vengeance and Damnation, Blood and Defamation: From Jewish Martyrdom to Blood Libel Accusations," *Zion* 58 (1993): 33–90, with its challenging thesis. On the melding of variant host and murder elements, see again Stacey, "From Ritual Crucifixion to Host Desecration," and the literature he cites, whose point is that Host elements, the insertion of Marian and Eucharistic motives, are present in the thirteenth-century ritual crucifixion account of Adam of Bristol.

47. Thomas of Monmouth, *The Life and Miracles of St. William of Norwich*, ed. Augustus Jessopp and M. R. James (Cambridge, 1896), 25–27. The text says that the Jews wandering about with William's body were immediately suspicious, because they were surprised out of doors on Holy Thursday, an element Thomas could—and would—have used only were it to ring true to readers. Much later, in fifteenth-century Italy, scenes of crucifixions also sometimes place Jews indoors, e.g., Philadelphia Museum of Art, inventory no. 1295, an anonymous "Predella panel of Jesus Christ being led to Calvary" (I thank Magda Teter for this reference).

48. On Agobard, see nn. 51, 52, and 67 in the Introduction above. Guibert is cited in J. F. Benton, *Self and Society in Medieval France* (New York, 1970), 115, and see the immediately following stories of magic, too; and the original in *De vita sua*, ed. E. R. Labande (Paris, 1981), 246–48. See also the reference in Trachtenberg, *Devil and the Jews*, 213.

49. Martí, *Pugio fidei*, pt. 3, distinction 3, chap. 16, par. 13.

50. Theophilos's story is found in Valerie Flint, *The Rise of Magic in Early Modern Europe* (Princeton, 1991), 344–47, and retold in Despres, "Mary of the Eucharist," among many other places, although in a slightly different light.

51. See Delumeau, *Sin and Fear*, 437.

52. See Linder, trans. and ed., *Jews in Legal Sources*, no. 1139. Communion here means social aggregation, of course, not the Eucharist. This text amplifies the Syriac *Teaching of the Apostles*, "15. The apostles further appointed: That whosoever loves the Jews, like Iscariot, who was their friend, or the pagans, who worship creatures instead of the Creator—should not enter in amongst them and minister; and moreover, that if he be already amongst them, they should not suffer him to remain, but that he should be separated from amongst them, and not minister with them again" (www.ccel.org/fathers2/ANF-08/anf08-145.htm [accessed June 29, 2005]). The derivation from 1 Cor. 10 is patent.

53. There is, however, a proto-libel, which actually precedes the blood libel, certainly at Fulda in 1235, and possibly that in the chronicle, as we shall see below, of Guillaume le Breton, who died in 1223. The context is a conversion story, in which the wafer works magic, turning coins into other wafers. The story appears in a letter of Innocent III; see the text in Grayzel, *Church and the Jews*, 1: 137, no. 29, and the discussion of the letter in Chapter 6.

54. Leah Sinonoglou, "The Christ Child as Sacrifice," *Speculum* 43 (1973): 491–509. And see, too, Despres, "Mary of the Eucharist."

55. This is the theme of Rubin, "Desecration of the Host."

56. See Chapter 1, n. 13, above, and Rubin, *Corpus Christi*, passim.

57. To the Magnesians (13.2), cited by Uriel Tal, "The Future of Jewish Christian Dialogue," in *Christians and Jews*, ed. Hans Küng and Walter Kasper (New York, 1975), 82.

58. On a somewhat less emotional level, but making a similar point—reminiscent also of what fifteenth-century Franciscans, as seen above, were saying about the "blood-sucking" of Jewish lending—the English (Protestant) political theorist James Harrington expressed himself, in 1656, in his *Oceana*, as follows: "To receive the Jews after any other manner [than agriculturalists] into a commonwealth were to maim it; for they of all nations never incorporate but, taking up the room of a limb, are of no use or office unto the body, while they suck the nourishment which would sustain a natural and useful member." James Harrington, *The Commonwealth of Oceana and A System of Politics*, ed. J. G. A. Pocock (Cambridge, 1992), 6. Harrington is cited by Holly Snyder, "Rules, Rights, and Redemption: The Negotiation of Jewish Status in the British Atlantic Port Town, 1740–1831" (to appear in *Jewish History* 20, no. 2 [2006]).

59. See Kertzer, *Kidnapping of Edgardo Mortara*, for a careful and dramatic retelling of this extraordinary story of the secret baptism of a sick child, followed by a "legal" kidnapping and the devoted personal protection of the child by Pius IX, who was unwilling to give Edgardo back to his parents, regardless of the disastrous political consequences for the papal state, which led to its collapse in 1860. Edgardo remained a Catholic and eventually took orders as a priest.

60. On Pius IX and St. Roche, see *Bibliotheca Sanctorum*, 11: 271.

61. St. Roche protects vintners as well, a role also accorded to Werner (see Vauchez, "Antisemitismo e canonizzazione popolare"). Perhaps Roche and Werner had become mixed up in Pius IX's thinking involving Edgardo.

Chapter Three. Richard of Pontoise and Philip Augustus

1. Vauchez, "Antisemitismo e canonizzazione," speaks of an interplay between popular emotion and clerical restraint alternating with clerical fervor.
2. On these motivations in ritual murder tales, see again Stacey, "From Ritual Crucifixion to Host Desecration."
3. On theological argument and the closing of the Roman banks in 1682, see Kenneth Stow, "The Good of the Church, the Good of the State: The Popes and Jewish Money" (in Hebrew) in *Economics and Religion,* ed. Menahem Ben-Sasson (Jerusalem, 1994); revised English version in *Christianity and Judaism,* ed. Wood, 237–52. See the Introduction for the relationship between Franciscans, lending, "Jewish dogs," and ritual murder, esp. at n.97.
4. *ActaSS*, March, 3: 591–92. The Bollandists are firm about this date; they in fact insist upon it, on the basis of their own textual comparisons. And were the date substantiable beyond question, it would be most important in the corroborating evidence to be adduced from the Hebrew texts. However, the date of 1179 is problematic. The various chronicled reports about Richard are virtually identical in language, but they assign his death to a number of dates. Moreover, in reporting his death, prefaced by "in those days," or some other nonspecific phrase, none ever say "in the year. . . ." Thus, the report is inserted under dates as diverse as 1156, in Geoffrey Voisin of Limoges (for the text, see Martin Bouquet, comp., *Recueil des historiens des Gaules et de la France*, ed. Léopold Deslisle [Paris, 1877], 12: 438), and 1163. This latter date appears in (1) the account of Lambert of Waterloo, who was dead before 1179 (Bouquet, comp., *Recueil,* 13: 520); (2) Robert of Torigny's discussion of Blois (*Chronicles of the Reigns of Stephen, Henry II, and Richard I,* ed. Richard Howlett [1884–89; repr. Liechtenstein, 1964], 4: 250–51); (3) Rigord's narration of Philip Augustus and his reactions to ritual murder accusations; and (4) in the later epitome *Ex Chronica Regum Francorum* (Bouquet, comp., *Recueil,* 12: 214), which suggests that the Innocents chapel with Richard's body was well established by 1179. Finally, there is Guillaume le Breton (Bouquet, comp., *Recueil,* 17: 66), who, the Bollandists say, pointedly inserts the death — as does all later tradition, however, following the Bollandists — into his discussion of Philip's accession in 1179, using the words "in those days." Were the Bollandists our sole source, I would not hesitate to say that 1179 is the real date of Richard's alleged martyrdom. But because of the varied dates in other chronicles, I must hold back. So do others: Jordan, followed by Stacey, gives 1163; Friedrich Lotter, "Innocens Virgo et Martyr, Thomas von Monmouth und die Verbreitung der Ritualmordlegende im Hochmittelalter," in *Die Legende vom Ritualmord: Zur Geschichte der Blutbeschuldigung gegen Juden,* ed. Rainer Erb (Berlin, 1993), 49, gives 1163; so

does Langmuir in "Ritual Crucifixion," in id., *Toward a Definition of Antisemitism*, accepting Lambert. But see Guerin, *Petits Bollandistes*, 3: 634–36, who accepts the Bollandist dating of 1179, even 1180; so do Butler and Attwater, and especially Vacandard, "Question du meurtre rituel," 330, on the basis of his own reading of Rigord and Le Breton. Vauchez does, too, in *Sainthood in the Later Middle Ages*, 150, and earlier in "Antisemitismo e canonizzazione," 489, admittedly on the basis of the Bollandist record alone; still, Vauchez, with his enormous knowledge of sainthood and its textual sources, cannot be dismissed out of hand.

5. This view of the expulsions repeats in Johann Jacob Schudt, *Jüdische Merckwürdigkeiten*.... (Frankfurt a/M, 1715-18), 1:145 (I thank Deborah Fischel for this reference). It obviously had a long history, and likely can be found in other later writers, too, as well as in earlier ones, e.g., in the *Fortalitium Fidei* of Alfonso da Espina, fol. 120, which, in fact, cites Rigord verbatim (I thank Magda Teter for this reference).

6. Rubin, *Gentile Tales*, 26.

7. See John W. Baldwin, *The Government of Philip Augustus: Foundations of French Royal Power in the Middle Ages* (Berkeley, 1986), 396–97, on Rigord and his writings.

8. *ActaSS*, March, 3: 593.

9. Actually, he seems to indicate 1183, but he really falls into the group that sees 1179 as the date when Richard died; see the discussion above.

10. Bouquet, comp., *Recueil*, 17: 5–6; with no reference to Blois itself, Rigord notes that in the time of Louis VII, many Jews were caught and burned; Rigord then proceeds directly to Richard. To be wholly honest, Rigord is not giving a precise date for Richard, although one must assume he thinks it at least contemporary with Blois, if not later.

11. *Oeuvres de Rigord et de Guillaume le Breton*, ed. Henri-François Delaborde (Paris, 1882–85), as cited in Jordan, *French Monarchy;* the pages are 17: 5–6, 9, 36, and 48 in Bouquet, comp., *Recueil*.

12. The one instance, that is, in the cases I have examined in *ActaSS*, which is especially important, since when discussing William of Norwich, the principal discursus is to mention other ritual murders. The treatment of Simon of Trent is not extended, except to cite selections from the enormously aggressive attack of the physician Tiberino, mentioned in the Introduction (*ActaSS*, March, 3: 494–502). Vernet, "Juifs et Chrétiens," 1703–9, supplies further examples.

13. This would be the same message the clergy under Bourbon reform were trying to send the Bourbon king; see again Kroen, *Politics and Theater* in Chapter 1, n. 49. The point, once again, is continuity of motifs.

14. See n. 16 below and the last section of this chapter.

15. See Butler, *Lives of the Saints,* ed. Attwater and Thurston, 1: 671.

16. Rigord, the Bollandists' fullest source, makes a direct link with Richard, the Jews' supposed annual murder of a Christian, and the burning of many Jews on ritual murder charges during the reign of Louis VII, although without men-

tioning Blois by name (Bouquet, comp., *Recueil,* 17: 5–6). The Bollandists also cite Robert of Torigny (*Chronicles,* ed. Howlett, 4: 250–51), who describes various libels, including the Blois story of 1171.

17. Jordan, *French Monarchy,* 30–31; the St. Denis chronicle, which is virtually copying Rigord in French translation here, has "vi kal." (in Bouquet, comp., *Recueil,* 17: 350), but this would have been a Sunday in 1180, more probably a confusion of dates, a single day off, but still not a secure date. William C. Jordan, "Princely Identity and the Jews in Medieval France," in *From Witness to Witchcraft,* ed. Jeremy Cohen, 262, suggests the redating to 1180 may require more proof.

18. Was there any real basis for this accusation? One may imagine Jews wishing they could do something like this, but prudence would have dictated otherwise. Besides, the chalice was surely deemed polluted, and contaminating, by an act, the Eucharist, that Jews considered idolatrous. Using it for food would have been out of the question. Ivan Marcus in his recent *The Jewish Life Cycle* (Seattle, 2004), 70–71, seems to differ. Marcus sees here a direct report of the Jewish ritual of learning-initiation, in which a young boy is fed honey cakes on his first day of school, which Marcus sees as what he calls a social polemic against the Eucharist (on which more in Chapter 6). Marcus translates *offas* as cakes, which makes sense. Yet, more probable is that Rigord is not reproducing a picture of actual Jewish doing, the mocking of the sacrament. Rather, this is his version—and interpretation—of the initiation ceremony; the introduction of the communion chalice as such is likely Rigord's invention.

19. Jordan, *French Monarchy,* 31, following his dating, takes this episode to be part of the original one reported by Rigord for 1180; our interest, to be sure, is not the actual date but the way the Bollandists, as opposed to Rigord, dated the episodes.

20. The commentary of Pagi for 1181 is found in notes to Raynaldus XV, continuing Cesare Baronio, *Annales ecclesiastici,* ed. A. Theiner (Bar-le-Duc, 1864–83), 504, 527, and the note on 1179 is no. 17.

21. *The Chronicle of Melrose,* ed. Alan Anderson and Marjorie Olgivie Anderson (London, 1936), 22. The chronicle itself dates from the thirteenth century. Our interest is in its subsequent use, not its factual accuracy.

22. Rigord has "relaxavit . . . a debitis iudaeorum, . . . sed exiit edictum" (see the text in Appendix One). An early summary of events, along with careful textual references, is found in Caro, *Sozial- und Wirtschaftsgeschichte der Juden,* 1: 357–61, and 504–5 for sources. By contrast, see Kenneth Stow, "Expulsion Italian Style: The Case of Lucio Ferraris," *Jewish History* 3, no. 1 (1988): 51. Ferraris, a Franciscan and judge of the Sancta Rota Romana, who wrote in 1756, reads the 1182 expulsion as a consequence of the Judaizing of 1181. Ferraris's stress on Judaizing was possibly tied to problems of modernity.

23. Jordan, too, feels that Philip was motivated in 1182 by an accusation, and he follows Rigord in seeing a link between 1179 and 1182 (*French Monarchy,* 17–19, 31, and n. 47 there); he queries whether there was a rumor about a child killed at

Orléans, a rumor he finds baseless. However, the reference in the text may be to another, ancillary accusation, one similar to that in the *Melrose Chronicle*. Perhaps, too, there was a retelling of another accusation made to seem like two separate murders; for instance, the chaplain of Cardinal Reginald Pole, G. Lillius (cited by the Bollandists in their discussion of William of Norwich, *ActaSS,* March, 3: 588), wrote, using an epitome of a thirteenth-century chronicle, the *Regum Anglorum,* that there was a second William of Norwich in 1235. This accusation is repeated freely by Hart in *Historia et cartularium monasterii Sancti Petri Gloucestriae,* ed. id., lv; Hart also notes that it appears in Capgrave et al., *Nova legenda angliae* (154); Hart assigns Robert of St. Bury to 1181, following, it seems Pagi(us); see n. 20 above.

24. Mary Minty "Kiddush HaShem in Christian Eyes in Medieval Germany," *Zion* 59 (1994): 234–35 (in Hebrew), and also 241n32, on the Eucharistic imagery associated with the story. Willis Johnson, "Before the Blood Libel," argues that views of Jewish mothers were especially negative. See also, on avariciousness, n. 76 below, especially on Bernard of Clairvaux.

25. McCulloh, "Jewish Ritual Murder," esp. 724–28; see also Robert C. Stacey "Anti-Semitism and the Medieval English State," in *The Medieval State: Essays Presented to James Campbell,* ed. J. R. Maddicott and D. M. Palliser (London, 2000), 163–77, on the need for patron saints, which ritual murder victims easily filled.

26. The Bollandists choose this point to mark the revocation of the expulsion in 1198. It could be that they felt they had no choice but to mention this event, since Rigord did, too. Nonetheless, since they are editing sources so highly, the revocation, too, must have its part in the whole.

27. On Philip's determination, see Jordan, "Princely Identity and the Jews in Medieval France," in *From Witness to Witchcraft,* ed. Jeremy Cohen, 261, noting, by contrast, Louis VII's supposed leniency toward Jews, which is balanced by Philip's seeking power and independence, yet with a sincere need to support the canons and perhaps also to listen to clerics. These desires of the young Philip would add, not detract, from the point being made here; see also Baldwin, *Government of Philip Augustus,* 51-52. At the same time, one must question how much Philip differed from his father, in particular, initially; on which, see nn. 55 and 59, below. Ephraim of Bonn, who blamed Louis for grave Jewish losses in 1147, would have doubted there was a difference; Haberman, *Sefer gezerot,* 121.

28. Rigord, in Bouquet, comp., *Recueil,* 17: 36, and Bollandists, March, 3: 592, on this passage; there are few details to add, including those offered by Ephraim of Bonn in Haberman, *Sefer gezerot,* 128.

29. Rigord, in Bouquet, comp., *Recueil,* 17: 6, and *ActaSS,* March, 3: 591.

30. *ActaSS,* March, 3:591.

31. Capgrave et al., *Nova legenda angliae,* 2: 39, and *ActaSS,* March, 3: 588; Thomas of Monmouth, *Life,* 93. This motif is found in Josephus, *Contra Apionem* (of the many editions in various languages, see most recently the Hebrew translation of Aryeh Kasher [Jerusalem, 1996], with full bibliography) that the Jews an-

nually fattened a Greek for sacrifice. That Thomas knew the story, however, is doubtful.

32. Capgrave et al., *Nova legenda angliae,* and *ActaSS*, both there: John Wilson, *English Martyrologe* (St. Omer, 1640; rpr. Ilkley, Eng., 1975) for June 29; and Thomas of Monmouth, *Life and Miracles,* 25–27.

33. St. Ioanettus in Bollandists, *ActaSS*, March, 3: 502; Vernet, "Juifs et Chrétiens," 1706, says there is no precise date for this death.

34. John T. Appleby, *The Chronicle of Richard of Devizes of the Time of King Richard the First* (London, 1963), 146–48, 331.

35. *Historia et cartularium monasterii Sancti Petri Gloucestriae,* ed. Hart, *Gloucester,* xxxix–li. Cf. Martí, *Pugio fidei,* ed. Carpzov, pt. 3, distinction 3, chap. 22, par. 22, who refrains from specifically the blood libel, but says Jews kill Christian children and throw them into wells (I thank Jeremy Cohen for this reference).

36. Wilson, *English Martyrologe,* [95] 29 June.

37. HaKohen, '*Emeq haBakh'a,* ed. Letteris, 94; the book was written after the middle of the sixteenth century. One might note the victim in the so-called Mainz Anonymous chronicle, who is said to have been boiled, which is a kind of variant on the water motif. However, the origin of this figure may be a much later insertion, since the chronicle as a whole is considered mid twelfth-century, before a full development of the motifs noted here; see Haberman, *Sefer gezerot,* 98, on the incident.

38. See Haberman, *Sefer gezerot,* 143.

39. Jordan is a bit more emphatic about this element in Philip's activity in "Princely Identity" than in *French Monarchy,* although, in this latter, too, he does point (17) to its importance. Based on the Bollandists, I would like to go a bit further to see it as an integrating, if not dominating, element, not one among many.

40. Guillelmus Armoricus in Bouquet, comp., *Recueil,* 17: 66; in this paragraph, Le Breton says Richard was "crucified in these days," and his date is 1179. On *communicare* in the sense of "to take communion," see above, Chapter 1, n.14 and the Latin cited there. The juxtaposition of *immolabant* and *communicabant* here, taken together with Rigord's remark about *sacrificio,* leaves little reason to assume that the term is not being used here in a sacramental sense, and we have shown that the ritual murder victim is perceived eucharistically; see especially Chapter 2, n. 26. Why the heart? Perhaps as the seat of life. We recall Aztec sacrifice, cutting the heart out, but one should not make facile comparisons between societies.

41. See Langmuir, "Ritual Cannibalism," in id., *Toward a Definition of Antisemitism,* although he speaks (265) only of "sharing the heart of a murdered child," not the sacrificial addition.

42. Grayzel, *Church and the Jews,* 1: 271, and 2: 118, for letters of Innocent IV and Gregory X, respectively, on blood accusations; the first, in 1247, is to Germany, and because Valreas is technically within the Empire, Langmuir, "Ritual Cannibalism," 265, identifies this episode as the one at Valreas. Grayzel, there, points

out, it seems correctly, that this is a statement of principle, responding to widespread charges, not a specific response to a specific accusation. One Jewish text, at least, records the accusation of eating Christians directly, "that we murder their children and consume the blood"; see *Jewish-Christian Debate,* ed. Berger, 54, on Jer. 10:25; and also 229; in which case, I am not clear why Berger, 343, cites Rigord and Le Breton as here, yet continues that Parkes and Trachtenberg are "incorrect" to say Rigord and Guillaume were accusing Jews of eating Christians. Literally, Berger is right, since they specify only the heart, but they are certainly making a blood libel, not one of ritual murder alone, and as said in the text, heart here is clearly a figure for blood. The *Nizzahon Yashan,* consistently brilliant, throws the libel of eating "human beings and the blood of Christian children" back into Christian faces, saying that it can be proved that "they too eat human beings, as it is written, 'For they have eaten up Jacob' [Jer. 10: 25]." The real brilliance is that the author knows very well that the Christians say that they themselves are Jacob/Israel. Is he suggesting they eat themselves, which would be to say—is he demonstrating a penetrating knowledge of the theology of the *Corpus Christi,* the Pauline unity of Christ and believers?—that in consuming the Eucharist, Christians are consuming themselves? This is irony at its best, and I am convinced the *Nizzahon*'s author intended it.

43. It is unlikely that somebody went back and put this line into Le Breton after 1235; on Fulda, see Aronius, *Regesten zur Geschichte der Juden,* no. 497, for Frederick II in 1236.

44. See once more Lampert, "Once and Future Jew," who reviews earlier literature, including Stacey and Rubin, and goes further than others toward the certainty of the linkage.

45. Trachtenberg, *Devil and the Jews,* 138, explains this phrase to mean only that "Jews *eat* Christians" (italics Trachtenberg's); Langmuir, "Ritual Cannibalism," in id., *Toward a Definition of Antisemitism,* 265, as said, writes of "sharing the heart" of a murdered child.

46. See recently Jordan in "Princely Identity," and *French Monarchy,* 9 and 17, where he also notes the opinion of others.

47. Confiscation—despite strong papal protest—was normally the rule; there are sufficient examples in Grayzel, *Church and the Jews,* 2: 121, 142, 173, 309, and many more. See also Minty, "Kiddush HaShem," 234. And see the translation, below, n. 25 in Appendix Two, on a possible Hebrew substantiation of these conversions. On possible forced conversion initiated by Philip, see Bouquet, comp., *Recueil,* 12: 215: "praefixit terminum [to leave . . . and steadfast of mind] recesserunt omnis qui baptisari noluerunt (ex chronica Regum francorum a trojana gentis origine ad annum 1368)."

48. Linder, trans. and ed., *Jews in the Legal Sources,* 607, 615, 636.

49. See on these issues the bull *Turbato corde* of 1267, Grayzel, *Church and the Jews,* 2: 102; and my "Conversion, Apostasy, and Apprehensiveness: Emicho of Flonheim and the Fear of Jews in the Twelfth Century," *Speculum* 76 (2001): 911–33.

50. Peter says that even if one defeats a Jew in debate, the Jew will not convert in his heart; cited by David Berger, "Mission to the Jews and Jewish-Christian Contacts in the Polemical Literature of the High Middle Ages," *American Historical Review* 91 (1986): 580. Berger's judgment about Peter's pessimism with regard to conversion may perhaps be expanded to say Peter feared that as experience showed, missionizing was more likely to create an apostate than a "new man." On Maestro Andreas, see Kenneth Stow, "Jacob of Venice and the Jewish Settlements in Venice in the Thirteenth Century," in *Community and Culture,* ed. Nahum Waldman (Philadelphia, 1987). See also the reference in the *Nizzahon Yashan. Sefer Yosef Hamekane* repeatedly has a *poqer,* from the Hebrew for heretic or atheist/agnostic, pose questions, intending, no doubt, converts, reversing for effect *qofer*'s consonants to read *poqer* (*p* and *f* are in Hebrew the same letter, the differing sound made through introducing a diacritical mark; and note that words in Italian, e.g., *albero,* often have consonants reversed in Spanish, *arbol,* tree).

51. Rigord is very clear about Philip's initiative; see Bouquet, comp., *Recueil,* 17: 36, and Jordan, *French Monarchy*, 37, for emphasis; and see n. 53 below. The Bollandist addition to Rigord goes: "Verum vel simulatam fuisse multorum qui remansere, [Col. 0592E] conuersionem, vel eos qui egreßi fuerant clam iterum regressos, non tantum ad ea quæ prius incoluerant loca, sed etiam ad vsitata scelera, intra decenniû patuit." Hyams's Internet translation of Rigord (see Appendix One) gives 1192 as the intended date.

52. See Kenneth Stow, "Papal and Royal Attitudes Toward Jewish Lending in the Thirteenth Century," *AJS Review* 6 (1981): 161–84; and see Shatzmiller's reproduction of Stow's arguments in *Shylock Reconsidered: Jews, Moneylending, and Medieval Society* (Berkeley, 1990), 43–67. Bollandist disillusion, even their sense of "Judaizing" betrayal, brought about by the recall of Jews in 1198, should, as already said, have been mitigated by the renewed restrictions on lending Philip instituted in 1206. Rigord certainly opposed Jewish lending, as seen especially in Jordan, *French Monarchy,* 9–10. One may ask whether there is any relationship between Innocent III's decrees on Jewish lending in 1198 (see n. 75 below) and Philip's recall.

53. Jordan, "Princely Identity," 261–62, citing Rigord in *Oeuvres de Rigord et de Guillaume le Breton*, ed. Delaborde, 1: 14–15; actually, Ephraim of Bonn, in Haberman, *Sefer gezerot,* 121, challenges this portrait, as already noted above, n. 27.

54. The Bollandists do not mention that Brie occurred shortly after Philip's return from the Crusades. Perhaps they did not want to liken him to the image of the Crusader wantonly killing Jews; more likely, they considered the Crusade too far afield from the matter of Richard and ritual murder to be considered.

55. Bouquet, comp., *Recueil,* 18: 248, the chronicle of Robert of Auxerre; Robert's chronicle squares well with the two other texts, the papal letter and the now lost, but surely once existing, royal petition to Pope Alexander, lending this report credence. Guido himself no doubt explained the exchange of correspondence to

Philip: "Orta est inter Guidonem archiepiscopum Regemque dissensio, eo quod archiepiscopus quaedam decretam concilii [the Third Lateran of 1179] nullatenus pataretur infringi [this was the decree nullum christianorum mancipium fieri Judaeorum]. Volebat itaque Rex his nequaquem teneri [and the archbishop protested, as well as against other royal] usurpationibus ... ira Regis incanduit, ut ipsum juberet aut sedem relinquere, aut suis iussibus assentire. Qui tamen maluit subire exilium quam contra iustitiam regium implere preceptum. Verum paulo post accepto saniori consilio, Rex, poenitentia ductus, exilem revocat."

Royal prerogative asserted in the face of ecclesiastical demand was not a new issue. True to this tradition, in his first days, Philip was ready to oppose ecclesiastical authority, even vehemently, in which light his subsequent initiatives against Jews were matters of principle, not bowing to the Church. The reference by Robert of Auxerre to royal penitence is either a topos, or perhaps it reflects Philip's real about-face concerning Jews; we can only speculate. For the letter of Alexander III, see Simonsohn, *Apostolic See and the Jews*, 1: 62, no. 59, and also Bouquet, comp., *Recueil*, 15: 968: "an sit appellationibus deferendum a carissimo in Christo filio nostro L. [*sic*] illustri francorum Rege pro iudaeis interpositis ... fecimus admoneri et credimus quod monitis nostris acquiescat [but he petitioned again, and it was Philip who received the answer via Guido of Sens]." In the light of all this, that the real Philip—as opposed to the Philip Rigord depicts—should, even as a youth, assert royal prerogative over that of the Church says much about Philip's determination to rule. Philip's resolve and initiative cannot be doubted. Nor was this the sole time Philip quarreled with the pope. Jennine Horowitz reminds me that on the question of his divorce from Ingebord, Philip held out at length, despite both his excommunication and an interdict on the realm. See also Baldwin, *Government of Philip Augustus,* 28-32, on Philip's associates, including bishops. Moreover, Philip's successors, too, in particular Philip III and Philip IV should be judged from the same perspective. Both issued ordinances forbidding the Inquisition to try Jews without royal permission, if at all—even though both tried Jews for the same offenses themselves. See Jordan, *French Monarchy*, 191, for Philip III in 1288, and *Revue des études juives* 2 (1881): 31, for a document of Philip IV's taken from Chartres Cathedral, for 1302. In 1290, Pope Nicholas IV complained about inquisitional abuses in unwarrantedly changing venues, on whom, see Grayzel, *Church and the Jews,* 2: 182-83; the kings were complaining about usurpation of jurisdiction outright, something quite different.

56. See John Gilchrist, "The Perception of Jews in the Canon Law in the Period of the First Two Crusades," *Jewish History* 3, no. 1 (1988): 9-24, on the history of early canons on the Jews. And see also various conciliar decrees cited in Linder, trans. and ed., *Jews in the Legal Sources*, such as the Council of Agde (506), that of Benevento in southern Italy (c. 900), and in the *Collectio Hispana, Excerpta*, the original about 656, and the excerpts in 700 and again 900 (for these texts, see Linder 466-67, 549-51, and 580-82, respectively). Philip III's charter of 1283 explicitly forbade domestic service (see the reference to this charter cited in n. 67 below).

57. Bouquet, comp., *Recueil,* 17: 6, "alia quamplurima nefanda," beside ritual murder.

58. Ibid., 36, where Rigord says that nobody knew ahead of time about this initiative. On the debate over lay or clerical advisors, see Baldwin, *Government of Philip Augustus,* 28-32, and also Jordan, "Princely Identity," 262, who speaks of reliance, a "crutch," but not subservience to a—temporary—clerical clique.

59. The issue is not, therefore, lenient Louis versus harsh Philip, but which legal approach was correct. Rigord, desiring to paint Philip as pious, pictures Philip as an enforcer, his father as lax. In truth, Louis's so-called laxity was really perplexity over a most serious issue: should old, hence, revered, legal custom be modified, which is what Philip did; and see n. 62, below. The anonymous chronicler is Bouquet, comp., *Recueil,* 15: 968, *Fragmentum Historicum vitam Ludovici VII,* noted by Bouquet himself next to the letter of Alexander (and see it in context in Bouquet, 12: 286, among Alexander III's letters): that Louis VII "graviter Deum offendit, quod in regno suo Judaeos ultra modum sublimavit, et eis multa privilegia Deo et sibi et regno contraria immoderata deceptus cupiditate [concessit]." Louis "gravely offended God, because he raised the Jews in his kingdom to an unfitting station, bestowing upon them many excessive privileges contrary [to the good] of the kingdom, that of God and of himself as well, all in the name of avarice. This text seems to echo the point. What a chronicler saw and reported, faithful to his own terms of reference, was not necessarily fact. The wording of the 1144 order of Louis VII (Bouquet, comp., *Recueil,* 16: 8c, *Epistolarum Regis Ludovici VII*) that Jews converted and returning to Judaism should leave the kingdom specifies that were these apostates to stay and be caught, they were liable "capitali damnarentur judicio vel membrorum portione multentur" (to be condemned to pay with their lives or by mutilation of their limbs). Recently, Gérard Nahon, "From the Rue aux Juifs to the Chemin du Roy," in *Jews and Christians,* ed. Signer and Van Engen, 327, has reexamined these questions and judges Louis "favorably," but he leans principally on the supposed facticity in just the texts whose "facticity" I am questioning; he also questions Ephraim's account of 1147, which almost surely reflects serious trouble. Ephraim's language is uniquely technical about the canceled loans; they were on contract, not against pawns, and Ephraim had no reason to manipulate his sources or even to invent his accusation. It is a rare case where one may trust—better, cannot explain away—chronicled detail; see Stow, *Alienated Minority,* 113–14, and the literature cited there.

60. For Henry IV and Wibert's reaction, see Aronius, *Regesten zur Geschichte der Juden,* no. 203; for Innocent IV, see Grayzel, *Church and the Jews,* 1: no. 113. Not to allow return was established by the time of Gratian, in 1140, although the actual canon describing the "absolutely forced conversion" that alone was not canonically binding was not issued until 1298, by Boniface VIII; see Grayzel, 2: 209.

61. Bouquet, comp., *Recueil,* 13: 320, for the *Appendice ad Sigebertum,* of Torigny for 1177: "quinta feria in Coena domini, occisus est Guillelmus a Judaeis Parisiis qui concremati sunt igne."

62. The right to employ these servants was granted by many royal and ducal charters through the twelfth century; see Friedrich Lotter, "The Scope and Effectiveness of Imperial Jewry Law in the High Middle Ages," *Jewish History* 4, no. 1 (1989): 48–49. It is only in the mid thirteenth century (again see n. 67 below) that English and French charters begin to specify that Jews might *not* have Christian servants, women in particular; we may assume that overall grants of good custom included the right to employ such women. An excellent testimony on the rights of Jews to "good custom" appears in a letter of Gregory the Great about moving a synagogue, Simonsohn, *Apostolic See and the Jews*, 3: "eos sicut mos fuit ibidem liceat convenire."

63. One might go out on a limb and say that Rigord's *nefanda* meant principally the failure of Louis to go hunting Jews after the Blois incident, but this limb might break with the slightest push.

64. By this time, as we shall soon see, Philip also knew how to mix realpolitik with anger at ritual murder.

65. Taken together, the texts of Rigord, Ephraim of Bonn, and most especially the letters of Celestine III and Innocent III cited in nn. 69 and 70 below leave little doubt that what Rigord reports corresponds to the general, if not the specific, course of events.

66. Beller, "Inquisition and the Jews in Modena," and see the Introduction for the term *strepitum*.

67. Gustave Saige, *Les Juifs du Languedoc antérieurement au XIVe siècle* (Paris, 1881), 233–34, as cited and conveniently translated in *Church, State, and Jew in the Middle Ages*, ed. Robert Chazan (New York, 1980), 186.

68. Simonsohn, *Apostolic See and the Jews*, 3, cited in n. 62 above: "eos sicut mos fuit ibidem liceat convenire."

69. *Etsi non displiceat*, cited in Grayzel, *Church and the Jews*, 1: 106, no. 14: "Usque adeo etiam, quod cum robore referimus, insolescunt, ut senonensi iuxta quandam ecclesiam veterem novam construxerint sinagogam, . . . in qua, non sicut olim prius quam fuissent eiecti de regno, demissa voce, sed cum magno clamore secundum ritum iudaicum sua officia celebrantes, divinorum celebrationem in eadem ecclesia non dubitant impedire." The complaint is that after 1198, and the Jews' return, the nuisance had begun again, when Philip, for a while, relaxed his policies. Innocent links new synagogal construction directly to noise, revealing clearly the intent behind the Third Lateran's prohibition.

70. Simonsohn, *Apostolic See and the Jews,* no. 65, a letter of Celestine III, May 14, 1193: "Philippus [in 1182] . . . synagogam ipsorum piis usibus deputavit." Rigord mentions such actions in previous years.

71. Interpretations of canon law held that Jews might be expelled for irremediable offenses, but this was a justification after the fact, except in the case of the accusations of magic, noted above, justifying the expulsions of 1569 and 1593 from the papal state. But these expulsions are unique in papal-Jewish annals.

72. Jordan, *French Monarchy*, 150, and see also 300, n. 44, which says this was by then traditional legislation. On Meir ben Simeon, see Chapter 4 and the texts cited there.

73. See the text in Chapter 2, at n. 42, above.

74. See Grayzel, *Church and the Jews*, 1: 104–9, 114–17, for, respectively, *Etsi non displiceat* sent by Innocent III sent to Philip in 1205, about noise from synagogues and employment of Christian servants; and *Etsi iudaeos*, of a few months later, not addressed directly to Philip, about violations of the Holy Week curfew; it also says Jews kill Christians, although not ritually.

75. Jordan, *French Monarchy*, 34, notes Philip's lack of influence over his barons with respect to Jews. The very mature Philip reversed himself again in 1206; see ibid., 88–89; although, Stow, "Papal and Royal Attitudes," would qualify that however these actions mollified radical clergy, they also expressed Philip's real underlying will, which his realpolitik—at which he was a master—did not always let him pursue. That Jews saw this politics as erratic—Jordan's term—I have no doubt. In real terms, it was just that; for Philip, I think, it was a question of being consistent with one's fundamental beliefs. How, nonetheless, do we confront the fact that in 1198, the year of the Jews' recall by Philip, Innocent III issued *Post miserabilem*, the first canon issued to touch directly on Jews and interest? Perhaps Philip (and his father Louis VII) had been seen as taking the lead, and ecclesiastical authorities were satisfied; now they had some doubts. Still, Innocent III's decree at the Fourth Lateran *quanto amplius* indicates that some measure of interest was acceptable when the lender was a Jew. Properly to judge Innocent III, it is necessary to put an end to the historiographical myth of the Fourth Lateran as a turning point *in terms of legal innovation*, for there was really none; see the texts in Grayzel, *Church and the Jews*, 1: 306–13, remembering that some were incorporated into Gregory IX's *Decretals* (10.5, 6). The Fourth Lateran Council, like the Third, was seeking to have enforced what previously had existed mostly, if not wholly, on paper. Chapter 6 explores why the decision was taken at this time to insist on enforcement. At the same time, if the Church succeeded in its endeavor, it was because kings decided on their own initiative that supporting the Church was correct, not because they were bowing to ecclesiastical pressure. The overall health of the kingdom, they must have thought, required observing canonical rigor.

76. Bernard of Clairvaux's taunt, calling clerical lenders "judaei nostri" (our [i.e., baptized] Jews), comes to mind; see Stow, *Alienated Minority*, 211, and the literature cited there. Recall Paul's notion, subsequently articulated by Cyprian and Agobard, that one who participates in the Jewish altar, that is, imitating Jews in any way, is Judaizing. Here, the king is Judaizing if he imitates the Jews' purported avariciousness. In fact, avariciousness linked to Judaizing is a topos; note the story in Minty, "Kiddush HaShem," 234–35, where the priest who aids the father dispose of his son is called avaricious and is eventually burned (one may assume as a heretic and even perhaps a Judaizer). And see this story above in the text.

77. Gerald Guest, review of Sara Lipton, *Images of Intolerance: The Representation of Jews and Judaism in the "Bible moralisée"* (Berkeley, 1999), *Medieval Review* on-line, www.hti.umich.edu/cgi/t/text/text-idx?c=tmr;cc=tmr;sid=bc95cdc39d63 bf167a8200e6b62f7bf7;q1=figure%20of%20the%20Jew;rgn=main;view=text;idn o=baj9928.0003.004 (accessed May 11, 2005).

78. Jordan, *French Monarchy*, 35, calls Philip a "fanatic."

79. Ibid., 44, 61, 89–91.

80. Langmuir, "The Knight's Tale of Young Hugh of Lincoln," in id., *Toward a Definition of Antisemitism*.

81. Stow, "Papal and Royal Attitudes," 179–82.

82. On the royal family, see Yves Sassier, *Louis VII* (Paris, 1991), and, more particularly, Baldwin, *Government of Philip Augustus*, 14-16, 25, 28, and 32, on marriages. The family of Champagne was outraged: Philip marries the daughter of the count of Flanders, "quod matri eiusdem Regis et matris fratribus valde displicuit . . . [and as a result] a filio expulsa, ad fratres confugit ac per hoc . . . eorumdem fratrum contra Regem simultas incandescit"; Bouquet, comp., *Recueil*, 12: 298, the chronicle of Robert of Auxerre.

83. The thesis of Jordan in "Princely Identity." Eventually, Philip reestablished his Champenois links.

84. See Jordan, *French Monarchy*, 36.

85. Ora Limor, "The Blood Libel," in *Jews and Christians in Western Europe: Encounter Between Cultures in the Middle Ages and the Renaissance*, ed. id. et al. (in Hebrew) (Tel Aviv, 1998), 5: 33–52 directs us to the main players between 1171 and 1182; all were close members of the royal family; see also Baldwin, *Government of Philip Augustus*, 17.

86. Hebes de Charenton, in Bouquet, comp., *Recueil*, 17: 6, Rigord, and again, there, 17: 350, *Chronicle of St. Denis*.

87. The case of Hugh of Lincoln simply did not offer the same rich and, particularly, extended narrative possibilities, despite Henry III's role. In other cases, kings were not involved.

Chapter Four. The Jewish Version

1. The manuscript was once held in Jews' College, London, MS 28 fol. 151–68, 1453, but it is now in private hands. A copy is housed in the library of the Jewish Theological Seminary, New York.

2. The manuscript contains the sole surviving copy of the long First Crusade Chronicle, edited in the Rhineland about 1147; Anna Sapir Abulafia, "The Interrelationship Between the Hebrew Chronicles of the First Crusade," *Journal of Semitic Studies* 27 (1982): 221–39.

3. This theme appears in the Shebet Yehudah of Solomon ibn Verga and is discussed by Yosef Yerushalmi in *The Lisbon Massacre of 1506 and the Royal Image in the*

Shebet Yehudah (Cincinnati, 1976), although it would be hasty to draw parallels between the two narratives.

4. See Robert Chazan, "The Blois Incident of 1171: A Study in Jewish Intercommunal Organization," *Proceedings of the American Academy of Jewish Research* 36 (1963): 13–31; id., "The Timebound and the Timeless: Medieval Jewish Narratives of Events," *History and Memory* 6, no. 1 (1994): 5–35; and id., *God, Humanity, and History: The Hebrew First Crusade Narratives* (Berkeley, 2000), 3–4. The letters are found as appendices to the German manuscript of the chronicle known as that of Shelomo bar Samson and have been published by Haberman, *Sefer gezerot*, 142-46. And see also Yuval, *Two Nations*, 203–7, and Limor's excellent overview in "Blood Libel." Susan L. Einbinder reopened the issues in "Pucellina of Blois: Romantic Myths and Narrative Conventions," *Jewish History* 12, no. 1 (1998): 29–46, esp. 30, and expands the discussion in *Beautiful Death: Jewish Poetry and Martyrdom in Medieval France* (Princeton, 2002), 45–69. As indicated, my reading takes Einbinder's as its starting point. Yuval, too, is aware that there are Christian motifs in the letters, but he concentrates on trying to find actual events and causes, despite the intrinsic difficulty of doing so in texts of this kind. Most important for understanding the texts is Wachtel, "Ritual and Liturgical Commemoration." Finally, see Schmitt, *Conversion d'Hermann le Juif*, esp. 47–49, which argues that there are levels of reality in accounts like these, but that they are always overlaid with theological intentions and interventions, and that we should not use the term "fiction" with reference to medieval texts in the way we use it today.

5. Grayzel, *Church and the Jews,* 2: 118: "a Judeis ipsis extorquere aliquam pecunie quantitatem . . . avaritie."

6. This is so irrespective of the time of its origin, which, perplexingly, is still contested. The most recent comment on this difficult text is in Kenneth Stow, "The Avignonese Papacy, or, After the Expulsions," in *From Witness to Witchcraft*, ed. Jeremy Cohen, 276–78, nn. 5 and 6, where the opinions of Richard Landes, "The Massacres of 1010: On the Origins of Popular Anti-Jewish Violence in Western Europe," in *From Witness to Witchcraft*, 79–111, and Robert Chazan (in his review of Stow in *Speculum*, 62 [1987]: 728–31) are considered; see also Kenneth Stow, review of *The Jews in Medieval Normandy: A Social and Intellectual History* by Norman Golb (Cambridge, 1998), *Medieval Review* on-line, www.hti.umich.edu/cgi/t/text/text-idx?c=tmr;cc=tmr;sid=f44ec5dba8aa585efad22a626c199e65;q1=Golb;rgn=main;view=text;idno=baj9928.9905.003 (accessed May 14, 2005). I date the text to the thirteenth century, Landes and Chazan to the early eleventh. Landes resorts to dramatic metaphor to categorize those who disagree with him; he calls them the "Lumpers," as opposed to "The Splitters," meaning those who sift the evidence finely, that is, Landes himself. Yet, truth be told, Landes's own "sifter" has let through a great deal of dross. Neither he nor Chazan has directly confronted the arguments for a late dating. Neither grapples with the terms and ideas that are found in the "1007 Anonymous" text, which were not in use prior to the

thirteenth century. Nor do they grapple with the 1007's verbatim citation of a full eighteen-word sentence from *Sicut Iudaeis non*, a text whose earliest existence containing this sentence is known not to predate 1119 and possibly dates from no earlier than 1179 (our first extant copy). Chazan's attempt to question the identification of coins discusses names but avoids numismatic chronology and problems of monetary circulation. Mostly, his review does not confront the 1007 text, as it is written, that is, as a story, which has perforce been edited (not to mention possesses a literary quality). Consequently, he ignores that the words of the same character (Jacob ben Yekutiel), whether to the pope or the duke in the tale, are ultimately the words of the author and represent the author's view. They must be evaluated as such, not as though they were "really" said.

What makes the opposition to the thirteenth-century date so strong is essentially emotional, or so I am persuaded. A late date destroys all hope of establishing the existence of early eleventh-century Jewish persecutions. Taken alone, the Latin texts of trials Jews supposedly faced at this time provide insufficient proof. They hopelessly contradict themselves about what happened, unless, like Landes, one arbitrarily wants to read them positivistically (literally), yet also selectively (contrary to the positivistic canon), to suggest, as Landes does in the end, that the Christian chroniclers present their events out of order. Who is to establish what the right order is? Second, accepting the "1007 Anonymous" as late and as a romance means that one must abandon the attempt to find "facticity"—recent shorthand standing for "real historical reporting"—even partially, in texts whose literary character is beyond serious question. Indeed, if one text is an intentional fiction, then the same perhaps applies to all the others of its ilk (I invoke Hippolyte Delehaye), and the search for "facticity" must perforce grind to a halt.

In any case, Norman Golb assigns the "1007 Anonymous" text to the twelfth century, and he is on the right track. Yet it is a new piece of evidence, hitherto overlooked for its apparent irrelevance, that provides the greatest argument of all for the late date of the composition of the "1007 Anonymous." I am referring to the broken *petil ha-zahav*, the golden tassel on the duke of Normandy's sword, which breaks when he raises it against the hero Jacob ben Yekutiel and which pierces the duke's hand, making him rethink his actions. As far as I can tell, this term appears but once in rabbinic literature, that of weaving strands of thread, hardly a context that would have any meaning here. On the other hand, the motif of a broken sword whose breaking has magical aspects is found in Chrétien de Troyes's *Conte de Graal*, which is from about 1180, and whose source is Celtic (I again thank Jennine Horowitz); see *Le Roman de Perceval ou le conte du Graal*, ed. William Roach (Geneva, 1959), verses 3654–85 (107–8). As the romance goes, any unauthorized person who tries to wield the sword discovers that it will break in his hands, but also—the broken sword motif itself is *not* unique to Chrétien—that its fringes are worth a *tresor* and that it has a *pommeau* of beautiful gold. This is the sword of the "1007 Anonymous" beyond a doubt, even if there, it is the hilt, not the blade, that breaks. Central in both cases is the sword's breaking because it is unjustly wielded. In the *Graal* romance, only Galahad, the new Christ, has the power to restore the sword to wholeness. In the "1007 Anonymous," this would be the pope, if not Jacob ben Yekutiel's intervention. Interestingly, Chrétien was in Flanders when he wrote, which is where Jacob ben Yekutiel is "sent" at the end of the "1007 Anonymous" narrative, and disappears; I doubt this is coincidence.

We should not neglect that the copying of the Galahad sword motif indicates an extraordinary level of Jewish acculturation to high culture, a high culture that is relatively secular, too, which means we must rethink the real levels of medieval Jewish acculturation. It is one thing to mimic a ceremony, to know theology roughly, even to quote papal theory and to parody it; we shall see the latter here. It is another thing to be acquainted with recently constructed literary motifs as precisely as was the author of the "1007 Anonymous." However, our immediate interest is not how representative culturally this writer actually was (on which see the reflections of Susan Einbinder, in "Signs of Romance: Hebrew Prose and the Twelfth Century Renaissance," in Signer and Van Engen, *Jews and Christians*, 224, discussing, not the "1007 Anonymous" text, but the story of Rabbi Amnon, contrasting Amnon's hesitation to that of Lancelot in Chrétien's "Knight of the Cart"). Our interest is that by introducing the late twelfth-century motif of the shattered golden hilt—one drawn from the highest rungs of high culture and that cannot be sloughed off as a popular trope—the author has unmistakably revealed both his chronological identity and his literary intentions.

Those who refuse to recognize both the literary foundations and the very, very late date of this text—hence, too, the enormous dangers of trying to tease out "facticity" from thoroughly stylized words—are doing so out of stubborn inertia. About the only defense left is (absurdly) to claim that the Celts and Chrétien were themselves copying from an earlier, completed "1007 Anonymous" text, and in perfect command of a highly difficult Hebrew style; the same, by the way, would have to be said about the Latin in the *Sicut iudaeis* text, that it copied the eighteen consecutive words it has in common with the "1007 Anonymous." The point of all this, I add, is not arcane scholarly polemic. It is the fundamental one of methodology in reading medieval Hebrew narrative texts, which clearly cannot be read solely from within.

This all said, I anticipate similar (emotionally driven) criticism from those who will cling to seeking from the Blois letters (about to be analyzed here) *was es eigentlich gewesen*. I have already received comments to this effect, that Blois was too holy in people's memory to have been the subject of parody, even irony. But this kind of criticism will not stick. I shall presently show that there is irony and parody in the Orléans Narrative itself and that the attached letters deal with Blois as a foil. Wachtel, "Ritual and Liturgical Commemoration," has pointed to problems with the fast the letters supposedly decree. And the greatest outside support for the "facticity" of the Blois letters, the existence of a supposedly pro-Jewish policy of Louis VII, has seriously been challenged. There is, finally, the most important evidence of all, the content of the letters themselves, as we shall see.

7. Robert Chazan, "Archbishop Guy Fulcodi of Narbonne and His Jews," *Revue des études juives* 132 (1973): 587–94.

8. Ephraim of Bonn on Blois in Haberman, *Sefer gezerot*, 30–34; *Das Martyrologium des Nürnberger Memorbuches*, ed. Sigmund Salfeld (Berlin, 1898), 16–17.

9. Haberman, *Sefer gezerot*, Orléans text and appended letters, 142–46.

10. Wachtel, "Ritual and Liturgical Commemoration."

11. Einbinder, "Pucellina," and more recently, id., ed. and trans., "The Jewish Martyrs of Blois," in *Medieval Hagiography: An Anthology* ed. Thomas Head (New York, 2000), 537–60; see, too, Shalom Spiegel, "*In monte dominis videbatur*: The Martyrs of Blois and the Early Accusations of Ritual Murder" (in Hebrew), in *The Mordecai Kaplan Jubilee Volume* (New York, 1953), 285–87; the poem Spiegel cites is reproduced in Haberman, *Sefer gezerot*, 258–59. Also valuable are Susan Einbinder, "Meir b. Elijah of Norwich: Persecution and Poetry Among Medieval English Jews," *Journal of Medieval History* 26, no. 2 (2000): 145–62; "Jewish Women Martyrs, Changing Models of Representation," *Exemplaria* 12, no. 1 (2000): 105–27; and, "The Troyes Laments: Jewish Martyrology in Hebrew and Old-French," *Viator* 30 (1999): 201–30.

12. On this genre and also *chansons de geste*, see Michel Zink, *Introduction à la littérature française du Moyen Age* (Paris, 1999), 37–50; some might even argue these letters are *chansons* rather than romances, but in either case, the text is literary. I leave the precise classification of the texts to those expert enough to decide.

13. The question of inversion merits particular attention. Parts of the actual account and much of the contents in the letters about to be discussed are a new stage in the development of what I like to call "inversion—or mirrored reflection—stories," pairs, like the story of the waxen image Jews in the town of Trier supposedly pierced to work sympathetic magic in 1066 (mentioned in Chapter 2), which is reflected in a Hebrew text that purports to be from 992. This Hebrew text, too, accuses Jews of piercing a waxen image, but in this version, the Jews are saved, not forced into baptism, or threatened with it, as in the Trier story. The Blois letters represent a new stage in these "inversions." Rather than offering mirror images of *literary* narratives, like the pair 992 (Jewish) and 1066 (Christian), they mirror, invert, reinterpret, and theologize images of reality, in which it is the Christian side that establishes the reality, to wit, the burning at Blois, while the Jewish one reduces it to a narrative, replete with divine intervention.

The simplest of these mirror stories, which best explains the phenomenon, is that of a wager between a Jew and Bishop Wazo of Liège (Blumenkranz, *Auteurs chrétiens*, 260). The bishop wins, and the Jew must convert. The story is told as part of Wazo's claim to sainthood. The Jewish version has a certain Hananiah wager against the bishop of Oria, and this time the bishop loses, although, to be sure, even in fiction, the Jews do not paint the bishop as converting, but as paying a prize (*The Scroll of Ahimaaz,* ed. Benjamin Klar [reprint, Jerusalem, 1974], 23–24). More than 1,200 miles (2,000 km) separate Liège in southeastern Belgium from Oria in the Italian Salentine Peninsula; these stories traveled. Stow, *Alienated Minority,* 36, 81, 85, gives examples of reflection-inversion stories, those with both a Jewish and Christian version, including the two about waxen images mentioned above, as well as mentioning a paired Jewish and Christian Theophilos story; the Christian version is noted above. On the problems of medieval narrative, especially historical narrative, see the comments in the Introduction, in particular, the reference to Karl Morrison. Even where the intention is to tell of real events, it is overshadowed by the desire to place them in a devotional, and sometimes soteriologically pietistic, framework.

14. Schaefer, *Mirror,* 200–201. On the furnace image, see also the Orléans Narrative; Haberman, *Sefer gezerot,* 144; and Yuval, *Two Nations,* 204–6. And see Einbinder, "Pucellina," and the text of Ephraim cited in id., "Jewish Martyrs of Blois," 546, as well as Hillel of Bonn's poem, 548–49, and its analysis by Einbinder there, 449–50: "The ties were severed from the children [of Israel's] hands/They cried out: "The fire has tested us and we have emerged innocent!" And see Appendix Two, notes, for a lengthier citation. This image reappears a third time in the so-called Loches letter. It is thus is definitely a motif.

15. See Schaefer, *Mirror,* 214, to the effect that the late ancient *Sefer Zerubbavel* creates a counter-Virgin in the mother of the Jewish messiah. In a parallel, I thank Edward Feld for pointing out to me—I believe the argument is originally Moshe Idel's—that Jewish prayer takes every opportunity to refute Christian claims about the Trinity or the powers of the Virgin by reasserting God's unicity and direct redemption. A perfect example is the paragraph beginning, "True and lasting [ʾemet va-yatsiv]" immediately following the last paragraph of the central Shema Yisrael section of the synagogue service. Nearly every line can be read as such a reassertion and reaffirmation. This would be the case in the Blois story, too: God saves, not the Virgin.

16. See Lampert's Croxton essay cited in Chapter 2, n. 28, above; but also Mary Minty, who emphasizes the Eucharistic symbolism; see Chapter 2, n. 46, above, and also Browe, "Hostienschändungen der Juden im Mittelalter," 182, for a similar story at Passau in 1477.

17. See Ivan Marcus, *Rituals of Childhood: Jewish Acculturation in Medieval Europe* (New Haven, 1996), passim, who goes so far as to speak of social polemic, actions imitated and reimitated, although see my comments in Chapter 3, n. 18, above, in which I suspect some of the polemic may have been in perceptions of Jewish actions, like that of Rigord's, more, or rather, than in the Jews' own intentions.

18. On the ordeal by cold water, where the condemned was supposed "to swim," not sink, see Robert Bartlett, *Trial by Fire and Water: The Medieval Judicial Ordeal* (Oxford, 1986), 23.

19. Haberman, *Sefer gezerot*, 125; Paul builds on Ezek. 20:25; this theme is ubiquitous in the early chapters of the Epistle to the Romans.

20. On copying, see discussion in this chapter of Shelomo bar Shimshon's First Crusade Chronicle. On these motifs, see Chapter 3, nn. 31–37, above, and Thomas of Monmouth, *Life*, 25–30, where William is left in a sack and tied by a cord in Thorpe Wood, and the body is discovered because it gleams. Water is a theme in the Crusade Chronicles, and in the "1007 Anonymous," too: pious women commit suicide by jumping into water; Haberman, *Sefer gezerot*, 19–21. see also Yuval, *Two Nations*, 188–98, on the repetition of the theme of water and on the antinomies of Jewish and Christian significations of water. I am not wholly convinced by Yuval's antinomies, especially when water becomes equated with blood, although antinomies there are, e.g., in Shelomo bar Shimshon (Haberman, *Sefer gezerot*, 59): at Weiselberg, the would-be Crusaders drown in the (Leitha) Danube, in whose waters they have baptized all of Regensburg's Jews. But see Ephraim Kanarfogel, *"Peering Through the Lattices": Mystical, Magical, and Pietistic Dimensions in the Tosafist Period* (Detroit, 2000), 234, n. 41, for the responsum of Judah He-Hasid. R. Judah tells of a Jewish apostate who, in order to atone for his baptism, drowns himself in a river. Here impure and pure waters—the river is clearly a *mikveh*, ritual bath, of purification—are patently opposed, but as water only, with the emphasis on the impure water's effect nullified by the water of purification; this, too, is an inversion story. One is also tempted here, but must proceed cautiously, to link these stories with that of the four hundred youths in the Babylonian Talmud, *Gittin* 58b, who drown themselves rather than be put to sexual slavery, an offense worthy of martyrdom (I thank Haym Soloveitchik for this reference); the motif reappears slightly adapted in Ibn Daud's *Sefer HaKabbalah*, ed. Gerson D. Cohen (Philadelphia, 1967), 64, citing this same passage in *Gittin*. Suicide by immersion in water is indeed purifying, making the inversion of the Christian motif all the more striking.

21. See Ulysse Chevalier, *Répertoire des sources historiques du Moyen Age* (Montbéliard, 1894–99), 1: col. 1272, Gastinais and Gastinois: in Hebrew, G-A-S-T-I-N-O-I-I-SH, same configuration as B-L-O-I-I-SH for Blois, hence, he is a Gastinois from the Gastinais, or Gâtinais. I am perplexed why scholars have regularly read here "Augustinian," to suggest the priest was a member of the Augustinian Order, rather than just a local country curate.

22. Chazan, *God, Humanity and History*, 8–11, tacitly rejects this reading, clinging to "lover," although he does cite Einbinder, "Pucellina."

23. On ʾ*ahavah* and ʾ*ohev*, see Ephraim himself in Haberman, *Sefer gezerot*, 117; ʾ*ohavo goi*, his Christian protector. See also *Haman ve ʾohavav* in the Book of Esther, and see Bouquet, comp., *Recueil*, 17: 126. The usage occurs in Latin, too; in 1182 (in the *"Philippidos"* of Guillaume Le Breton), "[the king] withdrew his protection, or support" (suo privavit amor) of and from the Jews; this was hardly alienation of affection. I note that in modern Spanish *amo* is patron, master, even boss, and, of course, feudal lord.

24. Chazan, sources cited in n. 4 above, reports three letters, but there are really as many as six, if not seven, if the few lines beginning with the phrase, "about the keys of the synagogue . . ." are, as they seem to be, a wholly separate missive, which likely should be taken as a reference to the royal confiscations of 1181 or 1182.

25. Following Wachtel, "Ritual and Liturgical Commemoration," I would not see this series of letters as falling into such a tight (legislative) mold. Nor do they present an integral whole. On the assumption that the letters are integral, Chazan's study set out to demonstrate how Jacob Tam assumed a kind of royal position by sending out written directives. In them, Jacob Tam also anticipated, as I have discussed in "Holy Body, Holy Society: Conflicting Medieval Structural Conceptions," in *Sacred Space: Shrine, City, Land,* ed. Benjamin Z. Kedar and R. J. Zwi Werblowsky (New York, 1998), the implementation of the representative principles found in the concept of "Quod omnes tangit ab omnibus approbetur," which translates loosely as "What applies to all must be aired before all." Chazan's study pointing the way toward this eventual resolution of Rabbenu Tam's intentions may be read in this light. The problem, of course, is that the close inspection of these letters carried out first by Wachtel and now here raises questions about both Chazan's and my own original conclusions with respect to this specific event. Chazan is convincing about Rabbenu Tam's *modus legislandi* in general.

26. Haberman, *Sefer gezerot,* 126, and see again the thesis of Wachtel, "Ritual and Liturgical Commemoration."

27. This is aside from the issue of the fast itself, and see Chazan's essays cited in n. 4, above.

28. There is one exception. Two of the letters mention a ransom, in the first, of 100 plus 102 pounds, and, in the other, 220 pounds. Yet rather than resolve problems, this common particular complicates them. In both cases, the ransom is for those alive (the second case says also to reclaim the bodies of the dead, but the emphasis is on "also"). At Blois, according to the narratives, everybody died. In which case, one might argue, the letters have nothing to do with Blois at all, but refer to another act of Theobald, a subsequent, or prior arrest of Jews. Or they might refer, as we shall see, to the affair at Loches, where there were survivors according to the tale. Alternatively, if the reference is to the aftermath of Blois, these figures suggest that the Orléans Narrative as we have it is telling only half the story, of those martyred, but not of the survivors, whose existence the narrative (apparently) hides. Both possibilities, nonetheless, are unwarranted and unsupported speculation, and we do best not to build on the "ransom" numbers. By contrast, from a purely literary angle, that the numbers do not *precisely* jibe suggests that the source of the original letters is not one and the same for all of them. A second issue is whether the "I" who pays the ransom in the first letter is identical with the Mr. Natan, the ransomer in the second; and on this see Appendix Two, n. 36, below. See also n. 42 there on the difficulties of blending the Loches letter with that concerning Troyes.

29. Various scholars have protested that this letter refers directly to Blois. Its opening, "Before the trouble," they say, obviously means the "trouble" in Blois, especially since the letter follows the Orléans Narrative immediately in the manuscript. However, the Hebrew *tsara* here repeats again in the Loches letter, where it refers to a forced conversion, *in Loches*; see Appendix Two and n. 30, below. The literary skill of the final, anonymous, editor of the letters was finely honed. It looks as though he almost purposefully was misleading his readers. The second *tsara* gives him away.

30. On Loches, see Marcel Pacaut, *Louis VII et son royaume* (Paris, 1964), 16, showing the town's importance to Foulque V, father of Geoffrey Plantagenet, count of Anjou; and see also Baldwin, *Government of Philip Augustus,* 195, on the town's being given by Philip to Dreu de Mello in 1205. This, of itself, is reason to suspect that the letters come from a later era, for instance, after 1204 and especially 1205, when Touraine was in French hands (Rigord, in Bouquet, comp., *Recueil*, 17: 39, indicates that Philip already possessed the town from 1194) and the letters as a uniform series would make more sense. Going in another direction, since there is a delator, a *malshin*, at Loches, within a tale of redemption, one wonders whether there is a connection to the Hebrew story (mentioned above, n.13, and Chapter 2, n.11) of Sehoq ben Esther Israeli, set in 992. The waxen image motif in this story may correspond, invertedly, to the Latin story of Eberhard of Trier in 1066, where there is also a waxen image. The 992 story was most likely written after that of Trier. Yuval, *Two Nations*, 197–98, suggests a possible link with 992, going so far as to propose that perhaps the delation in the Loches letter is the real explanation for what happened at Blois. This is a logical first supposition. Yet once Loches is removed jurisdictionally from the county of Blois, such a possibility fades; there is always a limit in trying to read reality out of texts like these, which problems like this political one here stymie—over and above the problems of the texts' literary genre. Indeed, it is to just this literary side of the texts that Yuval's extremely perspicacious association of the *Alenu* prayer in the Orléans Narrative with the Christian *Te Deum* points. It reminds us of how heavily the texts are laden with topoi and motifs and, hence, of their nature as romances or *chansons de geste*. The heavier the topoi and the more heuristically narrative an entire text, one might say, the less justification there is for imagining it contains *identifiable* "historical fact." Yuval discusses Loches the *Te Deum*, in *Two Nations*, 203–18; and the 992 incident at Le Mans (or Limoges as the text states), 180.

Beside all this, the expression in the Loches letter, noted above, "we hope the trouble did not bring shame on them," cannot refer to Blois. In context, it refers to baptism *and apostasy*, hence, the probable reason for the burning at Loches. This would be significant. It may be a first, certainly very early, instance of such a punishment for this "crime." Whether real or fictional, it is the *idea* of such a punishment for apostasy that counts. Escaping the fire, too, may reflect primitive ways of burning, tying with cords only, which burned, allowing the victims to try to escape—unless we do better just to see this description as a variant on the three boys in the furnace motif of the biblical Book of Daniel. Once again, the biblically added context in the Blois narratives leaves one in the dark, with the author clearly out to stress, for theological purposes, the survival of the corpses intact. In addition, why would Theobald of Blois be angry with those who pressed escaping Jews back into the fire? Was he exerting his authority, or was this "justice?" And what does the reported successful escape of the people of Loches signify in relation to Blois? The more one tries to see the Loches letter as related directly to Blois, the murkier matters become.

There is a final possibility, that this letter is the second of two originals pasted together (much of whose original text has been lost). One phrase in the surviving (compound) letter, "remembering after I have written," suggests that one of the two originals was about Blois—thus the description in the Loches letter of the fire—the second original being this one about a difficult event in Loches. This interpretation is forced, extremely forced, to say the least. And to sum up this involved discussion, one must accept that there are too many questions, too much internal confusion. A complete answer about Loches likely will never be had. Whether as a historical or literary text, this letter is best declared a mystery, except for one thing. It is not about Blois.

31. The information about Philip comes from *Revue des études juives*, 2 (1881): 31, which contains a French summary of a text housed in the Treasure of Chartres, saying Philip IV (1285–1314) renews and confirms a perpetual exemption from the tithe given in 1180 by Philip Augustus to a converted Jew named Philip and his descendants. It is not clear from the *REJ* whether the letter was written at Loches, or to Loches, or about someone at Loches, although common practice was for a king itinerating through his possessions to renew local privileges at the place where they were bestowed. That is, Philip IV was in Loches and so were the descendants of the original recipient; it is difficult to imagine the convert Philip being from elsewhere. This text does pose a problem in that it dates the conversion to 1180, while it is difficult to suppose that the conversion and, more particularly, the exemption predate Philip's assumption of power over Loches in 1194 (Rigord's date for the event, although Philip's full powers in Loches may have been acquired only a decade later). The late thirteenth-century scribe must have backdated the conversion, either out of sloppiness or ignorance, or perhaps for propagandistic purposes.

32. Admittedly, one never knows precisely why a given text is included in a larger medieval manuscript. A shared motif like burning could be sufficient. In other cases, we are dealing with sheer accident. But even with the motif of burning in common, anyone insisting on seeing the letters as a unit—and on insisting that the king is Louis VII—and that the letters were contemporaneous with the Blois events would be hard-pressed to refute the historical and literary evidence presented here. The historical cases are especially problematic. To insist that the

Loches letter is contemporary with Blois means that the letters are speaking of two kings, not one: Louis of France and Henry II of England, the respective rulers at that moment; albeit strictly speaking, Henry II was a vassal of the French king and in fact did homage to him (Baldwin, *Government of Philip Augustus*, 263), surely nobody would think of the French king as the real or direct ruler in Loches. On the other hand, if the king in the letters is one, Philip Augustus, and their subject is royal action, then the Loches letter fits neatly into the authorial intention to point out royal danger. This is so even if the neophyte Philip is not the convert the Loches letter mentions. A single king also makes the letter postdate 1180, since Philip was the first Capetian king to rule Loches and Blois together, however directly. Yet the editor of the letters seems to have forgotten this fact. Or perhaps he never knew it, because the transfer of ownership from Angevins to Capetians had occurred too far back in his own past.

33. Jordan, *French Monarchy*, 9; note that the second letter says that the original was sent elsewhere, that it is not at hand, and that what is being put down now (and sent along) is a memorandum. And see the translations and the notes on this point, which confirm Jordan.

34. Jordan, "Princely Identity," 261–62; but see Stow, *Alienated Minority*, 113–14, on Ephraim of Bonn's negative assessment; see also, and especially, the discussion in Chapter 3, nn. 55 and 59, above. Louis appears as precise; the picture is not that of a king who would go out of his way "to favor" Jews beyond what was theirs by formal privilege. The figures in the letters, the king especially, even discounting possible hyperbole, bend over backwards, even breaking, or virtually breaking, the law.

35. Haberman, *Sefer gezerot*, 145–46, *hevel*-nonsense and *le-khabdam pi shnayim*, for double honor; the first letter says to honor them, but not "double." On honor as possibly a reference to the Roman law concept of status and office, both forbidden the Jews, see Appendix Two, n. 18, below, in the translation of the letters.

36. For the Hebrew, Henri Gross, *Gallia Judaica: Dictionnaire géographique de la France d'après les sources rabbiniques* (Paris, 1897), 442–43; Gross identifies the usages here as unique to these Blois letters, itself an indication that one ought to question them. He resolves the contradiction by dropping *Rirt* and *Kefar* in his entry; the bracketed *o* in *P[on]tiyeh* indicates the lack of a *vav* in *P[o]tiyeh Rirt*, *Peynun*, rather than *Pey-vav-nun* in *Kefar Pontiyeh*, a difference Gross overcomes simply by offering both spellings. For the Latin, see J. G. Grässe and Friedrich Benedict, *Orbis Latinus* (Berlin, 1922), 245. *Briva* seems to mean town, but standard medieval Latin dictionaries, including Niermeyer and Latham, do not list it.

37. See, Chapter 3, n. 17, above, and Bouquet, comp., *Recueil*, 13: 520 for Lambert (1163), 12: 438 for Geoffrey of Voisin (1156), and 13: 320 for the *Appendice ad Sigebertum* of Torigny for 1177.

38. See Chapter 3, n. 4, above, for a complete discussion of the sources.

39. Vauchez, *Sainthood in the Later Middle Ages*, 150.

40. I thank William C. Jordan for his help.

41. See Baldwin, *Government of Philip Augustus,* 19; and Sassier, *Louis VII,* 443–46.

42. In the first Parisian letter, the Jews meet the king in (the then suburb of) Poissy.

43. Aronius, *Regesten zur Geschichte der Juden,* no. 497.

44. See the text cited in Chapter Three, n. 40, above, once more stressing that *communicare* can mean to receive and share the Eucharist (rather than the standard *communire*); the use of "share" as by Grayzel and Langmuir, does not do justice to the setting.

45. Stow, "Conversion," 914.

46. *Sefer Yosef HaMekane,* 14; and now see Jeremy Cohen, *Sanctifying the Name of God: Jewish Martyrs and Jewish Memories of the First Crusade* (Philadelphia, 2004), whose thesis rests on the idea that the Hebrew Crusade Chronicles are full of irony, even parody.

47. See the citation at n. 35 above.

48. For example, Aronius, *Regesten zur Geschichte der Juden,* nos. 168 and 170. And Thomas Rymer, *Foedera* (London, 1816), 1: 1, 51.

49. And so is the continuation: Haberman, *Sefer gezerot,* 145, "to preserve their persons and property" (lishmor gufam ve-mamonam).

50. See again Baldwin, *Government of Philip Augustus,* 195. The fragmentation of secular power before 1200 meant that "full jurisdiction over Jews pertained to any lord with high justice or who permitted them to reside under his jurisdiction," according to Gavin Langmuir, "*Tanquam Servi*: The Change in Jewish Status in French Law About 1200," in id., *Toward a Definition of Antisemitism,* 184. The context here is such that one thinks of a direct relationship, not an intermediary one, between king and nobility, as established at Melun in 1230. This, in turn, suggests that the letters may derive from much later in the thirteenth century, under Louis IX, for example, when royal power was direct over all French Jews; Louis IX, of course, enlarged on the Jewry policies of Philip Augustus.

51. Exodus 1, "a new Pharaoh arose" Was this what the author was thinking?

52. It might be precisely for this reason that German Jews, reflecting on their changing status in the thirteenth century and on continued physical attack, might have decided to copy these letters, reminding themselves that kings were fickle at best, even in France. There were massacres in Frankfurt am Main in 1241, and other massacres, known as those of Reindfleish and Armleder, respectively, in 1298 and 1336, the last two connected directly to libels.

53. See n. 49 above.

54. On Guillaume, see Marcel Pacaut, *Louis VII et les élections épiscopales dans le royaume de France* (Paris, 1957), various places. The archbishop in the letter is specified as the brother of Theobald. This is *not* the same Archbishop Guido of Sens, mentioned above, who was instructed by Alexander III to persuade Philip Augustus to restrict the Jews' use of Christian servants. Guillaume, the Champenois brother, was archbishop of Rheims when Philip was crowned.

55. Spiegel is cited in Limor, "Blood Libel," 5: 46–47; and also Haberman, *Sefer gezerot*, 258–59. Browe, "Hostienschändungen," 189, cites the chronicle of one Nicolai Triveti, for which Browe gives no date, who says that the Jews of Blois were burned except those who converted, on which see Jordan, *French Monarchy*, 19.

56. Kenneth Stow, "Church, Conversion, and Tradition: The Problem of Jewish Conversion in Sixteenth-Century Italy," *Dimensioni e problemi della ricerca storica* 2 (1996): 26–35. The stance imputed to the archbishop here is distant from that of Alexander III (Simonsohn, *Apostolic See and the Jews*, 1: 52, no. 50) and his contemporary, the archbishop of Canterbury, both of whom seem to have allowed backsliding, or considered it inevitable, especially when converts lacked means of financial support, which was frequent, as the many papal letters ordering subsidies for converts attest. (See Stow, *Alienated Minority*, 119, and the texts cited there.) In the letter here, the archbishop of Sens seems actively to encourage backsliding, inquiring who would like to return, as though actually assisting—although, as is about to be noted, he does nothing to help these Jews get back lost monies and goods. The archbishop seems to be going backward and forward at the same time. He breaks the law and says "return," but then, by implication, he seems to be trying, as Gregory the Great had suggested in the canon *Iam vero*, C. 23, q. 6, c. 4 in Gratian's *Decretum*, to impoverish these "apostates," hoping that they return to Christianity, then to receive a subsidy. In short, the Hebrew author treats the archbishop like a fool. A possibly true countercase, showing episcopal support for conversion's permanence, is that of the bishop of Liège, about 1220, as told by Caesarius of Heisterbach and Thomas of Cantimpre in the story of Catherine Parc-aux-Dames, both later melded into one tale by the Bollandists, May 4, 1: 532–34; a good translation of the original texts, along with references, is in Michael Goodich, *Witnesses at the Margins of Medieval Society* (Philadelphia, 1998), 26–31. However, in this case, the Jews were alleging the use of force and the baptizing of an underage child against parental will, which the chroniclers freely admit. The bishop of Liège was obligated to give the Jews a day in court. At Blois, the converts—were there in fact such—technically fell under the heading of conditional force. They chose to be baptized rather than die, and they were also, it seems, of the age of reason. Assisting their return was—would have been—canonically wrong. For Louis's order of 1144, see Bouquet, comp., *Recueil*, 16: 8, *Epistolarum Regis Ludovici VII*, and Chapter 3, n. 55, above.

57. Grayzel, *Church and the Jews*, 1: 95–99, nos. 6 and 8; the fear of confiscation also motivated Alexander III, for example, to insist on subsidies for converts, noted in the letters cited, esp. Simonsohn, *Apostolic See and the Jews*, no. 50.

58. See n. 62, below, and see the letter of Innocent III approving one such consecration, Grayzel, *Church and the Jews*, 1: 104–5.

59. *Memshelet reshutekhah*. Rabbinic literature contains no such expression, so Haym Soleveitchik has kindly informed me. The Paris letter uses *memshalah* for

"realm." *Memshelet reshutkhah* in the "1007 Anonymous" text is thus "in the realm of your authority," your lawful jurisdiction, or rightful authority.

60. *The Standard Prayer Book*, ed. S. Singer (New York, 1957), 58, *shemoneh'esre* on *memshelet zadon*.

61. Commentary on Judg. 19:4–5, found in any standard rabbinic Bible with commentaries, of the late fourteenth century Levi ben Gershon, but whose origin no doubt is in earlier sources.

62. Haberman, *Sefer gezerot*, 146, in the totally opaque letter about the keys to the synagogue, where a *shalit* (ruler) is mentioned, but neither named nor given a title. See, too, the Brie incident in Haberman, *Sefer gezerot*, 128, where Ephraim of Bonn calls Philip a "wicked king . . . [whose] wickedness endured from first to last." One wonders whether Ephraim's opaque remark concerning Blois, that the king left the youths under the age of 13 "in peace and to escape with their lives [lit., souls]," hints that he pushed them into Christianity, and they would have been the ones ransomed. This is speculative, especially since this is Ephraim's invention, who was removed in place and time from the events and otherwise, as Wachtel has shown, leaned fully on the Orléans Narrative.

63. Bouquet, comp., *Recueil*, 17: 9d; here Rigord makes an oblique reference to Louis VII's failings. Philip, he says, acted "unlike his predecessors; the Jews easily bent Louis to do their will" (alios reges praedecessores suos ad voluntatem suam faciendam facile [the Jews] inclinare consueverant). The reference must be, again, to domestic servants, but in context, it seems to be directed against all of Louis's actions, as opposed to Philip's thorough "reform" program concerning Jews.

64. Guillaume le Breton, Bouquet, comp, *Recueil*, 17: 126.

65. They were fleeing in fact, on which see Langmuir, "Tanquam servi."

66. Unless one believes the narrative of the "1007 Anonymous," which, as said, has not a shred of historicity with respect to the events it describes. That story is also one of forced conversion or death. Theobald had executed Jews charged with ritual murder, which is something else. For this, there was no precedent.

67. Jordan, *French Monarchy*, 191, identifies no blood or ritual murder charge with royal participation after Philip's time, but he does point to Philip IV's total acceptance of the Host libel. There was also the libel at Troyes in 1288. Royal participation, if not initiation in the attack on the Talmud also falls under the heading of countering menace. It is not that the Talmud was heretical—it was judged to contain heresies. Judaism itself is not, nor can it be, heresy; canonically, this is impossible. On the other hand, as Ramon Martí would say about 1278, the Talmudic doctrine of the rabbis "stinks" and is "revolting." It is infectious, just like all other Jewish practice, and, among other things, it encourages ritual murder; see Introduction, n. 106, above.

Chapter Five. A Usable Past

1. The expression comes from the English title of Karl Marx's *Die Judenfrage,* ed. Stephan Grossman (Berlin 1919), which hopes for exactly this, with its own picture of Jewish assault on society through finance capital, a modus operandi that Marx says Christianity has adopted for itself. See Marx, *A World Without Jews,* trans. Dagobart G. Runes (New York, 1959); this translation of the German original is picked up on many web sites, including neo-Nazi ones, e.g., www.zundelsite.org/english/zgrams/zg1999/zg9909/990917.html (accessed May 13, 2005).

2. See David Sorkin, *The Berlin Haskalah and German Religious Thought* (London, 2000), 79–94, for thinking on this and similar subjects in the modern period.

3. See Sonne, *Mi-Pavolo*, 23n2, who discusses the awareness of this kind of transference on the part of Jewish authors like Benjamin ben Elnatan, and see the texts cited in Chapter 2, n. 10, above.

4. Browe, "Hostienschändungen," 195–96.

5. Kornberg, "Ignaz von Döllinger's *Die Juden in Europa,*" passim.

6. See also Grayzel, *Church and the Jews,* 1: 109, no. 14, and 271, no. 116, for Innocent III and Innocent IV, respectively, and 2: 118, no. 31, where Gregory X is specific: "their law expressly prohibits" consuming blood, of animals, let alone humans. Note especially that Innocent IV says Jews are persecuted without proper "[legal] accusation, confession, or conviction," that is, without "due process," which he sees as an inalienable right. See, too, Langmuir, "Historiographic Crucifixion," in *Toward a Definition of Antisemitism*, 286–87, as well as other places in that book.

7. See *Die Päpstlichen Bullen über die Blutbeschuldingung* (Munich, 1900), 77–143, however, for various papal letters through the eighteenth century rejecting the blood libel.

8. See Browe, "Hostienschändungen," 189, who mentions the case, one of a Christian woman stealing the Host for magical ends, or so says Winterthur.

9. On this episode, see Trachtenberg, *Devil and the Jews,* 135; Ram ben Shalom, "The Blood Libel in Arles and the Franciscan Mission in Avignon in 1453," *Zion* 63 (1998): 391–408, esp. 399 (in Hebrew); and Mario Esposito, "Un Procès contre les Juifs de la Savoie en 1329," *Revue d'histoire ecclésiastique* 34 (1938): 785–801, who also reproduces the texts. see Vauchez, "Antisemitismo," 499, for the Flemish verses. No image, of course, could be more "un-Jewish" than this one: the Jewish conception of the unquestioning acceptance of the "yoke of commandments" as defining Jewish behavior and obligation has no relation to the Christian idea of salvation gained through membership in the *Corpus Christi*, confirmed by receiving the Eucharist. Nonetheless, Christians had apparently been in the habit of linking the eating of matzoh and bitter herbs with consuming Christian bodies and blood; see *Jewish-Christian Debate,* ed. Berger, 54, line 5. For related views of *haroseth* as a danger, see Yuval, *Two Nations*, 258–64.

10. On the Damascus affair, see Jonathan Frankel, *The Damascus Affair: "Ritual Murder," Politics, and the Jews in 1840* (Cambridge, 1997).

11. See Carlo Ginzburg, *Storia notturna* (Turin, 1989), 44–45; trans. Raymond Rosenthal as *Ecstasies: Deciphering the Witches' Sabbath* (Chicago, 2004).

12. On justice and virtue, see Kantorowicz, *King's Two Bodies*, 137.

13. On due process in the Middle Ages, see J. A. Watt, "The Term '*Plenitudo Potestatis*' in Hostiensis," in *Proceedings of the Second International Congress of Medieval Canon Law*, ed. S. Kuttner (Vatican City, 1965).

14. For Innocent's text, see B. Z. Kedar, "Canon Law and the Burning of the Talmud," *Bulletin of Medieval Canon Law* 9 (1979): 79–82.

15. See *Päpstlichen Bullen über die Blutbeschuldingung*, passim.

16. See the initial discussion with references above.

17. On de' Giudici and Sixtus IV at Trent, see Stow, "Papal Mendicants."

18. I refer, especially, to the Internet, which has become the source for easy access to enormous hate literature, whose seriousness or cynicism defies decoding. Blood libels have been adopted especially by ultra-right-wing white American Protestant fundamentalists. *Jewish Ritual Murder* by Arnold Leese (London, 1938) has been republished electronically on http://churchoftrueisrael.com/streicher/jrm/ (accessed on June 30, 2005), a site that linked to www.posse-comitatus.org, of similar provenance, and also www.aryan_nations.org (sites that often change their contents, however). There are also the writings of Pastor Bob Jones of Nevada and G.O.A.L., God's Order Affirmed in Love, and its Reference Library for Reconstructing a National Identity for Christians, featuring the writings of Malcolm Ross, which can also be accessed through the pseudonymous Poppy Dixon, www.postfun.com/pfp/features/98/oct/bloodlibel.html (accessed June 30, 2005) whose stated goal is to expose these organizations. G.O.A.L. explains itself simply: "We need a preservationist ethic to replace the *Racial Nihilistic* Judeo-liberal, 'tolerant', egalitarianism that is destroying the races as God created them." A full discussion of these sites, however necessary, must await another occasion. However, it is important to note that between the time this note was first composed and the date of publication, some of these sites have either been closed, their names changed, or the domain reassigned. Melvig.org, as noted in the Preface, is now a catch-all vendor. For additional discussion, see Introduction, n. 8, and Chapter 1, n. 3.

19. See again Stow, "Papal Mendicants," on the political intrigues forcing the papal hand, not to mention that already executed punishments could, obviously, not be reversed. Getting children back to their (actually baptized) mothers was something else, and this de' Giudici and Sixtus did achieve.

20. For a summary on medieval Dominican censorship, see Stow, *Alienated Minority*, 251–59, especially on Innocent IV.

21. See Introduction.

22. Joassart, *Hippolyte Delehaye*, 2: 769–70, doc. 275: October 1, 1903. Joassart provides the remarks of the censor in their original Latin; the French, also original,

is François van Ortroy's. The censor, one of a number appointed to oversee Bollandist writing at that time and whose names are unknown, was taking apart more than just the review of Divina. He was also having a go at van Ortroy's review of *Layettes du Trésor des chartes*, vol. 4: *De l'année 1261 à l'année 1270*, by E. Berger (Paris, 1902): The give and take with the censor is reconstructed by Joassart as below. The review of G. Divina is *Storia del beato Simone da Trento* (Trent, 1902), *Analecta Bollandiana* 23 (1904) 122–24.

> "aberrations, véritable acte de folie." Haec violenta sunt. Satis erat quod scriptor in pag. 21 v. 22 dixerat: "erreurs, tors involontaires." Immo nonne S. Ludovicus hac in re potius deceptus fuit quam erravit? [Van Ortroy observes that this is a piece of history conceived and executed with a profound understanding of the subject . . . yet an admiration that did not blind the author for an instant to the errors] "bien involontaires d'ailleurs, des son héros. . . . La seconde croisade fut en effet une de ces aberrations, quelque noble et généreux qu'on suppose le dessein." "Plus d'une fois, au témoignage des Souverains Pontifes, ces représailles ne reposaient que sur des impostures mises en circulation par des princes. . . ." Dubito satisne manifesto id colligatur ex Bulla Innocentii IV quae profertur. Itan enim incipit, 'Lacrymabilem Judaeorum Alemanniae quaestionem recepimus, quod nonnuli [*sic*] tam ecclesiastici quam saeculares principes . . . '; ubi Pontifex innuit obiurgationem suam niti *testimonio iudaeorum* [emphasis in original]. [Van Ortroy says more fully: " . . . plus d'une fois, au témoignage des souverains pontifes, ces terribles représailles [= exactions contre les Juifs accusés de violence contre les enfants chrétiens] n'avaient pour origine que des impostures mises en circulation par les princes avides de satisfaire des instincts rapaces et sanguinaires. C'est ainsi que le pape Innocent IV met en gard les éveques d'Allemagne quod nonnulli tam ecclesiatic quam seculares principes, ac alii nobiles et potentes vestrarum civitatum et diocesum, ut eorum bona iniuste diripiant et usurpent, adversus ipsos impia consilia cogitantes et fingentes occasiones varias et diversas, falso imponunt eisdem quod in ipsa solemnitate se corde pueri communicant interfecti." (p. 123, 6–14) Quidquid est, scriptor Boll. recte opinatur eiusmodi argumentum prudentissime tractandum esse; et quae circa casuam Tridentinam particulatim animadvertit suam profecto vim habent.—Verumtamen processus legitimum est monumentum; neque ulla ratione positiva demonstratur fidem ei adiungi non posse. Ad eius auctoritatem repudianam haud sufficiunt coniecturae.—Item crediderim bullam Sixti IV maioris esse ponderis quam in pag. 29 indicatur.—Ipsam vero conclusionem: "situation fort équivoque, où les haines de races ont joué un rôle . . . prépondérant (p. 123, 20ff.), hoc vel alio simili modo mutare oportet." . . . 'situation' difficilem, ancipitem, in quam 'les haines de races' forsitan magnum influxum habuere.

The discussion of censorship and the order is in Joassart, *Hippolyte Delehaye*, 1: 144–316, where he details the various stages of the battle between the Bollandists and Rome that went on over three decades.

23. See again Joassart as cited in the preceding note.

24. Simonsohn, *Apostolic See and the Jews*, no. 999.

25. For examples, see the discussion above, especially the reference to the English *The Month*, cited in Chapter 1, n. 4, above.

26. The Amsterdam consultation is cited above with respect to the date of Werner's passion, in Chapter 2. This is not to open the entire question of previous intellectual contact between Jews and Christians, or the special situation of Jews, Muslims, and Christians in medieval Spain. In the event, in northern (extra-Iberian) Europe, with the possible—conjectural—exception of late twelfth- and early thirteenth-century Paris, the purpose of studying with Jews was normally exploitative. This includes the study of Kabbalah later on, in Italy, by Pico della Mirandola and others. Here, I am speaking of true mutuality.

27. Joassart, *Hippolyte Delehaye*, 288, 326, 373, 561–62.

28. Some of Duschesne's work was considered so modernist that it was placed on the Index of Prohibited Books.

29. On these events, see Norman Stillman, *The Jews of Arab Lands* (Philadelphia, 1979), 4.

30. Louis Duschesne, "Le Massacre des Chrétiens Himyarites au temps de l'empereur Justin," *Revue des études juives* 20 (1890): 220–24.

31. Isidore Loeb, summary of Duschesne's "La Question de la Pâcque au Concile de Nicée (325),"* *Revue des études juives* 2 (1881): 157–58. (**Revue des questions historiques* 28 [1880] : 5–42.)

32. *Revue des études juives* 11 (1890): 73–77.

33. Joassart, *Hippolyte Delehaye*, 336, cites this letter.

34. *Analecta Bollandiana* 43 (1925): 211 and 44 (1926): 183.

35. The web site Holywar.org continues this tradition, citing both of these popes as praiseworthy.

36. Joassart, *Hippolyte Delehaye*, 204.

37. The term "defenders of the text" was introduced by Anthony Grafton. The *mos gallicus* has been clearly described by Donald Kelley. See Anthony Grafton, *Defenders of the Text: The Traditions of Scholarship in an Age of Science, 1450–1800* (Cambridge, Mass., 1991), on scholarly textual study and faithfulness to textual traditions, especially in the Low Countries, and Donald R. Kelley, "Budé and the First Historical School of Law," *American Historical Review* 72 (1967): 807–34, on the *mos gallicus*, the attempt to find original meanings in legal texts that the traditional Italian *mos italicus*, as Kelley explains, viewed in terms of contemporary relevance.

38. Delehaye, *Works of the Bollandists Through Three Centuries*, 87–116.

Chapter Six. Purity and Its Discontents

1. See the Introduction, n. 66; and on direct infection through syphilis, see Anna Foa, "The New and the Old, The Spread of Syphilis," in *Sex and Gender in*

Historical Perspective, ed. Edward Muir and Guido Ruggiero (Baltimore, 1990). See especially nn. 42 and 51 below, on pollution and its threats among Christians themselves, with clear parallels to the pollution feared from Jews.

2. Haym Ibn Attar, *Or hahayim* (Jerusalem, 1986), on Exod. 35:12: the holiness of the tabernacle and the altar are like the holiness of the table.

3. Linder, trans. and ed., *Jews in the Legal Sources,* 1143, 631; and see on Agobard, Introduction, above.

4. Cyprian, according to Eusebius, saw even a physical defilement through heresy, necessitating a rebaptism following repentance; see Introduction, n. 38, above.

5. See Nirenberg, "Conversion, Sex, and Segregation," 1071, on clerical concubines corrupting their priest partners, a version of the concept of the *lapsus*. In fact, they are said to make the priest do dishonor to the Eucharist, just a step from corrupting it; again, the impossible—and heretical—but no doubt imagined. The corrupted priest would transfer his personal pollution to communicants, or so Agobard and his ilk seem to have thought. Moreover, though the sacrament itself remained holy, those polluted did not receive its saving benefits.

6. Brundage, "Intermarriage," 25–40, discussing sexuality, notes the many times Gratian and the *Liber Extra* refer to prohibited relations between Christians and Jews.

7. Brundage, "Intermarriage," 25–40, 283, and Oronozo Giordano, *Religiosità popolare nell'alto medioevo* (Bari, 1979), 123.

8. See above, Chapter 1, n. 60.

9. *Catechism of the Council of Trent,* in *Canons and Decrees of the Council of Trent, Original Text with English Translation,* ed. H. J. Schroeder (St. Louis, 1960; repr. of 1941): "It also restrains and represses the lusts of the flesh, for while it inflames the soul more ardently with the fire of charity, it of necessity extinguishes the ardour of concupiscence." There are many editions, including on the Internet.

10. The bull *Etsi judaeos* in Grayzel, *Church and the Jews,* no. 1: 114, no. 18, and Hostiensis, cited in Grayzel, 2: 71; cited also by Rubin, *Gentile Tales,* 99. See Jacob Katz, *Exclusiveness and Tolerance* (New York, 1961), 24–27.

11. See the discussion of milk and blood in Charles Wood, "The Doctor's Dilemma: Sin, Salvation, and the Menstrual Cycle in Medieval Thought," *Speculum* 56 (1981): 711–27. For Jewish attitudes to Christian mother's milk, see the sixteenth-century *Shulhan Arukh* of Josef Karo, *Yoreh De'ah,* 81:7, especially the later (Ashkenazi) commentary of Moses Isserles, there, that "the milk of an Egyptian [pagan, non-Jewish] woman is like that of an Israelite woman. Still, babies should not be nursed by an Egyptian if an Israelite is available. For the milk of idolators [including—indeed, especially for Isserles—Christians] makes the heart foolish and instills [into the child] a wicked disposition." The comment, Isserles notes, goes back to the medieval Solomon ibn Adret (I thank Magda Teter for this reference).

12. Hayes, *Gentile Impurities and Jewish Identities,* "Conclusion," notes that among Jews, impurity was not passed on from generation to generation. Hence

it was genealogy and the acceptance of the commandments that defined membership in Judaism, or exclusion from it, making the birth of Christianity as a distinct religion inevitable. Gentile Christians qualified for neither of these categories. This may be true in the sense of one's indelible identification. The matter of temporary impurity, voiding or corrupting one's status as a member in good standing, is something else. In Agobardian terms, such corruption is extraordinarily serious, since the communicant is affected. In Jewish terms, it is a matter of knowing when one can and cannot mix, although mixing might also mean seduction into apostasy.

13. See the reference to Eusebius in Introduction, n. 38, above.

14. See above, Introduction, n. 55.

15. See especially the comments of Simo Parpola, cited in the Preface, n. 10, above.

16. See the text cited in the Introduction, n. 28, above.

17. On variations in Christian sacred space, see Jonathan Z. Smith, *To Take Place: Toward Theory in Ritual* (Chicago, 1987), passim; and Natalie Z. Davis, "The Sacred and the Social Body in Sixteenth-Century Lyons," *Past and Present* 90 (1981): 40–70.

18. The late Gerson D. Cohen presented these ideas at a graduate seminar at the Jewish Theological Seminary in 1968. He never published them. Hayes, *Gentile Impurities and Jewish Identities*, various locations, has independently come to the same conclusion, although she refers only to Ezra. I am delighted that these important conclusions are finally in print. I should add, as Hayes does as well, that the core of Ezra's concept of purity is genealogy. One is pure by descent. And this, one spots in Christian thinking too; see here the text immediately to follow.

19. On these issues, see Foa, "Religious Orders and Conversion," and Stow, "Church, Conversion, and Tradition."

20. To clarify: I am not engaging the thorny issue of the Catholic Church and racial laws. What I am saying is that a doctrine that preaches physical separation, if purportedly to protect belief, is a doctrine that is uncomfortably close to racism. From this, there is no escape.

21. *Jewish-Christian Debate,* ed. Berger, 206, no. 210; Num. 19:13, for the phrase, "in the tent," which is the clear basis for Haggai and Hosea: "Any who touches the dead and is not purified sullies the tabernacle (the tent) of God. This person is to be 'cut off.' For he [or she: unsaid, yet understood in the original, which speaks generically of persons] has not been washed with the water of the *niddah* [that purifies the menstruant or other impure people]"; my trans. from the Hebrew. Water cannot be baptism, since the offending Christian has already been baptized.

22. Official, *Sepher Joseph Hamekane,* ed. Rosenthal, no. 91a. Official himself lived in the later thirteenth century.

23. See Babylonian Talmud, *Abodah zarah* 48b, that idolatrous offerings communicate defilement within covered space; see also there 47a–b, that idolatrous

shrines in general defile, a concept that, as noted, Jews invoked when speaking of Christian holy places for medieval Jews, and, finally, 54b, "You call the idol a dog," cited and discussed in the Preface, n. 11, above. For Ahimaaz's remark, see *Megillat Ahimaaz*, ed. Benjamin Klar (Jerusalem, 1973), 18.

24. Rubin, *Corpus Christi*, 38, 313.

25. Ibid., 14, on Thomas and the nature of the Eucharist; and also Rubin, *Gentile Tales*, 93–10.

26. *Nizzahon*, no. 213, p. 207.

27. Innocent IV says explicitly that Jews petitioned (Grayzel, *Church and the Jews*, 1: no. 116, and see, too, no. 113). See further, Chapter 3, n. 42, on the *Nizzahon* saying that it can be proved that, "they too eat human beings, as it is written, 'For they have eaten up Jacob' [Jer. 10: 25]." He is punning on Jacob, Israel, true Israel = *corpus Christi*. They eat Christ.

28. *Mekane*, no. 14; and see also Rubin, *Gentile Tales*, 97.

29. Robert Stacey tells me that from the twelfth century, various Christian anti-clericals were making similar statements about excrement in relation to bread, and the idea was especially popular among the fifteenth-century Lollards. If so, then Official is demonstrating, and exploiting, a great acquaintance with what Christians were saying.

30. *Mekane*, no. 174, page 184, and no. 212, page 207, respectively. One might think the barking refers to the Dominicans, the "dogs of God" (*Domini canes*), as they were known. Perhaps, yes, but if so, then with the Dominicans standing for all Christians. I suspect, rather, that the author was speaking of Christians generally. Indeed, following the text cited in n. 23, above, Babylonian Talmud, *Abodah zarah* 48b, equating dogs with idols, this reading makes special sense, since Christians were considered at this stage idolators.

31. Moses of Coucy, *Sefer mitzvot hagadol* (Jerusalem, 1973), 65.

32. *Mekane*, no. 91a.

33. Cited also by midrash *Sifrei to Deuteronomy*, par. 81, 4: 5, trans. (from Hebrew) Reuven Hammer (New Haven, 1986).

34. The issue here was really to ensure that the idolatrous nature of Christianity not be denied, Babylonian Talmud, *Abodah zarah* 2a.

35. *Sefer ha-roqeah ha-gadol* (Jerusalem, 1967, par. 296, p. 164; *mehankhim*, means "to educate," as well as "to consecrate." Cited in Marcus, *Rituals of Childhood*, 26.

36. Marcus, *Rituals of Childhood*, 31 (I thank Magda Teter once again for this reference). Marcus uses Gentile; for consistency, I have emended to goy.

37. See Chapter 2, at n. 47, above.

38. *Sefer selah ha-qodesh* (Jerusalem, 1993), *shaʿar haʾ-otiʾot, ʾot daled, derekh ʾeretz*, 23.

39. *Sefer ha-roqeah*, par. 317, p. 202, and see Marcus, *Rituals of Childhood*, 69–71, citing the original source in *Baraita ha-Niddah*. In truth this passage con-

tinues, saying "should she come into contact with an ass, her children will be foolish like the heart of the ass; should she have contact with a bumpkin, so will her children be bumpkins." The essence, of course, is purity. The ass and bumpkin may, or may not, signify the goy, too. But it is hard to think otherwise about the dog.

40. See here Despres's comments in "Mary of the Eucharist," 378–79.

41. It was after having written this section, that I saw Hayes, *Gentile Impurities and Jewish Identities*, 14, and there I read the following: "Through carnal (i.e., sexual) connection, the moral impurity of the morally defiled *body* [Hayes's emphasis] of the unbeliever is communicated to the holy *body* of the believer, resulting in a carnal (i.e., fleshly) defilement. *Paul's new 'carnal impurity'* [Hayes's term, my emphasis] conflates the characteristic features of moral and ritual impurity. *It is a moral impurity, and yet it resides in the flesh and may be communicated to others by carnal contact* [again my emphasis]. The theme of carnal impurity figures prominently in the writings of the early church fathers." She elaborates on p. 93: "Believers are members of the body of Christ; their bodies, being identified with the body of Christ, are holy bodies. . . . A believer's union with a sexually immoral woman joins the holy body of Christ with her impure body—and so defiles not only the believer but also Christ himself." Substantially, Hayes and I are saying the same thing; her point of entry into the argument is the question of purity as a boundary. Hayes relies heavily on Pauline texts from Corinthians, esp. 1 Cor. 6:15–20, as do I.

42. See the Introduction, n. 11, above, citing Neusner and Chilton, *Jewish and Christian Doctrines*, 84, recognizing that the doctrine of purity is a real, physical one, not spiritual. Their concentration is on Paul's thinking per se, whereas here the emphasis is on its social and cultural implications. See, too, Zerubavel, *Fine Line*, 38, and its citation in the Introduction above, n. 52. Zerubavel's argument touches all the issues here. Sexual penetration and emission is sensed as breaking barriers, rendering "the individual [into] an open sieve, . . . liable to [physical] contamination." More, as put by Dale Martin, *The Corinthian Body* (New Haven, 1996), 173, "The individual offender is merely the breach in the wall that Paul so desperately attempts to build to keep the cosmos out of the church and *sarx* [flesh] from contaminating pneuma"; and see 176, on I Cor. 6:15. See also n. 51, below.

43. Cyprian, *Three Books of Testimonies Against the Jews*, treatise 12, bk. 3, par. 94; the treatise is a long collection of headings and scriptural citations.

44. "God had acted to expose and remove such bishops, and thus to prevent contact between the clean and the unclean; returning them to office would pollute the altar and infect the community with the sin of one who had served Satan," Burns comments in *Cyprian the Bishop*. Whether there is any significance to the location of this paragraph in Cyprian's *Three Books of Testimony* should perhaps not be pressed, unless Cyprian was making a similar contrast between Jewish and Christian systems of altar-contact purity, as Paul does in 1 Cor. 10: 16–18.

45. *John Colet's Commentary on First Corinthians,* trans. and ed. O'Kelly and Jarrott, 133.

46. Cited already in the Introduction at n. 61.

47. Mary Douglas, *Natural Symbols* (1970; rpr., New York, 2003), 93, 110, 111.

48. Ibid., 111.

49. On social drama, see in particular Victor Turner and the associated literature cited in Stow, *Theater of Acculturation,* Introduction, nn. 73 and 75; see, too, Clifford Geertz, *Negara: The Theater State in Nineteenth-Century Bali* (Princeton, 1980). One might judge Jewish martyrdom, *Kiddush haShem,* by similar criteria.

50. See Schaefer, *Mirror,* and comment in Chapter 2, n. 24, above. Lisa Lampert conveyed to me that this discussion, including the overall discussion of Douglas, recalled for her "abjection" theory as proposed by Julia Kristeva, *Powers of Horror: An Essay on Abjection*, trans. Leon S. Roudiez (New York, 1982), esp. chap. 1. The "abject" is a jettisoned object, which may be presented, and represented, in the guise of pure and impure, parts of the self (temporarily) rejected, feared, and then sometimes reintegrated, often visible with respect to food or religious laws and rituals. This theory expands considerably the cognitive frontiers of what we are discussing, although our more pertinent interest here is in the tangible historical confrontation between pure and impure in Christianity and Judaism. Lampert uses this theory in *Gender and Jewish Difference from Paul to Shakespeare* (Philadelphia, 2004).

51. See Introduction, at nn. 55–65. The texts of the Fourth Lateran and subsequent papal elaborations make the linkage between sexuality and special dress directly; see Grayzel, *Church and the Jews,* 1: 296–98, Third Lateran texts, and 306–13, the texts of the Fourth Lateran. For years, I have argued (see Chapter 3, n. 75) that the council did not innovate, taking this position based on what was *not* new in legislation. The traditional view looks only at the legislation, especially the special clothing in its eventual—rather than its original—sense of a "badge of shame." But this view came about without the perspective now available through the studies of Linder, Brundage, and others, which is the basis of my rejection of novelty. Traditional views also hold that the aim of the legislation was to repress. It certainly did curtail privilege. But this was far from the mind of the legislators, as the discussion here clarifies, whose goal was to prevent eucharistic impurity. This approach links the new turn to Jews to specific new turns in the Church itself—as it should be. On sexuality, the Eucharist, and the dangers of pollution caused by contact with—Christian—women, whether to the individual, especially the celebrant priest, as well as to the corporate body of the Church (with overtones of possible contamination of the Eucharist itself and the transmission of contagion, like that of Cyprian's *lapsus,* to others), see Dyan Elliott, *Fallen Bodies: Pollution, Sexuality, and Demonology in the Middle Ages* (Philadelphia, 1999), *passim,* but esp. 100–106, and 122–26. She cites Peter Damian: "What business have you [the married priest] to handle the body of Christ, when by wallowing in the allurements of

the flesh you have become a member of antichrist . . . ?" (104); Elliott also speaks (122) of "active [feminine] malice," going beyond the "passive pollution" women, and priests' wives in particular, may cause. Heresy, too, was considered to contaminate (154). The parallels are obvious to the charges made against Jews, as described in this study, and which Elliott herself notes. See also Dale Martin, *The Corinthian Body*, 176, on the body of the individual polluting that of Christ and the Church, but also vice versa, 177: " . . . the man's penetration of the prostitute makes Christ a penetrator of the prostitute also," a fear which is expressed in ritual murder libels like that of Werner, in particular, as described above.

52. See above, the Introduction, at n. 64, the *Summa Coloniensis*, which speaks of circumcision or forcing people to observe Jewish rites, which was truly offensive and boundary-breaking. The text is borrowed from a Toledan council and includes, too, the prohibition of Jews holding office, which also has clear polluting overtones.

53. See Stow, *Alienated Minority*, 248.

54. Brow, "Religiöse Duldung," 30; see also Chapter 2 at n. 47.

55. It is notable that the renewed Jewish presence in the Low Countries in their day did not deflect the Bollandists from emphasizing martyrdom. The real, and recent, memories of the Henrican martyrs must have been far more pressing for them than imaginings about what real Jews "might do."

56. Cited by Browe, "Hostienschändungen," 179; the *Summula* was printed in Paris in 1516, here fol. 28.

57. Grayzel, *Church and the Jews*, 1: 137, no. 29; Grayzel's translation.

58. Ibid., 140, no. 31.

59. See Trachtenberg, *Devil and the Jews*, 109–21, for similar miracles, like the Host sticking to the palate, and also the discussion above of the Croxton play.

60. Ezekiel Kaufman, *The Religion of Israel* (London 1960), passim, touting this as the real monotheistic difference, not just one God, but one God above all nature, including magic. In fact, even medieval Jews sometimes seem to perceive God as a great magician, blocking, for instance, the prayers of those besieged during the first Crusade with a cloud, as though wanting their martyrdom.

61. Langmuir and Rubin in various works cited above have spoken of doubt, especially Langmuir, "Doubt in Christendom," in id., *Toward a Definition of Antisemitism*, doubt about the Eucharist itself as God. Here, the issue goes beyond that to the Eucharist's immunity from corruption. This is much as observed above that stories of martyrdom prove the Host's invincibility.

62. "Nam quia Iudeus non commederet cibos paratos a Christiano, hac ratione Christianus se inferiorem videtur facere, et ita loquitur conclium Agatense predictum, de quo in docto c. omnes, 28. q. 1. Sed quando Christianus non commedit cibum a Iudeo paratum, et e converso commedit cibum ipsum quem Iudeus sprevit et pro se parare noluit, hoc *fatiendo non facit se inferiorem Iudeo, sed maiorem potius*, quia profitetur Apostolum et legem Christianam non distinguentem cibos,

ut constat recte intuenti. Alias sequeretur quod commedere omnia illa que Iudei spernunt secundum legem suam peccatum esset, quod est *ridiculum* dicere; et nolle illa commedere esset potius cibos distinguere, et *sic Iudaizare et peccare*, quam velle commedere, ut etiam constat recte intuenti." Cited in Angelo di Castro, "'Cibus iudaei': un 'consilium' quasi inedito di Angelo di Castro sulla macellazione con rito ebraico e una 'reprobatio' di san Giovanni da Capestrano," ed. Hélène Angiolini, in *La storia degli ebrei nell'Italia medievale: Tra filologia e metodologia*, ed. M. G. Mazzarelli and Giacomo Todeschini (Bologna, 1990).

De Susannis, *De Iudaeis et aliis infidelibus* 1.4.19, says one may buy food from Jews, since there is no pollution. This is a bit out of character for him, just as when he says Jews may attend schools, but sometimes de Susannis surprises. However, he did believe blood libels. Possibly he knew di Castro's position, just as he downplayed Alexander de Nievo on taking interest. Finally, de Susannis allows wet nurses outside the home, even without a dispensation.

63. In Angiolini (cited in the preceding note), "'Cibus iudaei': tamquam reliquiis effusis per nephandas et putridas manus infidelium et perfidorum Iudaeorum . . . quoad vinum quod suis pedibus calcant non dedignemur sumere, tanquam si essemus eorum servi empticii."

64. Gerhard Ladner, "Homo Viator: Medieval Ideas on Alienation and Order," *Speculum* 42 (1967): 233–259.

65. See *Alienated Minority*, 236–40; and note that Angelo follows his more famous father, Paolo, a student of Baldus's, on allowing Jews to take interest.

66. Capistrano had prohibited wine of any kind trodden by Jews, which, like the Christian consumption of unfit meat, he saw as indicating a servile status vis-à-vis Jews; see the Latin text in n. 63, above.

67. See the fuller discussion of these letters in the Introduction at n. 77.

68. In trying to decipher the reason for special clothing, I suspect that most, as I myself did in the past, have thought of this legislation in terms of Ashkenazim, who, as far as we know, were already distinguished from Christians by their beards or hats. Innocent's decree was therefore puzzling, and this led to much speculation about belittling Jews and the like. However, Innocent III, a Conti, who was born in Anagni and died in Perugia, saw another kind of Jew, as said in the text above, one whom he might be able to identify as a Jew on the basis of appearance only if the individual was known to him personally.

69. We must ask whether Innocent, or anyone at his court, knew the story Johannes Buxtorf (1564–1629) ascribed to the *Yalkut Shimoni*, 229.3—in fact, it is par. 750; see *Yalqut Shimʿoni ʿal ha-Torah*, ed. Dov Heiman (Jerusalem, 1986), 311, with the origin in the Babylonian Talmud, *Menahot* 44a—of a young Jew, overcome by lust for a Christian prostitute, who, when about to fulfill his desires, stopped short when he began to remove his own ritual fringes, reminded of his duties to God. So impressed was the prostitute that she converted to Judaism, then married the youth, with whom she produced many pious offspring; for Buxtorf,

Synagoga Judaica, trans. Corré, chap. 4, www.uwm.edu/People/corre/buxdorf. Innocent's reasoning literally inverts the story—whether knowingly, of course, cannot be said. For Innocent, even a prostitute is corrupted by sex with a Jew (there were, in fact, precise penalties for this, as de Susannis spells them out). The midrash sees the lust that led to intercourse as a gateway to the prostitute's eventual sanctification through marital sex as a Jewess (as is said to occur for all Jews in marital sex; see, e.g., the last chapter of the *B'alei ha-Nefesh* by Abraham ben David of Posquierres [Bnei Brak, 1990]).

70. Cited with no reference by Grayzel, *Church and the Jews*, 1: 300–301; see again Corré, chap. 27.

71. See the Introduction at n. 69 for the full verses.

72. David Friedenreich, at the time of this writing a doctoral candidate of Robert Somerville's at Columbia University, kindly showed me a draft of a paper he was preparing that stresses the idea of inferiority found repeatedly in the commentaries of the canonists and in the texts Gratian included in his *Decretum* that go back to earlier canons and councils. As I read these texts, the concern with inferiority sublimates fears of contamination and masks Christian imitation of Jewish concepts of physical purity and impurity.

73. See again Hayes, *Gentile Impurities and Jewish Identities*, 93–98.

74. On Jewish mechanisms of principled self-defense in the Middle Ages, see Katz, *Exclusiveness and Tolerance*, 24–27.

75. Stow, "The Avignonese Papacy," 292.

Chapter Seven. Denouement

1. See especially Talya Fishman, "Changing Early Modern Jewish Discourse about Christianity: The Efforts of Rabbi Leon Modena," in *The Lion Shall Roar: Leon Modena and His World*, ed. David Malkiel (Jerusalem, 2003). For twentieth-century views of Christianity by Jewish thinkers, see the anthology edited by Fritz A. Rothschild, *Jewish Perspectives on Christianity: Leo Baeck, Martin Buber, Franz Rosenzweig, Will Herberg, and Abraham J. Heschel* (New York, 1990).

2. Attilio Milano, "L'impari lotta della comunità di Roma contro la Casa dei Catecumeni," *Rassegna mensile di Israel* 16 (1950): 355–68, 408–19.

3. Mario Rosa, "La Santa Sede e gli ebrei nel Settecento," in *Gli ebrei di Italia*, ed. C. Vivanti (Turin, 1996), 2: 1071–72. That Polish bishops were profiting from moneylending is the same kind of corruption that ensues from shared commensality. The Judaized bishops—St. Bernard had referred to clerical lenders saying: "these are our Jews"—thus became contaminated, and they passed on the contamination to all those with whom they had contact. Moreover, had not fifteenth-century Franciscans seen Jews lending as dogs devouring the blood of the town? By implication, all recipients of the Eucharist in Poland were in a state of contamination and received no benefit from the sacrament. This would never have been stated, but it is hard to escape that this was the intention.

4. One should note Pope John Paul II's encyclical *Ecclesia de eucharistia* of April 17, 2003, which details current teachings. The full text in English is available on the Vatican web site: www.vatican.va/holy_father/special_features/encyclicals/documents/ hf_jp-ii_enc_20030417_ecclesia_eucharistia_en.html (accessed June 29, 2005).

5. On a much lesser, but still indicative, scale, a review published during the summer of 2002 in *La civiltà cattolica* 2, 3–11, no. 3643 (full text on www.david kertzer.com/pdf/patj_civilta.htm [accessed May 19, 2005]), attacking Kertzer's *Popes Against the Jews*, justified attitudes in the earlier twentieth century by saying that enmity toward Jews derived from the great Jewish affinity for Bolshevism at that time. The idea that Judaism and the threat of modernity are one and the same had been neatly revived. That the popes of the earlier twentieth century saw Bolshevism as the Church's greatest foe is well known, on which see Kertzer, *Popes Against the Jews*, passim, and also James Carroll in *Constantine's Sword*.

6. Agosín and Sepúlveda, *Amigas*, 13.

7. *Ante-Nicene Fathers*, vol.10, www.ccel.org/fathers2/ANF-10/anf10-14.htm #P5028_613432 (accessed June 29, 2005); and see the Greek original in M. R. James in *Texts and Studies* (Cambridge, 1891) 2:109-26, from an Ms. in the Bodleian Library, which he assigns to the eleventh century. The original he conjecturally assigns to the ninth century.

8. González Salinero, *Antijudaísmo cristiano occidental*, 94, citing Augustine, Ep. 82 to Jerome.

9. "La pastorale collettiva dei vescovi cattolici di Germania," *La civiltà cattolica*, 89, 4, no. 2119 (October 1, 1938): 68–77: "Noi, Vescovi cattolici tedeschi, abbiamo già in precedenti Pastorali caratterizzato con opportuni richiami e moniti questa lotta che ci è stata imposta. Oggi pure, dopo varie esperienze, dobbiamo riconoscere che gli assalti non sono divenuti per nulla più moderati e più sopportabili, ma piuttosto più acerbi e più violenti, scoprendo più chiaramente gli scopi voluti. Si vuole, cioè, impedire e dissanguare la vita cattolica; ancor più, si vuole distruggere la Chiesa cattolica in mezzo al nostro popolo, e perfino sradicare lo stesso Cristianesimo per introdurre una fede che con la vera fede divina e con la fede cristiana circa la vita futura non ha assolutamente nulla a che vedere. . . . Ma è appunto questo che al presente, in certi luoghi, si cerca in tutti i modi: la totale distruzione della fede cattolica in Germania."

10. See n. 5 above. A direct linkage by Catholic forces, albeit not ecclesiastical ones, between Bolshevism and Jews appeared in Poland between the wars and afterward: "The struggle against the Jews," wrote Zbigniew Dymecki, "is also a struggle against the communist gangrene" (radical fifteenth-century Franciscans used this term, too, with respect to Jewish lending); Dymecki in *Alma Mater* 6 (1938) (in Polish), cited and translated by Joanna Michlic-Coren, "Anti-Jewish Violence in Poland, 1918–1939 and 1945–1947," *Polin* 13 (2000): 41, where Michlic studies this phenomenon in some depth. Apropos of the entire argument here, she adds: "The ethno-nationalist version of national history intertwines the myth

of Polish victimhood with the myth of the Jew as the Threatening Other" (p. 49). "Threatening Other" is Michlic's term, which well coordinates with the ideas of Jews as creators of martyrs and martyrdom, the Jewish predator, as expressed in this study.

11. Apparently, there never was a clear or unambiguous call of the German bishops as a unified episcopate to alleviate the plight of the Jews; see, e.g., James Carroll, "The Catholic Church and the Holocaust," *Atlantic Monthly*, 284, no. 4 (1999): 107–12. This review of John Cornwell's controversial *Hitler's Pope* is typical of the debate, certainly in presenting the issues. Was this really the stance of the German Church (as I said much earlier, I shall not enter the Pius XII debate)? Of many of its prelates? We cannot know, including whether the absence of any outcry was out of duty to a papal lead. There most certainly were acts of individual clerical courage, but the initiatives were private.

12. The sections of the document are those found in all traditional papal texts or letters: greeting, *proemium* (theological introduction), *actio* (what is happening, or has happened, and what ought to be done), and conclusion (or a penalty clause).

13. Paper delivered at the International Catholic-Jewish Liaison Committee, Jerusalem, May 23–26, 1994.

14. See n. 4, above, for a reference to the full text: Par. 20 ". . . all who take part in the Eucharist [must] be committed to changing their lives and making them in a certain way completely 'Eucharistic.' This fruit of a transfigured existence and *a commitment to transforming the world* in accordance with the Gospel splendidly illustrates the eschatological tension inherent in the celebration of the Eucharist and in the Christian life as a whole."

15. Linder, trans. and ed., *Jews in the Legal Sources,* esp. text no. 1158.

16. This article on "The Holy See and the Jews!" was first published in 1939 in a special number of the *Revue internationale des sociétés secrètes* (described as the "Organe de la Ligue Franc-Catholique contre les sociétés secrètes maçonniques ou occultistes ou leurs filiales"), founded by Msgr. Ernest Jouin. According to www.holywar.org/holysee.html (which reproduces the article; accessed June 30, 2005), it has now been republished by the Ligue Franc-Catholique, whose address is given as 11 bis, rue Portalis, Paris. Its books are for sale at www.galaxidion.com/home/catalogues.php?LIB=perigord&CAT=17606&sortOrder=alpha, and www.livre-rare-book.com/Matieres/jd/4980f.html (both accessed June 30, 2005).The League describes itself on the Internet as "a lay group of Catholics for patriotic and social defense, founded by Monseigneur Jouin, Apostolic Prothonotary, Cure of St. Augustine parish, Paris in 1913. The magazine was founded March 23, 1918, with the approval of the Holy See. This League publishes and sells many books and tracts, among which are the following: *Sources and Discipline of Jewish Imperialism: the Talmud, the Shulchan Aruch, the Zohar, the Kahal* and *Jews and Masons,* both by Mgr. Jouin," as well as the infamous *Protocols of the Learned Elders of Zion*. Jouin is

said to have been "a recognized authority on Jewish history and objectives and the necessity for exposing the facts in defense of Christianity. The Vatican formally praised him for this work of enlightenment as far back as June 20, 1919, in a letter signed by Cardinal Gasparri, Papal Secretary of State. Monseigneur Jouin died in 1932." See also on Jouin and his writings www.catholicism.org/pages/jouin.htm (accessed on June 30, 2005).

17. One such site, unmentioned till now, Catholicism.org, even reprints materials by the late Leonard Feeney S.J. who was excommunicated by none other than Pius XII for teaching that "outside the Church there is no salvation," by which he meant that all who were not Catholics *in good formal standing in their parishes* would go to hell, literally. This site links to others selling books on such subjects as why the reversal of the Spanish expulsion of 1492 is a disaster.

18. Alberto Asor-Rosa, *La guerra: Sulle forme attuali della convivenza umana* (Turin, 2002), 97–102. An alternate version of Asor-Rosa is the "senior French official" cited in the *International Herald Tribune*, June 23, 2003, saying that Israel is "not European, not by geographical, not by historical, not by cultural terms." This statement, seemingly preposterous, is not that at all—if one realizes that this is a veiled reference, however consciously, to the "Asiatic" quality often ascribed to Jews, for instance, by Marx's opponent Bruno Bauer, among many others. Jews are thus cultural outsiders, unassimilable, and they threaten the modern polity, now, the European Community, to which the French official was referring, as it considered the question of Israel's membership. Similar themes in contemporary England are noted by Melanie Phillips of the *Daily Mail*; the essay appeared in the "Week's End" supplement of *Haaretz*, November 7, 2004, B4, analyzing why Michael Howard could be acceptable as Conservative Party leader, while Israel as a state is considered illegitimate.

19. See Chapter 1, at n. 29, above.

20. Augustine, *Ps. 58 Enarr.* 1.2.22: "testes iniquitatis suae et veritatis nostrae."

21. A teacher in a public kindergarten in Rome, about 1997, was severely reprimanded, however, for telling—at Eastertide—the tale of the Jewish children running in hot pursuit of "il bambin Gesù." One of the parents gave me this information.

22. It cannot be overemphasized that if there is an Augustinian doctrine of witness, it is this, not of the testimony contained in Jewish books. See Introduction.

23. Kurt Hruby, "A Christian View," in *Christians and Jews*, ed. Küng and Kasper, 88–90; see here Biddick, *Typological Imaginary*, 1–2.

24. Nonetheless, at a talk by Cardinal Kasper delivered at the Centre for the Study of Jewish-Christian Relations, Cambridge, MA, December 6, 2004, he seems to have qualified himself in what was a very scholarly context. Kasper presented recent sentiments under the sign of an "unabrogated covenant." The word supersession is replaced by "substitution theory." Yet the context easily remains that of Paul in Romans, who, too, flatly denied the (old) covenant's abrogation. The idea of fulfillment of the (old) covenant remains also firmly in place and, even more, the idea of a theological interdependence between Judaism and Christian-

ity; "The Relationship of the Old and the New Covenant as One of the Central Issues in Jewish-Christian Dialogue" (www.bc.edu/research/cjl/meta-elements/ texts/ cjrelations/resources/ articles/ Kasper_ Cambridge_6Dec04.htm [accessed July 3, 2005]).

25. See Grayzel, *Church and the Jews,* various places, for this last idea. The Council statement cites the official Vatican statement issued under the name of Cardinal Johannes Willebrands in 1985, "Notes on the Correct Way to Present Jews and Judaism in Preaching and Teaching in the Roman Catholic Church," part 6 (www.vatican.va/roman_curia/pontifical_councils/chrstuni/relations-jews-docs/rc_pc_chrstuni_doc_19820306_jews-judaism_en.html [accessed July 1, 2005]). Readers unfamiliar with the story should be apprised that in the thirteenth century, the Church discovered the talmudic text and judged it blasphemous if not a theological novelty, a *nova lex*, which was other than the biblical Judaism that was approved. The result was a burning of the Talmud. See Stow, *Alienated Minority*, 251-59, for a summary of literature and discussions on this large subject.

26. What Paul meant by salvation (of the soul) is not something that most Jews would have seen as Judaism's end. In the present context, however, this is not the issue.

27. John Paul II's Address to Delegation of the World Jewish Congress (excerpts):

Your visit brings to mind the bonds of friendship which have developed between us since the Second Vatican Council issued the Declaration *Nostra Aetate* and placed relations between Jews and Catholics on a new and positive footing.

God's word is a lamp and a light to our path; it keeps us alive and gives us new life (cf. Ps. 119: 105, 107). *This word is given to our Jewish brothers and sisters especially in the Torah. To Christians this word finds its fulfillment in Jesus Christ.* . . . In light of the rich common religious heritage we share, we can consider the present as a challenging opportunity for joint endeavors of peace and justice in our world.

> www.zenit.org/english (accessed May 19, 2005). ZENIT is an international news agency aiming "to provide objective coverage of events, documents and issues emanating from or concerning the Catholic Church."

28. *Nostra aetate* ("Declaration on the Relation of the Church to Non-Christian Religions . . . October 28, 1965"): "As Holy Scripture testifies, Jerusalem did not recognize the time of her visitation, nor did the Jews in large number accept the Gospel; indeed not a few opposed its spreading [Rom. 11:28]. Nevertheless, God holds the Jews most dear for the sake of their Fathers; He does not repent of the gifts He makes or of the calls He issues—such is the witness of the Apostle [Rom. 11:28-29; cf. *Lumen Gentium* (Light of Nations) *AAS* 57 (1965) p. 20]. In company with the Prophets and the same Apostle, the Church awaits that day, known to God alone, on which all peoples will address the Lord in a single voice and 'serve

him shoulder to shoulder' (Soph. 3: 9) [Isa. 66:23; Ps. 65:4; Rom. 11:11–32]" (www.vatican.va/archive/hist_councils/ii_vatican_council/documents/vat-ii_decl_19651028_nostra-aetate_en.html [accessed May 20, 2005]). Footnotes appear in brackets in slightly edited form. See also the recent statement by Prof. Riccardo di Segni, Chief Rabbi of the Jewish Community of Rome: "Steps Taken and Questions Remaining in Jewish-Christian Relations Today," Rome, October 19, 2004, 5 Heshvan 5765, at the Pontifical Gregorian University (www.bc.edu/research/cjl/meta-elements/texts/center/conferences/Bea_Centre_C-J_Relations_04-05/DiSegni.htm [accessed July 3, 2005]).

29. Gavin Langmuir, "Anti-Judaism as the Necessary Preparation for Antisemitism, in id., *Toward a Definition of Antisemitism*, 85, citing E. Boshof, *Erzbisch Agobard von Lyon* (Cologne, 1969), 42. See, too, Introduction, n. 5.

30. "de *ex illis* es." The farce is enhanced subtly, because quartermastering was a traditional Jewish profession, one sometimes practiced by *conversos*. More, *ex illis* actually refers to Peter, as he is identified as one of Jesus' circle in Matt. 26:73 (Vulgate: "accesserunt qui stabant et dixerunt Petro vere et tu ex illis es"). The quartermaster, the *converso*, possibly a crypto-Jew as well, is the real disciple. Finally, the *maravillas*, the wonders, are not only those on stage, but miracles, which only true believers are favored to see. Whether the *retablo* should be understood in its theatrical sense, as a "short play" or whether in its sacral meaning, as the frame, the retable, behind the altar, or pictures on the altar, suggesting various meanings about *true* altars, is left to the reader's imagination. The text of the play is found in *Teatro español del siglo de oro,* ed. Bruce W. Wardropper (New York, 1970), 364–86 (I thank Estela Harretche for this reference).

Appendix One

1. I translate the Latin here, *offas*, as balls of dough; Marcus says "cakes"; see above. Following Lewis and Short, *offas* may mean abortion, which might be another way of expressing the idea of ritual murder, but this seems extreme.

Appendix Two

1. In Hebrew, *tsara*; the reference is to some kind of forced conversion, apparently, as is deduced from the word's second use: "we do not know whether . . . this *tsara hiv’ishah ’otam*," the trouble brought shame on them, with the last expression a euphemism for "brought them to accept baptism," perhaps not wholly by force. Should this be the case, and conversion, and apostasy, be the reason for what happened, then we certainly have a different set of events from those at Blois—unless, of course, there was conversion and relapse at Blois, but the chroniclers chose *not* to report it (highlighting once more the literary nature of the texts).

2. This is a rare indication of family units operating at more than the nuclear level, which most other texts argue; see Kenneth Stow, "The Jewish Family in the Rhineland: Form and Function," *American Historical Review* 92 (1987): 1085–1110.

3. Meaning, they were truly married; betrothed equals here *matrimonium*, Hebrew, *le-qadesh*. The problem of secret marriage was continuous. Ultimately, it was said a marriage, a betrothal, was legitimate only when performed before ten witnesses, including close relatives, including, preferably, the parents; see Kenneth Stow, "Marriages Are Made in Heaven: Marriage and the Individual in the Roman Jewish Ghetto," *Renaissance Quarterly* 48 (1995): 452–91.

4. The abomination is surely the secret marriage, and by "will not work," the father means he will force the two to divorce through rabbinic-communal pressure, a claim that rested as much on bravado as real expectation. However, the youth, as the account goes, was either frightened or brazen enough to take the following step (or the author is merely pointing to how precarious Jewish life had become). The ability to control what went on within the community was small, the threat of outside interference constant.

5. Here, *sar*, later, *shilton*; both are generic, but they seem, in the context of these letters to translate well as "prince," or even "king," or just "ruler." In the letter to follow about the synagogue keys, *shilton* refers almost surely to the king; and see the expression, *"sar ʾo melekh,"* (prince [high officer] or king), in Maimonides, *Mishneh Torah, Hilkhot ʾishut*, 15:20, and the *Tur, Yoreh deʿah*, 254.

6. About what? Some secret: that they were lending at too high a rate of interest, or had Christian servants? This is doubtful. At the most, the penalty would have been a fine to the count's benefit. Could the reference have been to previous apostasy, hence, the use again of the term "the trouble," or "shame?" Here the possibility—together with the capital punishment—is real. This, however, would indicate a significant change since 1096, when "apostates" freely returned to Judaism with imperial assent. Indeed, it contradicts the action of the bishop of Sens in the letter below. One would like to know more about how and when this change occurred: under Louis VII, with his threatening letter of 1144, discussed above, in Chapter 4, or later.

7. In these texts, *litpos* usually has the sense of imprison, not simply taken, surely translating the Latin *captio*; see Jordan, *French Monarchy*, *captiones* in the index on page 360.

8. Apart from the central question: which bodies and what event, the language is hazy. Were the people escaping killed by the wood thrown at them, or was the wood used to heighten the fire, or just to push the people back? Compare the stanza in the poem commemorating the Blois massacre by Hillel of Bonn/Blois, Emunei-Shelumei Yisrael, trans. Einbinder, "Jewish Martyrs of Blois," 449–50:

> When the flames reached the bonds of the Jewish priests' hands,
> The ties were severed from the children [of Israel's] hands.
> They cried out: "The fire has tested us and we have emerged innocent!"
> The kings and princes of the earth are stationed [Ps. 2: 2]!
> The tormentor's rage against them did not diminish.
> He commanded his servants to return them to the fire,
> Beaten and wounded. They were struck with clubs and with their staves—

9. Does he mean he wrote the letter, put it down, and is now adding something, or that he had sent an earlier letter? *Kadosh/kedoshah* is the term used for those who died "to sanctify God's name" as martyrs. By "forgotten," the writer may mean a number of things, but most likely, that they had not recovered her body at first.

10. *Le-daber be-seter,* "to speak in secret." This is the verse alluding to Judges 3:19, *davar seter yesh li ʾailekhah,* as spoken by Ehud ben Gerah to the king of Moab, whom Ehud would then slay with his "two-edged sword."

11. Note, *migdol,* not *migdal,* a tower.

12. See Gross, *Gallia Judaica,* 442; and see above Chapter 4, n. 36, on the problems with the name Pontiyeh, which is missing the *zayyin* in the normal orthography of the town name (of Pontoise) in Hebrew. Ponte Demir, or Ponte Derir are clearly identified by Gross with Pont Audemar, which is a town not otherwise known for a ritual murder charge. Jordan, *French Monarchy,* 234, mentions the town as Norman, but not in the context of a libel. The variants on the name in J. G. Grässe and F. Benedict, *Orbis Latinus* (Berlin, 1922), 244–45, offer no help with the variant Ponte Rirt. Both Janville and Pontoise are relatively near to Paris in the Île-de-France, Pontoise to the northwest and Janville to the southeast.

13. The term *ʾumot ha-ʿolom* is used by Raul Glaber among others (see *MGH, Scriptores,* 4: 136) and cited in Blumenkranz, *Auteurs chrétiens,* 256–58.

14. Not in Gross; see in the second Parisian letter, where this town is mentioned again, with the reference being undeniably to Pontoise; see again, above, Chapter 4, n. 36.

15. So the reader is intentionally made to believe, regardless of how much later the letter was originally drafted.

16. Did the author know the words of Johannes Teutonicus (1175–1245), the author of the *Glossa Ordinaria* to Gratian's *Decretum,* that Jews are "our neighbors, whom we are bound to love as ourselves"? Notwithstanding his remarks cited above about "deception between courses," Johannes did say this. Cited by James Brundage, "Intermarriage Between Christians and Jews in Medieval Canon Law," *Jewish History* 3, no. 1 (1988): 31–32.

17. Lit., "if they should do the same to our enemies." The phrase is most difficult. Do we have a fantasy likened to revenge on Haman, but which, in context, would be ironic: Jews could never expect real vengeance, but they should be able to expect the king to provide the protection he now promises—and which, of course, he was not providing. Even this hope, therefore, is expressed in exaggerated, almost bombastic, terms.

18. *Kavod,* translated into Latin as "honor" (much as *ʾahavah* is translatable back into Latin as *amor,* which, as in the Hebrew, means protection), flirts with the legal concept of high, or honorable status, even office. Roman law and all its medieval commentators prohibited the Jews from possessing "honors," just as did the canons. If the play on meanings is, as I suspect, intentional, the irony is extraordinary: the king would make the Jews princes, courtiers, even judges. Certainly!

The author is being subtle and ingenious, as well as highly informed. On "honor," see de Susannis, *De Iudaeis et aliis infidelibus* 2.6.

19. First *ʾishon*, and now *babat*, which is the more common usage. The author's Hebrew vocabulary is noteworthy; the variant is surely for emphasis.

20. Theobald's brother, as is Henry of Troyes; Louis's wife is Theobald's sister.

21. The term *ʿanus*, forced one, is untranslatable. It means those who were required to convert to Christianity, but it normally appears in medieval Hebrew texts to designate all converts. In Jewish parlance, and especially in written expression, willing conversion is a virtually unacceptable category. The Hebrew calls these "prisoners" sons of either the *hasidim*, the righteous, or, as is surely more correct, sons of righteousness. The masculine plural indicates the abstract, e.g., *sar hamishpatim* (plural) = minister of justice (abstract singular). In the Blois story, as the Orléans Narrative tells it, there are only martyrs, no surviving *ʾanusim*.

22. This term, *shohad*, which appears in medieval Hebrew texts time and again, is always problematic, at least for me. In modern Hebrew it is bribe, but in the Middle Ages, one normally paid fees for justice, which was not "publicly funded." Where did the line pass, then, between bribe and acceptable payment for services? I prefer "payment" as a translation, therefore, consonant with the modern concept of court costs and attorneys fees, not money to win over rulers or judges. One should note here, too, the very strong medieval concept of proper justice.

23. Guarantees, pledges, surely not hostages.

24. This, of course, is the surprise of the letter, and see Chapter 4 at n. 56, above. The Hebrew is a bit vague whether it means he asked whether they wanted to return, or just requested them to return.

25. "[va]yavʾo-u u-veyad ramah u-ve-zeroʿa netuyah." The subject must be the prisoners. The image is biblical, and it appears in the Bible three times. Twice, in Exod. 14:8, and Num. 33:3, it refers to the pride, the raised heads, with which the Jews left Egypt, a fitting phrase, therefore, for Jews released from prison or allowed to return to Judaism after forced conversion. However, Num. 15:30 uses the phrase quite differently, threatening excommunication, the "cutting off from the people," of those who would blaspheme. One wonders whether, beside the first meaning, the expression of pride in those who returned, there is not a second meaning also, a contrapuntal reference to those who reneged and did not return to Judaism when "asked" by the archbishop. Or is there a hint to a lack of forgiveness for those who once converted and returned, contrary to the usual portrait of Jews forgiving returned converts? One is reminded of Rigord's reference to Jews who did not reconvert after Philip's confiscations of 1182; see Chapter 3 at n. 47, above. These two texts—Rigord and the letter—are not connected. Yet, on the grounds that the king intended by the letters is actually Philip, not Louis VII, one may ask whether the figure of conversion and prevarication both texts paint did not register a reality Philip's actions generated. The form of "came" (*yavʾo-u*) is a future, but no doubt a *vav* has fallen, the *vav-hahipukh* of biblical grammar,

which the writer has just used in *va-yahtom*, that turns future into past tense: "they came."

26. The term *hovot* means debts, but in this context, it also means bonds, their credits, the monies owed them.

27. The text is slightly imprecise about the antecedent for "he." However, since the first one who put something into writing according to the letter was the archbishop, rather than the count, I take it to be the same here. It would be cynical, in any case, for the count to say—or to have attributed to him—that there would be no more libels. At the same time, within the contrived context of the letter, almost anything is possible.

28. This term has been translated otherwise as "count" here, but the intention must be the king. The reference is likely to the synagogues Philip confiscated and consecrated as churches; on which, see Chapter 3 above.

29. The letter is so opaque as to have been questioned as a separate missive. But separate it is. Its contents are independent; the curses refer, no doubt, to the daily (generic) reference in prayer by Jews to wipe out the *memshelet zadon*, the evil kingdom. The letter might serve as an introduction to the implied idea, in the next letter, and as discussed in Chapter 4 above of Jews as faithful servants whom the king trusts; but whom, in fact, he does not trust, and whose faithfulness he suspects.

30. Possibly, the real letter is what is called the "first letter," above. The "memorandum" here would have served as an excuse for changes and embellishments. Or are both part of a larger romance fiction?

31. Once again reminiscent of Judg. 3:19, the story of Ehud ben Gerah; and see the comments to the first letter from Paris, above.

32. Note how the Jewish author plays on the Christian concept of mortal sin; more interesting is the inversion. Christians say Jews are destroying the image of God; the Jews respond, no, your accusation is a mortal sin, hence, you are betraying the faith, not us.

33. Compare with the terms in the first Parisian letter, and here the reference is directly to Richard of Pontoise

34. Lit., voice, *qol*, much in the sense of *vox populi*, or *vox dei*, or *vox Regis*. The meaning here is public declaration.

35. *Haver*, lit., friend, usually means some kind of associate, someone almost a rabbi, but the term's meaning is never absolutely fixed, and, hence, it is better left untranslated. The question, however, is whether this Mr. Natan is identical to the "I" in the letter about the archbishop of Sens. We have no clue. The discrepancy in the sum suggests, once again, however, that this identity should not be sought out. Admittedly, were the "I" and Mr. Natan one, we would have reason to seek out some real historical chain here—although any reference to real events may not be to Blois at all.

36. In Hebrew, the letter *R*. standing alone means Mr. as often as it is Rabbi (see the martyr lists in Sigmund Salfeld, *Das Martyrologium des Nürnberger Memorbuches* [Berlin, 1898]), and here all the more so, since Natan has already been identified as a *haver*.

37. Again I prefer the more neutral "ransom" instead of *shohad*; see n. 22 above.

38. The victims of Blois were already dead, or at least they should have been in the standard reading of this material; see Chazan's reading cited in Chapter 4, n. 4, above. Hence, the reference could be to the bodies of the victims, or to a wholly different group of people—unless the letter purports to be retelling what happened in between the seizures by Theobald and the execution. However, this explanation creates inordinate difficulties, and, although it must be considered, it seems best rejected.

That the author may have in mind the seizures of Philip Augustus is another matter. In which case, the letter has to do with the death of Richard of Pontoise and possible royal action, apart from that reported by Rigord. This is tempting and tantalizing, and possibly correct. But evidence will permit us to go no further. Nonetheless, if the suggestion is correct, then the theatricality of the letters is enhanced a thousand times over: Philip Augustus denying—in the letter—the very thing he was doing in fact. This would be parody and satire almost beyond belief.

The future tense of the verb used at the end of the sentence, surely a subjunctive, and not a corruption, in this case, of biblical grammatical usage: that he should succeed—in releasing "those arrested," not the bodies of the dead—stirs the historical imagination even more. Regrettably, however, this is the stuff of speculation, mental diversion, and no more. Also highly speculative is to suggest that the final editor of the letters has conflated Blois with a hitherto unidentified episode at Loches, where there were apparently survivors and forced converts. Such a conflation would make sense out of some of the strange passages. In the event, there is no way to know this, since everything, real and imagined, has been pressed into the service of irony.

39. As noted in Chapter 4, at n. 2, the use of Heinrich suggests a German origin for the letter/memorandum's author/scribe, at least the writer of the text as it has reached us in the Speyer MS.

40. What the exact charge was is unknown. Its identification would certainly help in dating these letters. This time, *qol* translates as rumor. As for the reference to Easter [*pesach*, but surely Easter not Passover], it shows especially the pitfalls of trying to read texts like these as though they reflect precise and identifiable chronological realities. Chazan, too, saw this, I believe, in freely translating ʾ*etmol*, yesterday, as "recently." This is not absolutely incorrect, but it is still interpretative. Rashi, for example, on Exod. 5:14, speaks literally of "the third [day]," which is the day before yesterday (ʾ*etmol*); and Rashi's usage comes from roughly (and linguistically speaking) the same time period as the letters, but, most importantly, it predates them, meaning the sense of ʾ*etmol* as literally yesterday existed in the letters' day.

The problem facing the reader, or translator, is that if "yesterday" is read literally, then—apart from the problem of accounting for this otherwise unknown episode at Épernay—we must accept that Henry/Heinrich was speaking about something that took place either before Blois (Passover falls in April, and the

Blois incident/massacre occurred after Passover, in Sivan/June, actually May 26, 1171) or it occurred a year later. Before seems impossible; but a year later (April or so) means ten months *after* Rabbenu Tam's death, and all the letters are supposed to be directed to the *living* Jacob Tam, who died two weeks following the Blois episode. In short, an interpretative quagmire! Does substituting the noncommittal "recently" for the literal "yesterday" allow overcoming it? The reader may decide for him or herself, yet with the understanding that a reading that insists on treating the letters as factual reporting cannot enjoy the luxury of emendation and accommodation when the "facts" go out of kilter. Attempts to skirt the problem by establishing criteria for "facticity" or "patterning" fall short for just this reason.

41. It is not clear why an outside match would be seen as violating a time of mourning, presumably over the Blois episode, unless the purpose is to avoid the well-attested pageantry with which outside brides or grooms were often received; see, e.g., Louis Finkelstein, *Jewish Self-Government in the Middle Ages* (New York, 1964), 240.

42. One cannot escape thinking that this reference somehow harks back to the Loches letter, with its discussion of secret betrothal. Communities tried many tactics to avoid secret betrothals, as noted above in n. 4. And perhaps this letter and that of Loches are a pair, neither of which concerns Blois? The common subject would be the dangers to the community, not just families, of secret marriage. Yet, once more, this is to speculate. Besides, Troyes is in Champagne and Loches in Touraine, making such a pairing highly improbable.

What is clear is that this letter—which Wachtel thinks may have been a later addition to the whole—betrays a certain confusion among the Jews of twelfth- or thirteenth-century France and a climate of no little fear. This letter, together with the others, no matter how much their central interest is made to appear the Blois episode, seems to meld together a series of crises not with the idea of reporting events, as has been emphasized, but to indicate the dangers Jews faced and to suggest possible remedies, for instance, circumventing the king and (as in the "1007 Anonymous") appealing (as Jews did) to the pope. It may be hoped that we shall someday fathom the issues better.

43. The second person plural used is not clear in this context, which otherwise is consistently first person plural.

44. The blood of which *hasidim* required atonement? And which converts are meant? Or is it those noted in the letter to Loches, should the speculation in nn. 38 and 43 bear out?

45. Just how much it was necessary to be concerned about informers remains to be seen in future research. Convert-informers plagued Italian Jewry during the Renaissance, and the thirteenth-century case of Nicholas Donin at Paris is well known.

Select Bibliography

Abulafia, Anna Sapir. *Christians and Jews in the Twelfth-Century Renaissance*. London, 1995.

———. "The Interrelationship Between the Hebrew Chronicles of the First Crusade." *Journal of Semitic Studies* 27 (1982): 221–39.

Acta Sanctorum a Ioanne Bollando S.I. colli feliciter coepta. A Godefrido Henschenio et Daniele Papebrochio, S.I., aucta.... Antwerp, 1668. Reprint edited by the Socii Bollandiani. 69 vols. Paris, 1863–1940. Cited as *ActaSS*.

Agobard, Saint, archbishop of Lyon. *Agobardi Lugdunensis Archiepiscopi Epistolae*. Monumenta Germaniae Historica, *Epistolae Karolini Aevi*, vol. 3. Edited by E. Dümmler. Berlin, 1899.

———. *Agobardi Lugdunensis Archiepiscopi Epistolae contra Iudaeos*. Latin text with Hebrew translation. Translated and edited by Akiva Gilboa. Jerusalem, 1964.

Agosín, Marjorie, and Emma Sepúlveda. *Amigas: Letters of Friendship and Exile*. Austin, 2001.

Angelo di Castro. "'Cibus iudaei': un 'consilium' quasi inedito di Angelo di Castro sulla macellazione con rito ebraico e una 'reprobatio' di san Giovanni da Capestrano." Edited and with an introduction by Hélène Angiolini. In *La storia degli ebrei nell'Italia medievale: Tra filologia e metodologia*, ed. M. G. Mazzarelli and Giacomo Todeschini. Bologna, 1990.

Ante-Nicene Fathers, vol. 9, www.catholicfirst.com/TheFaith/ChurchFathers/Volume 09/virgin01.htm.

Apocalypse of the Virgin. Edited by M. R. James. Texts and Studies, vol. 2. Cambridge, 1891.

Appleby, John T. *The Chronicle of Richard of Devizes of the Time of King Richard the First*. London, 1963.

Aquinas, Thomas, Saint. *Summa Theologica*. Cambridge, 1964–81.

Archivio di Stato, Roma, Tribunale del Governatore, Criminali, Costituti.

Aronius, Julius. *Regesten zur Geschichte der Juden im Fränkischen und Deutschen Reiche bis zum Jahre 1273*. Berlin, 1902.

Aschheim, Steven E. "'The Jew Within,' The Myth of 'Judaization' in Germany." In *The Jewish Response to German Culture*, ed. Jehuda Reinharz and Walter Schatzberg. Hanover, N.H., 1985.

Asor-Rosa, Alberto. *La Guerra: Sulle forme attuali della convivenza umana*. Turin, 2002.

Attwater, Donald. *The Penguin Dictionary of Saints*. New York, 1965. Reprint 1983.

Augustine, Saint, Bishop of Hippo. *Contra Faustum*, 12.12–13. Translated in Jeremy Cohen, *Living Letters of the Law: Ideas of the Jew in Medieval Christianity*. Berkeley, 1999.

———. *De adulterinis coniugiis et de fidelibus puellis*. Jena, 1798.

———. *In Ps. 58 Enarratio*. In Corpus scriptorum ecclesiasticorum Latinorum, vol. 93. Vienna, 2003.

———. *Treatises on Marriage and Other Subjects: The Good of Marriage; Adulterous Marriage; Holy Virginity; Faith and Works; The Creed; Faith and the Creed; The Care to Be Taken for The Dead; In Answer to the Jews; The Divination of Demons*. Translated by Charles T. Wilcox et al. Edited by Roy J. Deferrari. Fathers of the Church, 27. Washington, D.C., 1969.

Baldwin, John W. *The Government of Philip Augustus: Foundations of French Royal Power in the Middle Ages*. Berkeley, 1986.

Baring-Gould, Sabine. *Lives of the Saints*. Rev. ed. Edinburgh, 1914.

Baron, Salo W. *A Social and Religious History of the Jews*. Philadelphia, 1952–69.

Baronio, Cesare. *Annales ecclesiastici, denuo excusi et ad nostra usque tempora perducti ab Augustino Theiner*. Bar-le-Duc, 1864–83.

Bartlett, Robert. *Trial by Fire and Water: The Medieval Judicial Ordeal*. Oxford, 1986.

Battista de' Giudici. *Apologia Iudaeorum; Invectiva contra Platinam: Propaganda antiebraica e polemiche di Curia durante il pontificato di Sisto IV (1471–1484)*. Edited by Diego Quaglioni. Rome, 1987.

———. *De Canonizatione beati Bonaventurae*. In Étienne Baluze, *Stephani Baluzii Tutelensis miscellanea novo ordine digesta et non paucis ineditis monumentis opportunisque animadversionibus aucta*. . . . 4 vols. Lucca, 1761–64.

Beeri, Emmanuel. "Civiltà cattolica." In *Encyclopedia Judaica*. Jerusalem, 1971.

Bell, Dean P. *Sacred Communities: Jewish and Christian Identities in Fifteenth-Century Germany*. Leiden, 2002.

Beller, Katherine Aron. "The Inquisition and the Jews in Modena in the Seventeenth Century." Ph.D. diss., Haifa, 2003.

Ben Shalom, Ram. "The Blood Libel in Arles and the Franciscan Mission in Avignon in 1453." *Zion* 63 (1998): 391–408. In Hebrew.

Benjamin ben Elnatan. Chronicle in Isaiah Sonne, *Mi-Pavolo ha-Reviʿi ʿad Pius ha-Hamishi*. Jerusalem, 1954.

Benz, Ernst. *Ecclesia Spiritualis: Kirchenidee und Geschichtstheologie der franziskanischen Reformation*. Stuttgart, 1934.

Berger, David. "*Dominus Iesus* and the Jews." Delivered at the 17th meeting of the International Catholic-Jewish Liaison Committee, New York, May 1, 2001. www.bc.edu/bc_org/research/cjl/articles/berger.htm (accessed July 17, 2005).
———. "Mission to the Jews and Jewish-Christian Contacts in the Polemical Literature of the High Middle Ages." *American Historical Review* 91 (1986): 576–91.
Bernard of Clairvaux, Saint. *Epistolae*, no. 365. In *Patrologia Latina*, ed. J. P. Migne, vol. 182.
Bialik, Hayim Nahman. "In the City of Slaughter." Translated by A. M. Klein in Alan Mintz, *Hurban: Responses to Catastrophe in Hebrew Literature*, 132–41. New York, 1984.
Biddick, Kathleen. *Typological Imaginary: Circumcision, Technology, History*. Philadelphia, 2003.
Biller, Peter. "Views of Jews from Paris Around 1300: Christian or Scientific." In *Christianity and Judaism*, ed. Diana Wood. Studies in Church History, 29. Oxford, 1992.
Birnbaum, Pierre. "Un Antisémitisme à la française." In *L'Antisémitisme éclairé: Inclusion et exclusion depuis l'époque des Lumières jusqu'à l'affaire Dreyfus*, ed. Ilana Zinguer and Sam Bloom. Leiden, 2003.
Bland, Kalman. *The Artless Jews: Medieval and Modern Affirmations and Denials of the Visual*. Princeton, 2000.
Blumenkranz, Bernard. *Les Auteurs chrétiens latins du Moyen Age sur les juifs et le judaisme*. Paris, 1963.
———. "Deux compilations canoniques de Florus de Lyon et l'action antijuive d'Agobard." *Revue historique de droit français et étranger* 33 (1955): 227–54, 560–82.
Bonfil, Robert. *The Jews in Renaissance Italy*. Berkeley, 1992.
Bouquet, Martin, comp. *Recueil des historiens des Gaules et de la France*, ed. Léopold Deslisle. Paris, 1877.
Boyarin, Daniel. *A Radical Jew: Paul and the Politics of Identity*. Berkeley, 1997.
Browe, Petrus. "Die Hostienschändungen der Juden im Mittelalter." *Römische Quartalschrift* 34 (1926): 167–97.
———. "Die Judenbekämpfung im Mittelalter." *Zeitschrift für katholische Theologie* 62 (1938): 197–231, 349–84.
———. *Die Judenmission im Mittelalter und die Päpste*. Rome, 1973.
———. "Die religiöse Duldung der Juden im Mittelalter." *Archiv für katholisches Kirchenrecht* 118 (1938): 29–30.
Brown, Peter. *The Body and Society: Men, Women, and Sexual Renunciation in Early Christianity*. New York, 1988.
Brundage, James. "Intermarriage Between Christians and Jews in Medieval Canon Law." *Jewish History* 3, no. 1 (1988): 25–40.
Burns, James Patout, Jr. *Cyprian the Bishop*. Routledge Early Church Monographs. London, 2002.

———. "The Eucharist as the Foundation of Christian Unity in North African Theology." *Augustinian Studies* 32 (2001): 1–24.

Butler, Alban. *Lives of the Saints*. Edited by Donald Attwater and Herbert Thurston, 4 vols. New York, 1956. Revised from 1938; with imprimatur by Francis Cardinal Spellman in 1955.

Buxtorf, Johannes. *Synagoga Judaica*. Basel, 1603. Translated by Alan Corré. www.uwm.edu/People/corre/buxdorf/chp27.html (accessed May 14, 2005).

Caliò, Thomasso. "Antisemitismo e culto dei santi in età contemporanea: Il caso del beato Lorenzino da Marostica." In *Il pubblico dei santi: Forme e livelli di ricezione dei messaggi agiografici*, ed. Paolo Golinelli. Rome, 2000.

Capgrave, John, et al. *Nova legenda angliae*. 2 vols. Edited by Carl Horstman. Oxford, 1901. Translated as *The Chronicle of England*, ed. Francis Charles Hingeston (London, 1858).

Caro, Georg. *Sozial- und Wirtschaftsgeschichte der Juden im Mittelalter und der Neuzeit*. 2d ed. 2 vols. Frankfurt a/M, 1924.

Carroll, James. "The Catholic Church and the Holocaust." *Atlantic Monthly*, October 1999.

———. *Constantine's Sword: The Church and the Jews. A History*. New York, 2000.

Catechism of the Council of Trent. In *Canons and Decrees of the Council of Trent*. Original text with English translation by H. J. Schroeder. 1941. Reprint. St. Louis, 1960.

Chazan, Robert. "Archbishop Guy Fulcodi of Narbonne and His Jews." *Revue des études juives* 132 (1973): 587–94.

———. "The Blois Incident of 1171: A Study in Jewish Intercommunal Organization." *Proceedings of the American Academy of Jewish Research* 36 (1963): 13–31.

———. *God, Humanity, and History: The Hebrew First Crusade Narratives*. Berkeley, 2000.

———. Review of *The "1007 Anonymous" and Papal Sovereignty: Jewish Perceptions of the Papacy and Papal Policy in the High Middle Ages* by Kenneth R. Stow (Cincinnati, 1984), *Speculum* 62 (1987): 728–31.

———. "The Timebound and the Timeless: Medieval Jewish Narratives of Events." *History and Memory* 6, no. 1 (1994): 5–35.

———, ed. *Church, State, and Jew in the Middle Ages*. New York, 1980.

Chevalier, Ulysse. *Répertoire des sources historiques du Moyen Age*. 2 vols. Montbéliard, 1894–99. Reprint. New York, 1975.

Christianity and Judaism: Papers Read at the 1991 Summer Meeting and the 1992 Winter Meeting of the Ecclesiastical History Society. Edited by Diana Wood. Studies in Church History, 29. Oxford, 1992.

Chronicle of Melrose. Edited by Alan Anderson and Marjorie Olgivie Anderson. London, 1936.

Chronicles of the Reigns of Stephen, Henry II, and Richard I. Edited by Richard Howlett. Rerum Britannicarum medii aevi scriptores, 82. 4 vols. 1884–89. Reprint. Liechtenstein, 1964.

Chrysostom, Saint John. *Eight Homilies Against the Jews*. Internet Medieval Sourcebook, ed. Paul Halsall, www.fordham.edu/halsall/source/chrysostomjews6.html (accessed May 13, 2005).

———. *Homilies Against the Jews*. Translated by Wayne Meeks and Robert Wilken in *Jews and Christians in Antioch in the First Four Centuries of the Common Era*. Missoula, Mont., 1978.

———. Homily XXIV, Homilies on First Corinthians. In *Nicean and Post-Nicean Fathers*, ser. 1, vol. 12. Grand Rapids, Mich., 1978–79.

Civiltà cattolica. Review of *The Popes Against the Jews: The Vatican's Rome in the Rise of Modern Anti-Semitism* by David I. Kertzer (New York, 2001). *Civiltà cattolica* 2, 3643 (2002): 3–11. Text at www.davidkertzer.com/pdf/patj_civilta.htm (accessed July 17, 2005).

Codex diplomaticus Majoris Poloniae documenta, et jam typis descripta, et adhuc inedita complectens, annum 1400 attingentia. 8 vols. Poznan, 1877–1989.

Cohen, Esther. "Symbols and Culpability and the Universal Language of Justice: The Ritual of Public Executions in Late Medieval Europe." *History of European Ideas* 11 (1989): 411.

Cohen, Gerson D. "Esau as Symbol." In *Jewish Medieval and Renaissance Studies*, ed. Alexander Altmann. Cambridge, Mass., 1967.

———, ed. *A Critical Edition with a Translation and Notes of the Book of Tradition (Sefer ha-kabbalah) by Abraham Ibn Daud*. Philadelphia, 1967.

Cohen, Jeremy, ed. *From Witness to Witchcraft: Jews and Judaism in Medieval Christian Thought*. Wiesbaden, 1996.

———. *Living Letters of the Law: Ideas of the Jew in Medieval Christianity*. Berkeley, 1999.

Cohen, Thomas V. *Love and Death in Renaissance Italy*. Chicago, 2004.

Colet, John. *John Colet's Commentary on First Corinthians*. A critical edition and translation by Bernard O'Kelly, with commentary notes by Catherine Jarrott. Medieval & Renaissance Texts & Studies, 21. Binghamton, N.Y., 1985.

Cristiani, Marta. *Tempo rituale e tempo storico, Communione Cristiana e sacrificio: Le controversie eucaristiche nell'alto medioevo*. Spoleto, 1997.

Crouzet-Pavan, Elizabeth. "Venice Between Jerusalem, Byzantium, and Divine Retribution: The Origins of the Ghetto." *Mediterranean Historical Review* 6 (1991): 163–79.

The Croxton *Play of the Sacrament*. In *Non-Cycle Plays and Fragments*, ed. Norman Davis, 58–89. Early English Text Society, suppl. ser., 1. London, 1970.

Cyprian, Saint, bishop of Carthage. *Sancti Cypriani episcopi opera*. Corpus Christianorum, Series Latina. Turnhout, 1972–76.

Davies, W. D. *Paul and Rabbinic Judaism*. London, 1960.

Davis, Natalie Zemon. "The Sacred and the Social Body in Sixteenth-Century Lyons." *Past and Present* 90 (1981): 40–70.

De Pomis, David. *Enarratio brevis, de senum affectibus praecavendis, atque curandis . . .* Venice, 1588.

Delehaye, Hippolyte. *Les Légendes hagiographiques*. 1903. 4th ed., Brussels, 1955. Translated by Donald Attwater under the title *The Legends of the Saints* (New York, 1962; Dublin, 1998).

———. *Les Origines du culte des martyrs*. Brussels, 1912. 2d ed., rev., Brussels, 1933.

———. *The Work of the Bollandists Through Three Centuries, 1615–1915*. Princeton, 1922. Appeared serially in *Études de Paris* in 1919; first ed. published in 1920 under the title À *travers trois siècles: L'Oeuvre des Bollandistes, 1615–1915*.

Delumeau, Jean. *Sin and Fear: The Emergence of a Western Guilt Culture*. Translated by E. Nicholson. New York, 1990.

Desportes, Henri. *Le Mystère du sang chez les juifs*. Paris, 1889, 1890.

Despres, Denise. "Mary of the Eucharist: Cultic Anti-Judaism in Some Fourteenth-Century English Devotional Manuscripts." In *From Witness to Witchcraft: Jews and Judaism in Medieval Christian Thought*, ed. Jeremy Cohen, 375–402. Wiesbaden, 1996.

Döllinger, Ignaz von. *Heidenthum und Judenthum: Vorhalle zur geschichte des Christenthums*. Regensburg: G. J. Manz, 1857.

———. *Die Juden in Europa: Rede, gehalten in der Festsitzung der Münchener Akademie am 25. Juli 1881*. Berlin, 1921.

Douglas, Mary. "Deciphering a Meal." *Daedalus* 101 (1972): 61–82.

———. *Natural Symbols: Explorations in Cosmology*. 1970. Reprint, New York, 2003.

Duschesne, Louis. "Le Massacre des chrétiens Himyarites au temps de l'empereur Justin." *Revue des études juives* 20 (1890): 220–24.

Einbinder, Susan L. *Beautiful Death: Jewish Poetry and Martyrdom in Medieval France*. Princeton, 2002.

———. "Jewish Women Martyrs: Changing Models of Representation." *Exemplaria* 12, no. 1 (2000): 105–27.

———. "Meir b. Elijah of Norwich: Persecution and Poetry Among Medieval English Jews." *Journal of Medieval History* 26, no. 2 (2000): 145–62.

———. "Pucellina of Blois: Romantic Myths and Narrative Conventions." *Jewish History* 12, no. 1 (1998): 29–46.

———. "Signs of Romance: Hebrew Prose and the Twelfth Century Renaissance." In *Jews and Christians in Twelfth-Century Europe*, ed. Michael Signer and John Van Engen. Notre Dame, Ind., 2001.

———. "The Troyes Laments: Jewish Martyrology in Hebrew and Old-French." *Viator* 30 (1999): 201–30.

———, ed. and trans. "The Jewish Martyrs of Blois." In *Medieval Hagiography: An Anthology*, ed. Thomas Head, 537–60. New York, 2000.

Elliott, Dyan. *Fallen Bodies: Pollution, Sexuality, and Demonology in the Middle Ages*. Philadelphia, 1999.

Enciclopedia cattolica. Rome, 1949–54.

Erler, L. "Die Juden des Mittelalters," "Die Päpste und die Juden," and "Die Judenverfolgungen des Mittelalters." *Archiv für katholisches Kirchenrecht*, esp. 42 (1879), 3–80, and see also in vols. 43, 44, 48, 50, 53.

Espina, Alfonso de, bishop of Orense. *Fortalitium Fidei*. Ca. 1464. Lyon, 1487.
Esposito, Mario. "Un Procès contre les Juifs de la Savoie en 1329." *Revue d'histoire ecclésiastique* 34 (1938): 785–801.
Fabre-Vassas, Claudine. *The Singular Beast: Jews, Christians and the Pig*. Translated by Carol Volk. New York, 1997.
Fishman, Talya. "Changing Early Modern Jewish Discourse about Christianity: The Efforts of Rabbi Leon Modena." In *The Lion Shall Roar: Leon Modena and His World*, ed. David Malkiel. Jerusalem, 2003.
Flint, Valerie. *The Rise of Magic in Early Modern Europe*. Princeton, 1991.
Foa, Anna. "Il gioco del proselitismo: Politica delle conversioni e controllo della violenza nella Roma del Cinquecento." In *Ebrei e Cristiani nell'Italia medievale e moderna: Conversioni, scambi, contrasti*, ed. M. Luzzati, M. Olivari, and A. Veronese, 155–70. Rome, 1988.
———. *Giordano Bruno*. Bologna, 1998.
———. "The New and the Old: The Spread of Syphilis," In *Sex and Gender in Historical Perspective*, ed. Edward Muir and Guido Ruggiero. Baltimore, 1990.
———. "The Religious Orders and Conversion." In *The Friars and the Jews in the Middle Ages and the Renaissance*, ed. Stephen McMichael and Susan Myers. Leiden, 2004.
Frankel, Jonathan. *The Damascus Affair: "Ritual Murder," Politics, and the Jews in 1840*. Cambridge, 1997.
Fransen, Gérard, and Stephan Kuttner. *Summa "Elegantius in iure divino" seu Coloniensis*. New York, 1969–90.
Gager, John. *Reinventing Paul*. New York, 2000.
Geertz, Clifford. *Negara: The Theater State in Nineteenth-Century Bali*. Princeton, 1980.
Gesta Boemundi archiepiscopi Treverensis. Monumenta Germaniae Historica, Scriptores, vol. 24. Hannover, 1879.
Gesta Treverorum. See Aronius.
Giesey, Ralph E. *The Royal Funeral Ceremony in Renaissance France*. Geneva, 1960.
Gilchrist, John. "The Perception of Jews in the Canon Law in the Period of the First Two Crusades." *Jewish History* 3, no. 1 (1988): 9–24.
Ginzburg, Carlo. *Storia notturna: Una decifrazione del sabba*. Turin, 1989. Translated by Raymond Rosenthal as *Ecstasies: Deciphering the Witches' Sabbath* (Chicago, 2004).
Giordano, Oronozo. *Religiosità popolare nell'alto medioevo*. Bari, 1979.
González Salinero, Raúl. *El antijudaísmo cristiano occidental, siglos iv y v*. Madrid, 2000.
Gonzalo de Berceo, *Los milagros de nuestra señora*. Edited by Brian Dutton. London, 1971.
Goodich, Michael. *Witnesses at the Margins of Medieval Society*. Philadelphia, 1998.
Gougenot des Mousseaux, Roger. *Le Juif, le judaïsme et la judaïsation des peuples chrétiens*. 1869. 2d ed. Paris, 1886.

Grafton, Anthony. *Defenders of the Text: The Traditions of Scholarship in an Age of Science, 1450–1800*. Cambridge, Mass., 1991.

Grayzel, Solomon. *The Church and the Jews in the Thirteenth Century*. 2 vols. New York and Detroit, 1966–89. Posthumous vol. 2 edited by Kenneth Stow.

———. Review of "Die Judenbekämpfung im Mittelalter" by Petrus Browe. Found attached to Grayzel's personal copy of Browe's essay, but with no reference as to its provenance; [probably] *Jewish Quarterly Review*, no. 122 or 123 (1939–40): 210, 212n5.

Gregory, Brad S. *Salvation at Stake: Christian Martyrdom in Early Modern Europe*. Cambridge, Mass., 1999.

Gross, Henri. *Gallia judaica: Dictionnaire géographique de la France d'après les sources rabbiniques*. Paris, 1897.

Guerin, Paul. *Les Petits Bollandistes: Vies des Saints*. 17 vols. Paris, 1888.

Haberman, Abraham. *Sefer gezerot ashkenaz ve-zarfat*. Jerusalem, 1945.

HaKohen, Joseph. ʿ*Emeq haBakhʾa*. Edited by Meir Letteris. Kraków, 1895.

Harrington, James. *The Commonwealth of Oceana and A System of Politics*. Edited by J. G. A. Pocock. Cambridge, 1992.

Hassig [= Strickland], Debra. "Iconography of Rejection: Jews and Other Monstrous Races." In *Image and Belief: Studies in Celebration of the Eightieth Anniversary of the Index of Christian Art*, ed. Colum Hourihane. Princeton, 1999.

Hayes, Christine E. *Gentile Impurities and Jewish Identities: Intermarriage and Conversion from the Bible to the Talmud*. Oxford, 2002.

Henry, Matthew. *The Complete Matthew Henry Commentary on the Bible*. www.gospel com.net/eword/comments/matthew/mh/matthew15.htm (accessed May 7, 2005).

Herbeck, Peter. *On "Dominus Jesus."* www.renewalministries.net/booklets/WWF.htm (accessed July 17, 2005).

Historia et cartularium monasterii Sancti Petri Gloucestriae. Edited by William Henry Hart. 3 vols. Rerum Britannicarum medii aevi scriptores, 33. London, 1863–67.

Hruby, Kurt. "A Christian View." In *Christians and Jews*, ed. Hans Küng and Walter Kasper. New York, 1975.

Hsia, Ronnie Po-chia. *The Myth of Ritual Murder*. New Haven, 1988.

———. *Trent 1475: Stories of a Ritual Murder Trial*. New Haven, 1992.

Hughes, Diane Owen. "Distinguishing Signs: Ear-Rings, Jews and Franciscan Rhetoric in the Italian Renaissance City." *Past and Present* 112 (1986): 33–34.

The Jewish-Christian Debate in the High Middle Ages: A Critical Edition of the Nizzahon vetus. Edited by David Berger. Philadelphia, 1979.

Joassart, Bernard. *Hippolyte Delehaye : Hagiographie critique et modernisme*. 2 vols. Brussels, 2000.

Johnson, Willis. "Before the Blood Libel: Jews in Christian Exegesis After the Massacres of 1096." MA thesis, Cambridge University, 1994. Typescript.

Jordan, William C. *The French Monarchy and the Jews*. Philadephia, 1989.

———. "Princely Identity and the Jews in Medieval France." In *From Witness to Witchcraft: Jews and Judaism in Medieval Christian Thought*, ed. Jeremy Cohen. Wiesbaden, 1996.

Josephus Flavius. *Contra Apionem*. Translated and edited by Aryeh Kasher. Jerusalem, 1996. In Hebrew.

Kanarfogel, Ephraim. *"Peering Through the Lattices": Mystical, Magical, and Pietistic Dimensions in the Tosafist Period*. Detroit, 2000.

Kantorowicz, Ernst H. *The King's Two Bodies: A Study in Mediaeval Political Theology*. Princeton, 1957.

Kaplan, Yosef. *An Alternative Path to Modernity: The Sephardi Diaspora in Western Europe*. Leiden, 2000.

Kasper, Walter. "The Jewish-Christian Dialogue: Foundations, Progress, Difficulties and Perspectives." Speech at the Israel Museum, Jerusalem, November 21, 2001. A revised and enlarged version of the address given by Cardinal Kasper at the conference of the International Council of Christians and Jews in Montevideo, Uruguay, July 8, 2001.

Katz, Jacob. *Exclusiveness and Tolerance*. New York, 1961.

Kaufman, Ezekiel. *The Religion of Israel*. London, 1960.

Kedar, B. Z. "Canon Law and the Burning of the Talmud." *Bulletin of Medieval Canon Law* 9 (1979): 79–82.

Kelley, Donald R. "Budé and the First Historical School of Law." *American Historical Review* 72 (1967): 807–34.

———. *The Human Measure: Social Thought in the Western Legal Tradition*. Cambridge, Mass., 1990.

Kertzer, David I. *The Kidnapping of Edgardo Mortara*. New York, 1997.

———. *The Popes Against the Jews: The Vatican's Rome in the Rise of Modern Anti-Semitism*. New York, 2001.

———. Review of *Under His Very Window: The Vatican and the Holocaust in Italy* by Susan Zuccotti. *Journal of Modern History* 74 (2002): 879–81.

Kieval, Hillel. "Death and the Nation: Ritual Murder as Political Discourse in the Czech Lands." *Jewish History* 10, no. 1 (1996): 75–91.

———. *Languages of Community: The Jewish Experience in the Czech Lands*. Berkeley, 2000.

———. "Representation and Knowledge in Medieval and Modern Accounts of Jewish Ritual Murder." *Jewish Social Studies*, n.s., 1 (1994): 52–72.

Kisch, Guido. *The Jews in Medieval Germany: A Study of Their Legal and Social Status*. New York. 1949.

Klar, Benjamin, ed. *The Scroll of Ahimaaz*. Reprint, Jerusalem, 1974.

Knowles, David. "The Bollandists." In id., *Problems in Monastic History*. London, 1963.

Kornberg, Jacques. "Ignaz von Döllinger's *Die Juden in Europa*: A Catholic Polemic Against Antisemitism." *Journal for the History of Modern Theology* 6 (1999): 223–45.

Kriegel, Maurice. "Un Trait de psychologie sociale dans les pays Méditerranéens du Bas Moyen Age: Le Juif comme intouchable." *Annales ESC* 31 (1976): 326–30.

Kristeva, Julia. *Powers of Horror: An Essay on Abjection*. Translated by Leon S. Roudiez. New York, 1982.

Kroen, Sheryl. *Politics and Theater: The Crisis of Legitimacy in Restoration France*. Berkeley, 2000.

Kurtz, Lester R. *The Politics of Heresy: The Modernist Crisis in Roman Catholicism*. Berkeley, 1986.

Ladner, Gerhard. "Homo Viator: Medieval Ideas on Alienation and Order." *Speculum* 42 (1967): 233–59.

Lampert, Lisa. "The Once and Future Jew: The Croxton *Play of the Sacrament*, Little Robert of Bury and Historical Memory." *Jewish History* 15, no. 3 (2001): 235–55.

Langmuir, Gavin. *History, Religion, and Antisemitism*. Berkeley, 1990.

———. *Toward a Definition of Antisemitism*. Berkeley, 1990.

"La pastorale collettiva dei vescovi cattolici di Germania." *Civiltà cattolica* (Rome) 89, 4, no. 2119 (October 1, 1938): 68–77.

Lease, Gary. *"Odd Fellows" in the Politics of Religion: Modernism, National Socialism, and German Judaism*. New York, 1995.

Lidaka, Juris. "The Book of Angles, Rings, Characters and Images of the Planets Attributed to Osbern Bokenham." In *Conjuring Spirits: Texts and Traditions of Medieval Ritual Magic*, ed. Claire Fanger. University Park, Pa., 1998.

Limor, Ora. "The Blood Libel." In *Jews and Christians in Western Europe: Encounter Between Cultures in the Middle Ages and the Renaissance*, ed. Ora Limor et al. Tel Aviv, 1998. In Hebrew.

Linder, Amnon, trans. and ed. *The Jews in the Legal Sources of the Early Middle Ages*. Detroit: Wayne State University Press; Jerusalem: Israel Academy of Sciences and Humanities, 1997.

Lipschitz, Leopold, ed. *Christliche Zeugnisse gegen die Blutbeschuldigung*. Berlin, 1882.

Lipton, Sara. *Images of Intolerance: The Representation of Jews and Judaism in the "Bible moralisée."* Berkeley, 1999.

Lotter, Friedrich. "Innocens Virgo et Martyr, Thomas von Monmouth und die Verbreitung der Ritualmordlegende im Hochmittelalter." In *Die Legende vom Ritualmord: Zur Geschichte der Blutbeschuldigung gegen Juden*, ed. Rainer Erb. Berlin, 1993.

———. "The Scope and Effectiveness of Imperial Jewry Law in the High Middle Ages." *Jewish History* 4, no. 1 (1989): 31–58.

Lucas, Leopold. *The Conflict Between Christianity and Judaism: A Contribution to the History of the Jews in the Fourth Century*. Warminster, Eng., 1993.

Luther, Martin. *That Jesus Christ Was Born a Jew*. Translated by W. I. Brandt in *Luther's Works*, 45: 195–229. Philadelphia, 1971.

Mack, Phyllis. *Visionary Women: Ecstatic Prophecy in Seventeenth-Century England*. Berkeley, 1992.

Macy, Gary. *The Theologies of the Eucharist in the Early Scholastic Period: A Study of the Salvific Function of the Sacrament According to the Theologians, c. 1080–c. 1220*. Oxford, 1984.

Marcus, Ivan. *Rituals of Childhood: Jewish Acculturation in Medieval Europe*. New Haven, 1996.

———. *The Jewish Life Cycle*. Seattle, 2004.

Marrow, James H. "*Circumdederunt me canes multi*: Christ's Tormentors in Northern European Art of the Late Middle Ages and Early Renaissance." *Art Bulletin* 59, no. 2 (1977): 167–81.

———. *Passion Iconography in Northern European Art of the Late Middle Ages and the Early Renaissance: A Study of the Transformation of Sacred Metaphor into Descriptive Narrative*. Kortrijk, Netherlands, 1979.

Martí, Ramón [Raymundus Martinus]. *Pugio fidei adversus Mauros et Judaeous*. . . . Edited by ed. J. Carpzov. Leipzig, 1687.

Martin, Dale. *The Corinthian Body*. New Haven, 1996.

Marx, Karl. *A World Without Jews*. Translated by Dagobart G. Runes. New York, 1959. This Philosophical Library translation is picked up on many websites, including neo-Nazi ones, e.g., www.zundelsite.org/english/zgrams/zg1999/zg9909/990917.html (accessed May 13, 2005).

Mathon, Gérard. "Richard of Pontoise." *Bibliotheca Sanctorum*, 11: 170. Rome, 1968.

McCulloh, John. "Jewish Ritual Murder: William of Norwich, Thomas of Monmouth, and the Early Dissemination of the Myth." *Speculum* 72, no. 3 (1997): 698–740.

Meens, Rob. "Ritual Purity and the Influence of Gregory the Great in the Early Middle Ages." In *Unity and Diversity in the Church*, ed. R. N. Swanson, 31–43. Studies in Church History, 32. Oxford, 1996.

Melamed, Abraham. *The Image of the Black in Jewish Culture: A History of the Other*. New York, 2003.

Messinio, A., S.J. "Gli elementi costitutivi della nazione e la razza." *Civiltà cattolica* (Rome) 89, 3, no. 2115 (August 6, 1938): 209–23.

Miccoli, Giovanni. "L'Italia cattolica e il fascismo." *Rassegna mensile di Israel* 69 (2003): 163–86.

———. "Santa Sede: Questione ebraica e antisemitismo fra Otto e Novecento." In *Gli ebrei di Italia*, ed. C. Vivanti, 2: 1371–1574. Turin, 1996.

Michlic-Coren, Joanna. "Anti-Jewish Violence in Poland, 1918–1939 and 1945–1947." *Polin* 13 (2000): 34–61.

Milano, Attilio. "L'impari lotta della comunità di Roma contro la Casa dei Catecumeni." *Rassegna mensile di Israel* 16 (1950): 355–68, 408–19.

Minerbi, Sergio. *Vatican and Zionism: Conflict in the Holy Land, 1895–1925*. New York, 1990.

Minty, Mary. "Kiddush HaShem in Christian Eyes in Medieval Germany." *Zion* 59 (1994): 209–65. In Hebrew.

Minucius Felix, Marcus. *Octavius*. Translated and edited by Jean Beaujeu. Paris, 1964.

Morrison, Karl F. *History as a Visual Art in the Twelfth-Century Renaissance*. Princeton, 1990.

Moyer, James C. "Hittite and Israelite Cultic Practices: A Selected Comparison." In *Scripture in Context II: More Essays on the Comparative Method*, ed. William Hallo, James Moyer, and Leo Perdue, 29–32. Winona Lake, Ind., 1983.

Muir, Edward. "The Virgin on the Street Corner: The Place of the Sacred in Italian Cities." In *Religion and Culture in the Renaissance and Reformation*, ed. S. Ozment, 28. Kirksville, Mo., 1989.

Niermeyer, J. F. *Mediae Latinitatis Lexicon Minus*. Leiden, 1976.

Nahon, Gérard. "From the Rue aux Juifs to the Chemin du Roy." In *Jews and Christians in Twelfth-Century Europe*, ed. Michael Signer and John Van Engen. Notre Dame, Ind., 2001.

Neusner, Jacob, and Bruce Chilton. *Jewish and Christian Doctrines: The Classics Compared*. New York, 2000.

Nirenberg, David. *Communities of Violence: Persecution of Minorities in the Middle Ages*. Princeton, 1996.

———. "Conversion, Sex, and Segregation: Jews and Christians in Medieval Spain." *American Historical Review* 107 (2002): 1065–93.

Nora, Pierre. *Realms of Memory*. Translated by Arthur Goldhammer. 3 vols. New York, 1998.

Nostra aetate. "Declaration on the Relation of the Church to Non-Christian Religions Proclaimed by His Holiness Pope Paul VI on October 28, 1965." www.vatican.va/archive/hist_councils/ii_vatican_council/documents/vat-ii_decl_19651028_nostra-aetate_en.html (accessed May 16, 2005).

O'Connell, Marvin R. *Critics on Trial: An Introduction to the Catholic Modernist Crisis*. Washington, D.C., 1994.

Oeuvres de Rigord et de Guillaume le Breton, historiens de Philippe-Auguste, publiées pour la Société de l'histoire de France par H. François Delaborde. 2 vols. Paris: Librairie Renouard, H. Loones, successeur, 1882–85.

Official, Rabbi Yosef. *Sepher Joseph Hamekane of R. Joseph b. R. Nathan Official*. Edited by Judah Rosenthal. Jerusalem, 1970. In Hebrew.

Oldradus da Ponte. *Consilia: Avrea qvidem svnt haec, ac pene divina responsa*. 1478.

Otto I, bishop of Freising. *Ottonis et Rahewini Gesta Friderici I. imperatoris*. 3d ed. Edited by Georg Waitz and Bernhard von Simson. Scriptores rerum germanicarum in usum scholarum ex Monumentis Germaniae historicis recusi, 46. Hannover, 1912.

Pacaut, Marcel. *Louis VII et les élections épiscopales dans le royaume de France*. Paris, 1957.

———. *Louis VII et son royaume*. Paris, 1964.

Die Päpstlichen Bullen über die Blutbeschuldigung. Munich, 1900.

Parpola, Simo. *Assyrian Prophecies*. State Archives of Assyria, vol. 9. Helsinki, 1997.

Patrologiae cursus completus: series latina. Edited by J.-P. Migne. 221 vols. in 222. Paris, 1844–1902.

Pichetto, Maria Teresa. "L'antisemitismo di mons: Umberto Benigni e l'accusa di omicidio rituale." In *Italia Judaica IV*, ed. Ministero per i beni culturali. Rome, 1993.

The Prophets: A New Translation of the Holy Scriptures. Philadelphia, 1978.

Prosperi, Adriano. "L'inquisitore come confessore." In *Disciplina dell'anima, disciplina del corpo e disciplina della società tra medioevo ed età moderna*, ed. Paolo Prodi and Adriano Prosperi, 187–224. Bologna, 1994.

———. *Tribunali di coscienza: Inquisitori, confessori, missionari*. Turin, 1976.

Raymundus da Peñaforte. *Summa de poenitentia et matrimoniae*. Rome, 1603.

Roach, William, ed. *Le Roman de Perceval ou le conte du Graal*. Geneva, 1959.

Rohling, August. *Der Talmudjude: Zur Beherzigung für Juden und Christen aller Stände*. Münster: Adolph Russell, 1872.

Rosa, Mario. "La Santa Sede e gli ebrei nel Settecento." In *Gli ebrei di Italia*, ed. C. Vivanti, 2: 1071–72. Turin, 1996.

Rothschild, Fritz A., ed. *Jewish Perspectives on Christianity: Leo Baeck, Martin Buber, Franz Rosenzweig, Will Herberg, and Abraham J. Heschel*. New York, 1990.

Rubin, Miri. "Choosing Death? Experiences of Martyrdom in Late Medieval Europe." In *Martyrs and Martyrologies*, ed. Diana Wood, 153–84. Studies in Church History, 30. Oxford, 1993.

———. *Corpus Christi: The Eucharist in Late Medieval Culture*. Cambridge, 1992.

———. "Desecration of the Host: The Birth of an Accusation." In *Christianity and Judaism*, ed. Diana Wood, 178. Studies in Church History, 29. Oxford, 1992.

———. *Gentile Tales: The Narrative Assault on Late Medieval Jews*. New Haven, 1999.

Rymer, Thomas. *Foedera*. London, 1816.

Saige, Gustave. *Les Juifs du Languedoc antérieurement au XIVe siècle*. Paris, 1881.

Salfeld, Sigmund, ed. *Das Martyrologium des Nürnberger Memorbuches*. Berlin, 1898.

Sanborn, Donald J. "A Critical Analysis of Ratzinger's Dominus Jesus." www.geocities.com/orthopapism/ahrs.html (accessed July 17, 2005).

Sartorelli, Augusto. "Ebrei e società cristiana ne pensiero tradizionalista cattolico." *Rassegna mensile di Israel* 69 (2003): 127–62.

Sassier, Yves. *Louis VII*. Paris, 1991.

Schaefer, Peter. *Mirror of His Beauty: Feminine Images of God From the Bible to the Early Kabbalah*. Princeton, 2002.

Schudt, Johann Jacob. *Jüdische Merckwürdigkeiten*. . . . 4 vols. Frankfurt a/M, 1715–18. I thank Deborah Fischel for this reference.

Shatzmiller, Joseph. *Shylock Reconsidered: Jews, Moneylending, and Medieval Society*. Berkeley, 1990.

Simonsohn, Shlomo. *The Apostolic See and the Jews*. 8 vols. Toronto, 1990.

Singer, S., ed. *The Standard Prayer Book*. New York, 1957.

Sinonoglou, Leah. "The Christ Child as Sacrifice." *Speculum* 43 (1973): 491–509.

Smith, Jonathan Z. *To Take Place: Toward Theory in Ritual*. Chicago, 1987.

Soloveitchik, Haym. *Principles and Pressures: Jewish Trade in Gentile Wine in the Middle Ages*. Tel Aviv, 2003. In Hebrew.

Sorkin, David. *The Berlin Haskalah and German Religious Thought*. London, 2000.
Spaccini, Giovan Battista. *Cronaca di Modena*. Edited by Albano Biondi, Rolando Bussi, and Carlo Giovannini. 2 vols. Modena, 1993–99.
Spiegel, Gabrielle. *Romancing the Past: The Rise of Vernacular Prose Historiography in Thirteenth-Century France*. Berkeley, 1993.
Spiegel, Shalom. "*In monte dominis videbatur*: The Martyrs of Blois and the Early Accusations of Ritual Murder." In *The Mordecai Kaplan Jubilee Volume*, 285–87. New York, 1953. In Hebrew and English.
Stacey, Robert. "Anti-Semitism and the Medieval English State." In *The Medieval State: Essays Presented to James Campbell*, ed. J. R. Maddicott and D. M. Palliser. London, 2000.
———. "From Ritual Crucifixion to Host Desecration: Jews and the Body of Christ." *Jewish History* 12, no. 1 (1998): 11–28.
Stillman, Norman. *The Jews of Arab Lands*. Philadelphia, 1979.
Stow, Kenneth. "Agobard of Lyons and the Medieval Concept of the Jew." *Conservative Judaism* 29 (1964): 68–75.
———. *Alienated Minority: The Jews of Medieval Latin Europe*. Cambridge, Mass., 1992, 1994.
———. "The Avignonese Papacy, or, After the Expulsions." In *From Witness to Witchcraft: Jews and Judaism in Medieval Christian Thought*, ed. Jeremy Cohen, 275–98. Wiesbaden, 1996.
———. *Catholic Thought and Papal Jewry Policy, 1555–1593*. New York, 1977.
———. "The Church and the Jews: From St. Paul to Paul IV." In *Bibliographical Essays in Medieval Jewish Studies*, vol. 2. New York, 1976.
———. "Church, Conversion, and Tradition: The Problem of Jewish Conversion in Sixteenth-Century Italy." *Dimensioni e problemi della ricerca storica* 2 (1996): 26–35.
———. "Conversion, Apostasy, and Apprehensiveness: Emicho of Flonheim and the Fear of Jews in the Twelfth Century." *Speculum* 76 (2001): 911–33.
———. "The Good of the Church, the Good of the State: The Popes and Jewish Money." In *Economics and Religion*, ed. Menahem Ben-Sasson. Jerusalem, 1994. In Hebrew. Revised English version in *Christianity and Judaism*, ed. Diana Wood, 237–52. Studies in Church History, 29. Oxford, 1992.
———. "Holy Body, Holy Society: Conflicting Medieval Structural Conceptions." In *Sacred Space: Shrine, City, Land*, ed. Benjamin Z. Kedar and R. J. Zwi Werblowsky. New York, 1998.
———. "Jacob of Venice and the Jewish Settlements in Venice in the Thirteenth Century." In *Community and Culture*, ed. Nahum Waldman. Philadelphia, 1987.
———. "The Jew as Alien and the Diffusion of Restriction: An Expulsion Text from Udine, 1556." In *Jews in Italy: Studies Dedicated to the Memory of U. Cassuto*, ed. Haim Beinart. Jerusalem, 1988.
———. "Papal and Royal Attitudes Toward Jewish Lending in the Thirteenth Century." *AJS Review* 6 (1981): 161–84.

———. "Papal Mendicants or Mendicant Popes: Continuity and Change in Papal Policies Toward the Jews at the End of the Fifteenth Century." In *The Friars and the Jews in the Middle Ages and the Renaissance*, ed. S. McMichael and S. Myers. Leiden, 2003.

———. Review of *The Jews in Medieval Normandy: A Social and Intellectual History* by Norman Golb (Cambridge, 1998). *Medieval Review* on-line, www.hti.umich.edu/cgi/t/text/text-idx?c=tmr;cc=tmr;sid=f44ec5dba8aa585efad22a6 26c199e65;q1=Golb;rgn=main;view=text;idno=baj9928.9905.003 (accessed May 14, 2005).

———. *Theater of Acculturation: The Roman Ghetto in the Sixteenth Century*. Seattle, 2001.

———. *The "1007 Anonymous" and Papal Sovereignty: Jewish Perceptions of the Papacy and Papal Policy in the High Middle Ages*. Cincinnati, 1984.

Strickland, Debra H. *Saracens, Demons, and Jews: Making Monsters in Medieval Art*. Princeton, 2003. See also under Hassig [= Strickland].

Susannis, Marquardus de. *De Iudaeis et aliis infidelibus*. Venice, 1558.

Tal, Uriel. "The Future of Jewish-Christian Dialogue." In *Christians and Jews*, ed. Hans Küng and Walter Kasper, 82. New York, 1975.

Thomas of Monmouth. *The Life and Miracles of St. William of Norwich*. Edited by Augustus Jessopp and M. R. James. Cambridge, 1896.

Toaff, Ariel. *The Jews in Medieval Assisi, 1305–1487*. Florence, 1979.

Trachtenberg, Joshua. *The Devil and the Jews*. New Haven, 1943.

Unity and Diversity in the Church: Papers Read at the 1994 Summer Meeting and the 1995 Winter Meeting of the Ecclesiastical History Society. Edited by R. N. Swanson. Studies in Church History, 32. Oxford, 1996.

Vacandard, Elphège. "La Question du meurtre rituel chez les Juifs." In *Études de critique et d'histoire religieuse*, 2d ed., 3d. ser., 311–77. Paris, 1912.

Van Engen, John. "Ralph of Flaix: The Book of Leviticus Interpreted as Christian Community." In *Jews and Christians in Twelfth-Century Europe*, ed. Michael Signer and John Van Engen. Notre Dame, Ind., 2001.

Van Ortroy, François. Review of Ministère d'état–Archives de l'Empire, *Layettes du Trésor des chartes*, vol. 4: *De l'année 1261 à l'année 1270*, by E. Berger (Paris, 1902). *Analecta Bollandiana* 23 (1904): 392–94.

———. Review of *Storia del beato Simone da Trento* by G. Divina, 2 vols. (Trent, 1902). *Analecta Bollandiana* 23 (1904): 122–24.

Vatican. Commission for Religious Relations with the Jews. "We Remember: A Reflection on the Shoah." www.vatican.va/roman_curia/pontifical_councils/chrstuni/documents/rc_pc_chrstuni_doc_16031998_shoah_en.html (accessed May 17, 2005).

Vauchez, André. "Antisemitismo e canonizzazione popolare: San Werner o Vernier (+1287) bambino martire e patrono dei vignaioli." In *Culto dei santi, istituzioni e classi sociali in età preindustriale*, ed. Sofia Boesch Gajano and Lucia Sebastiani. L'Aquila, Rome, 1981.

———. *La Sainteté en occident*. Rome, 1981.
———. *Sainthood in the Later Middle Ages*. Translated by Jean Birrell. Cambridge, 1997.
Vernet, Félix. "Juifs et Chrétiens." In *Dictionnaire apologétique de la foi catholique II*, cols. 1651–1764. Paris, 1910–12.
Wachtel, David. "The Ritual and Liturgical Commemoration of Two Medieval Persecutions." MA thesis, Columbia University, 1995.
Watt, J. A. "The Term '*Plenitudo Potestatis*' in Hostiensis." In *Proceedings of the Second International Congress of Medieval Canon Law*, ed. S. Kuttner. Vatican City, 1965.
White, Hayden. *The Content of the Form: Narrative Discourse and Historical Representation*. Baltimore, 1987.
Wilken, Robert. *John Chrysostom and the Jews: Rhetoric and Reality in the Late Fourth Century*. Berkeley, 1983.
———. *Judaism and the Early Christian Mind: A Study of Cyril of Alexandria's Exegesis and Theology*. New Haven, 1971.
Wilson, John. *The English Martyrologe: Conteyning a Summary of the Most Renowned and Illustrious Saints of the Three Kingdomes England, Ireland, & Scotland*. St. Omer, 1640. Reprint. Ilkley, Eng., 1975.
Wood, Charles. "The Doctor's Dilemma: Sin, Salvation, and the Menstrual Cycle in Medieval Thought." *Speculum* 56 (1981): 711–27.
Wright, David P. *The Disposal of Impurity: Elimination Rites in the Bible and in Hittite and Mesopotamian Literature*. Atlanta, 1987.
Yerushalmi, Yosef Hayim. *The Lisbon Massacre of 1506 and the Royal Image in the Shebet Yehudah*. Cincinnati, 1976.
Yuval, Israel Jacob. *Two Nations in Your Womb*. Jerusalem, 2000. In Hebrew.
———. "Vengeance and Damnation, Blood and Defamation: From Jewish Martyrdom to Blood Libel Accusations." *Zion* 58 (1993): 33–90.
Zerubavel, Eviatar. *The Fine Line: Making Distinctions in Everyday Life*. New York, 1991.
Zink, Michel. *Introduction à la littérature française du Moyen Age*. Paris, 1999.

Index

Anonymous, 100, 113–14, 115f, 123, 357–59, 262, 269, 292
Abraham, 2, 207
Abraham, children of, and Paul, xvi; Pope John Paul II on, 1, 205; Pope Benedict XVI on, 2
Acta Sanctorum, ix; and ritual murder narratives, xi–xii, 39, 54, 57, 129; and Werner of Oberwesel, 60, 189–97; and Richard of Pontoise, 76, 98, 177f
Adam of Bristol, 61–62, 85, 241, 243
Agobard of Lyon, on Christian purity, 15–17, 20ff, 134, 218, 274f; on Jews, 15–17, 34, 36, 71, 134, 214; on Christian society, 72, 173, 208; and Louis the Pious, 22, 51, 235
Alexander II, Pope, 21, 39, 118
Alexander III, Pope, and Third Lateran Decree, 19, 149, 226, 251; letter of, 90, 252f; and Louis VII, 90, 92, 99, 116, 252f; and Philip Augustus, 90, 92, 99, 267
Amalric of Metz, 6f, 36, 212
Analecta Bollandiana, 128–29, 130
Angelo di Castro, 136, 153–57
anti-modernists, *see* integralists
anti-Semitism, 48, 159, 164, 167, 204, 209, 222, 229, 232f
apostasy, 88–89, 90f, 112f, 151, 177, 251, 262; and Cyprian, 12; and Philip August, 93; and Louis VII, 254; in Loches letter, 264; and Gregory the Great, 268; in Blois letters, 287
Asor-Rosa, Alberto, 167f, 284

Attwater, Donald, 38, 229f
Augustine, St., 18, 24, 33ff, 35, 162, 168f, 225ff, 228
avarice, Jewish, 75–76, 152, 177; of Philip August, 96, 151; of kings, 100; and Louis VII, 253

banks, Jewish, 75
baptism, 18, 135, 143, 209, 214; of Jews, 26, 32, 91, 93, 255, 262; forced, 36, 112, 268; of martyrs, 66, 82; of Edgardo Mortara, 73, 244; in Loches letter, 264
Battista de' Giudici, Bishop of Ventimiglia, 21, 42, 124f, 220, 228
Bea, Cardinal, 168
Benedict XVI, Pope, and supremacy of Catholic Church, 1f, 34; and Abraham, 2; respect for Judaism, 34; inaugural address, 207
Berger, David, 206–7, 251
Bibles moralisées, 96, 116
Blois, Jewish martyrs, xi, 32, 77, 93, 99, 101–2, 109, 202, 261, 263, 287–89 *passim*, 291
Blois, ritual murder charge at, x, 81, 83, 85–86, 101, 106, 230
Blois letters, xi, xiiif, 99, 100–118, 259, 260–67, 289–90; translation, 198–202
blood, Jewish use of, xi, 9, 28, 31, 39, 62, 121f, 299, 140; eucharistic, 3, 6, 31, 51, 61, 135; Jewish sacrifice and, 10f, 86f, 133, 157, 213; Jewish lending and, 28, 244; baptism and, 66; menstrual, 135

blood libel, xv, xvii, 6, 29, 40, 51, 112, 122, 140, 159, 250; in papal letters, 48, 86–87, 270; and Bollandists, 55, 62, 67, 70; at Fulda, xi, 86, 109, 244; and Philip Augustus, xi, 115; definition of, 86; and popes, 121, 123, 229; denounced, 123; on Internet, 209, 271; and Martin Luther, 212
Bolland, John, 54, 56
Bollandist editing, 60f, 69, 77f, 80, 240, 248
Bollandist historicity, 55, 58, 78–79, 82, 98, 99
Bollandist scholarship, x, 42–43, 55, 64, 78, 120, 127f, 130ff, 237, 239f
Bollandist trials, 47
Bollandists, early, ix, xif, 47, 55–121, 127, 131–32, 236
Bollandists, modern, x, xiii, 47, 56–58, 120, 130f, 159, 232
Bollandists, seventeenth century, ix, xiif, 43, 47, 54, 56, 58, 64, 118–21, 131, 178
Bolsheviks, 163, 164
Bourges, Jewish boy of, 27, 61, 71, 82, 85, 102, 147; and Host libel, 240f
Brie, countess of, 97
Brie, victims of, 83–85, 117f, 251, 269; Jewish massacre, 84; Philip Augustus and, 88, 90, 93; and Rigord, 183
Browe, Peter, 41, 120, 232, 242
Burchard of Worms, the *Decretum* of, 17, 136
burning of Jews, at Blois, xi, 79, 99, 101,103–5 *passim*, 109, 260, 264f; Parisian, 91, 108
burning of Talmud, 123, 285
Buxtorf, Johannes, 17, 155–56, 217, 280

Campion, Edmund, 24, 64f
cannibalism, of Eucharist, 32, 88; Christian, 140, 142
canonization, 38, 42, 57, 64, 83, 122, 127, 131, 161, 237; of children, 42, 57; of Werner of Oberwesel, 60, 75, 189, 161, 210, 222; of William of Norwich, 67, 107; of Richard of Pontoise, 79, 107–9, 117, 199, 202; of Simonino of Trent, 37, 45, 229; of Gennaro, S., 128; of the Maccabees, 130

Capgrave, John, 59, 85, 239
carnality, Christian, 7f, 136, 140, 144, 147f, 153, 155f, 158
carnality, Jewish, 4, 133, 136, 153–55, 158; Paul on, 7–10, 35; 26, 53; Augustine on, 34–35; and Protestants, 53
Catholic Reformation, 57, 75
censorship, of van Ortroy, 47, 124, 125–26, 131; of Jewish texts, 116, 125; in Nazi Germany, 232; Dominican, 271f
Cervantes, 173–74
Charlemagne, Emperor of the Holy Roman Empire, 11, 104; laws of, 71
chronicles, Crusade, Latin, 88, 188, 256; Hebrew, 41, 88, 110, 257, 262
Chrysostom, John, on Jews as dogs, 4, 9, 17, 161; vilifies Jews, 8, 21f, 210; on Jewish contamination, 13f, 214; on supersession, 35, 141; on integralism, 124; on unity of Christians, 211; homily, 215
circumcision, 4f, 12, 14, 31f, 144
civil equality of Jews, *see* emancipation
Clement VIII, Pope, 58
Clement, Abbot of St. Andrew's Monastery, 27, 159, 242f
clothing, distinct Jewish, *see* dress
contact, sexual, *see* sexuality
contamination, of Eucharist, 6; of places, 6; Jewish, 8, 13; of food, 16f, 18, 20–22, 135, 216, 220; and domestic service, 19–20; eucharistic, 70, 159, 278, 281; of Christian altar, 94; of Jewish meat, 155; and sexual intercourse, 217, 277; and Judaized bishops, 281. *See also* pollution
conversion, Jewish, 10, 32, 34, 41, 83, 105, 152, 218, 251, 268; forced, 32, 36, 91–93, 112, 114, 226, 250, 253, 264, 269, 286, 289; false, 59, 89; and apostasy, 88ff, 93, 106, 112–13, 177; and Luther, 213
converts murdered, 26, 61, 82f; subsidies for, 268
corpses, contact with, 16f, 26, 134, 214, 275
Corpus Christi, 6, 43, 48–49, 52, 58f, 66f, 72–73, 93, 133, 147, 188, 235, 238, 250
Croxton play, 27, 62, 102, 241
Crusade chronicles, *see* chronicles

Crusade, First, 26, 88, 91, 279
Crusade, Second, 90, 106, 159, 255; Philip Augustus' return from, 251
Curialists, papal, 47f, 125
Cyprian, Bishop of Carthage, on Christian purity, lapsi, 11–15, 24, 69, 134–36 *passim*, 145–46, 154, 214–15, 218, 274, 277f; in the Middle Ages, 243

de Pol, Bishop Antonio, 51, 54, 68, 73
de Pomis, David, xviii, 205
de Prevot, Carol, 29
de Susannis, Marquardus, 18f, 21, 33f
dead, contact with, *see* corpses
Dead Sea Sect, xvii
Decian persecutions, 11, 22
del Val, Merry, Cardinal, 42, 47, 49, 124f, 127
Delehaye, Hippolyte, 40–43 *passim*, 45–46, 127–28
Delitzsch, Franz, 39f, 230f
des Mousseaux, Gougenot, 51f, 55f, 73,
Desportes, Henri, Father, 39f, 53, 73, 231
dialogue, Christian-Jewish, 2, 127, 129, 206–8, 211, 285
dining, common, *see* eating, mixed
Divina, G., 45–46, 123, 126, 272
dog, Jewish, xviif, 3–9 *passim*, 14, 25, 28–32 *passim*, 35f, 54, 66f, 74f, 122, 141–42, 153, 222, 224, 228, 281; Dominican, 276
Dogs and the Bread, The, 3–5, 160, 162f
domestic service, to Jews, 13, 90, 148f, 152; in *summa coloniensis*, 19, 149; Alexander III and, 19, 94, 149; Philip Augustus and, 89–90; Rigord and, 151; Philip III and, 252
Douglas, Mary, 144, 278
dress, distinct Jewish, 19, 149, 152, 155, 217, 278, 280; in Muslim lands, 220
Dreyfus, Alfred, 49–50
Duschesne, Mgr. Louis, 128–29

eating, mixed, 10f, 12, 14–17 *passim*, 20f, 71, 136, 220
Edgardo, *see* Mortara, Edgardo
Edward I, King of England, 96

Einbinder, Susan, 101, 103, 257, 259f
Eleazar the Rokeah, 143–44
emancipation of Jews, 48, 50
encyclopedias, Catholic, and ritual murder, 37–38, 44–45, 46, 120, 228–29
Ephraim of Bonn, 88, 90f, 101ff, 107, 226, 230, 248, 251
Erler, Ludwig, 44
Eucharist, and Jewish threat, xii, xv, 16f, 18, 22f, 62, 154, 240; purity of, xvf; 3f, 10, 12f, 14, 22f, 35f; indestructible, xvi, 23, 24; and Christian unity, xvi, 14, 27, 36, 69; as Christian "bread," 3, 6, 11–12, 14, 17, 20, 26; and Jewish contamination, 6, 12, 80, 133–35, 150, 153; and martyrdom, xii, 24, 27–28, 31–32, 52, 59, 60–61, 64ff, 68–70, 73, 147–50, 163; and impurity, 15, 23; declared annual obligation, 23, 68, 149; as Christian child, 26; as sacrifice, 59
eucharistic efficacy, 51, 58, 63, 66, 67, 142, 148
execution, 96f, 121
expulsion of Jews, 19f, 32, 219; from Udine, 33–34, 227; from papal state, 58, 254; from France, 76–77, 80f, 83, 93ff, 114f, 150–51, 177, 183f, 246f, 248; from England, 96; from Spain, 158, 221, 284
Ezekiel, 10–12 *passim*, 66, 93, 133, 137, 146, 157, 213–14
Ezra, Book of, 137, 275

Feuerbach, Ludwig, 53f, 154
Fisher, Bishop Eugene, 164, 169
Flanders, 97, 109, 201, 256, 259
food, contamination of, 16f, 18, 20–22, 216, 220; contamination by, 17, 21, 135, 156, 280; discrimination and, 153f, 216, 219
Frederick II, Emperor of Germany, 86, 109f, 112, 140
freedom of conscience, 3, 130, 172
French Revolution, 52, 235f
French state, secularized, 52–53

Gaguin, Robert, 76–77, 78
Ghetto, Roman, xvii, 31, 47, 50, 58, 237
ghettoization, 158

312 Index

Gibson, Mel, 223
Giovanni di Capistrano, 153–55 *passim*, 280
Gonzalo de Berceo, 27, 58, 224, 238
Gregory of Tours, 32
Gregory I, the Great, Pope, 5, 19, 32f, 219
Gregory IX, Pope, 17, 255
Gregory X, Pope, 121
Gregory XVI, Pope, 3
Gregory, Brad, 64–65
Guerin, Paul, 38, 246
Guido of Sens, 89, 92, 252
Guillaume le Breton, 76ff, 86–87, 109f, 115, 245, 250

Haggai, prophet, 15f, 134, 275
Halévy, Joseph, 128f
Halkin, Francis, 40–41, 43, 120, 130, 160, 232
Hart, William Henry, 38, 119, 230, 248
Hayes, Christine, E., 212, 218, 274f, 277
Hebrew Bible, 17, 134, 207
Hebrew Crusade chronicles, 41, 88
Hebrew texts, xi, xiii, 79, 91, 99, 103, 115, 117, 245, 259, 260
Henri, Count of Champagne, 109ff, 112
Henrican martyrs, 64, 66, 69, 279
Henry II, King of England, 111, 266
Henry III, King of England, 31, 96, 256
Henry IV, Emperor, 91, 253
Henry VIII, King of England, 64
Henry, Matthew, 4, 213, 225
Herbert of Huntingdon, 82
heresy, 59, 269; of John Paul II, xix, 172; Protestant, 56; Anglican, 59; and Henricans, 268; of Vatican II, 206; and Cyprian, 214, 274; of Apostolic Poverty, 223; of Talmud, 269; and Eucharist, 274; contamination of, 279
Herman the Jew, *Life* of, 5
Hittite texts, xvii, 6, 10, 204; temple, xvii, 10, 93; rule, 133
Hittites, xvii, 10
Holywar.org, 19, 24, 142, 172, 208, 273
Hosea, 11f, 23, 134, 137f, 145f, 214, 275
Host libel, 3, 6, 13, 62, 72, 122, 239; condemned, 41, 120; and Rindfleisch massacres, 32; and Martin Luther, 58, 66; and Bollandists, 58; roots, 70; evolution, 71, 87, 152; first, 72; and integralism, 159; and Werner of Oberwesel, 222; at Bourges, 241; at Troyes, 269; and Philip IV, 269
Hruby, Kurt, 169ff, 173, 207, 228
Hugh of Lincoln, 28, 37, 57, 59, 85, 96, 229, 256

idolatry, Jewish, 11, 13, 135, 211, 216; and Judaism, 16; Christian, 16, 23, 138, 140–43 *passim*, 216, 247, 274ff
Ignatius of Antioch, martyr, 16, 24, 65, 69, 73, 163
impurity, *see* purity
impurity, menstrual, 134–35, 143, 219, 275
In Our Times, see *Nostra aetate*
Innocent III, Pope, 48, 220, 244, 280; on Jewish wine, 23, 155f, 221; Eucharist, annual obligation, 23; and distinctive dress for Jews, 152, 155; *sicut iudaeis non*, 227; and Jewish lending, 90, 251, 255; on Jewish pollution, 94, 281; and blood libel, 121; on Jewish mother's milk, 135, 152; letter to archbishop of Sens, 151–52; protects Jews, 226
Innocent IV, Pope, 121, 126f, 231; on persecution of Jews, x, 48, 270; denounces blood libel, 86f, 109, 123–24, 140; against forced conversion, 91
Innocent XI, Pope, 75
Inquisition, 59, 93, 252; Modenese, 19; in Italy, 94
integralism, 43f, 47ff, 120, 127, 172, 232; and Host libel, 159
integralists, 2, 42, 48, 74, 121, 123ff, 130f, 235
interest on loans, 28f, 89, 90, 125, 255, 280, 287; and Eucharist, 28f; cancellation of, 80–81, 90, 93; restitution of, 89; Episcopal, 158
intermarriage, 3, 18, 212, 217, 274
Internet, xviiif, 2, 124, 134, 167, 172, 208f, 229, 270f
inversion, 102, 107, 112, 115, 117f, 142, 260–61, 262, 290
Isaiah, xviif

Israel, carnal, 133, 213; children of, 26, 35, 199, 200, 207, 213, 261; God of, 102; House of, 4, 5; Jacob, 276; poor of, 142; spiritual, 169, 171; State of, 167f, 220, 284; *Verus*, xvi, 9, 136, 173

Jacob Tam, Rabbi, 104, 263, 292
Jesuits, Italian; and ritual murder, xii–xiii, 40, 53, 236
Jewish threat, to Church, 5–9, 11, 14, 43, 49–50, 62, 95, 119, 163, 211, 282; to the Eucharist, xii, xv, 16f, 18, 22, 62, 73, 154, 240; social, 48–50, 70–74, 96, 117, 236, 284
John, 2, 16, 208f
John XXII, Pope, 223, 227
John XXIII, Pope, 168
John Paul II, Pope, prayer at Western Wall, 1, 205; and Abraham, 1; accepts Judaism, 1; accused of heresy, 3, 172; policy, 166, 170, 206; at World Jewish Congress, 285
Johnson, Willis, 25–26, 248
Jordan, William Chester, xix, 79, 93, 247ff, 255
Judaism, and Pope John Paul, 1; Catholicism and, 1, 13, 35, 134–36, 153, 158, 164–74, 211, 221, 229; and integralism, 2, 43; Agobard on, 16; Paul on, 8, 10, 32; Pope Benedict XVI on, 34, 207; medieval, 44; and modernism, 48, 56, 233, 282; and paganism, 59, 71; and Christianity, 158, 206f, 232, 285; and "We Remember," 164, 204, 206; rabbinic, 171; and Westernism, 209
Judaizers, ostracism of, 4
Judaizing, 2, 211; Paul on, 4, 7f, 14, 32f, 71, 210f, 219, 255; Chrysostom on, 8, 14, 21; nineteenth century, 50, 52f; and subversion, 53, 56; Rigord on, 80, 84, 177; in Rome, 130; of Christianity, 136; Angelo di Castro on, 153f, 156; in France, 184, 255; in Germany, 54, 236; in Spain, 221; and Philip Augustus, 251; of bishops, 281

kashrut, 5, 34, 216f, 227
Kasper, Cardinal Walter, 171–72, 208, 284–85

Kornberg, Jacques, 43, 120, 233

Lambert, Joseph, 53, 71–72, 73, 93, 135
Langmuir, Gavin, 67, 86, 230, 232, 239, 249f, 267, 279
lapsi, 12, 20, 24, 133f, 218, 274
Lateran Council, Third, 19, 89, 94, 148f, 217, 255
Lateran Council, Fourth, 19, 68, 102, 148f, 217, 255, 278
leaven, contamination of, xvi, 7f
lending, Jewish, 28–29, 80, 90, 244; and Richard of Pontoise, 75–76; and Philip Augustus, 76, 89, 94, 96, 112, 115, 251; and Louis VII, 90, 107, 287; and Benedict XIV, 158; Episcopal, 158; and Brie, 90, 117
lending at interest, 28f, 89, 90, 125, 255, 280, 287; and Eucharist, 28f; cancellation of, 80–81; restitution of, 89; Episcopal, 158; and Polish bishops, 281
Leo VII, Pope, 5, 20
Levites, 11
Leviticus, 12, 16–18 *passim*, 146, 156, 217, 219
liberalism, 42, 50, 127
loans, Jewish, cancellation of, 90, 93, 106, 183f, 253
Loches, 105f, 110f, 198f, 261, 263–66, 291f
Loeb, Isadore, 129
Lorenzelli, Monsignor, 50, 53, 56, 167
Lorenzino of Marostica, 51, 68f
Louis I, the Pious, Emperor of Holy Roman Empire, 22, 51, 235
Louis VII, King of France, and Hebrew letters, xi, 91–92, 99–101, 106, 109ff, 220; favors Jews, 89ff, 248, 259; and Jewish loans, 90; and apostasy, 90, 95, 106, 113, 253, 287; and Pope Alexander III, 90, 92, 99, 253; and Jewish domestics, 92, 269; and ritual murder, 93, 97; and Jewish massacres, 246
Louis IX, King of France, 100f, 267
Luther, Martin, 9f, 58, 136, 154, 212f, 214

Maccabees, the, 130
magic, Jewish, xi, 22, 58–59, 62, 70–72, 86, 88, 135, 254, 260; and Charlemagne, 11

marriage, mixed, *see* intermarriage
martyrdom, xvi, 57–58, 67–69, 119, 131, 147–50, 243, 262 ; eucharistic, xii, xv, 24, 27–28, 31–32, 52, 59, 61, 64ff, 68–70, 73, 147–50, 163; of Simonino of Trent, 31, 45f, 51; and Bollandists, 59–64, 119, 122, 279; of Werner of Oberwesel, xiv, 24–25, 59, 61, 63, 210, 222; and Cyprian, 69–70; of Richard of Pontoise, 59, 76–78, 184, 245; and avarice, 75–76; of Herbert of Huntingdon, 82
martyrs, Christian, xv, 24; child, 28f, 42, 57, 220; Henrican, 64, 66, 98, 279; English, 64; Maccabean, 130; Jewish, 261, 287
Marx, Karl, 167–68
massacre of Arian Christians at Himyar, 128
massacres, Jewish, 32, 112, 267; at Blois, 32, 77, 101, 202, 261, 263, 287–88f; Rhenish, 41; at Brie, 84; at Mantua, 68
Matthew, xiv, xvii, 3–5 *passim*, 7, 9–10 passim, 16, 19f, 34, 39, 140ff, 161, 169
matzoh, 7, 15, 122, 139, 229, 270
McCulloh, John, xi, xiii, 83, 86, 160
Melrose Chronicle, 81ff, 85, 108, 247f
Memorüchen, 101
mikve, 134, 215, 262
Mishnah, 212, 214
Modena, Leon, 158
modernism, and ritual murder 39–44; and fear of Jews, 47–48, 50, 127, 172, 232f
modernist crisis, 41–42, 124
Mortara, Edgardo, 73–74, 244f
murder of Christians, annual, 79, 84f, 96, 183, 246

Nazis, 41, 163, 165
neo–Nazism, 270
New Testament, 3–8 *passim*, 10–18 *passim*, 65f, 109
Nirenberg, David, 217–18
Nizzahon Yashan, 23, 137–42 *passim*, 161, 169, 250f
Nogent, Guilbert, 70, 72, 88, 135
noise, as disturbing, 6, 31, 68, 94f, 224, 254f
Nostra aetate, 2, 168, 170, 172, 205, 285

Observantines, 29
Odo of Cambria, 27, 63, 66, 221
Official, Rabbi Yosef, 110, 138–39, 140, 142
Oreglia, Giovanni, 50–51, 54, 129, 137, 146
Orléans Narrative, 99, 101–2, 103ff, 107, 259, 263f, 269, 289
ostracism, of Judaizers, 4; of impure Christians, 71; of Jews, 4, 94

paganism, 11, 59, 71; Christian, 140f, 214; Jewish, 11, 13–14, 17, 216, 218
papal infallibility, 43, 47
papal letters, 48f, 94, 208f, 227, 268, 270
papal state, end of, 31, 42, 48; expulsion of Jews from, 254
Paul, St., x; on Christian fellowship, xvi, 14, 48, 59; on Christian unity, xvi, 7f, 33, 62, 136, 159, 250; on Christian purity, xvi, 7–14 *passim*, 22, 93, 136; on supersession, xvi, 4, 8, 10–11, 35, 40; on Jews, xvi, 2, 4–9 *passim*, 15, 20, 31–34, 40, 170ff, 207, 211, 228; on Judaizing, 8, 14, 32, 71, 210, 255; on Eucharist, 10, 12, 72, 133, 145, 213, 219; on sexual morality, 7, 17, 145, 154; as a Jew, 32, 212; on paganism, 58; on Christ, 65; on martyrdom, 69f, 147; on Torah, 103, 171; on spirituality, 133, 136, 144, 154ff
Peter of Blois, 88
Philip V, King of France, 31
Philip II Augustus, King of France, cancels expulsion of Jews, 76, 81, 96; and Richard of Pontoise, 75–98; expulsion of Jews, 76, 151, 184; repression of Jews, 78, 95; suppresses Jewish lending, 76, 78, 112; and ritual murder, 83, 86, 245; executes Jews, 84; and Host libel, 87–88; defends apostasy, 93; and synagogues, 94–95; political attitude to Jews, 96; and Blois letters, 100, 105, 108f, 113, 115, 264, 266, 291; fears Jews, 118; and Inquisition, 252; excommunicated, 262
Pius V, Pope, 58
Pius IX, Pope, and Jewish dogs, xvii, 31, 50, 74, 94, 137; and freedom of conscience,

3, 131, 209; and modernist doctrine, 47; and Edgardo, 73–74, 244f; and Jewish pollution, 146
Pius XII, Pope, x; and freedom of conscience, 3
pollution, Jewish, 50, 94, 158, 205, 274; of Eucharist, 12, 80, 133–35, 150, 153; of Christians, 18–22, 32, 50–51, 80, 134, 151; of Rome, 50, 137; by noise, 6, 31, 94. *See also* contamination
prayer, Jewish, 31, 33, 50, 234; prohibited, 94; noise of, 31, 94f, 224, 254f; and God's unicity, 261
prayer of Pope John Paul II, 1, 205
proselytizing, 22, 213
Protestants, 40, 224, 243
Pucellina, 103, 111
purity, Christian, xii, xvff, 2, 7–15, 18–21, 36, 174, 277, 281; ecclesiastical, xiii, 158; eucharistic, xvf, 12, 14f, 20, 22f, 35, 145, 278; of holy places, xvi, 137; and supersession, xvi–xvii; of *societas fidei*, 22, 144; and martyrs, 24; spiritual, 54, 133; of Christian altar, 93, 134; bodily, 134–37 *passim*, 139, 144, 146, 218; of Rome, 137; of matza, 139
purity, Jewish, 10, 134, 136, 139, 143, 212, 215f, 274, 277, 281; of the Temple, xvii; of Matzoh, 139
purity, racial, 137, 275

Rabanus Maurus, 17, 136
rabbinic literature, 134, 143, 258, 268
rabbinic teaching, 8f, 31, 115
rabbinic texts, 125
racism, xviif, 134, 166; and Delitzsch, 40; anti-Semitism, 48, 126, 159, 164, 204, 208; Feuerbach on, 53; Van-Ortroy on, 125–126; modern, 137, 204, 236; and papal policy, 166; on Internet, 208, 271; twelfth-century, 225; in Germany, 236; and Catholic Church, 275; in the Book of Ezra, 275
ransom, 202, 263, 269
Rashi, *see* Yitzhaki, Solomon

Ratzinger, Card. Joseph, *see* Benedict XVI, Pope
recall of Jews to France, 77, 95f, 251, 255
Regino of Prum, 166, 211, 226
Reinach, Solomon, 127–9, 130
Revue des études juives, 128ff, 265
Richard of Pontoise, 38f, 45, 59, 64, 77–98, 107–108, 291
Rigord, 76ff, 80, 81f, 83–88, 90–93 *passim*, 95, 97, 99, 114–18 *passim*, 148, 150–51, 152, 177, 183–88, 246–54 *passim*, 269, 289, 291
rites de passage, 147f
ritual murder victims, *see under victim's name*
Robert of Bury St. Edmunds, 81, 108
Rogger, Father Iginio, 45–46
Rohling, August, 39, 44
Roman Curia, 47
Rupert of Deutz, 5, 25–26

sacrifice, Jewish, xi, xvi, 10, 13, 17, 21, 53, 134–35, 140f, 214; of Christian children, 84, 86f, 96; Christian, 7, 12–13, 139–40, 143, 153; pagan, 11; of Christ, 15, 63, 66, 157; of martyrs, 63f, 67, 73; eucharistic, 66, 73, 133, 138, 142, 173; in *midrash*, 142; in Rashi, 142–43; Aztec, 249
salvation of Christians, and the Virgin, 57, 82, 224, 240, 261; and Eucharist, 58, 67, 74, 142, 145, 270; and Christ, 63, 172; and martyrs, 24, 65–69 *passim*, 147–8; and the Torah, 103, 171
salvation of Jews, 51, 122, 171ff, 208, 285
Sanborn, Rev. Donald J., 205
Savoy trial of 1329, 121ff, 234
Schwabenspiegel, 18
Sefer Yosef HaMekane, 23, 110, 251
servants, *see* domestic service
sexuality, and impurity, xv, 8, 17ff, 51,135, 143, 217f, 281; and immorality, 7; Jewish, 71; and menstruation, 135, 143; and Jewish magic, 135; forbidden, xv, 149, 217f, 220, 277; and distinctive clothing, 149, 278
Shoah, 3, 164–68 *passim*, 283

Sicard of Cremona, 17–18, 51, 135–36
Simonino of Trent, xvii, 6, 21, 28, 31, 42, 45–47, 51, 85, 123, 126
society of faith, 16, 19, 22, 36, 73, 115, 220
spirituality, Christian, xvi, 5, 8, 35, 53f, 133, 136, 144–46, 153f, 156; of *Corpus Christi*, 48, 58, 74; of Eucharist, 139; of martyrs, 148; Jewish, 170, 206f
Stacey, Robert, xiv, 54, 235, 276
Stephen III, Pope, 13, 19
subversion, Jewish, xvii, 53f, 71, 135, 154
Summa Coloniensis, 19
supersessionism, xvi, xix, 34–36, 169, 236; and Paul, xviff, 8, 10, 35, 284; Pope John Paul II on, 1; Pope Benedict XVI on, 2, 34; Chrysostom on, 4, 35; Delehaye on, 130; and *Nizzahon Yashan*, 141, 166; on Internet, 167; and Kurt Hruby, 169–170, 173, 207; and Kathleen Biddick, 203–4; and Donald Sanborn, 206; and David Berger, 206; and Francois Gigot, 229
supremacy, royal, 65
synagogues, 79, 94; and Chrysostom, 8–9; Christian use of, 8, 22; confiscated, 94, 113, 290; new, prohibited, 94f, 106, 148; become churches, 94, 113, 290; closed, 95, 187, 224; and noise, 94f, 137, 255

Talmud, 8, 29, 109, 171, 269; Babylonian, 37, 204, 216, 262, 275f; burning of, 123, 285
Temple, the, xvii, 1, 135, 185; sacrifice, 53, 86, 133, 135, 155, 157, 173; destruction of, 1, 168, 171, 216; contamination of, 10, 93, 133, 221
Teutonicus, Johannes, 21, 23, 51, 288
Theobold, Count of Blois, 93, 99, 101, 103, 111, 116
Thomas Aquinas, 9, 68, 170, 212, 227
Thomas of Monmouth, 67, 70, 85–86, 239, 243, 262
Tiberino, Dr., 29, 39, 246
Toledan Council, Fourth, 88
Torah, 103, 109, 141, 171, 202, 130
trial, canonization, 21, 37, 46f, 60–61, 124ff, 189, 228

trial by ordeal, 102–3, 261
trials of Jews, 5, 49, 121–22, 124ff, 224, 258, 268

unity of Christians, 3, 6, 57, 62, 163, 165, 218; Pauline, xvi–xvii, 6f, 10, 33, 62, 145, 70, 136, 208, 250; eucharistic, xvi, 242; and Catholics, 2, 166; Gregory the Great on, 19; spiritual, 49; ecclesiastical, 59, 65; Chrysostom on, 211
unus panis, 6f, 10, 25, 36, 70, 159, 162, 164, 174, 234
usury, Jewish, 117. *See also* lending

Vacandard, Elphège, 39f, 43, 45, 246
van Döllinger, Ignaz, 43–44
van Ortroy, François, 45–47, 123–26, 131, 272
Vatican Council I, 43
Vatican Council II, 2, 38, 168, 206
Vauchez, André, 42, 109, 161, 210, 222, 237, 240
Vernet, Felix, xii, 43, 55f
Virgin, the, 58; and child martyrs, 57f; and Jew of Bourges, 27, 61, 71, 102, 147; saving intervention, 57, 224, 240, 261; and Werner of Oberwesel, 61; and Edgardo Mortara, 74; and Jewish avarice, 76, 82; and Richard of Pontoise, 76; *Apocalypse of*, 161, 166, 218

wax figures, 27f, 58, 147, 159, 238f, 241, 260f, 264
web sites, *see* Internet
Werner of Oberwesel, 24, 25, 62–63; sainthood trial of, 60; and Eucharist, 61f, 63, 222; martyrdom, 63
wet-nurses, Christian, 135, 143, 152, 274
William of Norwich, 38, 59, 67, 70, 83, 85–86, 91, 108, 239, 243; second, 248
William of Sens, Archbishop, 112f, 116, 151
Wilson, John, 59, 85
Winchester, ritual murder accusation at, 85

Yitzhaki, Solomon, Rabbi (Rashi), 29, 291

Zionism, 3